Web Design

The L Line,™
The Express Line to Learning

Web Design

The L Line,™
The Express Line to Learning

Sue Jenkins

1807
WILEY
2007

Wiley Publishing, Inc.

Web Design: The L Line,™ The Express Line to Learning

Published by
Wiley Publishing, Inc.
111 River Street
Hoboken, NJ 07030-5774
www.wiley.com

Copyright © 2007 by Wiley Publishing, Inc., Indianapolis, Indiana

Published by Wiley Publishing, Inc., Indianapolis, Indiana

Published simultaneously in Canada

For general information on our other products and services, please contact our Customer Care Department within the U.S. at 800-762-2974, outside the U.S. at 317-572-3993, or fax 317-572-4002.

For technical support, please visit www.wiley.com/techsupport.

Wiley also publishes its books in a variety of electronic formats. Some content that appears in print may not be available in electronic books.

Library of Congress Control Number: 2006939453

ISBN: 978-0-470-09628-4

Manufactured in the United States of America

10 9 8 7 6 5 4 3 2 1

1D/TQ/QR/QX/IN

WILEY

About the Author

Sue Jenkins is a Web designer, graphic designer, illustrator, teacher, and writer. For over ten years, she has provided Web and graphic design services to small and medium-sized businesses, consultants, writers, artists, and entrepreneurs through her company, Luckychair (www.luckychair.com). Jenkins designs and manufactures her own line of greeting cards and licenses her illustrations worldwide. Since 2004, she has been teaching courses in Macromedia Dreamweaver, Adobe Photoshop and Adobe Illustrator at the computer software training center, Noble Desktop, in New York City, and writing technical articles for the online e-zine, TechTrax. Sue recently moved with her son and husband, a philosophy professor, to Little Rock, Arkansas, from New York City.

Publisher's Acknowledgments

Acquisitions, Editorial, and Media Development

Project Editor
Rebecca Huehls

Senior Acquisitions Editor
Steve Hayes

Copy Editor
Virginia Sanders

Technical Editor
Dennis Short

Editorial Manager
Leah Cameron

Media Development Specialists
Angela Denny, Kate Jenkins, Steven Kudirka, Kit Malone

Media Development Coordinator
Laura Atkinson

Media Project Supervisor
Laura Moss

Composition Services

Media Development Manager
Laura VanWinkle

Editorial Assistant
Amanda Foxworth

Senior Editorial Assistant
Cherie Case

Senior Project Coordinator
Kristie Rees

Layout and Graphics
Brooke Graczyk, Heather Ryan, Erin Zeltner

Proofreaders
Laura L. Bowman, Brian H. Walls

Indexer
Estalita Slivoskey

Anniversary Logo Design
Richard Pacifico

Publishing and Editorial for General User Technology

Richard Swadley, *Vice President and Executive Group Publisher*

Andy Cummings, *Vice President and Publisher*

Mary Bednarek, *Executive Acquisitions Director*

Mary C. Corder, *Editorial Director*

Composition Services

Gerry Fahey, *Vice President of Production Services*

Debbie Stailey, *Director of Composition Services*

Author's Acknowledgments

Special thanks go to my intrepid agent, Matt Wagner, for offering me this exciting new project; to editors Becky Huehls, Virginia Sanders, and Dennis Short at Wiley for helping me help them craft a new book in a new series as well as for their fantastic editorial work; and to acquisitions editor Steve Hayes for his generosity in accommodating my cross-country move mid-book. I'd also like to thank my husband, Phil, whose love, encouragement, and humor helped me write this book.

Dedication

For Kyle.

Contents at a Glance

Contents

Preface

From the Publisher

Welcome to *Web Design: The L Line, The Express Line to Learning*. This book belongs to a new tutorial series from Wiley Publishing created for independent learners, students, and teachers alike. Whether you are learning (or teaching) in a classroom setting, or wanting to learn professional Web design skills while you build your own Web site, this book is for you. As rigorous and replete as any college course or seminar, *Web Design: The L Line* offers instruction for developing a designer's skill set.

Like all titles in *The L Line, The Express Line to Learning* series, this book's design reflects the concept of learning as a journey — a trip on a subway system — with navigational tools and real-world stops along the way. The destination, of course, is mastery of the key applications and core competencies of Web design.

From the Author

Web design is all about letting your creativity shine, but it's also about making a dream come alive by helping people connect in new ways — from a business reaching out to its customers to a young, emerging artist building an audience. Creating Web sites can be logically challenging too, because each site's requirements determines its own set of Web solutions. Many creative people get involved in Web design because they enjoy organizing and/or have a knack for technology. But if this doesn't describe you exactly, take heart; even if your organizational skills are not the best and/or you don't always take to new technologies like a duck to water, this book will walk you through every step of Web design so that by the final chapter you'll have the knowledge to build a complete Web site. If you enjoy whiling away an hour or two surfing the Web, as a Web designer, you're going to love being part of the worldwide network of people who help make the Web happen. This book shows you how.

Who Is This Book For?

As I wrote this book, I assumed you have some technical experience using computers and accessing the Internet but may be a beginner to the technology being presented. This book is designed for someone who likes a structured approach to learning and hands-on practice. Further, I presumed that readers of this book are seeking a professional-level understanding of the topic of Web design to become professional Web designers, or are hobbyists or do-it-yourself entrepreneurs who nevertheless want the same understanding of the topic that a professional would have.

If you have never built a Web site before, this book should demystify much of the jargon and answer many of your questions about building a site. Designing and building Web sites is actually a very fun and rewarding process when done right, especially because you can control what content will be displayed, how it will be organized, and what the site will ultimately look like. In fact, building a Web site is a terrific way to learn a lot about the business the site is being designed for. If you're using this book for your own site, you may find many of the earlier chapters invaluable when it comes to defining and refining your business goals. If you're embarking on a career in Web design, learning about the business of all your future clients will help keep your job interesting and expose you to a variety of industries you may not have ever learned about before.

If you're already familiar with some aspects of Web design, but you feel like your skills could use some guidance, organization, and improvement, you'll also gain valuable experience from following along with many, if not all, of the chapters in this book. To be sure, other Web design books and online tutorials exist, but none of them will teach you using the classroom style and techniques you'll find in these chapters. In reality, many tutorials often gloss right over some of the most important aspects of designing a site — such as good planning and organization, working with Web standards, and testing — that this book spends significant time covering.

What Will You Learn?

This book is divided into twenty chapters, organized chronologically by the topics you'll need to explore to build a site from start to finish, and you'll be covering a lot of ground, well beyond the actual designing and building of a Web site. Major topics include:

- Site planning and implementation
- Gathering and organizing content
- Domain registration and hosting
- Site architecture, layout options, and principles of design
- Design mockup and image optimization
- Working with Web standards
- Building Web pages, styling with CSS, and using JavaScript
- Search engine optimization techniques, validation, and publication

My ultimate goal for this book is not to teach you just what you need to know to be a Web designer; rather, I want this book to teach you how to be a good one. That means that by the end of this book, you should know how to effectively map out a site, organize site content, lay out the content logically, optimize graphics well, build standards-compliant pages, and continue to learn about ways to improve your design skills. Along the way you'll also learn a bit about the different software programs you can use for creating Web sites, how to create and use CSS (Cascading Style Sheets), as well as some easy search engine optimization techniques.

Although this book is primarily about how to build a Web site, you'll also learn some important things about promoting a business online. To get the most out of this book, I enthusiastically suggest that you use this as an opportunity to work on a real Web project. That way, everything you do will have a real context and will therefore be more meaningful to you. If you don't have an actual project in mind, think one up or consider offering your services free of charge to a worthy cause (a children's non-profit, an AIDS association, breast-cancer awareness, or something else) or to some small local business in exchange for using the completed site as a reference for your new Web design portfolio. Above all, this book should provide you with the specific knowledge you'll need to build a Web site plus a general understanding of designing for the Web, organization techniques, user experience strategy, and Web-related technology — all with the kind of encouragement, attention to detail, and sense of humor you'd typically find in a good classroom.

Because each lesson builds on the last, it is best to begin the book at the beginning and work your way through each chapter. All chapters include prereading assessment questions as well as clearly defined, step-by-step, hands-on instruction to master new skills and concepts. You'll also find a self-assessment quiz at the end of every chapter to reinforce key points in the material and evaluate how well you've met each chapter's learning objectives.

What You Will Need

To complete all the exercises in this book, you will need the following items, including hardware and software:

- A computer running either the Mac or Windows operating system
- Reliable Internet access
- Multiple browsers installed, preferably in the latest two versions (Safari, Firefox, Opera for Mac; IE, Netscape, Firefox for PC)
- Web design software including one raster, one vector, and one image optimization tool, such as Photoshop, Illustrator, and ImageReady or Fireworks, respectively

- A WYSIWYG/Code HTML editor, such as Dreamweaver. Alternately, while not as fun to use, any HTML code-only editor such as HomeSite or BBEdit will do

- An FTP Client software application (many are free, as you'll learn about in Chapter 20)

- Creativity, enthusiasm, dedication, hard work, and a desire to make good-looking, well-functioning, standards-compliant Web sites

This book is more about general Web design than about using any particular Web design application. In other words, after you learn the general structure of a Web page, feel free to use any software programs you like to generate the code, optimize images, and build Web sites.

That said, when I do talk about Web design in this book, I will often be speaking specifically in terms of using particular software programs, such as Dreamweaver, a WYSIWYG (What You See Is What You Get) editor by Adobe (formerly Macromedia), as well a few other graphics programs like Adobe Photoshop and Adobe ImageReady.

If you don't know how to use any of the particular software programs mentioned in this book, I strongly recommend you buy a tutorial book(s) and/or enroll in a comprehensive computer graphics class or two to learn the program(s) at a licensed, nationally recognized, software training school. An understanding, however cursory, of how to use these applications will both enhance your experience of learning using this book as well as speed up the process of creating your designs. Therefore, let me provide you with several great reasons to use these particular programs:

Why use Dreamweaver?

- Considered the best cross-platform (Mac and PC) Web development tool by professional designers

- Easy to use, and it keeps on getting better with each new release

- Reasonably priced, especially if you qualify to purchase the educational version of the software (Find authorized resellers of Adobe products here: http://partners.adobe.com/resellerfinder/na/education.jsp or search for "adobe educational software" in your favorite search engine)

- Great online tech support, forums, and more at Adobe.com

- Has its own built-in FTP panel for transferring files to a remote server

It's extensible (meaning you can improve the program's capabilities by installing 3rd party "extensions") and customizable (by editing the program's Preferences to make the user interface conform to your specific needs)

If the reasons listed above don't convince you, check out Adobe's Reasons to Buy Dreamweaver page at www.adobe.com/products/dreamweaver/productinfo/buy/

Why use Photoshop?

It's the most powerful professional raster image editor on the market

It lets you create graphics for both print and Web

Great for photo retouching and working with raw digital files

Comes with a free copy of ImageReady for image optimization

Why use ImageReady?

Easy-to-use interface, almost identical to Photoshop

Allows you to create rollover graphics and simple GIF animations

Has a special panel for optimization that lets you view and compare up to four different optimization settings

Generates optimized graphics with and without HTML and JavaScript

If you're coming to Web design with a graphic design background, you are probably very familiar with using QuarkExpress and/or InDesign. Though your comfort level may be strong in those applications, please do not use them as tools for your Web layouts. Neither Quark nor InDesign currently have a feature that allows you to export a designed page for print directly into a good working HTML Web page format. Therefore, for maximum ease of use, flexibility, and exportability, please rely on my experience as a Web designer and create your Web layouts using the Web design programs mentioned here, such as Photoshop, Illustrator, ImageReady, and Fireworks.

Throughout the book I may also make recommendations for other software programs, services, and online resources. None are meant to be viewed as product placements or endorsements. They are strictly meant as suggestions to help you meet the goals outlined in each chapter. Take what you need and leave the rest.

Conventions Used in this Book

To aid you in understanding new terms and concepts, this book uses the following typographical rules:

New terms: New terms introduced in this book are set apart with italics. For example:

> Two other unique attributes you have control over in a table are *cellpadding* and *cellspacing*, both of which, when added, uniformly apply to all the cells and cell walls in a table.

Code samples: The HTML code samples in this book are listed in monospaced text within a paragraph, like this: `<img src="bullet.gif">`, or set apart from the text, like this;

```
<!DOCTYPE html PUBLIC "-//W3C//DTD HTML 4.01
Transitional//EN"
    "http://www.w3.org/TR/html4/loose.dtd">
<html>
<head>
<title>My Page Title</title>
</head>
<body>
Page content goes here
</body>
</html>
```

Furthermore, when your attention needs to be drawn to certain parts of the code those parts will be listed in bold, as in

```
<body>
<p class="sidebarh1">Pancakes</p>
</body>
```

Cross-platform: Because PCs and Macs often use different keyboard shortcuts, anytime a keyboard shortcut is mentioned in this book, both platform shortcuts will be listed side by side such as, right-click (Windows) or Control-click (Mac).

Web addresses: Any time Web addresses are referenced in this book they shall be set apart in monofont, such as www.wiley.com.

In addition to the typographical conventions, each chapter in this book has a uniform look that includes directional navigation tools and symbols that build on the subway map theme. The following elements are found in each chapter:

Stations Along the Way: This element provides you with a quick overview of the chapter's learning objectives.

Enter the Station: These prereading questions act as a turnstile to the chapter. They give you an opportunity to consider what you already understand about the chapter's topic and outline the chapter's learning objectives so that you can read the chapter in a more focused way.

Step-by-step exercises: Numbered steps provide you with a tutorial approach to the material. Exercises typically walk you through a specific, real-world example and, if applicable, make use of example files. The tutorial part of a step is bold; any explanation follows the step and is not bold. Explanatory text might note alternatives to doing a certain task or help you to understand how a particular step illustrates a general concept.

Street Jargon: A mini glossary can be found at the end of each chapter, which reviews key technical terms.

Practice Exam: Your last stop before exiting a chapter is the Practice Exam, which will test you on the concepts you learn in each chapter. All answers can be found in Appendix B on this book's companion Web site (www.wiley.com/go/thelline).

Icons Used in This Book

The following margin icons are used in this book to assist with your understanding of the material and indicate points of particular interest:

Information Kiosk

These tip icons use the international symbol for information and point you to content of special interest.

Watch Your Step

Warning icons are placed next to information that can help you avoid making common mistakes

Transfer

These cross-reference icons direct you to related information found in another section or a different chapter.

Step Into the Real World

These icons can be found in sidebars providing you with case studies of real Web design situations that you might encounter in your own career. The information contained in them should help you determine how to apply what you've learned in the chapter to a real-life situation.

Using the Web Site

I truly hope you enjoy reading this book. But if that's all you do, you'll miss out on the real joy of this enterprise. For many of the tasks outlined in this book, you can find free sample files on the companion Web site so that you can follow along. (Go to www.wiley.com/go/thelline and click the book title.) You won't learn this stuff just by reading about it. You really have to get in there and do it yourself. Jump in, make some mistakes, and keep working away at the tasks outlined in this book to create your first (or second or third) Web site yourself. That's how learning really happens.

For Instructors and Students

Web Design: The L Line has a rich set of supplemental resources for students and instructors. **Instructors** can find a test bank, PowerPoint presentations with course and book outlines, and instructor's manual and samples syllabi online. Please contact Wiley for access to these resources.

Students and independent learners: Resources such as chapter outlines and sample test questions can be found on this book's companion Web site. Go to www.wiley.com/go/thelline and click the book title.

1

Starting with a Plan

STATIONS ALONG THE WAY

- O Figuring out a Web site's goals and purpose
- O Determining what benefits the site will offer the consumer
- O Constructing an identity for the site to improve the visitor's experience
- O Establishing what information and graphics to display on the site
- O Diagnosing whether the site needs a database to display information dynamically
- O Defining ways to drive additional Web traffic to the site

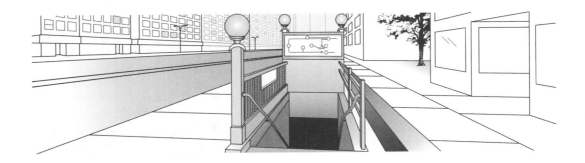

 # Enter the Station

Questions

1. What are the possible main functions of a Web site?

2. What tangible benefits can a Web site provide to visitors?

3. When thinking about a Web site, can you readily describe the image or identity of a site as if it were a person?

4. How do you decide what information to display on a Web site?

5. How can you determine whether a Web site needs to use a database?

6. To improve site traffic, what kinds of additional content can you add to a Web site?

Express Line

If your client will be handling site planning, or if you're already confident in your own Web site planning skills, skip ahead to the next chapter.

When you begin any Web site project, you — and your client, if you're designing for someone else — probably have a number of ideas about the final product. If those ideas are vague, you need to work on fleshing them out, and if they're specific, you need to keep them organized and understand the purpose behind them. In other words, you need a plan.

To get the project off to a good start and ensure these ideas and issues all get the consideration they deserve, you begin by pinpointing the purpose for building the Web site. Some people build Web sites because they have a product or service to sell. Others create sites to share ideas and information. Because the answer to "Why build a site?" is largely determined by the specific needs of the Web site owner, I've devised a series of brainstorming exercises in this chapter, which you can use as a guide to discovering that answer. By defining the site's purpose, you develop a foundation for the rest of the site planning. By the end of this chapter, you should have all the tools you'll need to establish a plan for building almost any Web site.

Determining the Site's Purpose

When you're ready to begin a new Web site project, the very first thing you should do — before you think of designing the site — is determine the ultimate purpose of the site. Start with a few simple questions: Why are you building this site? Will the site be professional, fun, silly, or informative? Will the site sell products, services, information, ideas, or some combination of these things? These are the kinds of questions you need to ask yourself right now, so read on.

Keeping up with the competition

The short answer to "Why build a site?" is that these days anyone who owns a business and wants to be taken seriously by savvy consumers should have a Web site. If you agree with the premise that, to be competitive, every business needs a Web site, you'll next need to figure out the site's main purpose. This step is often where you'll start your work as Web designer.

For the longer answer to "Why build a site?" you need to follow along as I take you on a quick walk down History Road: Since the boom of the Internet revolution in the late 1990s, every big company with a "brick and mortar" store learned that having a Web site would instantly make their products and services available to millions of site visitors each day. New Web sites sprouted up daily as more and more people purchased computers, learned how to use them, and began searching, finding, and buying the products and services they wanted online.

As the Internet continued growing in popularity, so did the idea that selling products and services exclusively online was a viable new form of running a business, mainly because it entirely negates the need for costly store overhead, which in turn can increase profits. Today, most businesses either have their own Web site, are in the process of creating one, or are in desperate need of having their current site redesigned and improved upon. People create Web sites to promote business services, sell products, share information, provide free resources, offer contests, coupons, tips, and advice, and more.

Gathering information

Oftentimes, a business will rely upon you, the Web designer, to assist it with determining the site's purpose. If you or your Web client haven't discussed this issue yet, read through the following questions and take careful note of the answers:

- **Will this site provide in-depth information about a particular topic?** The function of a political news blog or nonprofit organization is to share ideas and information with the public. A lawn mower company might want to offer lawn-care advice in addition to selling mowers.

- **Will the site be someone's personal Web site?** Personal Web sites are just for family, friends, and schoolmates. This could be a family photo album, a blog, or a place for online personal expression.

- **Will the site be someone's professional portfolio?** Professionals use portfolios to generate new business and showcase their talents. People who use portfolios include artists, illustrators, designers, writers, singers, photographers, musicians, poets, and academics.

- **Will the site sell any products, and if so, what kinds?** If the site will sell lots of products, find out how many product categories are needed and whether the products will be sold wholesale, retail, or both. Will the products be sold online or through an outside distributor?

- **Will the site market services?** A company, group, or sole proprietor (like a nonprofit arts organization, a law firm, or a marketing consultant) might want a site it can include on business cards and in advertisements in order to help spread the word about its services. Ask how many services the group offers and whether it wants to make pricing information available online.

Developing a purpose statement

Use the answers to the preceding questions to begin forming a vision of how the site will look and function. For example, a realtor's Web site that markets rental properties and realty services will necessarily look and function much differently than a nonprofit site for railroad veterans or one that showcases a watercolor artist's portfolio.

After talking over these questions with the site owner, you will find out whether you need to design the site to attract business, share information, provide feedback and advice, be a blog with text and photographs, provide a dating service, sell moving and relocation services, provide online banking, supply wholesale products to retailers, or some combination of these and other things. Then you'll want to take this information and boil it down into a purpose statement. Table 1-1 gives examples of several types of businesses and some purposes those business owners might come up with for their sites.

Table 1-1   Example Purpose Statements

Type of Business	Example Purpose Statement
Sole proprietor or entrepreneur, such as a business consultant, life coach, or private accountant	This site will market services to a wider audience, lend a sense of legitimacy to the business, generate more clients, and allow customers to register for a monthly newsletter.
Artist, designer, illustrator, photographer, poet, actor, musician, or band	This site will be an online portfolio for displaying and promoting work (art, music, photos) to art directors, editors, and other people in the industry. The site will help generate new business, share news and information, and sell a limited number of creative works.
Nonprofit organization	This site will promote services, provide industry-related information, educate the public, collect donations, offer public and private programs and events, list classifieds for members, and supply registration information for fund-raising events.
Small- to medium-sized business, like a greeting card company, a network backup hardware manufacturer, or an adventure tour company	This site will be an online storefront to sell products and services, answer FAQs, have a library of information related to products and services, and allow visitors to contact the business, receive customer support via e-mail and live chat, and subscribe to a weekly newsletter.

Take a moment to think about the purpose(s) of your Web site project and record your answers in the spaces provided here. If you don't have a project in mind, pretend you're planning a site for a marketing consultant who promotes art books. Whatever your particular answers happen to be, turn them into a purpose statement that you can keep handy throughout the first five chapters of this book; the statement will help you organize your ideas and plan the best Web site for your needs.

Type of business:

_____

Purpose of site:

1. _____
2. _____
3. _____
4. _____
5. _____
6. _____
7. _____
8. _____
9. _____
10. _____

Defining the Benefits to Visitors

Now that you know your (or your client's) site's general purpose, you'll need to begin constructing ideas about the tangible benefits to visitors. You definitely need to know what the visitors will get from visiting this particular site and purchasing particular products and services *before* you build it. The benefits are what will set your site apart from your competitors. For example, when you're designing a site for a fine wine and liquor company, if you know that its distinguishing benefits are (a) the number of years it has been in business; (b) the quality of its products; and (c) its reputation for expertly rating and evaluating the wines they sell, you can highlight those details in the design for the company's site. If you don't have this knowledge at the onset of the project, you might encounter design revision setbacks further down the line.

Benefits can help persuade visitors to purchase products, use services, tell all their friends, and return to the site often. To really understand what those benefits are, put yourself in the shoes of the consumer and look at the business from his or her perspective.

Discovering the true benefits

Opinions won't necessarily provide any tangible benefits to the customer. Benefits, on the other hand, can sway a buyer toward one product over another. For example, every pizza parlor across the country will tell you it has the best pizza. And to stay competitive in business, each parlor will probably have a legion of regulars who will swear up and down that the pizza there really is the best in their neighborhood, town, state, or country. To claim that the pizza is *the best,* however, is only an opinion.

Information Kiosk

A *benefit* is something that is useful, helpful, or advantageous and enhances or promotes healthiness, happiness, and prosperity.

Having the best pizza in town, then, while true, might benefit the consumers only if their lives will be improved by eating it. Therefore, rather than boasting on a Web site to have the best pizza in town, it makes better sense to market verifiable facts about the parlor — and build those elements into the design — like that it uses the best reduced-fat mozzarella, makes its own low-cholesterol pizza sauce from tomatoes grown fresh at local farms, is rated number 1 in the ZAGAT survey, or that two slices of its famous "salad pizza" are only 390 calories.

Seeing the visitor's perspective

Take a look at one possible type of business and see how you could convert someone's skills into benefits and clearly state why visitors should want to use the business's products or services. Suppose for a moment that you're a professional digital photographer looking to increase business by putting a portfolio Web site online. You have extensive studio experience, you've won some important industry awards, you've done a lot of fashion shoots around the world, and you're willing to travel for the right project.

Step into the Real World

What's in It for Me? When you purchase a product or service online, the benefits you'll receive from the item(s) are part of what makes you decide to make the purchase. Good online marketers know that those benefits need to appear front and center so you can decide quickly whether a product is right for you.

Take a few minutes right now to visit the following sites to see whether you can quickly identify at least two product or service benefits:

- **Dreamweaver 8:** www.adobe.com/products/dreamweaver
- **Firefox:** www.mozilla.com/firefox
- **Epson:** www.epson.com (In the Products area, note how features and benefits are highlighted for individual products.)
- **The Nature Conservancy:** www.nature.org
- **Julie Hasson, Chef:** www.juliehasson.com

Hint: Benefit statements often begin with action verbs such as create, manage, and develop.

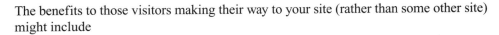

The benefits to those visitors making their way to your site (rather than some other site) might include

- Equipped; photographer owns her own studio and digital photographic equipment, so there will be *no hidden equipment fees.*

- Accomplished; hiring this award-winning photographer means you can *feel confident that your project will have quality results.*

- Experienced; with over ten years experience in the fashion industry, *you can rely on this photographer's skills, talent, and professionalism.*

- Global; photographer has traveled in the past with *Elle, Vogue,* and *Sports Illustrated,* and is *willing to travel anywhere in the world.*

To discover some benefits your particular Web site project can offer to visitors, try asking yourself what you would want to know if you were looking to do the following tasks:

- Hire someone who does what your client does. (For instance, your client might be an artist who paints faux finishes for home interiors, a clown who specializes in children's birthday parties, or a private marketing consultant for the knitwear industry.)

- Find a company that sells what your client's company sells.

- Find a business that provides services like your client's company.

- Find an artist with your client's particular skills and experience.

- Get information about a nonprofit agency like your client's organization.

You can easily convert the answers into benefits. Next, think about why visitors might want to use the products or services on your client's (or your own) Web site. Again, if you'd like a project idea to practice with, pretend you're creating a site for a marketing consultant who promotes art books. Record as many answers as you can come up with in the following spaces.

Benefits of this site to visitors:

1. _____

2. _____

3. _____

4. _____

5. _____

6. _____

7. _____

8. _____

9. _____

10. _____

Constructing an Image for the Site

The next important step to take with your project is to define the image that the Web site will project to the consumer. This image will establish the unspoken identity of your Web site to visitors — an identity that they will (hopefully) respond to both intellectually and emotionally.

To help construct this identity:

1. **Try thinking of the site as if it were your client's best salesperson, someone who fully represents the best about the company.**

2. **Come up with as many words as you can to describe this "person's" traits.**

   Is the person professional or laid back, serious or fun, creative or traditional? If the salesperson angle is a bit awkward for you and/or your Web client, think of the ideal image the Web site should project and find adjectives that describe that ideal. Table 1-2 lists descriptive terms you can use to begin defining the Web site's image; it's by no means complete, but should get you started.

Table 1-2   Describing a Web Site's Image

Professional	Casual	Innovative	Creative
Traditional	Cutting-edge	Popular	Honest
Open	Fun	Witty	Intelligent
Smart	Open-minded	Supportive	Caring
Technological	Trend-setting	Urban	Cultured
Educated	Contemporary	Organized	Efficient
Cost-effective	Reliable	Trustworthy	Friendly
Talented	Confident	Capable	Established
Savvy	Respected	Clever	Solution-oriented

Besides giving you a clearer sense of what you're doing with this Web project, the identity you construct for it will help you make aesthetic and organizational decisions about the site such as what colors to use, how to best lay out the content, and what graphics to include throughout the site. For instance, if your Web client will be selling football helmets, you'll probably decide to use bolder masculine colors over pastels in the design, and if your client is a consultant looking to advertise his services, you'll probably want to advise him to invest in some good royalty-free, industry-specific artwork for the site rather than display the often overused and amateurish-looking illustrations from the Microsoft Word Clip Art archive.

Right now, use the following spaces to list at least ten adjectives that describe the company image for your current Web site project:

1. _____
2. _____
3. _____
4. _____
5. _____
6. _____
7. _____
8. _____
9. _____
10. _____

Transfer

In Chapter 2, you'll do a similar exercise about the type of visitor you'd like the Web site to attract.

Determining Site Content Requirements

By now, you should have a pretty good idea about the site you want to develop. You have identified the site's purpose, determined what benefits visitors will gain from visiting the site, and made initial steps toward defining an identity for the site. With all that in mind, you can start thinking about what actual content needs to be presented on the Web site.

Certain content should be on every Web site, regardless of the site's purpose. Beyond that, anything else that goes on the site is up to you — the designer — and your client. That said, following a few general guidelines helps make most Web sites more effective, and I suggest you use this chapter and the rest of this book as a guide to assist you in defining content for the site.

Information Kiosk

The more informed you and your Web client are, the better. Although many creative people — including Web designers — are intuitive thinkers, you'll still benefit from learning about the general Web design issues that I discuss in the following sections and throughout this book. Even if you already know a Web page should look or work a certain way, being able to explain why can help you educate your client, who might also be able to give you more constructive input if he or she understands the concepts behind your design and the principles that drive content selection. (And if you or your client want an unconventional site, keep in mind that even Picasso painted realistic portraits and practiced technique before he broke away from the traditions of his time, so learning more about these guidelines will still be helpful to you.)

The bare minimum

At a minimum, your Web project will need to supply basic information, and your job during the planning process is to decide what content you or your client will need.

Transfer

Determining what information a site requires at this point in the planning process is helpful because it will give you a road map to work from when you begin gathering this content. Pulling the content from various sources is the focus of Chapter 3.

The following information is commonly found in some variation on most Web sites:

Home page information: The home page is the most important page on the site because this is where you'll need to introduce the site to visitors. This page should contain at least a paragraph or two of descriptive text (formatted in any way except as a graphic) generally outlining what visitors can find on the site. Whenever possible, *keywords* (descriptive terms used to find information on a specific topic) in the text should be hyperlinked to other pages on the site.

Watch Your Step

In the past few years, many sites have used the home page as a place to play introductory flash animations or to have a different set of graphics than found on the rest of the Web site. Although never really a good strategy even though it contained a bit of the "wow!" factor, this practice is no longer favored because a lack of meaningful, searchable content on the home page could prevent the site from being fully indexed by the most popular search engines. Furthermore, when visitors can't find what they're looking for by quickly scanning the home page, they'll leave. Make the most of the home page by including only relevant copy, links, and graphics on the page, using the same layout found on the rest of the site.

- **Contact information:** Be ready to provide the physical address of the company, the mailing address (if different), telephone and fax numbers, and a contact e-mail address. You might also want to include special contact information for various employees, departments, and services, as well as area maps, transportation directions, and hours of operation. Some sites also provide a form on the contact page where visitors can submit personal information, answer survey questions, provide comments and feedback, and/or request information.

- **Privacy Policy:** If you intend to collect any personal information (e-mail address, name, telephone number, and so on) from site visitors during registration or for purposes of responding to an inquiry, the site would benefit greatly from including some kind of privacy policy.

Information Kiosk

In the most general terms, a privacy policy should state how the company will care for the collected data, including any *cookies* (personal data collected by a visited site's server and saved to the visitor's computer so future visits to that site will run smoother) collected from the computer used to visit the site. For example, if the company will share or sell the data with other vendors, you need to state that expressly. Conversely, if the company plans to honor the privacy of visitors and closely guard collected information as if it were a priceless gift, state that clearly.

FindLegalForms.com has a generic policy (Privacy Policy Agreement #28152) you can purchase online for only $8.99, or if you want to generate a policy to match your specific business, you can use the Policy Wizard at the PrivacyAffiliates.com Web site for just $19.95.

- **Site map:** A site map is a page on a Web site that contains a list of organized text links to all the pages on the Web site. If you want your site to be accessible to as many visitors as possible, regardless of how simple or complex the site is, include a site map page.

Transfer

Site maps are not only good for long pages with a lot of content, they're also great for improving access to all the pages on a site by visitors with disabilities using assistive devices to access the Web. To learn more about how to make your sites accessible, see Chapters 11 and 19.

Footer: At the bottom of every page on a site, you should include the company name, copyright information, and a series of what I call *footer links* or navigation links to the most important pages on the site. At a minimum, include links to such pages as Home, About, Services, Contact, and Privacy Policy. This information will not only remind visitors whose site they're on, but also provide additional ways for them to navigate to other pages on the site. To really harness the full power of this often-overlooked Web real estate, treat this area like a mini site map and list links to not only high-level navigation destinations but also to more detailed subnavigation category pages.

Figure 1-1 shows an example of a site that includes all these basics.

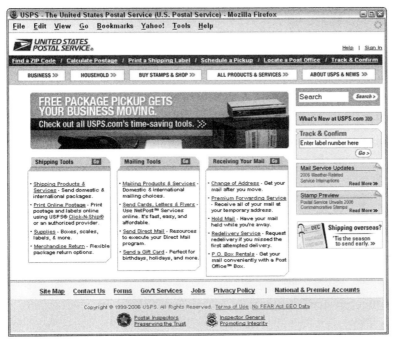

Figure 1-1: Most Web sites include this basic information.

Marketing and sales content

Whether the Web site you're designing is for a sole proprietor, entrepreneur, nonprofit organization, or a small- to medium-sized business, the rest of the content on the Web site should be geared toward promoting new business from visitors. You ought to provide ample information about the person, organization, or company and all the skills, talents, work, services, and/or products available plus anything else you can think of that will benefit the visitor and positively impact business.

Information Kiosk

As you make decisions about what information you do or don't want to include on a Web site, develop a keen awareness of the Web site's online and offline competition. For example, if you're designing a site for a children's ballet school, it should probably contain information that will help visitors choose to enroll their children as students, such as a schedule, photographs of the facilities and smiling children, a teaching philosophy, student and parent testimonials, and perhaps a price list. If the school's offline competitor happens to give students free tote bags, perhaps your client's dance school should also offer free tote bags and advertise that on the site.

The following list isn't meant to be comprehensive; rather, you can use it as a starting point for brainstorming about the content needed for each specific Web site.

- **Company Information:** This section of the site, usually called About Us or something to that effect, typically consists of either one page of company-related information or several pages of logically organized company details. The information here should describe the company to the visitor and include some form of the company mission statement. In addition, this section might include a directory with bios of the management team, a corporate history and philosophy statement, a resume or *curriculum vitae* (an academic's work history and accomplishments), and/or information about company internships and careers.

- **Biography:** Similar in scope to the Company Information section, the biography page (either called About Me, Bio, or Biography) usually includes historical and other interesting information about the artist, sole proprietor, or small business owner. This page, or series of pages, should provide information to stimulate interest in the services, skills, work, products, and so on being presented on the Web site.

- **Product/Service Information:** All products and services will require a detailed description. If the business is service oriented, describe what the business does, who needs this service, and how long the business has been operating. If the business sells products, the products need to be organized into logical categories and subcategories, such as Cat Products → Collars → Leather. In addition to a description for each main category, every individual product deserves its own description, including any information that might be interesting or necessary to purchasers, such as size, dimensions, color, weight, materials, ingredients, nutritional information, care instructions, country of manufacture, and warranty information. Also offer client/customer testimonials whenever possible.

Transfer

For any copyrighted material you intend to use on the site, including intellectual property, photographs, and illustrations, you must have permission to use it. This means paying royalty fees for rights-managed work, requesting and receiving written permission for non-rights-managed work, and otherwise obtaining the right to use and display the work created by another person or entity. To learn more about copyrights and permissions, see Chapter 3.

News and Press Information: This area typically contains current press releases, a press release archive, articles about the business or industry, and/or any news items in the form of media coverage. This area might also have information about upcoming programs and exhibitions, gifts and collections, relevant technology, a historical corporate timeline, an image gallery or media library, and a listing of literary publications.

Portfolio: This is the part of the site that displays an online version of an artist's portfolio, including photos and graphic examples of their work, a resume or curriculum vitae, video clips, sound files (MP3s), and more. The online portfolio is fast becoming the best way to market services to a global audience, generate new business, and share news and industry information with the public.

Frequently Asked Questions (FAQs): If visitors potentially have many questions that need answering, they'll benefit from viewing an FAQs page. Most FAQs cover information about contacting the site, searching for information on the site, customizing site preferences or membership accounts, getting more information, and using the site. If you don't have a list of information to create an FAQs page yet, start keeping track of questions the business gets asked. When a pattern begins to emerge, add those questions and answers to the frequently asked questions page.

Terms of Service: Similar in importance to the Privacy Policy, the Terms of Service page should state how the site provides services to — and the conditions under which those services must be accepted by — visitors. This may include concepts of intellectual property rights, usage, registration, security, payment, advertising, applicable law, legal compliance, indemnification, and more. Because the Terms of Service should contain legal content specific to the Web site's offerings, the best way to create the page is to consult with a lawyer. Do-it-yourselfers can download a generic Terms of Use Agreement from FindLegalForms.com for only $8.99.

Shopping Cart: Several kinds of Web shopping carts are available. The most basic is a cart that uses PayPal to process payments. Another option is to create an online store through Yahoo! Shops, which uses Yahoo!'s proprietary shopping cart system. For more customized solutions, you'll want something that's tailored specifically to your site's needs. With a simple search, you can find online shopping carts that are free and customizable, carts that are controlled by host providers, and carts that are powered by third-party software manufacturers.

Information Kiosk

In a 2006 Shopping Cart Software Report on TopTenReviews.com (`http://shopping-cart-review.toptenreviews.com`), ShopSite 7 Pro, MerchandiZer Pro, and Monster Commerce Pro were rated the best shopping cart software programs on the market.

Whatever cart you decide to use, take extra care to ensure that your visitors' personal information is safe and secure during the purchasing transaction. If the Web site will process credit card payments (instead of processing them through an outside service), you'll need to set up a special merchant account as well as purchase an SSL (Secure Socket Layer) digital security certificate for your domain. Your host provider should be able to assist you with these things.

Transfer

You'll find more information about merchant accounts, SSL certificates, and working with the different types of e-commerce shopping carts in Chapter 4.

Customer Service (Help): If you sell anything on your site, your visitors will need a place to contact you, get more information, ask questions, and resolve problems. Look to successful Web sites to gather ideas on how to set up this valuable area of your site. Consider having sections for ordering information, privacy issues, shipping and delivery, dealing with returns or damaged items, and accessing account information, just to name a few. The easier you make it for visitors to get answers, the more positive their experience on your site.

Site Credits: Want to toot the horn of the designer or design team (you!) that turned a Web dream into a Web reality? If you've included a clause in your client contract to do so, add a site credit link somewhere on the site, preferably embedded somewhere in the footer links. Otherwise, ask your client for permission to include the link. The site credit link itself can go directly to the Web site of the designer or open a page similar in layout to the rest of the site with contact information for the designer.

- **XHTML, HTML, CSS, and 508 compliance information:** If being accessible to any and all Web visitors is important to the site owners, the site should proudly display compliance information.

Transfer

You'll learn more about following guidelines set by online Web standards organizations in Chapter 9, which is entirely devoted to working with Web standards.

- **Site Search:** Though not at all required, providing a means for searching an entire Web site's content with keywords can improve the site's *stickiness* (the ability of a site to entice people to stay on the site longer). The most popular free search tool is Google Free. Get the code from Google at `www.google.com/searchcode.html`. As an alternative to this type of remote site search tool (where a search engine remotely searches and returns search results for a specified URL), you could also build your own server-based search tool, complete with a search results page. For further information about both methods, read the WebMonkey.com "Adding Search to Your Site" article at `http://webmonkey.com/webmonkey/00/09/index2a.html?tw=e-business`.

Diagnosing a Site's Dynamic Needs

A *dynamic* Web site refers to a site that uses a programming language, such as ASP, JSP, PHP, or ColdFusion, to gather specific records of information from a database, such as Microsoft Access or MySQL, and display that data on a Web page. Many sole proprietors, small businesses, and nonprofit companies might have little need (if any) to offer a Web site with dynamic capabilities. Having dynamic content on a Web site largely depends on the goals and budget of the site owner.

By organizing and storing data in a database, the content can be selectively pulled according to different scenarios or rules set up in advance. For instance, one business might want to display the ten most recent news items on a page containing news about the company. Presuming new data is regularly being entered into the database, the programming language can be set to check article publication dates and always pull and display the ten most recent files on a particular page.

You can use databases to store and retrieve all kinds of data. For instance, you might decide to use a database on your (or your client's) Web site to display

- Articles, papers, and documents sorted by date, author, and so on
- Store locations, hours of operation, and contact information

- Categories of products and product detail information
- Lists of services and service detail information
- A glossary of industry-related terms or FAQs
- Customer membership information or saved shopping cart details

In addition to dynamically accessing and using data, databases can be used to assist with adding, deleting, and editing content on a Web site. For an added fee, many programmers and host providers can now build a custom *Content Management System* (CMS) for a site, which allows site owners to easily control specific site content through a customized Web interface. Depending on the size of the project and the complexity of the dynamic needs, a CMS Web site component can cost as little as $1,000 to as much as $15,000 or more. This type of cost-effective tool can be extremely useful for sites requiring frequent updates.

Though admittedly slick, not every site needs to use a database. To determine whether your site needs to use one, take a good look at the type of content you intend to display. Ask yourself these questions:

- **How often will the content need updating?** Sites with daily and weekly update requirements might benefit from a database, whereas sites requiring less frequent modifications might be better off without the added expense.

- **Are more than 20 products or services being sold?** If the site is selling only a handful of products, though time consuming, each product can have its own Web page. However, if more than 20 products will be sold, using a database to dynamically create each product page would be more efficient.

- **What kind of growth does the company expect to achieve in the next year, three years, five years?** For some sites, there will be little to no intended growth, and therefore no real cost justification to using dynamic features. On the other hand, sites that project to grow their products and services over a few years might greatly benefit by building a site that can accommodate such growth.

- **Does the company need to collect and use visitor data?** E-commerce sites have good reason to collect data from purchasers, to both streamline the ordering process and provide future sale and promotional information, whereas a small business could just as easily manage that information by using a simple HTML form and an Excel file.

- **Is there or will there soon be enough dynamic content — such as a listing of store locations or the ten most exciting daily news articles — to justify the cost?** Depending on the complexity of the data processing, some things might be cost prohibitive for the start-up company yet affordable to the established business. Certainly the old adage "to make money, you need to spend money" pertains, but not everyone can afford to spend the money even when they want to.

The decision should be fairly clear after answering these types of questions. If you're still unsure whether to use a database, get quotes from programmers or hosting companies to see how it will impact the budget for your project. Money can sometimes be the great decider.

Defining Ways to Drive Traffic to a Site

When most people visit a Web site, they're typically looking for specific information about a particular product or service, like a 16.6-cubic-foot refrigerator. Although finding that information is important — presuming the products or services are the company's bread and butter — Web sites should also be sure to include other information that supports the product or service, such as the answers to frequently asked questions, company information, customer support, and contact information. Beyond that, any other information on the site is strictly optional — unless, of course, the site owners want to drive more traffic to the site, which they should.

Information Kiosk

Statistically speaking, the more traffic a site gets, the greater the likelihood is that it'll get visitors who will want the products and/or services being sold or will at least tell another person they know about your site.

Fortunately, you can use lots of great techniques to increase visitor traffic that have nothing to do with the product or service being sold. For instance, you or your client might decide to start a newsletter that offers industry-related tips, free downloads, or coupons, or the site owner (or you if he or she hires you to do post-launch site maintenance) might begin to post weekly articles on a variety of topics related to products or services. Other sites might post blogs, use polls, offer free calculator tools, or even have frequent contests with fun prizes.

In the following sections, you get a chance to look at a few of these options in greater detail. As you compare these options and decide which ones you might want to include in your plan, keep the site's purpose, benefit to visitors, and image at the forefront of your (and your client's) mind. These factors should help identify the best ways to make the site sticky.

E-newsletters

E-newsletters are a fantastic way to communicate regularly with customers through e-mail. An e-newsletter keeps a company or organization name, products, and services in customers' minds when they read it. And each one creates another opportunity to have a positive and meaningful exchange with site visitors.

Most e-newsletters are graphically formatted in HTML (but they might also be plain text, or you can offer both) and typically include the following:

- Some kind of topical news
- Sale offers
- Information about new products and services
- Upcoming events listings
- Links to articles or products online
- Company information, the date, instructions on how to subscribe and unsubscribe to the newsletter, and a few Web site links

Watch Your Step

Giving readers the choice to subscribe and unsubscribe is an important part of netiquette and will help you avoid looking like a spammer. With that in mind, I strongly recommend that, when sending e-newsletters, you take extra care to ensure that 1) you ask permission of your site visitors to add their e-mail address to your customer list *before* sending them anything, and 2) you include, in every mailing, a simple method for visitors to unsubscribe to your list. See the nearby sidebar for more about the art and practice of netiquette.

For exceptional information about writing and designing e-newsletters, check out the book called *Sign Me Up!: A Marketer's Guide to Creating E-Mail Newsletters That Build Relationships and Boost Sales,* by Matt Blumberg and Michael Mayor, published by Return Path Books.

To send newsletters, you can choose from a variety of e-mail programs, though the best supported applications are for PC only. Alternatively, if you'd rather outsource the management of your e-mail list to another company, several great online services can handle the job. Table 1-3 lists two mail programs and two newsletter services that have great reputations.

Table 1-3   Third-Party Newsletter Services

Product	Web Site
Direct Mail (PC & Mac)	http://ethreesoftware.com/directmail
Outlook Express (PC only)	www.microsoft.com/windows/ie/ie6/ downloads/critical/ie6sp1/default.mspx
Mail Chimp	www.mailchimp.com
Constant Contact	www.constantcontact.com

Step into the Real World

The Importance of Netiquette   Nowadays, purchase anything online and you're probably automatically added to the selling company's e-newsletter. If you enjoy learning more about towel sales, electronics equipment, and office supplies (for instance), seeing these e-mails in your inbox might be somewhat of a pleasant surprise for you each time they arrive. But when unwanted newsletters arrive — especially when you didn't expressly authorize the enrollment to the e-mail list — these kinds of missives can seem more like spam.

When sending e-mails and otherwise communicating over the Internet, do you use your best online manners? Network etiquette, or *netiquette,* is the set of unspoken rules everyone online should follow whether sending personal or professional messages. Each interaction online should be polite, courteous, kind, and considerate — using a sort of "do unto others" set of e-ethics to guide all your online correspondence and transactions.

To find out how your Internet manners rate, take the Netiquette Quiz at `www.albion.com/netiquette/netiquiz.html`.

Tips and articles

If marketing a service is the main thrust of a Web site, e-mailing industry-related tips to subscribed members and publishing regular articles on the site are both smart ways to provide tangible benefits and build a positive relationship with visitors. And remember that the more positive contact a site has with its audience, the greater the likelihood that audience will want the site's product or service.

Coming up with ideas for tips and articles is quite easy, really. Just think of all the things you know about your client's business that could help visitors and then jot them down. For example, if the site you're designing is a dog-grooming business, the tips might include the following:

- How to choose a dog-grooming brush
- A review of the best dog shampoos
- How to keep a dog's teeth clean
- Exercise tips that keep dogs fit

Tips within the e-mail can also help bring visitors to your site to read more tips, as well as learn more about and potentially purchase the site's products and services. Take the CliffsNotes Web site (`www.cliffnotes.com`) for example, shown in Figure 1-2. There visitors can sign up for newsletters; browse for literature, test prep guides, and other titles; and get free advice on studying and student life.

Figure 1-2: Good e-newsletters include tips that get readers to visit the authoring Web site.

Take the same idea and apply it to your projected Web site. Try to come up with at least 12 ideas that you could conceivably use for tips or articles over the next 12 months.

Blogs

Blogging is fast becoming the best way for Internet readers to learn about and provide feedback on nearly every topic of interest. That's because blog news travels fast. Blogs encourage instant feedback from readers and are a place for readers to share information and experience. Best of all, participation in the blogosphere provides instant cachet in the Internet world. When combined with business goals (like increasing Web traffic and online sales), blogs provide business owners with the opportunity to communicate directly with their target audience.

So what is a blog? The name is short for Web log, and it typically refers to a Web site that posts short articles (or just a few paragraphs) of information related to particular products, services, news, careers, hobbies, thoughts, beliefs, or ideas. These articles tend to be published on a regular basis (daily is most popular) and listed on the site in reverse chronological order, with the newest articles at the top of the page and older articles below. In addition to newer articles, most blogs contain archived articles, pictures, and links to other sites and blogs.

One popular feature of blogs is the ability to allow visitors to e-mail the author and/or respond directly to any given article by posting their comments to it, thereby creating a forum for online exchanges between the blogger and the blog's audience. Having a blog that offers advice and feedback from other consumers can be a very effective sticky site tool.

As you consider whether to include a blog in the site you're designing, here are some points to keep in mind:

- **A blog needs people who can add new content on a regular basis.** To maintain the sticky factor, you need to be able to post new and interesting content frequently. It's what will keep people coming back to your site. Some blogs post one or more short articles per day. Others post content a few times per week.

  To spread out the responsibility for authorship, blogs can be set up for groups or businesses where there can be multiple blog authors in addition to full participation in commenting and feedback.

  Be sure to learn some basic blogging rules and authoring styles prior to starting your own blog. One helpful book is *We Blog: Publishing Online with Weblogs*, by Paul Bausch and company (Wiley). It takes you through the steps of setting up a blog, points you to some great tools, and even covers promotion and syndication.

- **A visually appealing blog makes a good impression.** Besides the content, the look of the blog is all important because a visually captivating blog will be more welcoming than one that obviously took no care to lay out. Fortunately, sites like Createablog.com contain useful, free layouts, scripts, graphics, and more to assist with the blog look and feel.

  In addition to the overall look, adding pictures to your blog posts adds appeal, too. Though having images on a blog isn't a requirement, it's a nice feature to include, and most blog hosts allow you to upload photos to each post as a way to enhance or editorialize an article. Some even let you upload photos and text straight from your mobile camera phone.

  Figure 1-3 shows how the folks at CHOW.com incorporate a blog (The Grinder) right into the main content on the site.

- **Take time to decide what blogging tools you'll use.** When you add a blog to your site, it can either be off your main URL, hosted by a special blog-hosting service (such as `www.blogger.com`), or on your main URL by using special blog software on the server used to host your site. The four most popular offsite blog hosts are Blogger.com, TypePad.com, BlogHarbor.com, and LiveJournal.com.

Figure 1-3: CHOW.com uses a blog to allow its writers to communicate directly with site visitors.

To find out which blog tool works best for your Web project needs, you (and/or your client) should test as many of them as you can by creating sample blogs. Most blog hosts offer either free basic blogs or 30-day trials of fee-based blogging services. After you've learned to use each of the tools, you can select the one that best meets your needs.

Some tools offer enhanced blogging services for a fee, such as TypePad.com, which has three tiers of pricing from a simple one blog per author ($4.95/month) to a professional multiple authors with unlimited number of blogs ($14.95/month), or BlogHarbor.com, which offers full features at different pricing tiers (from $8.95/month to $34.95/month) that vary by bandwidth (1GB to 40GB) and hard drive space (100MB to 5GB).

You can help draw visitors to your blog with a profile. When the blog is live on the Internet, you can create a profile (like an About page on a Web site) for the author or group. The profile identifies the blogger's interests by category (such as worldwide volunteerism, CSS hacks for Web designers, or organic foods and recipes), by statistics, and by outside blog links. This profile helps people with common interests find the blog. Profiling is key so that the audience visiting the site belongs to the demographic group the blog is concerned about. For example, if you create a blog for your client on the topic of fundraising for education, the target audience might not necessarily include train hobbyists unless one or more of the posts on the blog has to do with using hobby trains as a means to raise funds for education.

Information Kiosk

Beyond these basics, you can add other elements to a blog to enhance the visitor experience and generate revenue for the blog owner. For example, you can use AdSense, a tool by Google that automatically places content-relevant ads on registered users' blogs. Each click on an ad by a reader earns money for the blog owner. There are also ways of globalizing content through blog syndication (news feeds with ATOM or RSS) whereby the blog host generates machine-readable versions of the blog for display on special newsreaders, hand-held devices, and Web sites. Bloggers might also benefit from enrollment in blog services (such as Bloglines.com or Technorati.com) that allow for enhanced blog searches and sharing news feeds, among other things.

On the plus side, with very little overhead, blog posts can and often do spread news and information faster than most traditional media sources, such as TV, newspapers, and radio. Similar to some forms of guerilla marketing where information is passed through word of mouth, blogs far surpass traditional marketing avenues, because they're global and typically reach an audience who's interested and takes active participation in getting the news rather than passively having advertising and ideas presented to them.

On the minus side, regularly posting to blogs can be a very time-consuming task, so you'll need to consider in advance what kind of posting schedule to maintain, be it daily, a few times a week, or weekly.

Watch Your Step

An abandoned or unkempt blog can be more injurious to a business identity than no blog at all. A blog with little to no content — as well as one with little to no feedback — can give visitors the impression that the blogger doesn't care about visitors, which in turn can make visitors not care about visiting. And, if no one cares, why bother reading posts, exploring the adjoining Web site, and possibly using the site's products and services?

Additionally, keep in mind that blog audiences currently reach only about 20 percent of the total Internet population. (That's worldwide, with most of the audience living in the United States rather than abroad.)

The bottom line for blogging is that, because the blogosphere is rife with illiterate, uninteresting, and infrequently updated or abandoned blogs, it's probably going to be a good idea only if a person or business is willing to devote time to adding to and improving the blog, to implementing ways to drive relevant traffic to it, and ultimately to saying something interesting *and* saying it well.

Polls

Because people love to give their opinions as well as learn about what other people think, polls are great tools to add to Web sites where opinions matter. For example, folks who are crazy about *American Idol* can visit the entertainment section of America Online to (unofficially) vote for their favorite idol. Likewise, movie-goers who want to give their opinion about whether a book was better than the movie version of it can sound off with a poll at MoviePhone.com.

Polls generate buzz at the water cooler, and that kind of talk might generate more business. Like blogs, polls can be hosted remotely or added to a site by installing poll software on the server. Basicpoll.com, Pollhost.com, Bravenet.com, and Sparklit.com, among many others, offer free or subscription polling services. Or, if you're more technologically minded and want to configure a poll yourself, go to `www.javascriptkit.com/howto/polls.shtml` to find information about installing a polling program on your site by using PHP, CGI, or ASP.

Calculators

Depending on the type of business you're designing a Web site for, having a calculator somewhere on the site could help increase traffic from the target demographic. For instance, if the Web site offers mortgage loans, consider having a mortgage calculator on the site that crunches different monthly payments and interest rates for prospective clients. Or, if you're designing a site for a travel company, add currency and temperature calculators to the site as a special aid to travelers.

Because calculators are a great value-added feature for Web sites, and the JavaScript code for many online calculators can be found and used for free, the following exercise will walk you through the steps you'd take to find and use a calculator on any one of your Web site projects. For your own projects, I highly recommend you first visit `www.calculator.com` to get a general overview of the kinds of online calculators that exist, and then spend some time searching for free calculators to find Web sites that offer free JavaScript code.

For this exercise, you'll search for, find, and use a particular calculator script that converts file size (or bandwidth) into bytes, kilobytes (K), megabytes (MB), and gigabytes (GB). For example, if you want to know how many bytes are in a gigabyte, the answer is 1,073,741,824.

1. **Open a blank Web page in your preferred HTML code editor.**

To create one by using a simple text editor such as Notepad or TextEdit, open a new, blank document and type the following code:

```
<!DOCTYPE html PUBLIC "-//W3C//DTD XHTML 1.0 Transitional//EN"
"http://www.w3.org/TR/xhtml1/DTD/xhtml1-transitional.dtd">
<html xmlns="http://www.w3.org/1999/xhtml">
<head>
<meta http-equiv="Content-Type" content="text/html; charset=iso-8859-1" />
<title>Untitled Document</title>
</head>
<body>
<!-- Insert calculator script below this line -->
</body>
</html>
```

2. Point your browser to `www.javascriptkit.com/script/script2/`
`bandwidthcal.shtml`.

This page contains a free script that will calculate different bandwidths based
on user input.

3. In the scrollable text area below the word Directions, select all the code and
press Ctrl+C (Windows) or ⌘+C (Mac) to copy it onto your computer's
Clipboard.

Figure 1-4 shows an image of the page with the code selected.

Figure 1-4: To select the code, click inside the code box and then choose Select All from the Edit
menu. To copy the selected code, press Ctrl+C (Windows) or ⌘+C (Mac).

4. **Paste the copied calculator code from the javascriptkit.com Web site between the opening and closing `<body>` tags on your blank Web page.**

   If you created your own page by using the code from Step 1, paste the calculator script below the line of code that says `Insert calculator script below this line`.

5. **Choose File → Save As, give your Web page a filename such as *calculator*, and save the page with the `.html` or `.htm` file extension.**

6. **View the calculator in action by opening the saved HTML file in a browser window.**

   To open the page in a browser, either double-click the file to launch it in a browser or drag and drop the file by its icon into any open browser window.

7. **To test the calculator script, enter any number in the first form field, select a unit of measure from the drop-down list, and click the Calculate button.**

   For instance, you might type **2300MB** to find it is equal to 2,411,724,800 bytes, 2,355,200KB, 2,300MB, and 2GB.

Contests and Sweepstakes

Contests can consist of anything you can think up. Raffle off a car. Give away a free computer class. Send winners on an all-expenses paid vacation. Affiliate your company with a worthy cause and offer cash to winners while increasing awareness about an important issue. Sponsors of events will often provide valuable prizes for your contests at no cost in exchange for the free publicity, such as offering winners a $500 Cingular gift card, ten passes to the new IMAX movie, or 100 free Betty Crocker cookbooks. Enrollment in the contest can happen automatically after a visitor signs up for the e-newsletter, registers for membership, or completes an online contest entry form.

Watch Your Step

If you do decide to have an online contest or sweepstakes on your site, be sure to follow the strict federal legal guidelines to ensure your contest is fair. Read the article "Online Contest or Illegal Lottery?" on the legality of contests and the pitfalls of illegal lotteries at www.techfirm.com/InternetContests.htm as a starting point to learn more about what legal rules to follow. You might also want to seriously consider hiring an outside firm, like Nationalsweeps.com, to organize and administer the contest for you.

blog: A Web site that publishes a person's thoughts, ideas, opinions, and impressions (like an online journal) on a topic and solicits feedback from visitors. A person who has his or her own blog or writes for one is called a blogger. For a handy glossary on blogging, see `www.samizdata.net/blog/glossary.html`.

blogosphere: The world of blogging.

CMS: Content Management System. A tool developed by a programmer, typically with some kind of Web interface, that ties into a Web site's database and allows the operators of a site to easily manage specified parts of the site's content without having to know any programming languages or HTML.

cookie: Small data file containing personal information (name, address, phone, username, password, IP address, shopping cart contents, and so on) about a site visitor and the time spent on a particular Web site. A site's server automatically sends a cookie to a visitor's computer. The cookie file is automatically saved to the visitor's computer so that future visits to the same site will run smoother and give the visitor faster access to his or her online accounts.

database: A collection of information, like a spreadsheet, with data organized into categories that can be easily retrieved by a computer program or by programming language on a Web site. Many Web sites use Microsoft Access or mySQL for the database and ASP, PHP, JSP, or ColdFusion as the programming language used to retrieve and display the data.

dynamic: Dynamic data or dynamic content refers to the way information can be automatically pulled from a database with special programming code (ASP, JSP, PHP, or ColdFusion) and displayed on a Web page on the fly. For example, a site can dynamically display the three most recent news articles, show a different image on part of the page each time the page is loaded or refreshed, or display search results based on a visitor's search input.

home page: This is the first page on a Web site that visitors see when they type in your Web address, such as `http://www.yourwebsite.com`. This page should include the company name and/or logo, navigation to the rest of the site, and text describing the site's products or services.

netiquette: The art of being respectful on the Internet. The term was coined by Virginia Shea in the early 1990s and refers to the good manners and interpersonal and professional etiquette that Web users should practice when sending and receiving e-mails and otherwise communicating over the Internet.

continued

 **continued**

standards-compliant: The World Wide Web Consortium (www.w3.org) and other noted groups set Internet standards to help streamline the process of creating similarly architected Web sites that are accessible to the widest possible audience and use the latest, tested technology. Following these standards will make your Web site standards-compliant.

stickiness: The ability of a site to attract and retain visitors. Ideal sticky site goals are to get the most traffic, keep visitors on the site as long as possible, and get visitors to return to the site as often as possible. Content such as blogs, e-newsletters, polls, games, contests, calculators, and the like can increase stickiness.

Last Stop

Practice Exam

1. True or False: If a Web site doesn't sell any products, it doesn't need a privacy policy page.

2. True or False: A site map is a Web page that has hyperlinks to all the pages on a Web site.

3. What are two reasons why a person, organization, or business might want to have a Web site?

_____

_____

4. How can defining the purpose of a Web site assist with building a site?

_____

_____

5. Describe three ways to use a database on a Web site.

_____

_____

6. What two file formats can you use to e-mail newsletters to registered visitors?

A) JPEG or TIFF

B) DOC or HTM

C) Plain text or HTML

D) XML or CSS

7. Why is it important to construct an identity for a Web site?

A) The client needs a way to ensure quality control of the site so that the branding or identity conforms to standards he or she might have set for other forms of communication.

B) The identity is something visitors can connect with both intellectually and emotionally, and it assists you with making aesthetic decisions about the site before it gets designed and built.

C) Having an identity for a Web site makes it more memorable to visitors and gives them a way to find the site again, boosting its search engine optimization.

D) By starting with an identity, you can more easily base a design on premade templates that come with Web page editors such as Dreamweaver, and using these templates saves time and reduces the amount of programming required to design a site.

8. Name some advantages and disadvantages of keeping a blog on a Web site.

_____

_____

_____

_____

9. A client comes to you to design and build a simple Web site for her eyeglass frames stores in the greater Atlanta, Georgia, area. The site is mostly static content, but she says she'll need to update the 100 or so photos of eyeglass frames about once every 6–8 months, and she wants to have a store locator where a visitor can type in a zip code to see the location, address, map, store hours, and contact information for the closest store. Would you recommend that this client add a Content Management System to the site? Why or why not?

_____

_____

_____

_____

CHAPTER 2

Defining Your Audience

STATIONS ALONG THE WAY

- Performing market research
- Gathering information on the target audience's computer usage
- Assessing a site's competition
- Learning how to characterize a target audience
- Preparing a site for multilanguage display

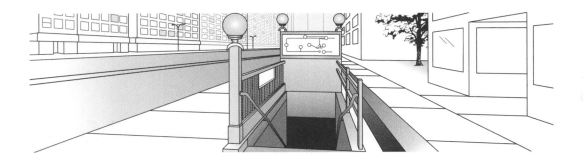

 # Enter the Station

Questions

1. What can online browser statistics teach you about the computer usage of the site's target audience?

2. What kind of research can you do to find information about the site's competition in local, regional, national, and global markets?

3. How might you go about defining the ideal site visitor?

4. If the site owner will be doing business overseas or worldwide, what do you need to consider in terms of the site's technical needs as well as its content and design?

Express Line

Some of your clients might have already done the kind of market research outlined in this chapter. If that's the case, move on to Chapter 3, where you'll learn about ways to organize the client's Web content.

Most Web site projects tend to have a logical flow of development, a type of evolution, that when followed can streamline the entire design process:

1. Planning Phase
2. Contract Phase
3. Design Phase
4. Building Phase
5. Testing Phase
6. Site Launch

After the planning steps, which you followed in Chapter 1, you should have enough information to successfully move into the contract phase, where you'll estimate fees for the project and then draft and submit a proposal to the client.

Information Kiosk

After the client gives verbal approval of the proposal, you can write up an official written contract and present it to the client for signatures. At the same time, you can collect financial retainers or deposits from the client along with any content or materials needed to begin development of the site. Try to get at least a 25 percent deposit from the client before you do any work. This shows good faith on your part for doing the work, and good faith on the client's part that he or she is serious about having you do the work and is willing to pay part of the fees to retain your services.

After you get the contract and deposit, you can safely enter into the design phase, which is where this chapter begins. Identifying the target audience (the first part of the design phase) is an information-gathering process that helps you make a Web site's design effective.

In this chapter, you will focus on defining the target audience by learning everything you can about the audience members — what their computer usage and Internet surfing habits are, where they fall demographically, what their buying preferences happen to be, and more. You'll also spend a little time doing your own informal market research by taking a good look at the competition to help give your Web project an extra edge.

Transfer

You continue to work on the design phase in later chapters of this book. Chapter 3 will cover organizing content; Chapter 6, defining a layout; Chapter 7, creating the design (and getting design approval); and Chapter 8, optimizing Web graphics.

Understanding Market Research

Market research is one of the best ways to begin the design phase of a Web site project. With specific regard to Web design, you can do a few things to make the most of your market research time:

- The first task is to gather some general information about the computer usage and Internet browsing habits of Internet users. Knowledge of who is out there using the Internet will greatly assist you in making important decisions about the site's size, layout, and accessibility features.

Information Kiosk

If you don't know much about market research, take a look at the KnowThis.com Web site, which bills itself as the Marketing Virtual Library — a place where visitors can learn about market research, marketing, advertising, and more. Besides the general marketing information, you'll also find many useful articles, tutorials, and even free research reports there. Another great resource on marketing and market research is the Marketing section on About.com (http://marketing.about.com).

- The second thing to do to with your marketing research time is to see what other businesses in the same field have already done with their Web sites. By looking at Web sites of competitors, not only can you find out what was already done poorly and take steps to avoid those mistakes, but you can also learn a lot from what the competition has done well and make plans to implement similar ideas in your Web project.

- For the third marketing research task, you'll define the ideal site visitor based on the demographic information you can glean from your own informal marketing research. The clearer your understanding of where the target audience lives — what their ages, income levels, buying habits, and interests are — the more customized to their tastes you'll be able to make the site design. You'll use this information when you get to Chapter 6 to make important decisions about the site's layout, color palette, image usage, and navigation scheme.

The following sections of this chapter will address each of these three marketing strategies.

Gathering Internet Usage Statistics

Before you gather any specific demographic information about your target audience, go find out about Internet users in general by reviewing the latest statistics regarding computer usage and Internet-browsing habits.

1. **Visit one or more online resources that offer information on computer usage and browsing.**

One of the best is W3Schools.com, where they list detailed, long-running (since January 2002), up-to-date browser, OS, and computer usage statistics.

For additional statistical data on Internet usage and browsing habits, visit

```
www.thecounter.com/stats
www.upsdell.com/BrowserNews
www.webreference.com/stats/browser.html
www.ews.uiuc.edu/bstats/latest.html
```

2. **Note the information about browser usage. Get the percentage of browser users on the most popular browsers, including Internet Explorer, Firefox, Mozilla, Opera, Netscape, and America Online.**

3. **Find out which operating systems (Windows, Mac, Linux) are the most popular among people accessing the Web.**

4. **Find out what people going online have their monitor resolutions and bit depths set to.**

Resolution refers to the number of pixels used horizontally and vertically to set the screen size of the monitor. The most common size these days is 1,024 x 768. After the resolution size is set, monitors use bits of color to create the actual display. The more bits used, the clearer the image and the more colors can be displayed. For example, an 8-bit monitor can display only 256 colors, whereas a 24-bit monitor can display millions of colors!

5. **Note the percentage of Internet users (90 percent) who leave the JavaScript enabled in their browsers.**

JavaScript is an easy-to-use, easy-to-learn, simple scripting language that when added to a Web page's HTML code can perform interactive functions such as opening new browser windows, changing an image when a visitor moves the cursor over a graphic, and displaying the current date.

Based on W3Schools.com analytic data as of May 2006, over 50 percent of all computer users were surfing the Internet with the Internet Explorer 6 browser, and another 25 percent were using Firefox; a whopping 74 percent of all Internet consumers are PC users running the WinXP OS while only 3.6 percent on the Web use Mac; and, because new monitors come factory preset resolutions of at least 1,024 x 768 pixels, nearly 60 percent of all computer users who go online leave the monitor's resolution that way.

This kind of information clearly tells you that, at minimum, you absolutely need to test Web page development in an IE 6 JavaScript-enabled browser on a PC with a 24-bit-depth monitor with a resolution set to 1,024 x 768 prior to site launch, because these are the facts about of most of the online population that is likely to visit the Web site.

Information Kiosk

After the Web project is completed, the site can harness the power of real-time Internet traffic reports to gather statistical data about actual site visitors, including geographic origin, search term usage, entry and exit pages, and more. Three well-respected services providing Web statistics and analysis are Opentracker.net, Omniture.com, and ClickTracks.com. Although costly, this kind of data can help site owners identify marketing strategies that aren't working so they can make site improvements based on actual visitor preferences.

Looking at Competitors' Web Sites

No matter what business your Web project happens to be in, you can evaluate scores of Web sites representing competitors in the same field for their apparent successes and failures. The beauty of this strategy is that it's free, and as long as you have access to a computer, you can do this market research online any time, 24 hours a day.

Begin your research by doing several keyword search engine searches for similar businesses in the local, regional, state, national, and global arenas, regardless of your specific Web project's anticipated marketing scope. For example, if you're working on a Web project for a local catering company that does business only within a 100-mile radius of its offices, be sure to also search for catering company Web sites across the entire country. If you do that, you're bound to find some great catering Web sites in other geographic regions that can be used for design inspiration as well as a springboard for defining and refining your project's site content requirements.

Keywords — if you didn't already know this — are any specific words or phrases that define the thing, person, or place a site visitor is searching for in a search engine, database, or catalog. For example, if you wanted to find a new hairdresser, you might do a search engine search for the keywords *"hair salon"* along with the name of your city and state, such as *"hair salon, San Francisco, CA"*. After submitting the keywords to the search engine, the Web page would then display a listing of results that contained the same keywords. Although most often used within the context of normal content on a Web page, you can also use keywords within page titles, headings, and Meta data as a means to drive additional traffic to a Web site.

How will you know what keywords to use to find competitors' Web sites? Think of the words you would use to find your client's business or your own.

To illustrate how to perform keyword searches at the local, state, and global market levels, presume you want to assess the competition of your Web client, an award-winning BBQ catering service based in Little Rock, Arkansas, and follow these steps:

1. **In the search field of your favorite search engine, type the following local search terms:** BBQ Catering, Barbecue Catering, Little Rock, Arkansas, champion, award, first place.

   The local search includes the name of the client's city and state, which will help the search engine narrow the focus of the returned results. Results should include a listing of other restaurants in the same town that also do BBQ catering. Take a look at the top ten or twenty links and review each site, making notes about the content and layout.

2. **Do a statewide search by entering these keywords into the browser search field:** BBQ Catering, Barbecue Catering, Arkansas, champion, award, first place.

   This search doesn't include the city of Little Rock, which allows the search results to include BBQ catering businesses across the entire state of Arkansas. Results now are geared more toward BBQ champions within the state, other catering companies, and even BBQ blogs. Again, click through to the top 10 to 20 links in the search results listings and note any interesting content and layout features that appeal to you and might be useful to mention to your Web client.

3. **The last search will be national or global in nature by the omission of any geography. Search for** BBQ Catering, Barbecue Catering, champion, award, first place.

   This search provides links to other BBQ catering businesses across the country, as well as restaurants that have won awards, BBQ classes and special events, and other resources for the BBQ aficionado. In this search results listing, you might want to search deeper than 20 entries to find other relevant competitors' sites, because this search result will include a wider variety of results that might or might not suit your needs.

The search results listings for each of these keyword searches will be geared to the specific geographic areas contained in the keyword string, each providing you with more insight to the world of BBQ catering across the city, state, and country. What you're likely to find by doing wider searches like this is that companies doing national and even global business tend to have the better-looking, better-functioning sites when compared to their local/state counterparts.

Look closely at the content presented on the result Web sites and work with your client to ensure that his or her site includes content that visitors will want to read. In the case of BBQ catering, that might mean including things on the site like Company Information, Menus, Directions to the Restaurant (if the catering is part of the main business of running a restaurant), Press Releases and Awards, Visitor Comments, Specialty Sauces for Sale, and possibly Dine-In Coupons.

Even when your client provides you with all the content before you begin the design phase of the project, you should still perform a keyword review of the competition to ensure that the client hasn't forgotten anything. This will also really help you to make important decisions in regard to layout and design so the site will stand out from the competition.

Information Kiosk

Another way to find relevant keywords is to look at the competition's keywords, which are typically placed in the Keywords and Description Meta tags in the HTML code. To find these keywords, open a competitor's Web site in a browser window and choose View → Page Source. The browser will open a separate window containing the HTML code of the page displaying in the browser. Scroll down just a little until you see the Meta tags and review the Keywords and Descriptions. Not all sites use them, but the good ones do.

In the next exercise, create a list of applicable local, state, and/or national/global search keywords for each of the three following pretend businesses. *Tip:* Sometimes several individual key phrase searches might be necessary to find competitors' sites, such as doing one for *"camping in Alaska"* and another for *"Alaskan camping"*.

1. A safari adventure company, based in Boston, Massachusetts, that books luxury tent safari tours to South Africa, Kenya, and Tanzania.

Local/State:

National/Global:

2. A small food tour guide service in New York City that provides walking food tours that explore the boroughs' unique neighborhoods and samples of Greek, Indian, Puerto Rican, Cuban, Chinese, Korean, Jewish, Caribbean, Italian, Polish, and Russian cuisines.

Local/State:

National/Global:

3. A modern, off-beat interior design firm in San Francisco, California, that specializes in residential loft design and renovations.

Local:

State:

National/Global:

Here are some possible answers for each example site:

- **The safari adventure company:**

  Local/State: Boston, Massachusetts, luxury African safari, tours to Africa, South Africa, Kenya, and Tanzania

  Global: African safari, luxury tours, Africa, South Africa, Kenya, and Tanzania

- **The small food tour guide service:**

  Local/State: food walking tours, New York City

  Global: food walking tours, food tasting tours, culinary walking tours

- **The interior design firm:**

  Local: San Francisco, California, interior design, residential, lofts, renovations

  State: California, interior design, residential, lofts, renovations

  Global: interior design, residential, lofts, renovations

If you're working on a project now, use the following space to come up with keywords to define that business so you can perform your own local, state, and national/global search.

Local:

State:

National/Global:

Next, using either your current Web project or one of the three example businesses from the preceding list, perform both a local/state and a national/global keyword search and review the Web sites of any competitors listed in the search results.

Take copious notes about your findings when looking at the competition. You'll use this information later in the chapter to define the ideal site visitor.

Here are some questions you might want to ask yourself when reviewing competitors' sites:

- Can you determine where the target audience lives: the suburbs, the country, the city, everywhere?

- What kinds of photographic images seem to appeal to them?

- Do competitors' sites seem to use any particular colors for this audience?

- What is the target audience's age group: Teens? Kids? Seniors?

- Does the target audience seem to have any particular hobbies or group interests, like being a sports fan, cook, artist, or gamer?
- Can you guess what kinds of values (religious, ethical, political, and so on) the audience might have?
- Can you identify any specific needs of the target audience?

Pay particular attention to site details, like colors, shapes, fonts, photographs, and other design elements that are consistently used on competitors' sites. When you know what everyone else is doing, you have the opportunity to decide whether to follow suit or break the mold in a unique and interesting way. If you're developing a new site for a company in the finance industry, for instance, and you notice that almost all the competitors uses navy blue as the primary color and burgundy as the secondary color, consider using two different but similar colors for your design, like a light blue and a rusty tan.

Also pay attention to the marketing messages other sites use to sell their products and services. These messages often shed revealing light on the target audience's buying preferences, habits, likes, and dislikes.

Other good resource areas for market research are the industry-related associations and organizations, as well as government agencies. You can often find Web sites for these groups by doing a search on your favorite search engine using terms like *"INDUSTRYNAME Association of America"*, *"American INDUSTRYNAME Association"*, or *"Association of INDUSTRYNAME of America"*.

When you're done with your research, organize the information into logical categories and summarize the details into a few definition-packed sentences of information. For example, if you performed keyword searches on the San Francisco interior design company, you might have discovered that many design companies favor using black, white, gray, and earth tones in their Web site designs, display lots of photographic examples, and tend to present their services to an audience who is well educated, cultured, and moneyed. Thus your summarized details might read, "Black, white, gray, and earth tones, clean, linear layouts, sophisticated audience that needs to be wowed with photographic examples of the client's work." With your summary completed, you can move on to the third marketing task of defining the ideal site visitor.

Describing the Ideal Site Visitor

At this stage, after gathering general computer usage information, the market research that is most valuable should have already been done by the company hiring you as a designer. If the client did his homework, he already knows the detailed demographic information about the people using his products or services and can pass that data on to you. Your role in the demographic market research, then, is really one of gathering and distilling what the client gives you to help define the ideal site visitor.

Ask your client for a demographic profile of his target audience. If that information isn't available, you can do what I call *research by proxy,* which is essentially harvesting information about the target audience by looking at competitors' Web sites and other industry-related sites.

Having a clear understanding of the ideal site visitor is an essential element of the design phase because that description will guide you to making important decisions about the site design. For instance, if you were going to develop a healthcare Web site for an audience composed mostly of seniors, you might deduce that font size might be an important issue and thus choose to make special modifications to the site's Cascading Style Sheets (by using percentages or other measurement units for the font size rather than pixels) that will give those visitors the ability to adjust font sizes through their browsers.

When starting to describe the ideal site visitor, begin your assessment with the demographic details of the target audience provided by your Web client. If that information doesn't exist, perform a keyword search for the business and gather relevant demographic data based on the Web sites of your client's competition.

Use the following questions to help define the ideal site visitor. To illustrate how you might answer each question, I'll use the example of a client seeking a Web site to sell his designer, screen-printed, organic cotton, men's and women's T-shirts.

1. Is the ideal visitor a man or woman, or does that matter?

A Web site for a mostly male audience might look very different from one that has a mostly female audience, whereas a site that should appeal to all visitors, both male and female, can (and probably should) use more gender neutral colors.

T-shirt site: Because the client is selling both men's and women's T-shirts, the audience must include both men and women. However, because women shop more than men, the ideal visitor is probably female.

2. Is the ideal visitor young, old, or somewhere in between? What age range does he/she fall in?

Having an age range for the ideal site visitor can assist you with making artistic and accessibility decisions. For example, a site for mostly college-aged student visitors can be more alternative in design layout, color, and font usage than a site that needs to appeal to white-collar business people in their 40s or 50s.

T-shirt site: Designer T-shirt wearers tend to be anywhere in the 12- to 42-year-old age range, depending on the grade of cotton, the sophistication of the design, and the intended retail outlets, if any. Presuming the client wants starlets like Paris Hilton and Lindsay Lohan wearing them, we can narrow the age range to 18 to 30 year olds.

3. Answering the next set of questions, which might rely solely on your imagination, can assist you in making other design and layout decisions.

Does the ideal visitor

- Smoke or drink alcohol?
- Attend a place of worship?
- Eat organically?
- Participate in sports?
- Clip coupons?
- Watch TV?
- Read newspapers?
- Own any pets?

Really get down to particulars and describe your ideal site visitor as clearly and vividly as you would a person sitting right next to you. The more you understand who will be visiting a site, the better that site can look.

T-shirt site: Because the trendy people often break the rules, presume the ideal visitor is a female that goes to parties, attends church on holidays, occasionally eats organically, doesn't play sports but skis and/or snowboards, barely watches TV or reads newspapers, spends most of her free time with friends, and has (or really wants to get) a tiny pet dog.

4. Using adjectives or descriptive statements, create a list of ten or more identity traits that define the ideal site visitor, similar to the exercise you performed on constructing an image for the site in Chapter 1.

Is the ideal site visitor smart or of average intelligence? Is she urban or suburban? Is she organized or messy, confident or timid, silly or serious? Who is this person?

T-shirt site: Single, urban, confident, a little irresponsible, fashionable, outgoing, makes good grades, image-conscious, sassy, and fun to be around.

5. Using the ten or so adjectives you generated in Step 4, write an identity statement for your project's ideal site visitor.

The identity statement will become your guiding statement of who to design the Web site for.

T-shirt site: A single, 22-year-old female who is an urban, confident, sometimes irresponsible, fashionable, outgoing person that overspends on fashion, likes to dance, have fun, meet new people, and try new things, goes to parties, drives a fun car, and lives with roommates.

Table 2-1 offers some examples of identity descriptions for a variety of businesses. Each description is unique to the type of business it represents, and each speaks to the creation of a different look and feel for the site design. The specific account of the ideal site visitor for your project will help you make intuitive, informed decisions about the site's colors, fonts, navigation, images, and more when you get to Chapter 6.

Table 2-1   **Example Identity Descriptions**

Type of Business	Description of the Ideal Site Visitor
Life coach	Smart, educated, middle-class, hard-working male or female entrepreneur in any industry who is or will soon be making a major life change and needs assistance getting organized, making decisions, meeting deadlines, and setting and achieving goals.
Alternative rock band	Urban, hip, trend-setting, open-minded, cutting-edge, casual, friendly 20- or 30-something person who wants to hear new music in clubs, download music, and/or write positive reviews about us for e-zines, magazines, and newspapers; and professional, honest, intelligent, open-minded, efficient, friendly, capable, and respected A&R music executive who is looking to sign record contracts with new alternative rock bands.
Global warming prevention non-profit organization	Smart, informed, educated, caring, concerned, active, supportive, reliable, and solution-oriented human (of all ages, races, sexes, and religions) who will take steps in his or her life to reduce global warming, as well as take an active role in educating others about this serious issue.
Start-up greeting card company	Fun, open, honest, witty, creative, professional, 20-to 80-year-old woman owner of retail greeting card store who is looking to buy new card lines and establish long-term wholesale buying relationships with a start-up greeting card company.

Planning for a Multilanguage Site

When learning about a target audience, one thing you might discover is that a significant portion of the audience might speak (or prefer to speak and/or read) another language besides English. This is particularly true when doing business worldwide, if the site intends to import or export products and services, or if you (or your client) are looking to expand a business by growing partnerships and buyers overseas. By giving visitors the option of accessing a site in another language, a business can significantly improve visitor browsing experience, increase market awareness about a Web site's products and services, and most importantly, positively impact business.

You can develop multilanguage sites in several different ways, so you'll need to explore options and choose a method in the early stages of the design phase after clarifying the picture of the ideal site visitor.

The three most popular methods of creating multilanguage sites are Total Site Replication, Full Dynamic Site Creation, and Selective Site Replication. The following sections explain these options and how to choose the best method for your site.

Understanding the options for organizing content

The three methods for creating the multilanguage site each require unique organizational structures and technical implementation on the remote server hosting the Web site.

The remote server can be any computer connected to the Internet that provides services to other computers through a network connection. Services include things like processing files with a remotely hosted application, sending and receiving e-mails, and retrieving information from a database. In the case of a multilanguage site, a remote server will hold all the files appearing on the Web site and shall deliver those files to a browser based on visitor input.

The three methods are

- **Total Site Replication:** In this method, a complete separate site is created for each language. The main language site is then hosted at the root level (the entry level) of the remote server, and additional language sites are stored in a subdirectory (folder) off the root level of the main language site, as shown in Figure 2-1. Visitors can jump from one language to another by using some kind of navigation linking system within the Web site's design. For example, the main site can present a menu from which visitors may select an alternative language to view the site in.

- **Full Dynamic Site Creation:** With a dynamic site, a database helps control how the content gets presented on the Web page. When each language has its own set of graphics and content, Web pages can use a programming language (such as ASP, JSP, PHP, or ColdFusion) to present the appropriate files to the viewer. In other words, this type of site can be dynamically generated based on the language preference selected by the site visitor when the site includes something called *session variables* to help determine which content and graphics to display. The term *session variable* refers to the different values a programming language object can accept at any one time during the course of a session, or exchange, between a program and a user. Figure 2-2 shows how a database can contain multilanguage data and then display only the selected content based on a visitor's preferences.

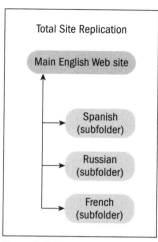

Figure 2-1: With Total Site Replication, each site is its own self-contained entity, sitting side by side on the remote server.

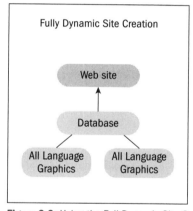

Figure 2-2: Using the Full Dynamic Site Creation method, a site can display content in the default language but can change when a visitor requests the site be viewed in an alternative language.

Selective Site Replication: The third method of creating a multilanguage site involves building Web pages that are dynamically generated based on the language preference selected by the site visitor. This means that instead of, say, specifically grabbing and displaying the Spanish About Us button (`sp_about.gif`) from the main images folder, all the content and graphics for each language are identically named but stored in different subfolders at the root level of the server, and they're dynamically parsed or pulled from the database before being displayed in a browser.

Figure 2-3 illustrates how this method uses a database to pull data from each directory before displaying the content on a Web page. For example, a graphic called `nav_01.gif` stored in an images folder in the English (`english/images/nav_01.gif`) subdirectory will have a Russian counterpart, also called `nav_01.gif`, stored in an images folder in the Russian subdirectory (`russian/images/nav_01.gif`). The differences between the language folders in this method are their organization locations on the server, the language the content contained within them is written in, and any language-specific text appearing on the graphics.

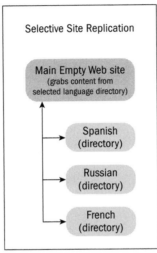

Figure 2-3: With Selective Site Replication, a visitor who chooses to view the site in French will see data pulled only from the French directory.

Choosing an organization method

Which organization method you choose for your multilanguage site ultimately depends on the client's budget and the number of languages the site needs to be displayed in. A simple two-language site, for example, could be built most affordably by using the Total Site Replication method, whereas sites with more than three languages, though more costly to implement, would benefit most from using the Selective Site Replication method.

To further assist you with choosing the best method for your multilanguage project, review Table 2-2, which outlines the benefits and drawbacks of each.

Table 2-2   **Multilanguage Organization Method
Benefits and Drawbacks**

Organization Method	Benefits	Drawbacks
Total Site Replication	Great for sites that have only 2 or 3 different languages but not too much content. Easy to keep track of content because each language site is totally separate from the other(s). Site replication can be somewhat automated when managing the site with a Web editor like Dreamweaver.	Changes to content (such as fixing bugs, updating text, or routine site maintenance) to one language site will need to be made to the attending page on the other language sites(s).
Full Dynamic Site Creation	Great for sites that have only 2 or 3 different languages but not too much content.	Slower browser page-loading times and changes to the site would need to be made directly to the database or to the database through a Content Management System.
Selective Site Replication	Great for multilanguage sites with three or more languages because all graphics and text for each language use identical naming conventions but are stored on the server in different subdirectories.	Modifying the site design can be complicated because many files will need to be re-created or modified to match any new content entered into the database or placed in the language subdirectories.

Transfer

If you choose to use either the Full Dynamic Site Creation or Selective Site Replication method of creating multilanguage sites, you might want to seriously consider hiring a programmer to assist you with the database development, programming, and deployment of the site. Chapter 4 speaks more in depth about hiring programmers to assist with the development of a site.

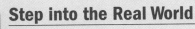

Step into the Real World

A Real Multilanguage Site   One of my clients, OonaHealth.com, a manufac-turer of women's herbal supplements, came to me when the company needed some help with the existing company Web site. Though the owner liked the design she already had, she wanted to improve the site's performance by cleaning up the code, changing a few graphics, implementing some site-wide page components, redesigning and programming the navigation, and updating content. She also wanted to create a mirror site in Spanish.

The client opted to use the Total Site Replication method for the Spanish site, leaving me with the task of designing and optimizing all the new graphics buttons for the Spanish site based on the client's original graphic designer's design, and using translation software to convert all the text, which was then pasted, page by page, into the Spanish version site. The client soon found, however, that the translation software didn't do a very good job because it seemed to pay no attention to context, destroyed referenced URLs in the text, and wasn't programmed to under-stand or interpret colloquialisms.

As a remedy, the client hired a Spanish-speaking translator who ended up reading through all the pages and manually making corrections to the text before giving them back to me so I could update the pages on the Spanish site. That process took a couple extra months, which meant the client had to choose between either having no Spanish site or having a badly translated Spanish site online until the updated content was ready. As a compromise, the client chose to leave the poorly translated version of the Spanish site online while the translator focused on correcting the most important pages first.

Having two sites in two languages means twice the work, but with only two languages, the sites are fairly easy to manage. Now both versions are online and running fine. When it comes time to make less-critical site updates, we follow the same procedure where the translation software does the bulk of the translations and a Spanish-speaking translator verifies content for spelling, context, and overall accuracy before we put the new information online.

Translating a site's content

After you choose the technique that works best for your project, you or your client might need to hire a translator or translation service to ensure that the text reads naturally as if spoken by a native of the target audience's country. It's especially important that the translation takes extra care with the translations of industry-specific terminology, slang words, and colloquialisms. Poor translations not only water down a company's message but also lower any potential customer's confidence in the new product or service. By contrast, good translations can foster trust in a new company's products and services, which in turn can increase brand identity in the new country or region and improve sales.

Watch Your Step

Finding a good translation service might prove somewhat difficult because services vary in ability and price and because the
translation service providers' sites, although helpful, aren't always the
best indication of quality. Though I have no personal experience directly hiring
a translation service, one company that seems to have a good reputation,
competitive pricing, and a nice Web site (in my opinion, a big factor in
determining whether to do business with that company) is Transware.com.

bit depth: The grayscale or color depth of an individual pixel of an image displaying
on a monitor. An 8-bit depth can display 256 colors, whereas a 24-bit color monitor displays 16.7 million colors.

demographics: A sociological term referring to the study of people and groups
within the population of a specific geographic region, including income, age, race,
sex, religion, marital status, and other characteristics.

global market: The world market wherein a company wants to offer their products
or services to consumers and/or other businesses.

ideal site visitor: A specific set of character traits culled from target audience
research that is used to define the ideal make-believe person who would be interested in using or purchasing a Web site's products or services.

JavaScript: A scripting language that can be added to HTML code to make Web
pages dynamic and interactive when viewed in a browser window.

keywords: Words that best describes a specific person, place, or thing that can be
used to search for information in a search engine, database, or catalog. Keywords
are often embedded in Web page text, titles, headings, and tags as a means to
drive additional traffic to a Web site.

market research: A type of research performed when information about a particular set of people needs to be gathered as an aid to making strategic marketing
decisions.

monitor resolution: Another way of saying "screen size," the resolution refers to
the number of pixels used to create the image on your monitor. Common resolutions are 800 x 600, 1,024 x 768, and 1,280 x 1,024.

continued

multilanguage: Web sites that are viewable in more than one language.

operating system: The main software on a computer, such as Windows XP for a PC and Mac OS X for a Mac, that manages the rest of the computer's software applications, handles communication with the computer's peripheral devices (such as the keyboard, monitor, and printer), and manages the storage of files and directories on the computer's hard drive.

parse: A term taken from linguistics used to describe computer processes that divide information into smaller parts that can then be translated into new forms, such as extracting collected data from online forms and entering that data into a database or sending the data to a predetermined e-mail address.

remote server: Any computer that provides services, like hosting Web sites, software applications, files, e-mail, and information, to other computers through a network connection.

root level: The main level of a folder or directory on a computer drive (which can be a hard drive, folder, DVD, CD, or any other media with folders and files) from which other files and directories can be accessed.

session variable: A computer programming term that refers to the different values a programming language object can accept at any one time during the course of a session, or exchange, between a program and a user.

subdirectory: A folder or directory inside another folder or directory. On a Web server, this typically refers to a folder sitting one or more levels up from the root level. Also sometimes called a subfolder.

target audience: The intended visitors of a Web site, as defined by their common interests, habits, and demographics.

Last Stop

Practice Exam

1. True or False: Web sites shouldn't use JavaScript because most computer users disable the JavaScript in their browsers.

2. True or False: Total Site Replication is the best solution for a multilanguage site that has five or more languages.

3. When performing keyword searches, you can isolate the competition by searching in the _____, _____, national, and global markets.

4. If you were designing a site that needed to be displayed in three languages, English, Spanish, and German, but the client had no budget whatsoever to hire a programmer, which multilanguage site organization method would you use?

_____

_____

5. List the six phases of a Web project that, when followed, can help streamline the design process.

_____

_____

6. To assist you with gathering statistical information about a Web site's target audience, what kind of computer usage data would be good to collect?

_____

_____

7. Besides looking at competitors' Web sites, where else online can you find information about a particular business?

_____

_____

8. Make a list of search keywords you might use to find competitors' Web sites in the same town if your client were a New York City florist that makes unique, modern, custom floral designs for weddings, including bridal bouquets and centerpieces, but also teaches classes in ikebana, the art of floral design, in her Soho shop.

_____

_____

9. What is one of the benefits of looking at competitors' Web sites before beginning the site design?

_____

_____

_____

_____

10. How does identifying the ideal site visitor impact the design of a Web site? Provide at least one example.

_____

_____

_____

_____

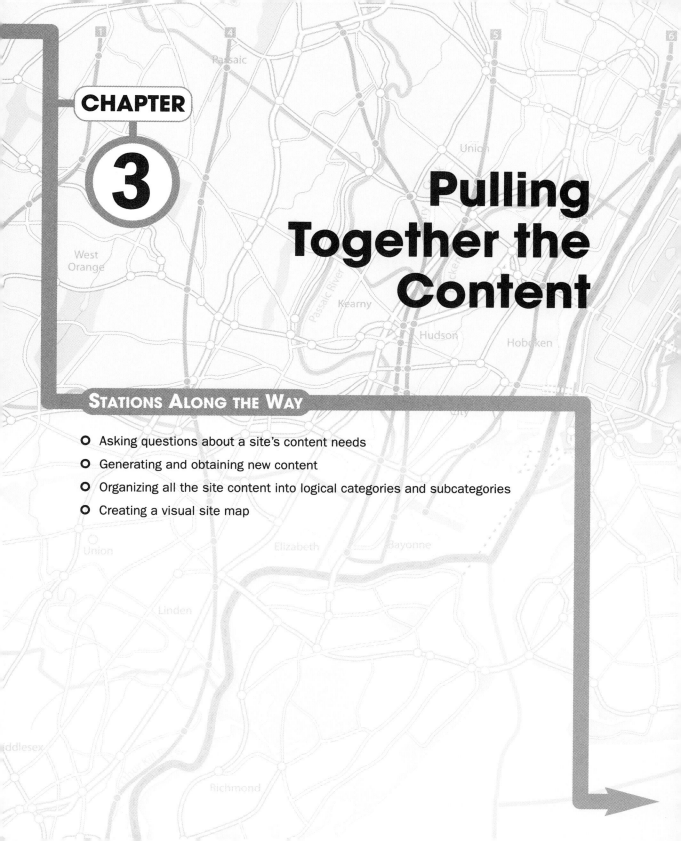

Pulling Together the Content

STATIONS ALONG THE WAY

O Asking questions about a site's content needs

O Generating and obtaining new content

O Organizing all the site content into logical categories and subcategories

O Creating a visual site map

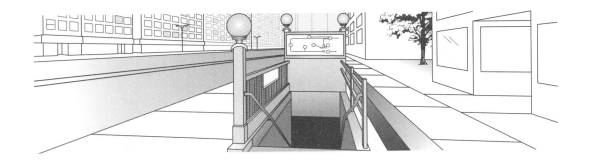

Enter the Station

Questions

1. To determine a site's content needs, what questions might you ask a client?

2. Who will be providing you with all the content needed for the site?

3. Why would you (and your client) want to determine the site's content needs before you begin working on the design?

4. What legal issues regarding images that will appear on the site do you need to be aware of?

5. How should all the site content be organized?

6. Why should you use a site map before creating the site design?

Express Line

If your client has completely worked out all the details about his or her new site before contacting you — from the wireframe to the navigation to the content — you can bypass the information here and go directly to Chapter 4, where you'll learn about Web site development tools and techniques. However, if you plan on designing a site map for the project, see the discussion at the end of this chapter.

You're now at the stage when you can begin guiding the client in the task of gathering content for the site. With luck, most of the site material has already been prepared for you, and your work will be just a matter of helping the client organize the information in a way that's best suited for the Web environment. What's more likely, however, is that the client has only a vague idea of what should go on the site, how that content should be organized, and what a visitor's experience on the site might be like.

To assist you with this large and what some think of as a tiresome task, I've arranged some tools and techniques in this chapter. For starters, you'll find a series of questions you can ask your client (or yourself if designing your own site) to help him or her generate ideas for content, page order, Meta data, and site navigation. Then you'll discover information and suggestions about where to obtain help with copywriting and editing and where to license or purchase photographs and illustrations online. The latter part of the chapter will deal with a Web site architectural technique called *wireframing,* and it will end with parts on content organization and the creation of a graphical site map of the entire project.

Discovering a Site's Content Needs

Now is the time to gather everything you can from the client to really lock down what will go on the site. This task includes getting all the text, logo and branding graphics, photos, illustrations, Flash movies, MP3s, QuickTime videos, and anything else that will appear on the site. Some of these things will already be prepared by the client, but other things might need to be created, licensed, and obtained. To be honest, most of this stuff is really the client's responsibility, not yours, but because many Web clients don't know what they're supposed to do (having never made their own Web site before), your role as the designer might include educating and guiding them through the content-gathering process.

I usually like to begin with a meeting or telephone conversation where I question the client about his or her vision for the site. During this conversation, I take careful notes of the client's answers.

Here are some of the questions that you might find helpful to ask your clients during your client meetings:

1. **We know there will be a home page — that's the starting point — but what other main pages do you want on the site?**

2. **Do you want an About page or About section where you'll provide information about your company?** Find out what the client would like to call this page/section. About, About Us, About Our Company? What subpages, if any, might go in this section?

Information Kiosk

Because part of the content-gathering task includes helping the client make decisions about what to put on their new site, try starting with things like what words to use for the labels on all the main navigation buttons and then what to call each page (the page header, the page filename, and the page title). If, for example, the client owns a hair salon and wants to have a section on his new Web site for "hair styling trends for long hair and summertime events," you might want to guide him to shortening the main navigation button to something like "styling trends" and then suggest including several subpages under styling trends for each of the trends he'd like to discuss on the site, like Men's Summer Styles, Women's Summer Styles, and Summer Weddings.

Watch Your Step

Pay close attention to what the client says because he or she might not realize the long-term implications of the choices he or she makes. In the case of the hair salon example, I'd make sure to ask the client whether he really meant he wanted to offer only summer trends or if in fact he really wants to display new trends each season, which would mean the navigation for those subpages will need to be updated quarterly. If he really wants to display only summer trend information, he'll need to be okay with the idea that for a substantial part of the year that summer trend information will be irrelevant. With that in mind, the client can decide whether he truly wants to update this section four times a year, for each of the seasons, or change the navigation and subnavigation to simply trends for men, women, and weddings, leaving off any reference to the season. The latter option is more generally labeled and would still allow for the client to update the page content to match the season if he wanted to.

3. **Do you want to have a Products page?** When considering this page, discuss whether the products, if any, will be merely described or also sold on this site. Be sure to find out how many products will be displayed and whether there are multiple product categories. The products page may include subpages, such as a product detail page for each product. All these factors impact the content you'll need from the client as well as determine somewhat how the pages need to be designed.

4. **Do you need a Services page where you'll list all the services your company provides?** Does each service warrant its own subpage, or can all the services be listed together on one page? Do any of the services require diagrams or other graphics to support them?

5. **What would you like to include on the Contact page?** For example, this page might list a single e-mail address or several e-mail addresses or have a contact form to collect contact data and comments, questions, and feedback from visitors. This section could also contain transportation information, directions, maps, or other details.

6. **Would you like to have a Clients page that lists clients alphabetically, by industry, or by project type?** This could be a list of past and current clients, including links to recent projects and/or links to client Web sites. Some client pages also include client case studies, and if so, you want to find out how many case studies will appear in this area.

7. **Do you want a page for your work, titled Our Work, What We Do, or perhaps Portfolio?** This page could be further broken down into categories that match the client's particular offerings, such as Planning & Urban Design, Landscape Architecture, and Interior Design; or Illustrations, Paintings, and Sculpture. Find out how many sample images, if any, will be shown in each category and how they will be displayed.

8. **How about a page for News or Press Releases?** Does the client need a news archive? How often will the news items be updated? How will the list of news items or press releases be displayed? By date, by topic, by title? Will they need to be sortable (which means you'll need a database)?

9. **What about an Events page?** What kinds of events will there be? How often will the events page be updated? Enough to justify having subpages in this section? Will events need to be presented by separating them into current/upcoming and past categories or will only upcoming events be listed?

10. **What about other industry-specific pages?** Do other pages on the site warrant having their own sections, with or without subsections?

11. **Will the site need any other pages that don't necessarily need main navigation links?** Some pages need not have main navigation links but should still be included on the site, accessible either through footer links, through the site map page, or through links on other pages throughout the site. Examples might include a page for Articles, Links, a Resume, Partners, Affiliates, Terms of Service, Privacy Policies, FAQs, a Site Map, or a page that links to an external blog.

12. **What elements should appear on every page?** Definitely include any branding information, including logos, tag lines, and the main navigation links, but what other things should be accessible from anywhere on the site? How about Join Mailing List, Location/Store Finder, Site Search, Help, Customer Service, My Account, Login, an e-mail address, or a toll-free number? These items can be graphics or text links anywhere on the page, such as at the top of the page or down in the footer, depending on their importance. If the site's design includes a sidebar on most or all the pages, elements like these can be placed there. Sidebars are often used for subnavigation, advertising, feature articles, and other site content that the site owners want you to pay attention to, and they will typically have different background colors, borders, text treatments, and graphics to visually distinguish them from the main content area.

13. **Will there be an e-commerce component on the site, and if so, what kind of shopping cart will be used?** Will the cart be something that came included in the

hosting plan, does it need to be purchased as a third-party software application, or will it be custom built by a programmer specifically for the client's products?

14. Does the site need to appear in multiple languages? If so, how many other languages and what are they? What technology will be used to create the sites? Does the client need to hire a translation service?

Transfer

Chapter 4 has more information about shopping carts and hiring programmers. You might have already discovered that the site will appear in multiple languages when you researched and discussed the site's audience in Chapter 2. If you learn about multilanguage needs for the site in this portion of the design phase, simply refer to Chapter 2 for details about organizing and translating content for multilanguage Web sites.

15. Who will provide graphics, photos, and illustrations? If the answer to this question isn't clear, you'll definitely want to learn about some of the sources I discuss in "Hiring illustrators and photographers" and "Licensing and buying stock images" later in this chapter.

16. Does anything else need to go on the site? Make sure you've covered everything the client or group you're working with has in mind for the site. Other content might include a photo gallery, a special password-protected, members-only section, a bookstore, a class listing, or a registration form.

At the end of the conversation, let the client know that there is still much to do during this stage of the Web design process, the responsibility of which mostly falls on her shoulders before you begin the design.

Concurrent with the gathering of the content for the site — which may include generating new content as well as culling content from existing company sources and/or hiring a copywriter — the client will need to produce, acquire, and/or license illustrations for the site.

After the content areas have been discovered, all that information must be organized to assist with creating a layout for the site. This can be done through the creation of wireframes, as you'll learn in the next section, to help identify what content is needed for each page on the site. Oftentimes, putting everything down on paper helps the client better envision what content to display and how the site will function.

Wireframes

An interesting technique called *wireframes* helps many clients when they're trying to determine what content to put on the individual pages of their site. As you can see in Figure 3-1, a wireframe is a text-only diagram, or blueprint, of a particular page in the Web site, and typically includes the following:

- **General site navigation:** Using text, the wireframes diagram the navigation and subnavigation elements, buttons, and other functional elements that show or describe how the visitor can enter and exit the page.

- **Content that appears on every page:** In addition to the navigation tools, the site may include components such as search boxes or mailing list signup links, page headers, page footers, or branding.

- **Interactive components:** This can include hyperlinks, navigation menus, hidden layers, games, rotating banner ads, rotating graphics, photo galleries, animations, video clips, movies, and other multimedia files.

- **Dynamic functionality:** Any data or images that will be dynamically pulled from a database and displayed on the page should be indicated on the wireframe to assist with the site layout and programming.

- **Content for each page on a Web site:** Include the page title and placeholder graphics and "dummy" text, which will be replaced with actual graphics and text. So, for example, your client might include notations such as "About Us page content" and "photo of boardroom" within the wireframe.

Creating a wireframe helps site owners plan how their sites will function, what each of the pages should contain, and generally what the layout might look like.

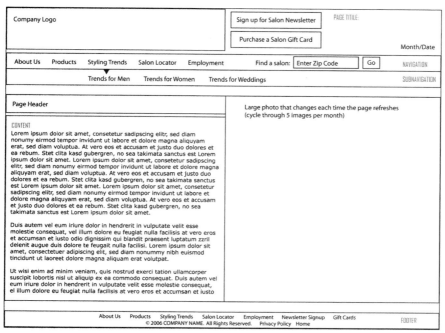

Figure 3-1: Wireframes are a text-only depiction of a Web site's navigation, interactive features, and content areas.

Because the making of wireframes is primarily the responsibility of the client, and most of your clients will have never heard of wireframes before, creating them often gets overlooked at this stage of the Web site's development. Make it part of your job to educate your client about how wireframes can be fantastic, time-saving, cost-effective, content discovery tools for them, and consider creating a sample wireframe for the client's home page as your special Web Design Value-Added Service. Who knows? The client might appreciate it so much that he'll consider paying you a little extra for you to help create more.

Because the wireframe typically contains only text, one of the key benefits of making wireframes for all the pages (or at least the most important ones) on the site is that the client can focus on user experience and content without having to think about design and layout decisions or coding and development issues. That stuff comes later. Only after that task has been accomplished should the client tackle what text the visitors will see on each page.

To create the wireframes, your client (or you) can draw them by hand on graph paper, mock them up in a graphics program like Illustrator, or use any other application that allows for the insertion and arrangement of text. A few software applications on the market, such as Microsoft Visio and Axure RP Pro 4, are specifically designed for creating HTML wireframes. These programs contain Web-like buttons, form fields, menus, and other page elements that can easily be dragged onto the wireframe diagram, making it easier for the client to foresee the content and its functionality pre-design. Or, if your client would rather go low-tech, he or she can certainly create wireframes in a program such as Microsoft Word or Excel.

Step into the Real World

Wireframes need not be created for every single page on a Web site unless this is something the client expressly asks for and is amenable to compensating you to do it. A more likely scenario will be that you create a wireframe for the home page and possibly one or two additional subpages with distinct content and layout requirements, such as a shopping cart page, a product detail page, or a search results listing.

Primarily, though, this technique is to assist the client with any content-gathering issues she might have for the site. Similar in concept to a book's table of contents, the wireframe merely outlines or hints at the content in a particular section. With the wireframe, the client can focus on the general rather than the specific by noting what information should be displayed, even when the information such as text and graphics isn't available or hasn't been created yet. For example, if your client will be selling products on their Web site, she should plan on having at least a main products listing page and a product details page, both of which can be wireframed to show how the individual products and product details will appear in the browser. The details page wireframe can include information placeholders like the company logo, content, and page title areas in the example shown in Figure 3-1.

Step into the Real World

Wireframes in Dreamweaver   If you'll be assisting with the wireframe part of the project and you plan on building the site with Dreamweaver, you might be interested in downloading a copy of Eric Ott's free Wireframing V1.0.0 Dreamweaver Extension from the Adobe Dreamweaver Exchange Web site. The Dreamweaver Exchange is an area on the Adobe Web site where Dreamweaver designers and developers can exchange information, tips, and tutorials and download free and fee-based extensions for Dreamweaver. This particular extension is available for both Mac and PC and includes objects that allow designers to make page wireframing in HTML using CSS layers.

To download the Wireframing V1.0.0 Dreamweaver extension, follow these steps:

1. **Go to the page on the Adobe Dreamweaver Exchange Web site that displays the following extension:**

   ```
   http://www.adobe.com/cfusion/exchange/index.cfm?view=sn121&extID=
   51463
   ```

2. **Sign in or register with Adobe by clicking the Sign In button at the top of the screen.**

   You must register before you can download the free extension, but that should take only a few minutes, and it's completely worthwhile because you'll then have access to the Exchange as well as other resources on the Adobe Web site, such as support documentation, user forums, and blogs.

3. **Follow the on-screen instructions to register or sign in.**

   After you register or sign in, you will be taken automatically back to the Wireframing extension page.

4. **Click the Download button to begin the download of the free extension. Save the file to your desktop or to your Dreamweaver Exchange downloads folder.**

   The file will be saved to your computer with the .mpx file extension.

5. **Double-click the downloaded file called MX51463_Wireframing.mxp.**

6. **The Macromedia (Adobe) Extension Manager application, which comes with Dreamweaver, should launch automatically and prompt you to accept the extension's disclaimer from a dialog box. Click the Accept button to proceed with the installation or the Decline button to cancel the installation.**

   An alert window will pop up when the extension has been successfully installed.

7. **Close the Extension Manager. If you had Dreamweaver open during the installation, you must close and restart the program before you can access the Wireframing extension.**

8. **Access all the Wireframing objects through the Objects palette or the new Insert → Wireframes menu.**

   Layout objects include two box types, three button types, a navigation bar, check box with label, drop-down list, radio button with label, text block, text field with label, page title bar, and disclaimer.

Start the wireframe by inserting the names of the main navigation links, links to any subpages in the main category being wireframed, and footer links. Then add an area for branding and other elements to appear on the page such as search tools and newsletter signup links. Page titles and header information can go on this page, if desired, along with any other information that will assist in the design layout and page creation. Insert greeking text, if desired, as placeholder text for the actual content on the page, and lastly, insert notations regarding any interactive and dynamic content such as images and information pulled from a database.

Gathering all the written content

The client is likely to have much of the textual content already created in the form of existing newsletters, brochures, and marketing collateral. Ask the client to start pulling all these materials together for the site, generating new content, and rewriting existing copy as needed to fit into the specific pages you discussed in the content-gathering meeting.

The client might even need to enter parts of the content for the site into an Excel spreadsheet for later importing into a database of some kind if the site will have any dynamic functionality. If that's the case, how data gets entered into the spreadsheet (how files are named and numbered) might depend on the programming language (such as ASP, JSP, PHP, or CFML) chosen to make the site dynamic. That decision will most likely be made by the person doing the programming of the site, whether that's you or a subcontracted programmer. (Chapter 4 talks more about working with programmers.) Making this decision now can save time later when you need to import data onto the pages from the database.

Some page content, naturally, might not exist yet. In such cases, the client will need to decide whether to write the missing information or to hire someone to do it. If you're confident in your copywriting skills, you might want to offer your services for an additional fee. However, if writing isn't your thing or the client rejects your offer to do copywriting and the client isn't capable of it, then he or she will need to hire an out-side service either through an agency or online through a job-listing site or writing organization. The more promising-looking national copywriting services include Freelancewriting.com, ScribeGroup.com, Guru.com, Elance.com, and WriterFind.com, but you should unquestionably still search online yourself to see whether you can find someone to do the work locally.

Hiring illustrators and photographers

With regard to the illustrations and photographs that are to appear on the site, ask the client where he intends to get these things. Some clients already have an established relationship with other graphic designers and will get any needed site graphics, like icons and illustrations, directly from those people. Other clients will look to you for direction. If you're an artist or illustrator as well as a Web designer, offer your services to the client for an additional fee. Otherwise, be ready to suggest some local artists and photographers who would be happy to create the needed art and photos.

Of course, you could leave hiring these artists solely to the client, but many times the client will want or need you to take on this responsibility. Your role in this can be as big or as small as you feel comfortable with. For instance, you might suggest the client buy a digital camera and create his or her own photographs.

Alternatively, you might keep a list of freelance artists and photographers that you like available so that you can simply give the list to the client and then let him or her vet, select, and hire someone from your list. To generate this list, you'll need to do some homework. For instance, you can post ads on Craigslist.com or other local online communities with job boards; or join the local chapter of the Graphic Artists Guild (`gag.org`), join a MAC user group (`mugcenter.com` or `apple.com/usergroups`), or join some other local arts organization where you can network with other artists, photographers, and designers.

Because each project is unique, be open to making suggestions and let the client decide what works best, given the timeframe, needs, and budget.

Licensing and buying stock images

Alternatives to hiring an artist or photographer are to license or purchase the artwork directly from an online service or to buy an entire CD of royalty-free images on a particular theme, such as pictures of businesswomen or agriculture. Most CDs cost around $299 for 100 images, and most single images can be licensed for as little as $1 per image, depending on the image size and quality, license timeframe, and usage parameters. The drawback of royalty-free images is a high likelihood that other businesses, including potential competitors, will have also selected and licensed the same images for their projects.

Corbis.com is the leading provider of rights-managed and royalty-free stock photography and illustration. Eyewire.com and iStockphoto.com are also reputable services with similar price structuring. For those looking for less expensive options, check out ClipArt.com, FotoSearch.com, Comstock.com, GettyImages.com, RoyaltyFreeArt.com, Shutterstock.com, and Inmagine.com. You or your client can also subscribe to images services, like AbleStock.com, JupiterImages.com, and PhotoObjects.net, where you can download an unlimited number of images on a monthly, biannual, or annual basis for a flat rate. Or, if you want to go the super inexpensive route, consider buying The Big Box of Art (manufactured by Encore Software or Hemera Technologies) on Amazon.com for as low as $9.99.

Step into the Real World

Respecting the Copyright Before you seek images for use on a Web site, you should know a little about copyright protection. All the images that you see online belong to somebody. Someone took the time to take that photograph, draw that illustration, build that animation, and design that icon. Smart Web site owners will have registered their own custom graphics with the U.S. Copyright office and/or made arrangements to legally license or purchase the work of others. However, what are the implications if you or someone else copies an image from another site, without permission or payment, and then uses that image for another project? What rights might have been violated? The answers depend on your usage and intent.

Suppose you go to the Disney Web site and see a picture of Goofy that you love and want to turn it into your desktop wallpaper so you can look at it every day. In this case, your usage intent is for private use and isn't for profit; therefore, your use of that Goofy image isn't harming anyone or earning you any income. Disney actually knows that many visitors might use its graphics for personal use, so it includes a clause in its Privacy Policy and Terms to allow that, but it forbids visitors from taking images off the site to use in any way for profit. Of course, it has no way of tracking this information because no reliable way of accurately monitoring images that are copied off the Web site exists. Nonetheless, by stating its rights on the Web site, it's protecting those rights to the images in case it needs to file suit against someone who knowingly violates the copyright.

Therefore, if you need an image for your site — say a photograph of a sunset on Waikiki beach that you use as part of the home page design for a Luau event and catering company based in Los Angeles, California — the right thing to do is create it yourself, hire someone to create it for you, or license the image from one of the many stock art or clip-art Web sites.

Watch Your Step

Wherever the client decides to get images from, be sure you add only legally licensed artwork to your design for the site. Don't make yourself liable to any copyright infringements made by your client. In fact, you might want to add to your contract some kind of Permissions and Releases regarding Copyrights and Trademarks clause. This clause could state that the client either owns the rights to or is responsible for obtaining all permissions and rights from the lawful image owner provided for the site, and you, the designer, will be held harmless for using them in your design.

Information Kiosk

For more information about copyrights, trademarks, and fair use, visit the Web sites of the U.S. Copyright office (`www.copyright.gov`) and the U.S. Patent and Trademark office (`www.uspto.gov`).

Page titles and Meta tag data

In addition to the text and images that appear directly on the page, you'll need page titles and Meta tag information, which you'll include in the site's HTML. If you're creating a site for someone else, ask your client to create these but be sure to check whether he or she meets the criteria discussed in this section. If you're creating a site for yourself, this section offers tips for creating the text.

Page titles are pretty self explanatory; each page on a Web site needs its own unique title, which after being placed appropriately in the head area of the HTML code, will appear in the browser window title bar.

Titles need to identify the site as well as the content displayed on the individual page by using a maximum of 70 to 80 characters, including spaces and punctuation. For example, "Where to Get the Best Breakfast for Under $6 in New York City" would be a good title for a Web page with reviews of restaurants serving cheap breakfasts. Titles longer than 70 characters might get truncated, or cut off, by the browser, so if titles are a bit longer, put the most important words in the first 70 characters.

A good rule when coming up with page titles is to pack them full of keywords that visitors are likely to use when searching for pages containing desired information. Test your skills at thinking up page titles with the following scenarios:

1. **The daily Virgo horoscope Web page on the AstroLioness site, which lists daily horoscopes by zodiac sign**

2. **A Web page with a free online mahjong game on a site that offers both free online and downloadable games; however, the main objective is selling the full version of Flash poker and other Casino software games**

3. **The track-listing page of a well-respected Los Angeles DJ on an Internet free-radio Web site that bills itself as having the best house-music Webcasts in the world**

Meta tags are special HTML tags that also go inside the head area of the code on a Web page. The information contained in Meta tags won't be displayed on the Web page. Instead, the contents of these tags provide browsers with informational content about the client's company, which helps search engines rank the site in search results listings.

Watch Your Step

It's important to ask for this data from the client at this stage of the site development because the client is focused right now on getting the content to you and will more likely comply with your request. In my experience, if you wait until you start building the site to ask for it — even though realistically it should only take your client about ten or so minutes to generate it — the chances of you actually receiving it are slim.

Two Meta tags should be placed on every page of a site — the Meta description and the Meta keywords.

Description: The description of the site, which is written in sentences or short phrases and contains up to 150 characters.

Keywords: Use words or short phrases that you feel would be helpful when searching for this site; keywords (and/or keyphrases) should be separated by a comma either with or without a space, such as *"bread,cakes,pies..."* or *"bread, cakes, pies..."*. Place the most important seven words first, in order of importance.

Information Kiosk

If you do any reading on the uses of Meta tags, you'll quickly learn that keywords are much less important than the description. Because keywords were so widely abused by unethical site owners looking to improve site rankings at any cost, their importance was quickly diminished by the search engines doing the indexing and ranking. Today, only one search engine (Inktomi) still uses a database that supports the usage of keywords as a ranking tool, but in my opinion, one is enough to justify keeping the keywords listed in the code. As an alternative to listing the seven most important keywords in the Meta Keywords tag, some designers duplicate the Meta Description content there.

Here's an example of the Meta tag code that might be used for a (pretend) company in Santa Monica, California, that offers classes in surfing, boogie boarding, and wake boarding:

```
<meta name="keywords" content="Surfing classes, Boogie
board classes, wake boarding classes, Santa Monica, Venice,
Long Beach, CA">
<meta name="description" content="Sign up for surfing,
boogie boarding, and wake boarding classes in Santa Monica,
CA. We welcome riders of all levels. Courses available for
beginners, intermediate, and advanced riders.">
```

Transfer

Other Meta tags exist but are less critical to the function of indexing the site on a search engine. For instance, one Meta tag can forward a page to another URL, and another can prevent the browser from caching the content on the page. You'll learn more about Meta tags in Chapter 11, including how and where to add them to your Web pages.

Organizing Site Content

You can use a few techniques to organize all the content for a site. The best way, of course, is to have the client begin to organize it for you. Notice I say *begin to* because the client isn't always the best judge of how to effectively organize everything. The client might, for example, want to have a staff contact page on the site that lists the names, telephone numbers, and e-mail addresses of everyone in the company and might think this information should go on the site as part of a Company History page under the About Us section. That just doesn't make sense. A more logical location for a staff directory would be as a separate subpage of either the About Us or Contact Us page.

When I start my part of the content organization process, I like to write the names of the main navigation pages across the top of a sheet of paper. Then I look at all the other pages of content and decide where they'd best be placed. That way, I can establish logical categories and subcategories of information, which can be used later in the site design as the labels for the site navigation. Another useful technique for larger sites is to write all the page names on index cards and then order the index cards into main navigation and subnavigation categories. The final order of the cards can then be transcribed onto a single sheet of paper.

Take care not to make too many levels of subnavigation in your page organization. A Web usability principle states that it's better to have a wide navigation than a deep navigation. In other words, rather than embed subnavigation that has subnavigation on top of subnavigation with even more subnavigation (deep), it is more user-friendly to keep most of the content close to the top level (wide) so that all the content on a site is accessible in no more than three clicks from the home page. This technique works great for most sites with less than ten main categories of information. Over ten and the site might need to use a directory type of navigation with hypertext links, where users can click a category (think Yahoo! home page) to narrow down what they're looking for and will be taken directly to that section of a larger site.

When sites are fairly small, organizing the content comes quite naturally because most sites have at least three pages in common: Home, About, and Contact. However, when a site is a bit larger — over 15 pages, say — exactly where in the site architecture each of the pages should go becomes a matter of logical organization. Try to arrange the content from the top down, starting at the home page, then move on to the main navigation categories, and finally the subpages. If you happen to run across a page that you're uncertain about where it should go, ask the client where he or she thinks it should go or make a suggestion to them on where it might fit in. If there is no logical place for the content, it might benefit from combining with content on another page or being removed from the site completely.

To test your organization skills, try assembling the following pages into a logical layout for a Web site using the paper or index card methods described in the preceding paragraphs:

Contact Information

About Us

Our History

What We Do

Our Goals and Values

Publications

Upcoming Events

Home

Links

Events

Donate

Our Mission Statement

Staff Directory

1. **Select which pages will be the main navigation pages.**

2. **Pick the pages that will become subpages.**

3. **Did you find any pages that didn't quite fit anywhere? If so, what would you recommend the client does with the page(s)?**

When you're done, compare your solutions against these possible answers for each step:

⊙ For the main page, include Home, About Us, Events, Donate, Publications, and Contact Information.

⊙ For the subpages, under the About Us page, include What We Do, Our Mission Statement, Our History, and Our Goals and Values. Place Staff Directory as a subpage under the Contact Information pages, and Upcoming Events as a subpage under the main Events page.

⊙ The Links page doesn't quite fit. Recommend the client remove it from the site, add the page as a subpage of the About Us section, or add a new main page called Resources, which sounds better than Links.

Making the Site Map

A *site map* is a visual representation of a Web site's architecture, reduced down to its most important components, including pages with page names, attention to page ordering, and details regarding the navigation scheme. The site map has a totally different function than the wireframes and should be created by you, the designer.

Site maps can be sketched by hand or produced in any software program that allows you to add text and draw rectangles and lines. Acceptable-looking site maps can be created by the nondesigner in Word, Excel, PowerPoint, and Visio. Those with more design experience can create a site map by using the drawing, shape, and text tools in Illustrator or Photoshop.

My preference is to draw my client's site map in Illustrator because I can create more elegant site maps by using unique shapes, like rounded rectangles, as well as display the specific fonts and colors that will actually be used in the site's design. Figure 3-2 shows an example of a site map I created for the Social Intervention Group, a multidisciplinary research center at the Columbia University School of Social Work, who hired me to do its Web site redesign in July 2006.

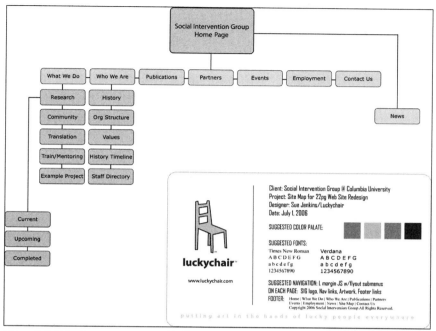

Figure 3-2: This site map was created in Illustrator.

To illustrate, you'll next create a sample site map using the answers you got from the organization exercise earlier, with the main navigation of Home, About Us, Events, Donate, Publications, Contact Information, in that exact order, and subpages of About Us: What We Do, Our Mission Statement, Our History, Our Goals and Values; Contact Information: Staff Directory; and Events: Upcoming Events.

Follow these steps to create a site map page using the drawing tools in Microsoft Word or any vector or bitmap graphics program such as Illustrator or Photoshop:

1. **Using a standard letter size page with a landscape layout, create a 2-inch-wide rectangle at the top, center of the page and label it with text that says "Home page."**

A good site map shows how each of the pages on a site are connected together from the home page as well as through navigation and subnavigation.

2. **Create a series of five equally sized rectangles in a row below the homepage rectangle to represent the main pages on the site, and label each of them with the following names: About Us, Events, Donate, Publications, Contact Information.**

Make sure these pages are listed in the order they'll appear on the site — from left to right for the main navigation and from top to bottom for any pages accessed through subnavigation links. This order will assist you in the site's design and building phases.

3. Connect all the rectangles together by drawing two lines; one line should flow horizontally behind each of the main page boxes, and the other line should connect the home page box to the first line.

Connecting the "pages" in this way can help to identify to the client how a visitor will interact with the navigation and experience visiting the site.

4. Now you'll add the subpages. Under About Us, draw four rectangles, labeled What We Do, Our Mission Statement, Our History, and Our Goals and Values, and draw a vertical line behind them to connect the subpages to the horizontal line connecting the main pages.

The line shows that the subpages will be accessible through the main About Us page. If any sub-subpages existed, you'd use the same technique to add those to the site map.

5. Under Contact Information, draw one rectangle and label it Staff Directory, and under Events, draw one rectangle and label it Upcoming Events. Then draw a vertical line behind each of the subpages that connect above to the main navigation page that spawned it.

You can now clearly see that both the contact and events pages have single subpages.

6. Most sites have at least one or more additional pages, such as a Terms & Conditions, Privacy Policy, or Site Map, that are not accessible through the main navigation but are accessible through footer and/or hypertext links. Create two additional rectangles on your layout, perhaps off to the bottom right of the page, and label them Privacy and Site Map.

No lines are necessary to connect these pages to the rest of the site map; they are indicated merely to show the client that the pages exist and are accessible through means other than the main navigation.

7. In a blank area of the page, type in notations about site details appearing on every page such as the logo, company slogan, toll-free number, footer links, site search features, and so on.

You may also include information about what colors, fonts, font sizes, layout attributes, and page dimensions to use.

8. In another part of the page, preferably on the bottom left or right side, add the date the site map was created along with your company name, logo, and contact information.

This information clearly identifies you, the designer, as the author of the site map.

9. **Save the file, and if you own a copy of Adobe Acrobat Professional, convert the page into an Adobe Acrobat PDF document.**

If you don't own Acrobat Professional, consider using a free online PDF file conversion tool, such as the one at www.pdfonline.com.

After my site maps are finished, I always convert them to Adobe Acrobat PDFs to present to the client. PDFs are wonderful tools to use because they don't require that the client own or purchase any design software to view them. If anything, the client will need to download and install only the latest version of the free Adobe Acrobat Reader software, which is readily available online at Adobe.com.

Information Kiosk

Any time you make contact with your clients, whether by e-mail, in person, or by phone, you have the opportunity to make another positive impression on them about you and the quality of your services. Friendly banter and a professional work ethic definitely go a long way toward fostering a good rapport with your clients, but so does the unspoken look of all your paperwork, e-mails, PDFs, and other correspondence. Make the most of every nonverbal communication by consistently adding your name, company logo, and contact information, including telephone numbers and e-mail address, to every document you present to your clients.

The completed site map should be reviewed by the client to ensure that it meets his or her expectations and includes all the pages of the site in a logical manner. If any changes need to be made to the architecture of the site, making those changes now can save you valuable time after you begin creating the site design. After the site map is approved by the client, get signed approval in writing before you proceed to the next step in the design phase — creating the design.

characters: Any letters, numbers, symbols, or other text entities, such as A, 23, ©, ⅗, and >.

content: Any text, logo, branding graphics, photos, illustrations, Flash movies, MP3s, QuickTime videos, plug-ins, and so forth that will appear on the site.

continued

 *continued*

greeking text: Dummy text, not unlike Latin, is used a) to show how text in a particular font will fill the desired space within the layout and/or b) as placeholder text in graphic layouts until the real content becomes available. Greeking text usually begins with the famous *Lorem ipsum dolor sit amet . . .* and looks very similar to English in its word size and distribution within sentences.

Meta tag: A component of HTML code that doesn't appear as content in a browser window but instead communicates information, such as keywords and a description, about a Web page to search engines, indexing spiders, and robots as well as identifying information, like character set and refresh rate, to browsers.

page header: A word (Contact), phrase (About Our Services), or short line of text (Sign In to Use the Control Panel) that identifies the content on the page and is placed above or away from the main body of text. Page headers can be formatted with CSS using the `<h1>` through `<h6>` tags, or can be graphics inserted onto a Web page.

page title: The title of a Web page as it appears in the title bar at the top of an open browser window. Page titles are set between opening and closing `<title>` tags in the HTML code of a Web page. Each page on a Web site should have its own unique title because this information assists Web crawlers index pages and entire sites.

placeholder graphic: A sample graphic used for placement only in a graphic or Web design layout until the final artwork becomes available.

rights managed: A term used in reference to licensing photographs and other artwork from an online service or agency or directly from the photographer, whereby, after paying a higher rate to license and use an image, there is less chance that other companies will have selected and used the same image in one of their marketing campaigns.

royalty-free: A less expensive way (than rights managed) of licensing photographs and other artwork for a Web or graphic design project.

sidebar: A section of a Web page, usually along the left or right margin, containing content separate from the main body text of a page.

site map: A visual illustration of a Web site's structural design, showing page navigation and subnavigation, page order, page names, and possibly some details about the site, such as what content will appear on all the pages sitewide, what colors and fonts will be used, and the total number of pages.

subpage: Although this can be any page other than the home page on a Web site, this term is more often used to refer to pages that fall one or more levels below a site's main navigation pages. Also referred to as a subnavigation page or an internal page.

wireframes: Text-only diagrams that depict an entire site or single Web page's general layout, navigation, interactive components, dynamic functionality, and content.

Practice Exam

1. True or False: It is always the designer's responsibility to decide what content should appear on each page of a client's Web site.

2. When licensing artwork for a Web design, the more expensive images are _____, which means there is less chance a competitor will also use them, and the less expensive images are _____, which means they are more likely to be used by more companies.

3. The term for creating a text-only representation of a Web page's navigation, content, and layout is a _____.

4. Visitors should be able to access all the pages on a Web site in no more than ____ clicks from the home page.

5. Name at least three things that would typically be included in the footer links on a Web page.

_____

_____

6. Make up a page title for the following fictitious Web page: A product detail page for supersoft, foam exercise mats on the FitForLifeExpress.com sports e-commerce site based in Yuma, Arizona.

_____

_____

7. Name the two Meta tags that should be placed on every page of a Web site.

_____

_____

8. Which of the following best describes the function of a wireframe?

A) A visual depiction of all the pages on a site that shows text and graphics exactly as they should appear in the design

B) A virtual map of the site that shows the architecture of the navigation and all the site's branding information

C) A text-only diagram for a particular page on a Web site that shows branding, navigation, common page elements, and placeholders or labels for page-specific content

D) A graphical diagram for just the home page on a Web site that shows navigation and example content

E) All of the above

9. It is better to make site navigation:

A) Deep rather than wide

B) Deep rather than tall

C) Wide rather than tall

D) Wide rather than deep

10. Describe what a site map is and what elements a site map should include.

_____

_____

_____

_____

Choosing Development Tools and Techniques

STATIONS ALONG THE WAY

- O Selecting a Web editor (HTML or WYSIWYG)
- O Learning the basics of HTML and code structure
- O Understanding programs and techniques for working with color in Web sites
- O Selecting the best shopping cart for an e-commerce site
- O Determining when to hire a programmer

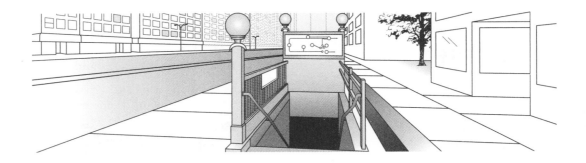

Enter the Station

Questions

1. Does it matter whether you hand-code Web pages by using an HTML editor or build pages visually with a Web editor?

2. What are the basic components of an HTML page?

3. What is the Web-safe palette and when should you use it?

4. What important considerations do you need to think about when choosing a shopping cart solution?

5. How will you decide whether a site's content warrants hiring a programmer?

Express Line

Designers who have a programming background (or plan on hiring a programmer) and understand the technical aspects of working with color on the Web can move ahead to Chapter 5, which deals with hosting plans, domain registration, and the creation of placeholder pages.

Now that you've pulled together all (or most of) the content for the site you're about to build, you're almost to the point where you can begin creating your site design. However, you first need to make a few decisions about the development tools you'll use and understand some basic techniques for using those tools.

You begin this chapter by learning about the basics of writing and using HTML. Not all Web-editing programs require that you know HTML, but having a simple understanding of its structure and use will definitely help you build the pages for the site. You also need to understand how to save files with the right extension and follow the proper naming conventions.

Second only to your page-creation tools are your graphics programs. You'll find details you might want to consider when selecting the right tools for the job. I recommend having at least one vector and one raster graphics program to create the design and another program to use for the optimization of all the images for the Web site. I also explain how your graphics programs can help you work with Web-safe color palettes and hexadecimal color values, both of which help ensure that the colors in your design look just right.

If the site you're creating has an e-commerce component or needs a way to process credit card payments, you'll need to look into shopping cart solutions as well. Your options range from a simple PayPal setup to third-party software or host-provided carts to custom-built shopping carts. Any option, except PayPal or outside credit card processing services, will require that the site owner gets a merchant account and an SSL (Secure Sockets Layer) certificate to process online payments.

Although you may want to design and build the site entirely yourself, some sites will have such customized and complex data-processing needs that you'll want the assistance of a professional Web programmer. For example, if your client wants a custom-built shopping cart that caters specifically to her products, hiring a professional programmer is a good idea. The last part of this chapter reviews criteria that help you determine when to call on a programmer, and offers suggestions on good places to look online to find one.

Working with Page-Creation Tools

HTML, which stands for HyperText Markup Language, is the foundation code of any Web page. It's a simple tag-based markup language for the World Wide Web that communicates information about how the hypertext links, formatting, and page structure of a document should be viewed in a Web browser. Almost anyone can learn HTML in a short period of time because it isn't a full-scale programming language and its structure is fairly uncomplicated.

You can write Web page code by using any plain text editor, such as Notepad or TextEdit, or by using a dedicated HTML (code) or Web (visual) editor. The editor will help you create the HTML and integrate other technologies, such as CSS (Cascading Style Sheets) and scripting, into your Web pages, as well.

HTML and Web-editing programs

You can use two types of Web-editing programs — code editors and visual editors — to build Web pages in HTML:

- **Code editors** are for people who know a little HTML and prefer to hand-code their HTML pages. Code editors can be as simple as the text-editing program that comes with your computer — whether that's Notepad on a PC or TextEdit on a Mac — or as complex as a program dedicated to writing HTML, such as BBEdit or HomeSite, which has tools, buttons, and code helpers to assist with the tasks of coding. If you're looking for a free coding editor, you might enjoy using BareBones' TextWrangler. Any of these and other editors you might find online are fine to use, as long as the editor assists you in writing HTML 4.01 compliant code.

Watch Your Step

Do not use applications like WordPad or Microsoft Word as code editors. Those programs tend to add extra characters and unnecessary markup to the code that can drastically increase the file size of the saved .html document.

- **Visual editors** allow designers to build pages by using a What You See Is What You Get (WYSIWYG, pronounced *wizzy-wig*) user interface. Visual editors provide you with buttons, tools, and drag-and-drop techniques for adding content to the Web page, so you don't need to know much HTML. Besides their user-friendly interfaces, visual editors closely mirror what the page will look like when launched in a browser window, making the page-building process much more fun and easy to do.

As an added feature, most visual editors also have built-in coding editors, so users can easily switch back and forth between code and visual editing modes, or in the case of Dreamweaver and GoLive, work in both simultaneously. The most popular visual editors are Dreamweaver, GoLive, and CoffeeCup. That said, this book uses Dreamweaver exclusively as the basis for steps in later chapters.

Information Kiosk

The Future of WYSIWYG Editing In late 2005 when Adobe bought out Macromedia, there was great speculation about which visual editor the new graphics behemoth would keep and which might be phased out. On the one hand, Adobe's visual editor, GoLive, is a decent enough Web editor, but hardly anyone was using it. On the other hand, Macromedia's Dreamweaver boasted being the industry leader in Web development with nearly 90 percent of all Web designers using it. Would the folks at Adobe keep GoLive because it was their own product, or would they dash it in favor of keeping Dreamweaver as the industry standard? The answer, at least a speculative one, came in a June 2006 article on Softpedia.com news ("Adobe to Drop Freehand and GoLive"), which stated that there were reports of Adobe phasing out GoLive in favor of Dreamweaver for Web development and FreeHand in favor of Illustrator for vector-based illustration. Both smart decisions, in the opinion of this seasoned designer.

Other editors are out there, of course. Freeware seekers might like FormBreeze's PageBreeze application or OpenOffice's BlueFish. I recommend staying away from old copies of Microsoft's FrontPage as an editor. I don't have anything against Microsoft, but besides having a non-intuitive interface compared to Dreamweaver and GoLive, FrontPage (like WordPad and Microsoft Word) adds way too much extra non-Web code to a page, making file sizes fatter than they need be. Though I personally haven't tested it myself, you may be able to safely use Microsoft's Expression Web tool to build standards-compliant sites without having the program insert extra unnecessary Microsoft data into the HTML code. If you'd like to do more research on Web editors before you make your purchase, check out the fairly comprehensive list of Web editors at the Desktop Web Site Editors section on About.com at `http://personalweb.about.com/cs/webpageeditors/a/aa031203a.htm`.

Introducing HTML tags

Even if you are uncomfortable with the idea of working with code, as a Web designer, you'll benefit from a basic knowledge of HTML, which uses small components called *tags* to mark up your text and graphics for presentation in a browser. Tags are essentially predefined words or acronyms written in all lowercase letters and surrounded by left (<) and right (>) angle brackets, for example, `<html>`. Just knowing a few basics about tags will help you understand much of the HTML code you'll see:

- **Most tags come in tag sets to mark the start and end of a text block or other object, such as an image, table, or layer, that will appear on a Web page.** Closing tags look identical to the opening tags but have a backslash directly before the tag name. For example, a sentence might be marked up with opening and closing paragraph tags:

  ```
  <p>HTML tags make your documents viewable on the
  Internet.</p>
  ```

- **The opening/closing tag rule has a few exceptions.** These exceptions include the use of Meta tags, line breaks `<br>`, horizontal rules `<hr>`, image tags `<img src="specify file">`, and a few assorted others, like the tags used to add form fields and embed media files on a Web page. Because these exceptions can be somewhat confusing to people who are new to HTML, unclosed HTML tags can be closed out either by closing all unclosed tags with a closed tag, like:

  ```
  <br></br>
  ```

or by borrowing from one of the syntax rules used in XHTML (eXtensible HyperText Markup Language), namely using a space and a backslash before the ending right angle bracket of the tag in question:

```
<br />
```

If desired, the opening tags can also contain elements or attributes that tell the browser how the tag or the content between the opening and closing tags appears, such as color, alignment, size, and style. Attributes (such as `width` and `align`) appear only in opening tags (never in the closing tags) using the syntax, $x="y"$, where x is the attribute and y is the value of that attribute:

```
<hr width="500">
<p align="center">This sentence will be centered on the page.</p>
```

You can list multiple attributes in the opening tag should the need arise:

```
<hr width="500" class="myrulestyle">
```

The rest of the available HTML tags deal with semantically identifying the different parts of page content. You can use the *basic tags* like <p> for paragraph and <h1> through <h6> for headings; *character formatting tags*, like <strong> for bold and <em> for italics to add emphasis; and then all the rest of the tags — including tags for inserting links, images, lists, tables, frames, and forms — for adding objects, programming, styles, and Meta data to the page.

Information Kiosk

For a complete listing of all the HTML tags you can add to your Web pages, visit the following sites:

```
www.w3schools.com/tags/ref_byfunc.asp
www.webmonkey.com/webmonkey/reference/html_cheatsheet
```

Understanding basic HTML page structure

Every Web page uses a similar fundamental structure. All tags are hierarchically nested between opening and closing <html> tags, and all code falls between either the <head> or the <body> tags:

```
<html>
<head>
<title>The page title goes here and displays in the
browser's title bar </title>
</head>
<body>
This part of the Web page contains all the content that
will appear in the browser window, including text and
graphics marked up by HTML tags with attributes.
```

```
</body>
</html>
```

The head area contains certain information about the Web page that will be interpreted by the browser, such as the page title, Meta tags used for page indexing by a search engine, style definitions in the form of CSS to control how content appears on the page, and JavaScript to manage simple site interactivity like rollover buttons. All the head data, with the exception of the title definition between the `<title>` tags, is invisible to the browser and won't appear anywhere on the finished Web page.

By contrast, the body area is where all the page's text, graphics, and other objects go. All content included in the body should be marked up with HTML tags to specify layout, style, and position. Anything between the opening and closing `<body>` tags — unless marked up with special comment tags — will appear as content on the page in the browser window.

Creating a page in a text editor

Now create your very first Web page by hand-coding in HTML. Follow these steps to see for yourself how easy it is to learn and use:

1. **Open a new document in your computer's text-editing program:**

On a PC, choose Start → All Programs → Accessories → Notepad.

On a Mac, launch your Applications folder and double-click the TextEdit icon.

A new untitled document should open automatically. If that doesn't happen, choose File → New to open a new file.

2. **Type the following HTML tags:**

```
<html>
<head>
<title></title>
</head>
<body>
</body>
</html>
```

3. Between the opening and closing **`<title>`** tags, **type** My First Web Page.

Your code should now look like this:

```
<html>
<head>
<title>My First Web Page</title>
</head>
<body>
</body>
</html>
```

4. Between the opening and closing `<body>` **tags, type** Hello world.

Now your code should now look like this:

```
<html>
<head>
<title>My First Web Page</title>
</head>
<body>Hello world.
</body>
</html>
```

5. Choose File → Save to open the Save As dialog box.

6. Set the Save In location to your computer's desktop.

7. In the File Name field, type index.html.

8. In the Save As Type field, select All Files.

9. Click the Save button to save the file with the settings you just entered and close the file.

10. Launch your favorite browser and open the window to roughly half the size of your desktop.

11. Drag and drop the copy of your new **index.html** page into the open browser window.

Your new Web page will appear with the words Hello world. in the body of the page, and the title, My First Web Page, will appear in the browser's title bar.

Congratulations! You've just created your first Web page. You can do a lot more to a page than include text, as you'll learn in future chapters. For now, feel free to experiment by adding more text between the body tags or changing the title.

Saving Web page files

When saving your files, you can use any name you like. Filenames can be any length, but it's more common to keep page names fairly short and succinct, and to avoid using spaces or odd characters with the exception of underscore (_) and dash (-). For example, a page name may be something like *about* or *email-signup*.

In addition to choosing a filename, you'll need to save all your Web page files with the appropriate file extension. It's important to remember to do this because the extension tells the browser the type of code used in the file so that the browser knows how to process and display the file's contents. Acceptable extensions for HTML are .html and .htm. Either extension will work; however, I recommend that you select one extension (I use .html) and use it for all the pages on a single site. Use other file extensions instead of .html if you end up adding any programming language or *Server-Side Includes* (a page containing HTML code that's embedded inside another HTML file) to the HTML page code. For example, acceptable filenames with extensions include `index.html`, `about-us.htm`, `articles.shtml`, `contact_us.asp`, `products.jsp`, and `services.cfml`. Table 4-1 outlines the file extensions you can use for different types of pages.

Table 4-1   **Saving with the Correct File Extension**

Type of Page	Extensions
HTML	`.html`, `.htm`
HTML pages with Server Side Includes	`.shtml` or `.shtm`
Microsoft Active Server Page	`.asp`
JavaServer Pages	`.jsp`
PHP script pages	`.php`
ColdFusion Markup Language pages	`.cfml` or `.cfm`

One page, however, must be deliberately named. In most cases, you should save the home page as either `index.html` or `index.htm`. Because the filename *index* is the default page name in a Web directory on most Web servers, visitors will not need to type in the filename and extension when they want to access the first (home) page on a site. For example, if I wanted to see the home page of the New York Public Library, rather than the typing the url and the filename plus the `.html` extension into my browser's address bar, `http://www.nypl.org/index.html`, I'd just type **http://www.nypl.org/** (or simply `nypl.org` if I felt particularly lazy) to get there.

Information Kiosk

Some Web sites might be hosted on different types of Web servers that require the home page to be named either `default.html` or `default.htm` instead. In my experience, this happens so infrequently, though, that I can usually figure this out myself by testing the `index.html` naming convention with a test page on the live server. If `index.html` doesn't work, `default.html` should. To save time, however, if you're unsure which filename to use, check with your (or your client's) host provider or system administrator. The administrator should know.

Working with the Right Design Tools

Web designers need a few of the right software tools to successfully design and build Web sites. In this section, you'll learn about how to choose the right graphic software applications and work with color on the Web using the Web-safe palette and hexadecimal values.

Choosing graphics programs

One of the nice things about being a designer, in my opinion, is the fact that you get to make lots of important decisions throughout the Web design process, including what applications to use to create the design, to optimize the graphics, and to actually build all the pages on the site.

Graphics programs

To work with and create images for the Web, designers can freely use both raster and vector programs.

- A **raster** program uses pixels to represent each bit of an image at the size used to create the image. It's okay to scale down a raster image (which is also sometimes called a bitmap image), but you should try to avoid enlarging a raster image because the larger version will need to use a computerized guessing technique called *resampling* and will tend to look, well, pixilated.

- By contrast, a **vector** program uses mathematical algorithms to draw shapes and paths, which means that vector images can be scaled up and down a zillion times and still retain the sharpness and clarity of its lines and shape at any size. Vector programs should always be used to create branding and corporate identity such as logos and other artwork, as the work can be scaled without any loss of resolution.

The most popular raster graphics application in use today is Adobe Photoshop, which, while primarily being a raster (or bitmap) application, can also create vector shapes and incorporate placed vector graphics from vector programs like Illustrator. Originally developed as a digital photo retouching and image-editing program, Photoshop has since evolved its capabilities for use as a nice Web graphics design tool. For vector art, most designers choose to use Adobe Illustrator or Macromedia FreeHand. Both are feature-rich drawing programs that allow you to draw just about anything for use in print, Web, animation, mobile devices, and video.

At a minimum, I suggest you have access to at least one good raster and one good vector art program, preferably Photoshop and Illustrator, respectively. Use the raster program to lay out all the parts of the Web page in the mockup (which you'll learn more about in Chapter 7), and if the design requires any special shapes, drawings, or illustrations, you can create them in the vector art program and then copy and paste them into your raster mockup. You could also use the vector application exclusively for the layout if desired, but many designers find the filters and effects in a vector program somewhat limiting compared to the special effects that can be applied in raster programs.

There are, of course, other image-editing programs you can use to create your Web graphics:

- Fireworks, though not too many professional designers use it, is a very good all-in-one image-editing and image-optimization tool.

○ For a super low-end, cookie-cutter graphics option, check out NetStudio's Easy Web Graphics program or Xara's Webstyle software.

○ If you have no budget at all for purchasing software, you can use several free online applications, such as the image editor at `http://myimager.com`. You'll also find some good freeware, shareware, and 30-day trials of image-editing software programs through download Web services like `www.download.com` and `www.zdnet.com`.

That said, I highly recommend you make the investment to buy Photoshop and Illustrator if you don't already own them. They're really the best tools available right now.

Information Kiosk

If you don't own any of these programs yet or you have old versions of them and are in need of an upgrade, a smart choice would be to buy the Adobe CS2, Studio 8, or Adobe Web bundle directly from Adobe. Students who can prove they are enrolled in a K–12 school, privately licensed training center, community college, or four-year college or university can qualify to purchase software discounted for students. For example, the full version of the Adobe Web bundle costs around $1,899, whereas the educational version of the same bundle costs only $599.

Watch Your Step

Avoiding Page Layout Programs   Though some graphic designers use Photoshop and Illustrator as page layout programs for print projects like postcards, brochures, and business cards, most tend to use software programs designed specifically for page layout, such as QuarkXPress and InDesign. Don't use a page layout program for your Web layouts unless you absolutely have no other choice! Page layout programs were designed for print, not the Web, and therefore won't necessarily have all the same features you'd currently find in Photoshop, Illustrator, ImageReady, and Fireworks. To be fair, Quark 7 now allows designers to export graphics into HTML as well as perform a few other optimization-like features similar to the things you can do with graphics in ImageReady and Fireworks. InDesign, however, currently offers nothing in the way of exporting HTML or graphics optimization. What it can do is allow designers (since the CS version) to export only an InDesign tagged XML file. That file can then be imported into an predesigned Adobe GoLive template, which inserts tagged data into preset areas on a Web template and doesn't allow designers to take advantage of their own design layout.

Web graphic optimization programs

After the Web site is designed, you'll need a good image-optimization program. *Optimization* means compressing the graphics into acceptable file formats that are small enough to be displayed on the Web without losing too much in the way of image quality.

Transfer

Chapter 8 is completely dedicated to the topic of optimization, so rather than get into that here, I just focus on describing which programs are the best to use.

The application most frequently used for image optimization is Adobe ImageReady, which comes bundled with Photoshop and is also the engine that converts vector graphics to Web graphics in Illustrator. You could use Fireworks or any number of the free or affordable optimization programs for a PC or Mac, like DeBabelizer Pro and Ulead's SmartSaver. What makes ImageReady and Fireworks so good, though, is that they can both optimize graphics and export tables-based HTML files, which can greatly cut down on the time it takes to build a Web site in an HTML or Web-editing program.

Using Web-safe colors

To help ensure that visitors on PCs and Macs have uniform experiences when they visit a particular Web site, Web designers should take efforts to select some of the colors on the site from the browser-safe color palette and to specify all colors using hexadecimal values. This browser-safe color palette (called the *Web-safe palette*) is somewhat restrictive in scope, having been developed mathematically by programmers, not aesthetically by artists.

Information Kiosk

The Web-safe palette originated in the early days of personal computers and the Internet. Computer monitors were capable only of an 8-bit display, which meant they could handle showing a maximum of 256 colors on-screen. What's more, the 256 colors viewable in an IE, a Netscape, or a Mosaic browser on a PC running Windows were somewhat different than the 256 colors viewable in an IE, a Netscape, or a Mosaic browser on an 8-bit monitor connected to an Apple computer running the Mac OS. If you take the 40 non-overlapping colors out of the equation, you're left with the 216 colors that will render uniformly on those browsers in both platforms.

One would think these limitations were somewhat short lived because of improvements made to monitor resolutions and browser capabilities. Today, monitors capable of 16-, 24-, and 36-bit display can render millions of colors on-screen. It's suggested, however, that designers still design for (or at least consider) the lowest common denominator — the audience members still using old computers, old monitors, and old versions of browsers — and thus choose colors from the Web-safe palette for their Web designs. At the time of this writing, Internet users with monitors having an 8-bit display represent less than 1 percent of the installed base.

This isn't to say that you can't include other colors in your designs at all! On the contrary; if monitors can display the colors, you should use them, but you should use the other colors smartly, in ways that might not be so obvious to the visitor using old equipment. The recommendation for the Web-safe palette is to use these 216 colors for large flat areas of color on a site, such as background colors (for pages, tables, and layers), logos, and illustrations saved as GIF files. For other parts of a site, such as photographs and graphics that can be saved as JPGs, using other colors might be fine, as long as you and the site owner understand the ramifications of potential color shift when viewed on older computer equipment. You'll learn more about color, file formats, and optimization in Chapter 8.

Introducing hexadecimal color values

When you're creating graphics for the Web in a vector or raster software program, you can specify color in RGB or hexadecimal values. However, when you're working in an HTML code editor, all colors, Web-safe or otherwise, must be specified in hexadecimal values preceded by the number symbol (#) to display properly on a Web page. The hexadecimal numbers, often called simple *hex colors,* refer to the RGB (red-green-blue, the additive colors used to display color on a computer monitor) values written in three pairs of numbers (from 0 to 9) or letters (from a to f), as shown in Table 4-2:

Table 4-2		Example Hexadecimal Values		
Color	Hexadecimal Value	Red	Green	Blue
Black	#000000	0	0	0
White	#ffffff	255	255	255
Red	#ff0000	255	0	0
Green	#00ff00	0	255	0
Blue	#ffff00	0	0	255

Transfer

Before CSS, designers used to add color attributes right to individual tags in the code, as in `<body bgcolor="#ffffff">`, to change the background color on a Web page. Today, using CSS, color attributes specified in hex values are added straight to the style definitions, which you'll learn about in Chapter 12.

Of the millions of colors that have hex values, only a handful have named equivalents, such as LightCoral for #f08080 and DarkSeaGreen for #8fbc8f, that are supported by most Web browsers and can be used in HTML code instead of the hex values.

To find the hexadecimal value of any RGB or CMYK (cyan-magenta-yellow-black, the subtractive ink colors used in four-color process printing) color, you must use a program that has a value conversion tool installed. Photoshop, Illustrator, Freehand, Fireworks, GoLive, and Dreamweaver all include Web-safe palettes and/or color tools that display converted hexadecimal values for colors.

If you'd like to use a standalone color conversion tool, you can find several freeware applications by searching online for a "free color picker." ColorPic, Color Cop, Color Spy, Huey, and ColorPickerPro all provide good RGB, CMYK, and hex conversions.

Looking up hexadecimal values in a graphics program

In this section, you learn how to look up hexadecimal values. Pretend you have a client who says that their new Web site must use certain preselected colors. The client doesn't have the hexadecimal color values but does have Pantone (a color-matching system used by designers and printers; see www.pantone.com), CMYK, and RGB equivalents. Here are the colors:

- **RGB:** R:246, G:191, B:0
- **CMYK:** C:52%, M:15%, Y:98%, K:1%
- **Pantone:** 297C

Your job is to find the equivalent hexadecimal color values for use in your mockup.

To do this exercise, you need access to Photoshop because its built-in color-picker tool allows for Pantone-to-hex conversion. If you don't have access to Photoshop, use a standalone color picker to make the CMYK and RGB conversions in Steps 8 and 12.

1. Launch the program and choose File → New to create a new document.

The New dialog box opens. Here you can enter the appropriate settings to set up your document.

You don't necessarily need a new document to use the color-picker tool, but in this exercise you will so that you can save the swatches for future reference.

2. Enter the following settings for the new document:

In Photoshop, enter **760 x 420** pixels for the Web page dimensions and **72** pixels/inch for the Resolution. For the Color Mode setting, choose RGB, 8 bit.

These settings are typical for Web design, and you can use them for most of your Web page mockups.

3. Click OK to close the dialog box and return to the new blank document.

4. With the rectangular marquee tool selected in Photoshop, click and drag on your document to create a rectangle shape and release the mouse.

In Photoshop, the rectangular marquee will create a selected area that you can fill with any color.

5. Click the top Foreground Color icon at the bottom of the Tool palette.

The foreground/background color selector icons are the overlapping squares. The foreground is on the top-left and the background is on the bottom-right.

This opens the Color Picker dialog box, shown in Figure 4-1, which has several options for viewing color.

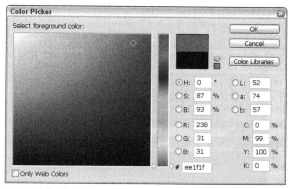

Figure 4-1: Most design programs have color tools that represent color in RGB, CMYK, and hexadecimal values, but some, like Photoshop, also allow for Pantone color conversion.

6. Select the Only Web Colors check box at the bottom of the dialog box.

This shifts the look of the colors displaying in the left of the color picker from showing millions of colors to showing only the 216 Web-safe colors. Because you're going to be looking at RGB, Pantone, and CMYK colors to find their hexadecimal equivalents, you don't need to be restricted to the Web-safe palette.

7. Deselect the Only Web Colors check box.

You want to see millions of colors.

8. To look up the first color, enter the following values in the R, G, and B fields: 246, 191, and 0, respectively.

As you enter the numbers into the R, G, and B fields, notice how the color shifts inside the Color Picker.

The hexadecimal value of your entered color will appear as a combination of six letters and numbers in the Hex field at the bottom of the color picker, beginning with a # symbol.

The hexadecimal value of this RGB color is #f6bf00.

9. **Click the OK button to close the Color Picker dialog box.**

   The rectangle shape will still be selected. Next you fill it with the new hex color.

10. **Choose Edit ➜ Fill to open the Fill dialog box and, under Use, select Foreground Color. Then click OK.**

    The yellow color fills the selected rectangle.

11. **To the right of the yellow rectangle, repeat Steps 4 and 5 to create another rectangle shape and open the Color Picker dialog box.**

    You'll use the same process to look up the hex value for the CMYK color.

12. **Look up the CMYK color by entering the following values in the C, M, Y, and K fields: 52, 15, 98, 1, respectively.**

    The hexadecimal value of this CMYK color is #89ac40.

13. **Repeat Steps 9 and 10 to fill the second rectangle with the new hex color.**

14. **To the right of the green rectangle, repeat Steps 4 and 5 to create a third rectangle shape and open the Color Picker dialog box.**

    You'll use the same process to look up the hex value for the Pantone color.

15. **To look up the Pantone color, click the Color Libraries button.**

    This changes the layout of the Color Picker dialog box.

16. **Under Book, select Pantone Solid Coated, then type the number of the Pantone color provided by the client: 297.**

    The color field automatically displays a range of blue color swatches with the Pantone 297C color highlighted.

17. **To convert the Pantone color into a regular color and find the hex equivalent, click the Picker button.**

    This changes the layout of the Color Picker dialog box back to the normal color picker mode. The same color blue is selected, but now instead of seeing a Pantone swatch, you can see that color's RGB, CMYK, and hexadecimal equivalents!

    The hexadecimal value of this Pantone color is #78c7eb.

18. **Repeat Steps 9 and 10 to fill the third rectangle with the new hex color.**

19. **Choose File ➜ Save to save the document.**

    Select a location on your computer to save your new file, name your file `HexSwatches.psd`, select the Photoshop format, and click Save.

Adding an E-Commerce Shopping Cart

If the site you're working on will be selling any products or services online, the site will need some kind of shopping cart to process payments coming from the purchasers. Payments can be processed in many ways, depending on the needs and budget of the site owner.

The most basic cart uses a payment processing service such as PayPal. The next tier of service is to create an online store using a shopping cart service's proprietary software, like Yahoo!Shops. Those, however, must reside on the service's server away from the site owner's main URL. Other shopping cart services include building more customized carts from either Web-host provided services or out-of-the-box shopping carts from third-party software manufacturers. While fancier, these solutions do have limitations and can be very frustrating to customize, even for the most experienced designers.

For clients looking for something really slick, the best option is to have a shopping cart custom built so that it's tailored specifically to the site's needs. This, however, can cost significantly more money and take a lot more time to build than the other shopping carts.

PayPal shopping carts

PayPal offers several payment solutions. The PayPal shopping cart is great for sites working within a budget or selling only a handful of products. What's more, PayPal accounts are easy to set up and easy to use. To use PayPal's services:

1. The client needs to set up a Merchant PayPal account linked to the bank she'd like to use to accept payments.

2. The client must also input data about all the products she'd like to sell on the site so that PayPal can generate Add to Cart PayPal buttons and HTML code for each product.

3. When that's done, as the designer, you need to copy and paste the code for those buttons from the PayPal site into the HTML pages that list the products on the client's site. That's all there is to it.

To use the shopping cart online, visitors click the button of the item they'd like to purchase and are taken to a special PayPal payment-processing page. Registered PayPal users can simply enter their payment information. Unregistered visitors can either choose to set up a PayPal account or simply enter their credit card information to proceed with the transaction. PayPal sends an automated e-mail to the site owner about the purchase. The site owner then has the responsibility of processing the order. PayPal processes Visa, MasterCard, American Express, Diners Club, and eChecks.

Third-party and Web host shopping carts

Two other methods of having an e-commerce site are either using a host-provided shopping cart service or purchasing a third-party software solution.

Most Web-hosting companies offer some kind of shopping cart service in one of their hosting plans. Host e-commerce plans often use their own, custom-built applications that allow site owners to add all the required products to their accounts, though some host providers have begun using a new service called GoogleCheckout, similar in concept to PayPal's Add to Cart buttons.

Although usually easy to configure and use, site owners should be aware of the greater fees associated with these types of e-commerce hosted plans. In addition to the monthly or annual hosting rate, site owners will also need to get a merchant account to process credit cards through their shopping carts, as well as pay for an SSL certificate to ensure that online transactions are secure. The cost of these extra fees and capabilities can increase the total cost of a hosting plan considerably (say from $50 per month to upwards of $200 per month). Because host-provided carts can vary drastically, be sure to test drive any you're considering before committing to using the service.

If the site owner is looking for a more customized but still reasonably inexpensive e-commerce solution, a third-party software application could be useful. Finding a good one, however, might prove challenging. In a "2006 Shopping Cart Software Report" on TopTenReviews.com (`http://shopping-cart-review.toptenreviews.com`), ShopSite Pro, MerchandiZer Pro, and Monster Commerce Pro were rated the best shopping cart software programs on the market. That said, I've actually used the program they rated at number four on their top ten list, but I'd never recommend it, even to my worst enemy. For that reason alone, I've stayed away from packaged solutions and instead favored either the PayPal or customized cart routes.

Believe it or not, some free shopping cart software applications are available. They will require a bit of coding to configure the cart, but a few of them are quite reputable. It would behoove you to do a Web search to learn more about your shopping cart options if you decide to go the third-party route.

Custom-built shopping carts

My favorite way to add a shopping cart to a site is to enlist the help of a programmer to build a custom cart that meets the client's exact specifications. With a custom-designed cart, every aspect of the ordering and checkout process can be customized, from the user interface to the checkout confirmation page. This kind of detailed customization is possible because the database is typically developed and integrated into the site as part of the e-commerce solution while the site is initially being built. All the e-commerce page layouts can be customized to the products being sold and have the same navigation, look, and feel as the rest of the site. Not only that, using the customized database means being able to customize the payment processing tasks, including sending e-mail receipts to the purchasers and creating administrative reports for the client.

If you don't have a background in database development and integration, you could either learn how to do these things yourself or hire a programmer to do them for you. If you have good split brain power and are motivated to learn, go for it. Personally, I'd much rather have someone who enjoys this kind of left-brain data manipulation do the work for me than to spend my own right-brain power trying to figure out how to do it myself. You learn more about hiring a programmer later in this chapter.

Planning for secure transactions

Whatever solution you decide to use, take extra care to ensure that the site visitors' personal information is safe and secure during the purchasing transaction. If credit card payments are going to be processed on the Web site (instead of through an outside service), the site owner needs to set up a special merchant account as well as purchase an SSL certificate for the domain.

A *merchant account* is a special bank account that handles the processing of credit card transactions. The merchant account collects payments electronically from the purchaser and then transfers the funds into the business owner's local business checking account. If you or your client decide to set up a merchant account, keep the following facts in mind:

- **Setup and Application Fees:** Merchant accounts can be set up through local banks, through host providers, and through billing software Web sites such as the Intuit site for QuickBooks. Most accounts cost about $25–$250 in setup and application fees.

- **Monthly Processing Fees:** Fees for merchant services can add up quickly! Most merchant accounts charge a minimum each month, in the $15–$30 range (this is sometimes called a gateway or statement fee) when the number of transactions processed is below a preset minimum, plus a nominal percentage of interest around $0.20–$0.30 on all transactions processed. If the monthly minimum is met in transaction fees, the monthly minimum fee is often waived. Thirty dollars might be merely a token savings if you do a lot of business online. For instance, at $0.30 per transaction, if you sell $10,000 in products a month, you'd pay $300.00 in transaction fees.

SSL stands for Secure Sockets Layer and refers to the digital security certificate that needs to be purchased by the site owner and configured for the domain by the host provider. A valid SSL certificate guarantees the site uses 128-bit or higher encryption to both keep visitors' personal information and credit card numbers secure and protect the Web site from hackers and credit card thieves.

The leading brand of SSL certificate is VeriSign, but several others are available at varying costs. All certificate issuers charge a one-time or annual fee, and the host provider might charge about $50 as a setup fee to obtain the certificate for you, though sometimes with specials, host providers will waive the setup fee. The first year always costs more than the renewal rates for subsequent years.

Annual rates vary from vendor to vendor depending on the bit encryption rate:

- VeriSign, $350–$895
- Thawte, $200–$500
- GeoTrust, $170–$1500

Knowing When to Hire a Programmer

In Chapter 1, you learned a little bit about diagnosing a site's dynamic needs. Adding dynamic features to a site adds cost and time to the project, and not all sites truly need it. Budget is often the primary factor for determining whether to add dynamic functionality to a site. Other considerations include expected growth of the site, the projected schedule for making updates, and the amount of data to be served on the site.

To refresh your memory, you might need to hire a programmer if you

- Have information stored in a database and want to have that data dynamically served on the pages of the Web site
- Want a site search feature that accesses a database and returns results based on selected search criteria, such as an alphabetized listing of store locations
- Want a custom-built shopping cart for the site's products, which will allow you to customize the user's experience throughout the entire purchasing process
- Would like a Content Management System built for the site so you (or your client) can manage content on the site
- Need to create an area of the site that requires a username and password for secure login to a database of accessible records
- Need to create a multilanguage site using either the full dynamic site creation or selective site replication methods, as described in Chapter 2
- Want to allow visitors to choose how data will be displayed on a page by clicking the category heading of a table of data to re-sort the records, as with the Sort by Price shopping feature found on most e-commerce sites
- Want to collect information from site visitors who've completed an online form, add that data to a database, and use that data to generate newsletters and e-mail blasts
- Would like to dynamically display information such as product descriptions, course listings, job opportunities, and real estate listings

Dynamic sites are really great, and some things you just can't do without a database and some programming. Even an inexperienced designer can learn and handle the simpler programming-like tasks. For example, a novice can easily learn to hard-code hypertext links to individual pages and add the appropriate actions, hidden fields, and script configuration settings to a Web page form so that a Perl script provided by a Web host can process the form.

Transfer

Perl scripts are often used to process data collected in online forms. The scripts themselves must typically be placed inside the CGI (Common Gateway Interface) folders at the root level of the Web host server to function properly. You'll learn more about forms and form processing in Chapter 16.

The two most common types of databases are created with MySQL and Microsoft Access, both fairly easy programs to learn. After the database has been constructed, you can easily learn the appropriate code to add to a Web page that will pull the data from a database, at least if you're using a program like Dreamweaver. This book, unfortunately, doesn't delve into those advanced techniques. However, if you're inclined to learn, I recommend a book that does cover those topics; check out the range of titles available at www.wiley.com.

If you prefer to hire a programmer, you need to go about finding someone to hire. The following steps will help you get started:

1. **Craft a "programmer wanted" ad to post somewhere. In your ad, be as clear as you can possibly be about your programming needs and how you'd like applicants to respond.**

   For instance, if you know you need to collect e-mail addresses so the site owner can generate and mail monthly e-newsletters, state that. Also, if you know the language you want the programmer to work in, whether it's ASP, JSP, PHP, or ColdFusion, specify it.

   Similarly, if you really need someone who can come to your office and work with you side by side, specify in your job posting that the applicant must live in your town. If you want to hire only seasoned programmers, request to see evidence of the programmer's portfolio. Always ask for references from everybody, even the student who might be charging next to nothing to build his or her portfolio.

2. **Post your ad. Fortunately, some of the best places to look for a programmer are online.**

   You can find programmers through an agency like Monster.com, or the less-formal job listing sites like Elance.com and GetACoder.com. Other, perhaps smarter, places to look are Craigslist, local programming school job boards, programmer blogs, forums, and even by word of mouth in programmer chat rooms.

3. **Ask the applicants (who, by the way, will be responding from around the globe) as many questions as you want about their experience, fees, and the timeframe it may take them to complete your project.**

Use your e-mails going back and forth with applicants as a way to weed out the less capable candidates.

4. **When you've whittled your list down to two or three promising programmers, try them out, if you can, on the same small project (different from the reason you're hiring them) to see whether they're reliable, friendly, hardworking, responsible, and capable programmers.**

If you're lucky, you'll end up with at least one, but hopefully two programmers you can begin working with on all your dynamic projects.

hexadecimal: The six-letter/number combination that represents RGB values of a color displaying in a Web browser. Numbers range from 0 to 9 and letters can range from a to f, as in #ffff00 for the color blue.

HTML: HyperText Markup Language. A Web page markup language that communicates how the content on a page should be displayed in a browser window.

optimization: A method for compressing graphics that are small enough to be displayed on the Web into acceptable file formats for the Web (.gif, .jpg, and .png), while retaining as much of the original image quality as is possible.

raster: A graphic created in bitmap or raster software programs (such as Photoshop) that use pixels to represent each part of the image. Raster/Bitmap programs are great for photographic retouching and building Web site mockups; however, these graphics don't look good when scaled larger than their original size.

SSL: Secure Sockets Layer. A digital Web certificate that guarantees that visitor data collected on a particular Web site will be transferred to and from the server using 128-bit (or higher) encryption methods.

vector graphics: Graphics that use mathematical algorithms to construct their shapes and paths. These graphics often have smaller file sizes than their raster-based bitmap counterparts, and they will always retain their crispness and clarity regardless of their size after rescaling.

Web-safe palette: The 216 cross-platform colors that Web browsers can display on an 8-bit computer monitor.

WYSIWYG: What You See Is What You Get; pronounced *wizzy-wig*. For example, a WYSIWYG Web editor has a design interface that closely matches what the page will look like when launched in a Web browser. These types of Web editors often use drag-and-drop tools, buttons, and other methods for inserting and styling objects and text on a page.

XHTML: eXtensible HyperText Markup Language. A stricter version of HTML that allows data on a page to be used as an application of XML.

Last
Stop

Practice Exam

1. True or False: All the pages on a Web site can be saved with any name as long as the proper extension is used.

2. In HTML code, the `<title>` tags go between the opening and closing _____ tags.

3. Content that will appear in a browser window should be coded between the opening and closing _____ tags.

4. Hexadecimal numbers contain _____ pairs of letter/number combinations.

5. The _____ symbol must precede a hexadecimal number in the HTML code so that the color displays properly in a browser window.

6. Which of the following are acceptable Web page names with extensions?

    A) `index.htm, butters.shtml, fly_fishing.asp`

    B) `tennis.cfml, aboutus.html, travelinfo.plp`

    C) `case study.jsp, marketing.asp, open-house.html`

    D) All of the above

7. Why would you not want to use a graphics layout program like QuarkXPress or InDesign to create your Web site design?

    _____

    _____

8. Name the two types of Web-editing programs.

    _____

    _____

9. Sites using third-party, Web-host provided, or custom-built shopping carts must also have what things to safely and securely process orders online?

_____

_____

10. Name three Web site features that would warrant having to hire a programmer for a site.

_____

_____

11. Explain the difference between a raster program and a vector program with regard to scaling.

_____

_____

_____

_____

12. If a site will be selling only six products and the site owner has a small budget, what type of shopping cart would you recommend? Why?

_____

_____

_____

_____

EXIT

Registering a Domain and Getting a Hosting Plan

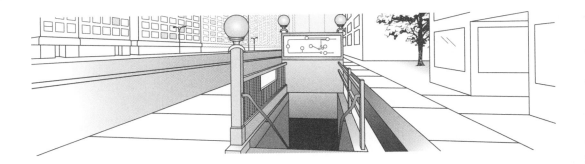

Enter the Station

Questions

1. What is the best way to choose a domain name for a business?

2. How can you verify whether the domain you want is available?

3. What online tools can you use to help generate ideas for a domain name?

4. Where should you go to register a domain name?

5. What services should you look for in a good hosting plan?

6. What is a *placeholder page* and why should a domain have one before the site is built?

Express Line

If your client has already procured and registered a domain name and acquired a hosting plan, skip to the last section on creating a customized placeholder page or move on to Chapter 6, where you'll learn how to define a site's look and feel.

To make a site available on the Internet, the site first needs to have an address. The Web address itself is commonly referred to as the *domain name.* The process of procuring a domain name involves quite a bit of work. To start with, someone needs to think of a name for the site. Then the name's availability needs to be verified. If it is free, the name needs to be registered, either with a domain registrar or host provider. After that, the client will need a hosting plan in order to publish the site, and if building the site might take some time, the client also might want to have you design and upload a customized placeholder page to the domain until the new Web site is ready.

Some clients will have already done all of these things before contacting you about your design services. Others will need a little hand-holding through each of the steps. It's really helpful that you know this stuff fairly well, because being able to provide information about these topics to your clients who don't know about them yet will enhance their experience with you as a designer. Remember, happy clients are more likely to return and/or refer business to you if they feel confident in all your Web-related skills.

If you've never dealt with domains before, you might want to practice these skills by setting up your own Web site before handling these tasks for a client.

In this chapter, you learn about domain name selection, name generators, domain verification, and domain registration. There's also a section about finding a good hosting plan, including what to look for in a plan, where to find a host, and general pricing structures. The last part of the chapter provides step-by-step instructions for creating a customized placeholder page, which is a single, simple Web page with company branding, e-mail, and other contact information that will hold the place on a new domain until the new Web site is built and ready to publish.

Choosing a Domain Name

Selecting a domain name for a Web site is something that you, in your role as a designer, might or might not be involved in with your clients, depending on their needs and how Web savvy they are. Some Web clients will have already selected a domain, registered it, and secured hosting, whereas others will say they don't really understand all that stuff and are relying on your experience to help them figure it all out. Some clients, of course, will fall somewhere in between, needing a little help with some but not all of these domain-related responsibilities.

To help guide you in these tasks, I'll assume you have a new client who needs help with everything, starting with selecting a domain name. As a matter of fact, part of your services might include explaining to a client what a domain name is before you go about assisting the client in selecting one.

A *domain name* is just a name used to identify an address on the Internet for Web sites and e-mail, as in `http://www.super8juice.com` and `info@super8juice.com`. The Web address itself is composed of four distinct parts:

- **protocol:** The first part of a Web address, `http://`, is the HyperText Transfer Protocol (HTTP) which identifies the protocol that allows a computer to browse the Web by getting information from a remote server. Secure access to the Internet (that is, anytime a domain has an SSL certificate installed on the host server for encrypting private data) requires the use of the `https://` (note the *s* for secure) protocol.

- **www:** The second part refers to the World Wide Web and identifies the type of page that will be delivered in a browser window. You might notice that some sites will still display in your browser without the www part of the address, such as typing just **super8juice.com** into your browser's address bar instead of **www.super8juice.com**, but that function is typically server-dependent and isn't a universal feature of domain names. Another type of Web address includes domains where the www is replaced with a different word, such as `products.super8juice.com`. This type of address refers to a subsite that resides on the main domain but is separate from it.

- **domain name:** The third part identifies the name of the Web site as registered by the owner of the site. Domain names may contain any combination of upper- and lowercase letters and numbers. In addition, though less often used, domain names may also include hyphens but not any other special characters.

- **extension:** The fourth part identifies the type of site visitors should expect to see at the address, such as `.com` for business sites and `.edu` for educational sites.

Though several unrestricted extensions are now in use by all kinds of companies across the globe, the most familiar ones must be used appropriately. For instance, `.org` is for nonprofit organizations and `.gov` is used exclusively for government sites. In addition to the more familiar extensions, several others identify the country of origin, such as `.co.uk` for the United Kingdom. Table 5-1 lists all the available extensions. Actually, about 30 extensions are available, and Web site owners can often select the one that best fits their needs at the time of domain registration.

Table 5-1   Web Domain Extensions

Extension	Typical Usage
.com	Commercial, but is commonly used for just about anything
.net	Internet administrative site, but is commonly used for other types of sites as well
.org	Organization

Extension	Typical Usage
.info	Information
.biz	Business
.us	United States
.name	Personal Web sites
.at	Austria
.be	Belgium
.bz	Belize
.cc	Cocos (Keeling) Islands
.cn	China
.de	Germany
.eu	European Union
.gs	South Georgia & the South Sandwich Islands
.ms	Montserrat
.mx	Mexico
.nz	New Zealand
.tc	Turks and Caicos Islands
.tv	Tuvalu, but often used for television
.tw	Taiwan
.uk	United Kingdom
.vg	British Virgin Islands
.ws	Western Samoa, but is often used for Web sites

Your job in helping the client choose a domain name necessarily involves helping to select the appropriate extension. That said, some domain names with the desired extension might (and probably will) already be taken by another company with the same name. In those cases, the client will need to use a different extension with the desired domain name, alter the spelling of the desired domain name, or come up with a similar but different domain name. I'll discuss domain availability later in this section.

The first item to look at when choosing a domain name for a company is the name of the client's business. If, for example, the client's company is called Bartoli Interior Design, the most fitting domain name for the company would be bartoliinteriordesign.com. With an unusual or unique business name, selecting domains can be quite simple really. But what about the client whose company name is so common across the country that the domain with the desired extension is already taken?

In those cases, the domain the client actually uses will need to be tinkered with by adding a state or city reference, inserting a hyphen between letters, or using abbreviations. For example, if the company name was Edgewood Apartments and it's located in New Jersey, the client could consider using `edgewood apartmentsnj.com`, `edgewood-apartments.com`, `edgewoodaptsnj.com`, or `edgewood-apts-nj.com`. Conversely, the client might also consider using another extension, either with or without the other name adjustments, such as `edgewoodapts.info` or `edgewood-apartments.us`.

Using a domain name generator

Finding a workable domain name can at times be quite frustrating. When that's the case with me, I often enlist the help of several online domain name generators, which can be great for suggesting ideas based on real-time domain name availability. The generators take whatever word or words you'd like to include in the domain name, then shake them out in a variety of combinations either with or without other words, and present a resulting list of potential names for you to choose from.

My two favorite online domain name generators are NameBoy.com and DomainsBot.com.

- At **NameBoy.com,** you can enter a primary and optional secondary word to begin the search and choose whether returned results include hyphens between characters and rhyming, which can sometimes make the domain name easier to remember. It also allows you to verify domains you're interested in with its handy WHOIS search form. You can even search for and register domains that have expired or are about to expire.

- **DomainsBot.com,** by comparison, has a few more features for searching desired domain names. In addition to finding keywords or specific domain names, you may also search for domains by entering in a short phrase or sentence. Another cool feature of this service is that, as you type your keywords into the search box, you can actually see site name availability before you click the Search button! When the search results appear, you can further refine the results list by limiting the specific extensions you'd like to see, selecting whether the domain name should include hyphens and/or numbers, and checking on all the domains' current status (available, expired, for sale). If you happen to find a domain you'd like, the site provides the option of selecting from among five different registrar services to handle the domain name purchase checkout process.

Verifying domain name availability

Even if you didn't require the services of an online domain name generator, you'll still need to verify that the selected name(s) you and your client decided upon for the Web site are truly available for registration. In other words, you'll need to make sure that no one else is using, or has already registered but isn't using yet, the domain you want. Verification is free and quick to do on a number of Web sites, including many of the domain registrar sites. With a good verification tool, finding a good name is only a matter of a little time, patience, and open mindedness.

Information Kiosk

I like using the domain verification tool on NetworkSolutions.com because the site provides superfast results, including automatic name suggestions should the entered name be taken.

In the following exercise, you'll use the domain name selection and verification tools at NetworkSolutions.com and DomainsBot.com to practice what you've just learned.

1. Open a browser window and go to the NetworkSolutions.com Web site, at `www.networksolutions.com`.

2. In the Find A Domain text box, type edgewoodapartments **and click the Search button.**

The `.com` check box should already be selected. Leave it selected and leave the other boxes deselected.

The search results indicate that the `.com` and `.info` extensions are unavailable. Other extensions are available, such as `.net`, `.org`, `.use`, and `.name`.

3. Scroll down on the page to view the Recommended Alternative Domain Names.

The ten names in this section are similar to the domain, and all use the familiar `.com` extension.

4. Do another search on the same site. This time, enter the domain name edgewood-apartments **and click the Search button.**

Aha! This domain name is available with the `.com` extension and could be registered today if you wanted it (presuming no one has registered this domain since the time I wrote this).

5. Now go to the DomainsBot.com Web site and type edgewood apartments **into the search field.**

Before you click the Search button, notice how a message window pops open to reveal the availability of domains using the two words in the search field. The `edgewoodapartments.com` domain name is unavailable.

6. Click the Search button.

The search results on this site are quite a bit more detailed and offer tools to refine the search based on selected criteria. To modify the results, adjust the settings in the LiveBot panel on the right side of the page.

7. Adjust the search results. Under Apartments, select lofts and suites, and under View Only, *deselect* all the extensions except .com and *deselect* Expiring and For Sale. Click the Update Results button.

The results list updates automatically to show only availability of domains matching the new search criteria. Among the options, you might find one the client wouldn't mind using. If the apartments are located in a downtown area somewhere in New Jersey, for example, the site might do well if it were called edgewoodcitypads.com or edgewoodcitysuites.com. However, if the domain name really needs to match the company name, the client might choose edgewood-apartments.com after all.

Registering a Domain

Registering a domain name is essentially like reserving a car; to use the car, you must go to the car rental agency, sign a contract, and provide payment information before the agency gives you the car keys. Likewise, registering the domain is simply a means of placing the name on reserve for later use.

To enable visitors to access an actual site through that name, you must secure a hosting plan and activate the domain name through what's called a *DNS transfer*. The transfer involves shifting the domain name from the registrar to the host provider. This assures that the domain points to the server hosting the site so that the site can be properly accessed by everyone on the Web. You'll learn how to select a hosting plan later in this chapter.

Information Kiosk

The DNS (Domain Name Server or Domain Name System) is like a permanent address for every domain name. After a domain has been registered, it typically must be relocated to a new destination for hosting. And because each computer has its own IP address, rather than finding sites by their IPs, it's easier to park a domain name on an IP address and allow people to search for a site by its domain name. The domain name, then, becomes the alias for the host computer's IP address.

Although the particular services might vary, you can expect the following from any domain registrar service:

- **The ability to select the length of the domain registration:** Typical terms for domain registration are for one, two, three, five, and ten years.

- **Rates from $1.67 to $12 per year, for the affordable domains:** These services might come with or without e-mail accounts. Most fall in the $8 to $9 range. The `.com` domains are the most sought after domains and tend to cost more, whereas the less trendy `.info` extension domain names can now be snagged for under $2.00 a year from most registrars.

So with literally thousands and thousands of Web sites offering online domain name registration, how should one go about finding a reputable domain registrar? The answer depends on your timeframe, budget, and needs.

Most registrars, in fact, provide additional services such as domain verification, domain name generators, domain transfers, hosting, and Internet access.

Watch Your Step

The most popular domain name registration services are the ones that charge the least amount of money. Remember, though, that while cheap, those services might not necessarily provide the best customer care, and depending on your level of knowledge, that might be an important factor to you and your client. Therefore, shop wisely and do research before you procure a domain for your client, or recommend your client registers the domain himself, from a particular company.

If you just need to register the domain name for a time before the site is ready to publish, but aren't interested in e-mail or hosting until right before the site gets launched, I think it's okay to go with one of the cheaper domain registrar services. However, if you need other services such as e-mail, Web hosting, site design, and e-commerce, go with one the companies that also provide those services, such as GoDaddy, NetworkSolutions, DomainDirect, Dotster, DirectNic, BulkRegister, Register.com, and Hostway, or any of the myriad hosting services that might have been recommended to you.

Before you do that, however, consider your long-term needs. If the site is ready or will have a short turnaround time (say, 30 days or fewer), I see no problem with speeding up the domain registration process by registering the domain through the host provider that will be hosting the site. On the other hand, until the site is ready for publishing and if you expect it to have a month or longer turnaround time, you have no need to secure hosting. For this reason alone, most site owners prefer to register the domain with one company and use another company for hosting, with the knowledge that they'll need to do the DNS transfer when the hosting plan has been secured. In case you decide to at least investigate the option of choosing a hosting service that's separate from the registration service, the next section will explain how you find a good hosting plan.

Finding a Good Hosting Plan

A hosting plan is like a monthly or annual parking space for a Web site in that you rent out a space on a host provider's server to park your site for a specified period of time. While there, and as long as the domain is directed to the host's servers, the site will be accessible to anyone surfing the Internet with knowledge of the Web address.

Like domain registrars, host providers are everywhere (possibly even more abundant that registrars), and deciding which service to choose is often difficult. What things should you look for in a hosting plan, and how can you tell whether you're getting a reasonable rate, good technical support and customer service, enough Web space on the server, the right number of e-mail accounts, decent reporting tools, or special services? Here are a few tips that can help you get started:

- **Word of mouth can often be the best method for finding a plan.** As a Dreamweaver teacher, I occasionally have designers in my classes who already have some experience in the Web world, and when I do, I often ask them which hosting plans they have used and like or dislike. Though I'm more likely to trust another designer's experience with multiple hosting plans than I am novice Web users who have only ever registered a single site (their own), I've gathered a decent list of providers that I refer to when the need arises.

- **The single most important feature in a hosting plan is customer service.** Having 24-hour telephone and e-mail support is essential for two reasons. First, should anything go awry on the server side, I like to know someone is there, 24/7, to fix the problem or answer technical questions. Second, being self-employed, I tend to keep irregular work hours and like knowing that my questions at 3:00 in the morning will be answered by a knowledgeable, friendly technician just as readily as the questions I have at 3:00 in the afternoon. In addition to word of mouth, you can get a sense about a company's customer service by noting what level of customer service it offers when you inquire about its plan. Also, ask what type of customer service it offers with the hosting plan or plans.

- **Look for the ability to access the site and upload files by using FTP (File Transfer Protocol).** Some host providers offer only a custom built "site console" or "control panel" with limited capabilities for uploading files. With FTP access, you have better control over uploading files when it's time to publish the site.

Hosting plans tend to come in four distinct flavors: the bare-bones starter plan, the small-business plan, the big-business plan, and the e-commerce plan. Each tends to have certain features in common, as shown in Table 5-2. Although I've seen monthly

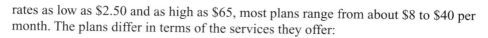

rates as low as $2.50 and as high as $65, most plans range from about $8 to $40 per month. The plans differ in terms of the services they offer:

Uptime: The total time within any 24-hour period where the site is accessible to visitors on the Internet. Any time a host provider's server goes down, for whatever reason, domains on that server will go offline, which is commonly referred to as downtime. Uptime of 100 percent is the ultimate goal of all host providers.

Hard drive space: This is the total number of MB or GB of space allotted for the domain on the host provider's server. To determine your client's hard drive space needs, multiply the number of pages they intend to have on the site by 30K and then factor in enough space for the file sizes of all the graphics, documents, and multimedia files to be hosted on the site as well. Typical small sites can make due with 500MB of space, whereas e-commerce sites can require upwards of 3,000MB, depending on the number of products being sold.

Data transfer and page views: The data transfer and page view figures refer to the maximum allowable number of times visitors access the pages (that is, the text, graphics, and other content) on the hosted site within a given timeframe, such as a 30-day period. If the site is very popular, there could be over 30 million page views in a month!

Dedicated IP address: Domains with a dedicated IP address will be hosted on their own servers. This type of plan is more expensive than Web sites that use a shared IP address but is ultimately more reliable because a dedicated server can more accurately monitor its own Web traffic and provide faster server response times. A dedicated IP address is also a requirement for sites needing an SSL certificate.

User account: Depending on your client's needs, the plan can accommodate anywhere from one to several user accounts. Each account provides password-protected host server access to site management tools such as passwords, e-mail setup functionality, billing information, and more.

Domain pointer: This is a feature of some hosting plans that allows one domain to send visitors to another. Domain pointers can often be useful when a business wants to provide for misspellings of a domain name so that anytime visitors try to view the misspelled domain, they're automatically directed to the correctly named site, such as mypinapples.com pointing to mypineapples.com.

Web-based statistics: Web-based stats can help site owners track the number of visitors to their site, including such details as the entry and exit URLs, the number of hits and page views, keyword analysis, and the number of returning versus new visitors.

Table 5-2 — Typical Hosting Plan Features

Feature	Starter	Small Biz	Big Biz	e-Commerce
Monthly Fee	**$8**	**$14**	**$19**	**$40**
Account	24-hour uptime, customer service, technical support			
Technical	500MB hard drive space, 100GB data transfer, 10 million page views, dedicated IP address, 1 user account	1,000MB hard drive space, 300GB data transfer, 30 million page views, dedicated IP address, 5 user accounts	2,000MB hard drive space, 400GB data transfer, 40 million page views, dedicated IP address, 10 user accounts	3,000MB hard drive space, 500GB data transfer, 40 million page views, dedicated IP address, 20 user accounts
Domains	Dedicated domain name, registration of new domains, domain pointers, and so on			
Site management	Online control panel, Web site builder, FrontPage extensions (scripts that provide dynamic functions on sites built with FrontPage), FTP access, free Web-based statistics, access to raw log files, and so on			
E-mail	50 accounts + 125MB hard drive space, virus protection, online e-mail access, and so on	200 accounts + 250MB hard drive space, virus protection, online e-mail access, and so on	400 accounts + 500MB hard drive space, virus protection, online e-mail access, and so on	500 accounts + 750MB hard drive space, virus protection, online e-mail access, and so on
Scripting	ASP, ASP.NET, CGI-BIN folder, Perl, PHP support, and so on			
Databases	mySQL max, 5MB hard drive space	+ mySQL server, 2 ODBC data source names, MS access, 50MB hard drive space	+ mySQL server, 4 ODBC data source names, MS access, 100MB hard drive space	+ mySQL server, 6 ODBC data source names, MS access, 300MB hard drive space
E-commerce	SSL secure servers, shared SSL certificates, merchant tools with and without credit card processing, and so on			
Data	Firewall and antivirus protection, daily backups, redundant servers with power backups, and so on			

Information Kiosk

Other good resources for finding hosting plans are the various online hosting review sites, like WebhostingInspector.com,

TheHostingChart.com, and Hosting-Review.com. Most likely, if you see a particular hosting company on more than a couple top ten lists, chances are it's a good host provider. Remember though, a host provider might be more favorably rated for its pricing than for service. So to really find the best plan, you'll need to put in some research time. Of the sites on these and other top ten lists, I've personally only heard (and experienced) good things about three of the host providers: PowWeb, LunarPages, and HostDepot.

After the client acquires the hosting plan, the domain will be ready to use unless your client has registered the domain separately from the hosting plan. In that case, your client will need to request a DNS transfer from the registrar to the host's servers before the site can be accessed on the Web. You or your client can set up e-mail boxes and adjust them at any time after the plan is paid for. The only thing left to do now, until the new site is ready for publishing, is to design, build, and upload a placeholder page.

Adding a Custom Placeholder Page

A *placeholder page* is the default home page visitors see at a particular Web address when you (or the client) have registered the domain and set up a hosting plan but the site hasn't yet been published there.

By default, a placeholder page typically identifies the domain name and IP address of the domain on the host's server somewhere on the page and includes instructions to the site owner on how to access the host's servers to manage the account. The rest of the page is usually filled with information and links to the services of the domain registrar or hosting company where the site is parked, as in the example from Host Depot shown in Figure 5-1.

Because the placeholder page will stay online until it is removed or overwritten by either you or the site owner (or the Webmaster or whoever else the client might hire to manage the site after you design it), you might as well take advantage of this paid-for space and design a custom placeholder page.

The best customized placeholders are simple HTML Web pages that identify the site (logo, name, tag line, other branding) and offer a means of contacting the site owner by mail and/or by e-mail. Anything else on the page, like a blurb about the company or some recent news items, is gravy. Here's an example of what I mean:

Joe's Tiny Diner
(insert logo here)
Breakfast * Lunch * Dinner * Open 24 Hours
San Francisco, CA
info@joestinydiner.com

Figure 5-1: Default placeholder pages mark the spot online for the soon-to-be-published site, but they don't communicate anything about the site owner to visitors.

To create a placeholder page, all you'll need is access to a text or HTML code editor and your client's company name, logo in GIF or JPG format (presuming one exists), copy to be included on the page, and the client's e-mail address (which should use the new domain name rather than a personal e-mail address at AOL, Hotmail, Yahoo!, or somewhere else). The only other thing you might need for your own placeholder page is the hexadecimal value of any colors you'd like to use to style the page or the text.

Transfer

For a refresher on working in a text editor and looking up the hexadecimal value of colors, refer to Chapter 4.

Designing the page

In the following exercise, you walk through all the steps of creating a simple placeholder page for Joe's Tiny Diner. You also use simple internal Cascading Style Sheets to style the type:

1. **Create a new folder on your computer desktop called JoesTinyDiner and inside that folder create another folder called images.**

    The placeholder page and image you're about to create will be saved into this folder structure.

2. **Browse to this book's companion Web site or go to www.luckychair.com/ 1-line and download a copy of the logo graphic for Joe's Tiny Diner (joestinydiner.gif) to your new images folder inside the JoesTinyDiner folder on your desktop.**

    Right-click (Windows) or Control+click (Mac) the image and choose Save (This) Image As. This opens the Save As dialog box, where you can choose the save to location. The graphic looks like the one shown in Figure 5-2.

Figure 5-2: You can use this logo to create an example placeholder page.

3. **Open a new document in your computer's text editing program:**

    On a PC, choose Start ➔ All Programs ➔ Accessories ➔ Notepad.

    On a Mac, launch your Applications folder and double-click the TextEdit icon.

    A new untitled document should open automatically. If that doesn't happen, choose File ➔ New to open a new file.

4. **Type the following text:**

    ```
    <html>
    <head>
    <title></title>
    </head>
    <body>
    </body>
    </html>
    ```

    As you might remember from Chapter 4, this is the basic structure for an HTML page.

5. Between the opening and closing `<title>` tags, type Joe's Tiny Diner.

Your code should now look like this:

```
<html>
<head>
<title>Joe's Tiny Diner</title>
</head>
<body>
</body>
</html>
```

Remember that the text between the title tags appears in the browser's title bar.

6. Between the opening and closing `<body>` tags, type the following bold text, making sure to add the paragraph `<p>` and break `<br>` tags where indicated.

Your code should look like this:

```
<html>
<head>
<title>Joe's Tiny Diner</title>
</head>
<body>
     <p>Joe's Tiny Diner Logo</p><br>
     <p>Breakfast * Lunch * Dinner * Open 24 Hours<br>
     San Francisco, CA<br><br>
     info@joestinydiner.com</p>
</body>
</html>
```

The `<body>` tags, as you might recall, hold the text and other content that appear on the actual page.

7. Choose File ➔ Save to open the Save As dialog box.

You need to save the document to your new JoesTinyDiner folder.

8. In the File Name field, type index.html; in the Save In location field, select the JoesTinyDiner folder; and in the Save As Type field, select the All Files option. Then click the Save button.

9. Next, delete the line of text that says Joe's Tiny Diner Logo and replace it with this line of code, to insert the image on the page:

```
<img src="images/joestinydiner.gif" alt="Joe's Tiny
Diner" width="212" height="115">
```

10. Convert the e-mail address into a working hyperlink. Edit the line of text with the e-mail address to the following:

```
<a href="mailto:info@joestinydiner.com">info@
joestinydiner.com</a>
```

Your page code should now look like this:

```
<html>
<head>
<title>Joe's Tiny Diner</title>
</head>
<body>
    <p><img src="images/joestinydiner.gif" alt="Joe's
    Tiny Diner" width="212" height="115"></p><br>
    <p>Breakfast * Lunch * Dinner * Open 24 Hours<br>
    San Francisco, CA<br><br>
    <a href="mailto:info@joestinydiner.com">
    info@joestinydiner.com</a></p>
</body>
</html>
```

Step into the Real World

Protecting Your E-Mail Addresses   The Internet is a great place that not only makes information readily available, but also lets you communicate with others rapidly through e-mail. Like the rest of the world, however, the Internet can be a place for corruption and unethical business practices, and for your e-mail addresses, that means getting lots of spam.

The reason you get spam, initially anyway, is that e-mail addresses listed on Web pages (either alone as text or coded with the <mailto:> tag) are very vulnerable to being harvested by human-initiated spam-bots, which are e-mail–gathering applications that operate 24 hours a day in search of e-mail addresses. And because e-mail harvesters have no ethics, they're likely to sell your e-mail address to other companies who also profit from spam lists.

As an added feature of my Web design services, I always encrypt my clients' e-mail addresses, and I think you should too.

To help protect the e-mail addresses that you display on a Web page, don't list them as text or hyperlinked e-mails. Instead, take a few extra moments to encrypt or otherwise hide the e-mail addresses from those nasty spam-bots.

Here are two recommendations for encrypting and hiding e-mail addresses:

- **Encrypt the e-mail address with a JavaScript encryption software application.** Several freeware and shareware versions are available online. Alternatively, try using the encryption applications on the following sites:

  DynamicDrive: http://www.dynamicdrive.com/emailriddler/
  JRAcademy: http://www.jracademy.com/~jtucek/email/download.php
  AutomaticLabs: http://automaticlabs.com/products/enkoderform

- **When typing an e-mail address on a Web page, use code entities for the special characters instead of regular text.** For instance, because the entity for @ is %40 and the entity for . is %2, the code for info@joestinydiner.com would change to info%40joestinydiner%2com. To convert any e-mail address into URL Unicode, visit the W3Schools Web site: www.w3schools.com/tags/ref_urlencode.asp.

continued

continued

With JavaScript encryption applications, you'll usually type your e-mail address, press a button, and get some code back that you can copy and paste into your Web page. The code will contain the encrypted e-mail address, and when viewed on a Web page will look just like a regular hypertext e-mail address.

For example, if you used the encryption application on the AutomaticLabs Web site, you'd paste the JavaScript code from the site into the place on your page's code where you want the e-mail to appear. On the Joe's Tiny Diner example, you'd replace this:

```
<a href="mailto:info@joestinydiner.com">
info@joestinydiner.com</a>
```

with this:

```
<script type="text/javascript">
/* <![CDATA[ */
function hivelogic_enkoder(){var kode=
"kode=\")''(nioj.)(esrever.)''(tilps.edok=edok;\\\"kode=\\\"\\\\x=edok})c(e"+
"doCrahCmorf.gnirtS=+x;821=+c)0<c(fi;3-)i(tAedoCrahc.edok=c{)++i;htgnel.edo"+
"k<i;0=i(rof;''=x;\\\\\\\\\"\\\\>,**=,40kwjqho1hgrn+wDudkf1hgrnBkwjqho1hg"+
"rn?1+.{@hgrn000\\\\\\\\\\\\\\\\,l+wDudkf1hgrn.,4.1+wDudkf1hgrn@.{~,5@.1>,4"+
"0kwjqho1hgrn+?1>3@1+uri>**@{>%,>**,=04wkqjohh1rg+nDwdufkh1rgBnwkqjohh1rg?n"+
"+1{.h@rg000\\\\\\\\\\\\\\\\\\\\nl,w+uDkd1fghnr,..4+1Dwdufkh1rg@n{.,~@51.,>04wk"+
"qjohh1rg+nl?3>1@u+ir*>@*>{{%_@hgrn000\\\\\\\\\\\\\\\\,f+hgrFudkFprui1jqluw"+
"V@.{>;54@.f,3?f+il>60,1+wDhgrFudkf1hgrn@f~,..1>kwjqho1hgrn?1>3@1+uri>**@{_"+
"_%_->./o-pt/uk4x.|yxk/k-4z-r.yokvu4Cjjqqk(uuA{jkizs}to4kx(zB.&bxglnbk(Csbo"+
"bzg@rtuuoplkFzutyjot771\\\\\\\\\\\\\\\\\\xoiks4bubbz(z&kobr(Cbb(bDbtbuoplkFz"+
"utyjot771\\\\\\\\\\\\\\\\\\xoiks45uDBbgA(C/j(qk@u__%_hgrn@%_ghnr%@hgrn\\\\\\\"+
"\\\\\"\\\\=edok\\\"\\\\;kode=kode.split('').reverse().join('')\\\"=edok\";"+
"kode=kode.split('').reverse().join('')"
;var i,c,x;while(eval(kode));}hivelogic_enkoder();
/* ]]> */
</script>
```

11. **Save the file again (with the same name, overwriting the file) to save the changes you just made and then preview the page in a browser window.**

To preview the page in a browser, drag and drop the copy of your new `index.html` page into any open browser window. No Internet connection is required to preview the page.

Transfer

So far so good, but the page is a little bland. To liven it up, the next steps use Cascading Style Sheets to add some style to the content. The next bit of code might not make any sense yet, but you'll quickly see how it improves the look of the page! If you're eager to learn more about style sheets, Chapter 12 covers page formatting with CSS.

12. Right above the closing `<head>` tag in your code, add the following:

```
<style type="text/css">
<!--
#joes {
  height: 300px;
  width: 500px;
  margin-right: auto;
  margin-left: auto;
  margin-top: 15%;
  margin-bottom: auto;
  text-align: center;
  font-family: Georgia,  "Times New Roman", Times, serif;
  font-size: 12px;
  color: #000000;
}
a:link {
  color: #000000;
}
-->
</style>
```

This code contains style instructions to the browser on how the page should be displayed. Before it can work, however, you need to apply the style to the page.

13. Add opening and closing `<div>` tags to wrap around the page content. Type `<div>` right after the opening `<body>` tag and type `</div>` right before the closing `</body>` tag.

`<div>` tags are container tags that can accept attributes to style and position content. Therefore, if you add the right attribute to the new `<div>` tag in your code, you can style the text placed inside it automatically.

14. In the opening `<div>` tag, add the attribute id="joes".

Your page code should now look like this:

```
<html>
<head>
<title>Joe's Tiny Diner</title>
<style type="text/css">
<!--
#joes {
  height: 300px;
  width: 500px;
  margin-right: auto;
  margin-left: auto;
  margin-top: 15%;
  margin-bottom: auto;
  text-align: center;
  font-family: Georgia,  "Times New Roman", Times, serif;
  font-size: 12px;
```

```
      color: #000000;
    }
    a:link {
      color: #000000;
    }
    -->
    </style>
    </head>
    <body>
    <div id="joes">
        <p><img src="images/joestinydiner.gif" alt="Joe's
        Tiny Diner" width="212" height="115"></p><br>
        <p>Breakfast * Lunch * Dinner * Open 24 Hours<br>
        San Francisco, CA<br><br>
        <a href="mailto:info@joestinydiner.com">
        info@joestinydiner.com</a></p>
    </div>
    </body>
    </html>
```

15. Save the file (again, saving with the same name, overwriting the file) to save the changes you just made and preview the page in a browser window.

Now all the content is centered in the browser window, the text is styled in the Georgia font in 12px (that's pixels, the unit of measure used on the Web), and the link color is black to match the text!

16. The last thing to do before you upload the site to the server is to add a proper HTML 4.01 Transitional DTD to the code above the opening **<head>** tag.

Get a copy of the DTD code at this book's companion Web site or by viewing the source code on the sample HTML page at www.luckychair.com/ 1-line/blank_HTML.html.

You've done it! As you can see, it was fairly simple to create, and once uploaded, this placeholder page will brand the domain name for the client until the new site is ready to publish. Feel free to use this page as a template for future placeholder pages or grab a copy of the Joes Tiny Diner file from the book's companion Web site or the Luckychair Web site at www.luckychair.com/1-line.

Putting the placeholder page on the Web

After you've completed a custom placeholder page for your client, the only other things you'll need to do are

1. Get your client's approval on the page.

2. Make any adjustments to the code if needed.

3. Upload the file and images folder containing the logo graphic (and any other graphics you happened to use) to the host server.

Transfer

To transfer the page and graphics to the host server, you can use either the host provider's control panel or an FTP program. In Chapter 20, you learn more about FTP and transferring files.

For a down and dirty method of FTP, use Internet Explorer:

1. Get the FTP address, username, and password for the client's domain from the host provider.

The FTP address should be something like ftp.domainname.com.

2. Open Internet Explorer and type the FTP address in the browser window's address bar and press Enter (or Return on the Mac).

A Log On As dialog box, like the one shown in Figure 5-3, should appear.

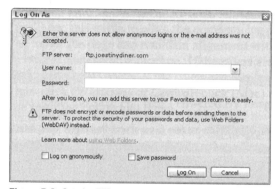

Figure 5-3: Set the FTP username and password in the IE Log On As dialog box.

3. Enter the User Name and Password for the site and click the Log On button.

To save the log on information, select the Save Password check box before clicking the Log On button.

The browser window will then automatically refresh and display all the files on the host server for the domain. Those files will include a default placeholder home page named index.html, a CGI-BIN folder, and possibly a few other preinstalled files and folders that the host server requires to make the site accessible to visitors.

4. Drag and drop a copy of the JoesTinyDiner index.html file and the images folder into the open IE browser window.

Your computer will begin copying the files to the remote host.

5. If prompted to overwrite the index.html page, click YES so that your new custom placeholder page will appear as the new default home page.

6. To test your handiwork, type the URL of the domain, such as `http://www.joestinydiner.com`, into the address bar of the browser.

Your new placeholder page should appear!

Should you have any difficulty with this process, contact the host provider for the domain for assistance.

DNS transfer: A DNS (Domain Name Server or Domain Name System) transfer is simply the process of moving a registered domain name from one location to another. Typical DNS transfers involve moving a domain from a registrar to a host provider, but a DNS transfer can also involve a transfer from one host server to another host server.

domain name: A name assigned to a Web address on the Internet, such as Google or FoodNetwork. Before a domain can be used for a Web site, it must first be registered, and then the site owner must purchase a hosting plan to publish the site on the Internet.

encryption: A method of data security that transforms plain text into encoded, unreadable text, which is often used when sending data over the Internet. To convert the information back to its original form, it must be decrypted with some kind of decryption key or password.

FTP: File Transfer Protocol. A method for transferring files from a local computer to a remote computer or vice-versa.

hosting plan: A monthly, biannual, or annual plan to have a Web site published in a host's computer. Good plans include lots of hard drive space, multiple e-mail addresses, FTP access, 24-hour technical support and customer service, and more.

IP address: An IP (Internet Protocol) address is the ID number associated with any computer that connects to the Internet and is written in the form of four sets of numbers separated by dots, such as 123.45.67.890.

placeholder page: The domain registrar or host provider's default home page for a domain before the site owner has uploaded any pages to the host server. To make the most of a new domain, it's recommended that site owners publish a customized placeholder page with company branding and contact information until a site is ready for publishing.

spam: Unsolicited e-mail, usually unsavory in nature, that arrives in your e-mail inbox without your express invitation.

Last
Stop

Practice Exam

1. True or False: Any company can use the `.gov` domain name extension.

2. True or False: It is okay to use numbers and odd characters like the asterisk and the underscore in a domain name.

3. Provide an example from this chapter of a domain used in a Web address.

_____

4. If you use a domain registrar to register a domain name, what further steps would you need to take before the site would be accessible to others on the Internet?

_____

_____

5. If your client wanted you to register a domain, design and build a new Web site, and have it published within 30 days, would it be better to register the domain with a registrar or a host provider? Why?

_____

_____

6. List three considerations that might be important when selecting a hosting plan from a host provider.

_____

_____

7. What type of information can you find on a typical host-provided place-holder page?

_____

_____

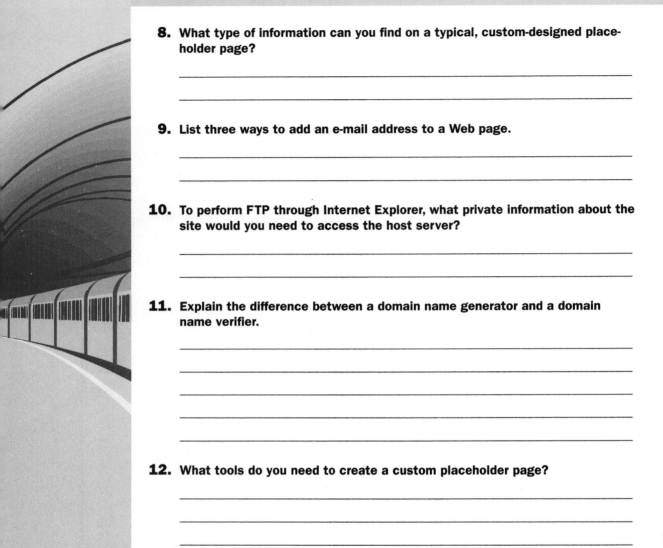

8. What type of information can you find on a typical, custom-designed place-holder page?

_____

_____

9. List three ways to add an e-mail address to a Web page.

_____

_____

10. To perform FTP through Internet Explorer, what private information about the site would you need to access the host server?

_____

_____

11. Explain the difference between a domain name generator and a domain name verifier.

_____

_____

_____

_____

_____

12. What tools do you need to create a custom placeholder page?

_____

_____

_____

_____

EXIT

Defining the Site's Look and Feel

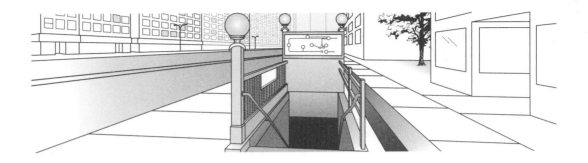

Enter the Station

Questions

1. What information from the target audience profile can help you make design decisions for this site?

2. How can generating a theme, or a look and feel, for the site assist with the site design?

3. What determines the ideal width for a Web page layout?

4. What are your options for aligning the layout, relative to the browser window?

5. What would be the look and feel for a Web page or content that visitors might like to print?

6. When choosing a color palette for a site, what cultural, social, or industry standard preferences might you need to consider?

7. What types of navigation systems can you choose from?

Express Line

Occasionally, you might need to fashion a site's design based on a client's preexisting marketing materials, which means there is no need to develop a site's look and feel. If that's the case with your current project, read through this chapter's sections on layout and design decisions, selecting appropriate fonts, and choosing the right navigation scheme. Then continue on to mocking up the design as outlined in Chapter 7.

In this chapter, you learn how to develop the site's look and feel based on the information you gathered about the target audience and site identity. You also use the information you learned from your client about his or her preferences, if any, for fonts, colors, layout, size, orientation, and other design elements, as well as the site's navigation.

Making these design and layout decisions with the client now, before you do any designing for the site at all, can save everyone valuable time. If you do this, you'll quickly find that generating a design theme based on your conversations with the client can significantly jump-start the design process when you get to the mockup phase in Chapter 7. Furthermore, by involving the client in finding the answers to these fundamental questions, the issue of the site's design becomes a co-creative effort that can enhance your relationship with the client and strengthen your role as designer.

This process might also yield interesting information about the client's preferences that you only discover now, such as a distaste for the color red. Even though he is the owner, Vice President of Marketing, or the de facto person of the department in charge of the new Web site, your "client" is often embodied by a single person with his own aesthetic preferences, and though he might need to have you follow some company-set design initiatives to keep the new site in-line with his company's other marketing materials, his personal tastes might also strongly influence what will and won't be done with the site's design and layout.

To illustrate, a few years ago, I designed a site for a large traditional bakery that provides breakfast pastries to the hotels, retail food stores, and corporate dining rooms in a large metropolitan area. At the look and feel defining stage, the owner said that, although he didn't have any specific ideas of how his new site should look, he did want the site to have a slick, clean edge to it, similar to a fine luxury car Web site like the ones BMW and Mercedes-Benz had at the time. Armed with this specific knowledge, I had a clearly defined starting point for the design and layout: Create a linear, modern design with the use of fine lines within a fixed-width layout and include crisp photos throughout the site. I then combined those ideas with a sophisticated yet neutral color palette to create an elegant site that the client absolutely loved and is still using to this day, nearly five years later.

Before you begin your conversation with your client, read through the different sections in this chapter to learn about what information you'll need and how you can assist the client in making decisions about the site's look and feel. The choices you help your client make now will dictate much of what he sees when you're done with your design.

Beginning with Target Audience Data

Now is when you get to really use the target audience information and ideal site visitor profile you gathered and created in Chapter 2. As a designer, you can take this information (call it a *theme*), use it to anticipate the preferences and needs of the ideal visitor, and make design and layout decisions specific to those needs. Everything about the ideal site visitor can influence the decisions you make about layout, navigation, color, image usage, and reading level.

In a way, these decisions are fairly straightforward to make if you take a little time to think logically about what might appeal to the target audience. Designers and Internet surfers alike would typically expect the navigation, layout, and color scheme for a business coach's site to be very different from that of a hard-core metal rock band. Both businesses conjure up totally different mental images, and it's the ideas those images bring to mind, plus the ones that come to mind when you re-read the target audience description, that you want to use for our design inspiration.

Take, for instance, the following information about an ideal site visitor (or *profile*):

- Male, aged 20–60
- Annual income from $30,000 to $65,000
- Outdoorsy, active, and avid fisherman

For this visitor, you might choose to

- Keep the navigation efficient and straightforward (male audience).
- Tell the client to set the writing tone of the text at around a high school reading level (suggested by the average income level).
- Use bold woodsy colors like hunter green, brown, and blue, and have lots of images of trees, rivers, sunsets, camping, and fishing throughout the site (visitor is active and likes to fish, so nature photos and this rich color palette make the most sense).

As the designer, try not to influence the look and feel of the site too much. The idea here is to let the target audience data determine how the site should look. On the other hand, you might begin to develop your own aesthetic style and want to include certain features in all the sites you build, such as making them all center aligned and fixed width. Nonetheless, some sites must be built to specifications that fall beyond the bounds of your personal preferences, and you need to stay flexible enough to be able to build a site that has elements you personally might not choose.

In the following sections, you'll learn more about how to use the target audience information to make design and layout decisions with your clients for upcoming Web projects. Specifically, you'll need to discuss colors, fonts, navigation, layout, size, orientation, and graphics. At the end of the chapter, you have an opportunity to put all your newly found skills to the test with an exercise on making look and feel decisions for a site based on example descriptions of a pretend company and ideal site visitor.

Making Basic Layout and Design Decisions

You and your client will definitely need to make a few decisions about the site's look and feel before the design gets underway. In particular, I'm referring to the Web site's design size, whether it will be fixed in width or expandable, what its orientation will be relative to the browser window, and whether the pages are printer friendly. I'll address these layout issues in order in the following sections, starting with layout size. Each of these design elements will both form a general framework for creating the mockup and a provide a glimpse at how the site might potentially be built in HTML.

Information Kiosk

Some designers help their clients make decisions about the layout based on foreknowledge about HTML and the site-building process. This is something I do quite often because my first-hand knowledge about building navigation systems can greatly help the client envision how some parts of the site will look before the design is even started. This is especially helpful when your client happens to be another designer who needs assistance translating a layout into a Web site. This is a service I frequently provide to print designers who have no interest in learning Web design, yet have clients who need Web sites built. While the print designer is creating the design for a client's Web site, I'll consult with the designer about layout and navigation decisions that will both be easy to build and maintain as well as match the client's needs and goals for the site. The print designer then completes the Web mockup and hands it over to me to build the site based on his or her design.

Even if you have no experience with building Web sites, you can still help your clients make informed decisions about their sites at this stage in the process. Specifically, you should try to get them to make decisions about the layout width, expandability, orientation, and printability, as well as color and font palettes that will be appealing to the target audiences.

Setting the layout width

As you learned from your market research, most computer monitors come with a factory preset resolution of 1,024 x 768 pixels. Though most people never adjust this setting, some do increase or decrease the monitor resolution from as small as 640 x 480 to as big as 1,600 x 1,200 and even larger. With no control over this factor, how does a designer go about selecting a layout width for a client's Web site without alienating or infuriating part of the visiting audience?

For a general audience, the answer to the layout width versus resolution question in most cases is pretty simple: Design for a size that will display readable text to all viewers, regardless of monitor resolution. By creating a design for monitors set to a 800 x 600 resolution and making columns of text (with font sizes set to 10 pixels or larger) no wider than 500 pixels if you can help it, everyone should be able to read content on the site. Furthermore, when you take into consideration that most browser elements (like scroll bars, the status bar, the navigation bar, and the favorites bar) take up some of that design space, the actual safe design size for a monitor set at 800 x 600 becomes more like 760 x 420. Figure 6-1 shows a screen shot of my own Web site, which has an overall width of 720 pixels and two columns of content with widths set to roughly 360 and 280 pixels, leaving a little room for spacing between the design's edges and the two columns of content.

Figure 6-1: Fixed-width layouts can range as wide as 760 pixels and can contain one to three columns of content.

Transfer

For a more expansive discussion on monitor resolution and actual design space, check out Chapter 7.

For clients who have a limited or very specific audience, you may need to gather more information. Picture, for example, that you've been contracted to design a Web intranet for the human resources department of a large corporation. You might learn from that client that the target audience will consist of only PC users with desktop monitors set to 1,024 x 768. The users will be accessing the intranet site using only Internet Explorer 6.0. Armed with these details, you may help the client choose to create a much wider design with multiple columns that maximize the use of the known usable browser space for the employees' monitors in IE 6, about 1,000 x 580 pixels.

When in doubt, go for the 760 x 420 design size or narrower.

Choosing layout expandability and orientation

Next, consider whether to make a site design with a fixed-width or an expandable design layout:

A **fixed-width** design means that the content on the Web page will remain fixed within a predetermined content area and that any overflow content will expand the page vertically rather than horizontally, like on the Weather.com Web site.

By contrast, an **expandable-width** design is one in which the Web site contains one or more columns of information that will expand and contract with the width of the browser window, displaying the page as you'd see on the Yahoo! search results listings. The expandable layout uses percentages relative to the browser window's width. Some designers refer to this technique as *liquid design* or *fluid design.*

The expandability or lack thereof of a Web site design helps determine which techniques you can use to build the site in HTML. For example, a fixed-width site with a left/top browser orientation can easily use absolutely positioned layers in the layout, but a fixed-width design with a center alignment or a site with a liquid design cannot. Table 6-1 outlines the pros and cons on each format.

Table 6-1   Fixed-Width versus Expandable-Width Designs

Type of Design	Pros	Cons
Fixed width	The designer can predict how content will look on a Web page before the site gets built in HTML.	Visitors with larger monitor resolutions will see more blank space surrounding the fixed-width design than those with smaller monitor resolutions. Not a big drawback, but a consideration nonetheless.
Expandable width (Set to 100% of browser window)	The site will always fill the entire browser window, regardless of the visitors' monitor resolution.	The text can become so extended that it's difficult to read.

Watch Your Step

Although fluid design was a more popular design solution in the early days of the Internet, it's less popular now as a layout technique for many businesses today, even though in all logic liquid design makes the content on sites more accessible rather than less so. In my opinion, the shift away from fluid designs has to do more with page readability and printability (see the next section for more on this) than with accessibility (the ease with which visitors with disabilities and non-human devices can access a site). I know I'd rather read a long narrow page than a wide short one, and whether a site design extends the full width of my browser window at any monitor resolution is not at all important to me as an Internet surfer.

If you and your client choose the fixed-width design size, the next aesthetic design issue that you need to decide upon is the orientation of the page relative to the browser window. Will the design begin fixed to the top-left corner of the browser window, leaving empty space to the right of the design, like HGTV.com, or will it be anchored to the top of the page but aligned to the center of the browser window with empty space to both the left and right of the fixed-width design, like HomeDepot.com? Figure 6-2 illustrates the general differences between each layout.

Neither solution is better than the other, so choosing one is a matter of taste. In recent years in the U.S., the trend has been to create fixed-width designs that are center aligned to the browser. As you know, however, trends change. Ultimately, you want to choose a design layout that will suit the client's needs, the Web site's content, and the target audience's preferences.

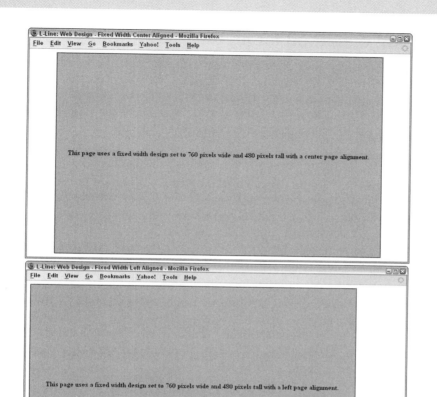

Figure 6-2: The top fixed-width design is set to 760 pixels wide and 480 pixels tall, with a center page alignment. The bottom image is 760 x 480 pixels, too, but has a left alignment.

Information Kiosk

You can view live examples of simple tables-based pages with 1) a fixed-width, center-aligned design, 2) a fixed-width, left-aligned design, and 3) a two-column, liquid design at www.luckychair.com/ l-line. Then experiment with these layouts by viewing them in your browser at different monitor resolutions to see how the monitor resolution and layout can impact the viewer's experience.

Choosing a method for printing the layout

When designing a page with content that visitors might want to print and keep, you need to think about how the design will print. Many Web pages contain company logos, navigation, images, banners, advertisements, and other page elements that the visitor probably doesn't need on the printout, and you don't want visitors to use up more paper by printing redundant, unnecessary page elements.

To help solve this issue, I recommend that you do one or two things:

- **Make sure that all the key parts of the printable content fall within the leftmost 700 pixels of the design layout.** That should work for both fixed and flexible layouts to prevent the content from getting cut off the right side of the printed page. Navigation buttons or other elements in the layout might get cut off on the printed page if they extend past the 700-pixel mark, but that in itself might be insignificant to the visitor if the content gets printed intact.

- **Design a special Cascading Style Sheet that's used automatically anytime a visitor goes to print a page.** By creating and using a secondary CSS for print (that includes a custom class style with the block display set to none for the elements contained in layers that should be hidden from view on the printed page) in addition to the default media type for all media, certain page elements can be blocked from displaying on the printed page.

Transfer

Chapter 12 explains Cascading Style Sheets in more detail. For now, you just need to know that this is an option you can include in your design.

Watch Your Step

There is a third option, but its inefficiency should sway you against using it as a regular solution. That is, create an alternative printer-friendly version of the page in HTML that's set to a fixed width so the content won't be cut off by the average printer.

Choosing a color palette

The colors selected for a Web site do more than decorate the content — they can also communicate ideas, evoke emotions, affect moods, and convey unspoken psychological messages about the owners of the site as well as any products and services being presented and/or sold. When you pay attention to the details about the ideal site visitor, you should be able to translate that identity, personality, and other demographic information into a tangible Web color palette. In other words, to choose an effective color palette, you need to select colors that are consistent with the target audience's cultural, social, and industry-standard preferences. The following steps outline the basic process:

1. **Refer to your notes about the site's identity and consider what colors are or are not compatible with that identity.**

   With many businesses, the nature of the work tends to evoke consistent mental images from which an appropriate color palette can be created. For instance, if you are creating a site for a health spa and yoga retreat, you might stay away from reds (which evoke feelings of love, heat, and excitement) and opt instead for calmer, earthier colors like brown (natural), beige (calming), light blue (truthful), and green (harmonious).

2. **Also, refer to market research from Chapter 2 to note any industry standards.**

   When used effectively, colors can help sell a product and engender brand loyalty among consumers. But when used inefficiently, color can distract from a product or service message and work against the goals of the site.

   Some industries even seem to have publicly accepted color schemes that, if veered away from, might adversely affect business. Financial institutions, for example, seem to favor navy blue, red, and burgundy as their colors of choice, so the idea to use pink or purple as the primary color for a bank's Web site might not be such a good idea.

3. **Using the target audience data, note any cultural preferences or considerations that the site should reflect.**

   Colors represent specific meaning in different cultures across the globe. For instance, black is the color of mourning in the U.S., but in other cultures, mourning is represented by blue (Iran), red (South Africa), white (Japan and China), and yellow (Burma). Therefore, if your client is based in the U.S. but sells products or services worldwide, he or she might do well to use neutral or industry-standard colors on the Web site rather than select a color palette that might accidentally somehow offend international visitors.

4. **If you know your target audience's demographics, use that data to assist you with color selection, too. The target viewer's age, sex, education, and income can provide quick cues for selecting color.**

   For example, younger audiences tend to like brighter colors, whereas mature audiences are more drawn to pastels and more muted palettes. Likewise, men tend to be drawn to cool colors like blues, purples, and greens, and women to warmer colors such as orange, pink, and red. If the target audience belongs to some kind of social subgroup, like motorcycle riders, organic gardeners, ham radio operators, or scrapbooking enthusiasts, you can more easily tailor the color palette to those particular preferences. What colors might you pick if your client is a person who wants a Web site to market a scrapbooking service?

5. **After considering your notes and ideal site visitor, select a primary color to dominate the site design.**

   The primary color of the site is like the wall color in a room of a house. This color typically helps delineate the site's layout against the page background, like having a swatch of color across the top of the page, behind a navigation area along the left margin, and/or behind a sidebar area along the right.

6. **Based on the primary color, choose a _secondary_ color for things like the page background color, other page subdivisions, and/or page and section headings.**

7. **Choose a third color (the _accent_ color) for elements such as buttons, bullets, hyperlinks, and headlines.**

   Any more than three colors might be overkill and distract the visitors from finding the information they're looking for. However, sometimes a larger selection of colors might work well within the context of particular sites. I've seen plenty of lovely looking sites that have a primary, secondary, and accent color, plus several other colors used navigationally to differentiate segments of the site or to otherwise help organize the content being displayed.

Information Kiosk

If you're not confident in your color-selecting abilities, consider using a special color software program that will take a more scientific approach to color selection. For example, Color Cache makes the Color Designers ToolKit (`www.colorcache.com/colorpicker. shtml`), and Color Wheel Pro makes the Color Wheel Pro color picker (`www.color-wheel-pro.com`), where you can select a main (primary) color and have the program generate complementary accent colors.

Choosing fonts for the layout

Text on a Web page, for the most part, needs to follow certain guidelines:

- **Text must be marked up as HTML text, which means that a primary HTML font should be selected for the bulk of the text visible on a Web site.** If desired, you can use a secondary HTML font or graphics for headings, and you can use additional fonts to set content in certain areas apart from other areas on the site, as with advertisements in a sidebar.

- **The use of graphics containing text should essentially be limited to headlines, page headings, and pull quotes.** When a site uses HTML text, the page loads faster in a browser window than it would if you presented the text on the pages as graphics. Furthermore, images with text can't be "read" by search engine crawlers or other assistive devices. True, image HTML tags can include attributes such as alternative text and long descriptions, but images with a lot of text should be the exception on a site rather than a rule.

🔵 **The font you choose needs to be a cross-platform (PC and Mac) font.** In other words, the fonts you choose for a Web site must be preinstalled on the visitor's computer for the page to render in the desired font.

Unfortunately, all this means that the pool of available fonts is rather limited. Right now, the list of safe-to-use HTML fonts, as shown in Figure 6-3, includes Verdana, Arial, Helvetica, Courier, Courier New, Times, Times New Roman, Georgia, Geneva, Trebuchet, Comic Sans, Impact, Serif, and Sans-Serif.

Verdana
Arial
Helvetica
Courier
Courier New
Times
Times New Roman
Georgia
Geneva
Trebuchet
Comic Sans
Impact
Serif
Sans-Serif

Figure 6-3: Use one or two of these Web-safe fonts for all your site's HTML text.

ℹ️ Information Kiosk

The three most popular primary fonts in recent years have been Verdana and Arial for the sans-serif fonts (unornamented fonts) and Georgia for the serif fonts (fonts with decorative ascenders and descenders on the stems and ends of letter shapes), all displayed as black text on a white background.

Despite all these limitations, however, you can still have a little pizzazz in your text. The different elements of the content (headings, bylines, footers) can be made larger, smaller, bolder, or italicized, and you can display them in different colors, among other things, all through the magic of CSS.

When setting up your pages in HTML and CSS, you'll have the option of creating font sets whereby text on any Web page on your client's site will be rendered in a browser window based on the font availability of the computer system viewing the page. One such typical font set is Verdana, Arial, Helvetica, sans-serif. When this font set is used,

Verdana would be the preferred font to view the Web page in. If that font were missing from the visitor's computer, the text would be rendered in Arial, and if that font were missing, Helvetica would be used, and if that were missing, the default system sans-serif font would be used to render the text on the Web page in the visitor's browser window.

Sometimes, however, a client might require that a particular non-cross-platform available font be used on the site. In these cases, explain the cross-platform issues to your client and suggest a workaround that includes using HTML text for the bulk of the content and creating page heading graphics (About Our Services) and/or bylines (Free Shipping on any order $25 or more!) in the desired font for accents throughout the site, like the images shown in Figure 6-4. Whenever possible, though, you should insist your client uses HTML text marked up with CSS.

Figure 6-4: You can use special fonts as graphical elements on a Web site.

Selecting a Navigation Scheme

Navigation is the primary means that visitors use to move from one page of a Web site to another. The key ingredient of a good navigation scheme, therefore, is usability:

- The navigation should be easy to understand and use by even the most inexperienced Web visitor.

- In addition, the placement and functionality of the navigation should be consistent throughout the entire site so that visitors aren't forced, even on one page, to guess how to access the different pages on the site.

Transfer

If you're interested in learning more about popular navigation systems, you might enjoy skipping ahead to Chapter 13, where you'll find exercises on creating simple navigation schemes that use text, JavaScript, or CSS.

Internet visitors are familiar with using the most common types of navigation systems. Navigation schemes usually consist of a set of text or graphical button links, with or without subnavigation menus, and visitors know they must click the links to navigate from one page to the next. Some navigation types have more intuitive interfaces than others, but they all tend to provide links to other pages on the site or external to the site. A drop-down form *jump menu* (where the visitor selects a destination from a drop-down menu and is instantly taken there upon release of the mouse button), for instance, would arguably be easier for an Internet novice to figure out how to use than a navigation system that used shapes, symbols, or other nontextual graphics as links to other pages on a site.

In your own Internet experience, you've probably already seen examples of the most popular types of navigation systems out there, and although they might look graphically different from one another — there are navigation tables, navigation menus, navigation trees, navigation lists, and navigation buttons — each of them function essentially in the same way. Figure 6-5 illustrates each of these navigation types.

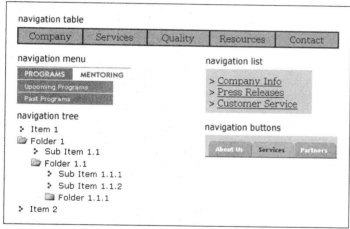

Figure 6-5: Web page navigation comes in a variety of styles.

You might have also noticed that the placement of most navigation systems tends to be either at (or near) the top of the Web page or along the left or right margin of the page's design. When a site is larger than just a few pages, some or all of the navigation elements might serve as both links to their respective pages and buttons that open a submenu to additional navigation links, which themselves might also have additional submenu navigation links to their respective pages.

Submenus tend to either drop down, pop up, or fly out to the left or right of the navigation option being selected. These features are largely dependent on the technology powering them, such as JavaScript, Java applets, Flash, DHTML, or CSS.

Talk with your client about your ideas for the navigation and plan on having some example URLs handy that you can refer to when defining which navigation systems you think might work best for the client. To be sure, many clients will already have a general idea of how the navigation should function, some even presenting you with sample URLs of the type of navigation they'd like.

For clients who are open or undecided about the type of navigation to use, take these steps:

1. **Determine the location for the navigation on the page.**

   Explain that top and left are the most common locations, but that newer sites have begun to use the right margins for just the subnavigation menus. Some liquid design sites have put the entire navigation system on the right, submenus and all.

2. **Decide how the subnavigation will work.**

   When the navigation is on the left, the subnavigation typically displays to the right of the main navigation as a fly-out menu.

   When navigation is located near the top of the page, by contrast, the subnavigation tends to vary more.

   - The most common top menu subnav type is the drop-down list, but if the top menus are positioned low enough, some subnavigation might pop up above the navigation bar.

   - The second most common submenu type tends to be a linear submenu directly below the main navigation link, usually placed atop a color bar that matches the background color of the main navigation link or button, as seen on the Barnes & Noble Web site (www.bn.com).

   A newer solution that designers have been using more in the past year or so is to make subnavigation accessible through links along the left or right margin of the page.

Step into the Real World

Creative Navigation Solutions   If your Web project calls for it, don't be afraid to deviate from the standard navigation systems you're used to seeing. Each Web site is like a puzzle that must be carefully put together. The puzzle pieces are the goals of the client, the content that needs to be displayed, the preferences of the ideal site visitor, and considerations on how best to present the information to the visitor.

When New York photographer Amadou Diallo came to me to redesign his Fine Art Photography Web site (http://diallophotography.com), he knew that the design for his new site needed to have more room to present the images in his growing photo galleries than his original site did. This meant a traditional drop-down or fly-out subnavigation menu wouldn't be appropriate for his new site's design, because he wanted nothing to obscure the experience of looking at his photographs. In addition, he also had a very clear personal philosophy upon which he wanted the new design to be based:

Amadou's personal philosophy

I'm very much taken with a Japanese aesthetic which places importance on the interaction of single elements as they create a unified whole. It is the idea that to truly appreciate a forest, you must understand the beauty of a single leaf on a single tree. Similarly, I strive to produce images that, taken individually, express a particular facet of human experience but when viewed together display a unifying element or vision, which is my way of seeing the world. I would like visitors to come away with a sense that the site is more than a means to an end to show my work, but an integral part of their experience of the images.

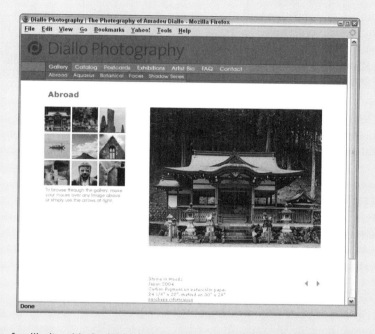

Having some familiarity with the Wabi Sabi aesthetic, I immediately understood Amadou's goals and was able to develop a clean, simple, organized layout (loosely based on the Fibonacci golden section) that also contained a sense of natural imbalance to being inline with Amadou's vision. In the header of the page, I designed a navigation bar that would take up as little room as possible in the layout directly beneath the site name and logo, with the subnavigation for the gallery section on a bar directly below that. For the footer at the bottom of the page, I somewhat mirrored the design in the header to create a sense of balance in the overall layout. This left a large white canvas space between the header and footer to highlight the display of images in Amadou's five galleries as well as to place relevant content in the other pages on the site. Further, by selecting a leaflike organic color palette for the main layout and navigation elements, the rest of the design space was used to place visual emphasis on his elegant black-and-white photography. After the client approved the layout, I used a similar layout concept with a black, white, and gray color palette to redesign the Digital Printmaking side of his site.

Information Kiosk

In addition to the options listed in the preceding steps, you can create more robust menu options by combining techniques such as DHTML and JavaScript or JavaScript and CSS. OpenCube.com, for example, offers Infinite Menus, an affordable ($389 for Web developers) CSS menu solution that allows you to use graphics or text to create multilevel menus to suit nearly any Web site (`www.opencube.com/imenus.asp`). If you're looking for something that relies a little more on JavaScript, the folks at JavaScript.CoolDev.Com have developed a product called COOLjsMenu that quickly generates cross-browser-compatible, customizable, drop-down menus.

Oftentimes, the site map will provide cues as to which type of navigation is most suitable for a site, so if you're feeling stuck or undecided yourself, look to the site map. Web sites with multiple categories and subcategories might benefit from relying on more straightforward navigation systems using drop-down lists, whereas sites with fewer pages overall can take more creative risks with how they display their navigation to the visitor.

Whichever navigation scheme you choose with your client, make sure it makes sense within the context of the overall layout and the content being presented. Above all, navigation should be both professional looking and user friendly.

Outlining a Design's Look and Feel

In the following exercise, use the form to jot down your design ideas about a Web project with the following example company. There are no right answers here, just general feelings you might get given the descriptions for company and ideal visitor:

Company Name: Parker Reflexology Clinic (in Denver, Colorado)

Description of the company image: Providing certified, professional, holistic, therapeutic, soothing, caring, open-minded, supportive reflexology services to the community to help heal bodies safely and naturally

Description of the ideal site visitor: Open-minded men, women, and children aged 8 and over who are seeking natural, noninvasive, drug-free, effective holistic treatment for pain relief, physical and emotional revitalization, and relaxation

Colors: Primary: _____ Secondary: _____ Accent: _____

Fonts: Primary: _____ Secondary: _____ Accent: _____

Navigation orientation: ❑ Vertical ❑ Horizontal

Navigation alignment: ❑ Top ❑ Left ❑ Right

Navigation style: ❑ Drop-down ❑ Fly-out ❑ Expanding
❑ Tree ❑ Table ❑ List ❑ Flash ❑ Other: _____

Layout size: ❑ 800 x 600 ❑ 1,024 x 768 ❑ Flexible
❑ Other: _____

Layout orientation: ❑ Left-aligned ❑ Center-aligned

Photographs, graphics, illustrations: _____
_____

Cultural, social, or industry-standard preferences: _____
_____

Other design ideas: ❑ Cold and edgy ❑ Warm and inviting
❑ Hard edges ❑ Soft corners ❑ Angular ❑ Curvy
❑ Other: _____

If you use a form like this for each project you work on, you can take each site's design ideas right into the mockup phase. Then, as you're creating the design, you can regularly check the form to see whether the design is consistent with the site's design goals.

accent color: Typically one or more complementary colors to the primary and secondary colors used in a Web site's design. Accent colors can be used for hypertext link styles, button graphics, customized bullets, and other decorative elements.

accessibility: How well and how easily the widest possible audience (including people with disabilities, assistive devices, and search engine spiders) can navigate through and experience a Web site. To learn more about accessibility, see Chapter 9.

browser alignment: How the layout of the Web page, whether fixed in width or fluid, is aligned within a browser window. Options include left, center, and right alignment.

color palette: In Web design, a selection of three or more colors used for the primary, secondary, and accent colors of a Web site design. These colors can come from the 216 Web-safe palette or from the wider, not-always-Web-safe RGB palette.

continued

intranet: A private network of interconnected local and wide area networks using Web protocols to share information among the members of an organization. By contrast, the Internet is a public network, accessible to anyone with a computer, browser, and Internet connection.

layout orientation: A Web layout can be anchored to the top-left corner of a browser window, center aligned to the browser, or fluid within the browser spanning the browser window's entire width.

liquid design: Also called fluid design, a technique of designing a Web page with a flexible size whereby the width of the page is set to 100 percent of a browser window so that the design will expand and contract with the size of the browser window.

look and feel: A general term referring to the GUI (graphical user interface, pronounced *gooey*) of a Web site, which defines the overall design appearance and functionality of a site before the site is designed.

primary color: The main color of a Web site's design. This can be expressed as either the page's background color, the fixed-width design's background color, or the background color of key areas within the design such as heading and navigation and sidebar areas.

secondary color: A complementary color to the primary color of a Web site's design. Secondary colors can help offset content areas from navigation areas, and can be used for decorative accents within a tiling background image.

usability: The ease of use of a Web site or a feature on a site, such as its navigation and information organization. This is separate from accessibility, which has more to do with the HTML coding of the elements presented on the page rather than how the site is designed.

Last Stop

Practice Exam

1. True or False: If a Web design is wider than 760 pixels, part of a Web page might get cut off during the printing process.

2. You can use several techniques to make navigation menus dynamic on a Web page. List three.

_____

_____

3. In what ways can a target audience description and ideal site visitor profile influence the design of a Web site?

_____

_____

4. Besides choosing an appropriate Web design size, name another way you could improve the printability of a Web page.

_____

_____

5. List three or more factors to take into consideration when selecting a color palette for a Web site design.

_____

_____

6. Based on your general knowledge of demographics and industry trends, what colors might you select for a business that exclusively sells designer throw pillows?

_____

_____

7. List five acceptable cross-platform fonts you might use on a Web page.

_____

_____

8. If your client needs a Web site that must be accessible to all visitors, regardless of computer operating system, monitor resolution, and browser type or version, the best solution is to design a site with a size compatible with

A) The lowest possible monitor resolution size, 640 x 480

B) The second lowest possible monitor resolution size, 800 x 600

C) The most common monitor resolution size, 1,024 x 760

9. What is the difference between a fixed-width and fluid Web page design?

_____

_____

_____

_____

10. Why is it better to use HTML marked-up text than graphics containing text on a Web page?

_____

_____

_____

_____

11. Complete the form shown in "Outlining a Design's Look and Feel" (earlier in this chapter) as if you were the designer for a hip urban knitting store that offers knitting classes and sells knitting supplies.

12. Use the form in "Outlining a Design's Look and Feel" to enter design decisions for the following company:

    Company Name: Wagner Family Dentistry (in Marin, California)

    Description of the company image: Providing the highest-quality dental care using the latest technology and a gentle touch. Our friendly and caring staff ensure that all our patients feel safe and comfortable. We're changing the world, one beautiful smile at a time.

    Description of the ideal site visitor: Men, women, and children seeking high-quality dental care in a professional, relaxed, and caring environment. Want a dentist who will remember their names and treat them like people, not numbers.

CHAPTER

7

Mocking Up the Design

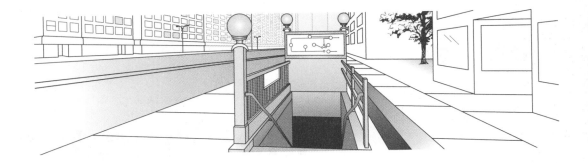

 # Enter the Station

Questions

1. What is the purpose of a visual mockup for a Web site?

2. How does using a visual site map help with creating a Web site mockup?

3. Does it matter whether you sketch the mockup first and then use a graphics program?

4. Where should certain page elements, such as branding and navigation, be placed in the mockup?

5. Are there areas of the mockup that are more "valuable" than others?

6. What additional graphics might you need to create after the mockup is complete?

Express Line

If your background happens to include training and/or work experience in graphic design, you might already be familiar with the process of converting text and graphics into a visually pleasing and marketable layout. Therefore, after glancing through the material and exercises in this chapter, if you believe you have a firm grasp of the information, move ahead to the lessons on graphics optimization in Chapter 8.

I n the previous chapters, you laid the groundwork for the Web site's look and feel: You determined the site's purpose and defined the ideal site visitor in Chapter 1, did market research and crafted an identity for the site in Chapter 2, gathered relevant content and created a visual site map for the Web project in Chapter 3, selected development tools and got a basic understanding of HTML code structure and usage in Chapter 4, registered a domain and secured hosting in Chapter 5, and made some important design decisions about the site's look and feel in Chapter 6.

In this chapter, you combine all that knowledge and research with your design decisions. Using the project's site map as a guide, you generate a unique, creative, and compelling Web page mockup that will best represent the project goals and vision for the site.

Creating a good design requires that all the elements of the site — content, fonts, colors, design elements, and so on — are strategically placed on the page. For some sites, this can be somewhat like solving a complicated puzzle, but if you take your time and follow the basic organizational rules outlined in this chapter, you should be able to come up with a suitable layout. One extremely useful rule is to include on the mockup a graphic example of the type of navigation system the site will use, preferably with one of the navigation links shown in the rollover state when applicable. This example will greatly help your client envision how the completed Web page will look when converted into HTML.

Transfer

Although you had a brief introduction to navigation systems in Chapter 6, if you want more in-depth knowledge of navigation systems available for Web sites, you might want to jump ahead to Chapter 13 to read about three of the most popular navigation options before building the mockup.

Understanding the Value of a Mockup

Before you start designing the mockup (or mockups, if you've contracted to create more than one), you might find it helpful to understand the purpose or value of it:

Visual representation: First and foremost, the mockup is meant to provide your Web client with a visual representation of how the completed site will look in a browser window before you actually spend any time generating the graphics or building the Web pages. The mockup becomes, then, a kind of blueprint that both designer and client can refer to when communicating about how the site will look and function.

- **Easy modification:** Should the design require any adjustments (which it inevitably will), you can more easily modify a single graphic mockup than rebuild or modify the code on all the pages on a Web site. Most Web clients do like to have some say in the design process. Allowing for client feedback during the design phase is a nice way to share the decision-making power and arrive at the best possible final design.

- **Design unification:** Ultimately, the mockup allows you to put all your design ideas in one place from which you'll generate all the graphics for the site and have a single, unified vision of the site's look and feel as you build the site.

- **Satisfaction:** For many Web clients, the site mockup has an emotional component. Not only is an approved mockup a clearly definable milestone within the Web design process, but it also provides the client with a great sense of accomplishment toward the finished project.

You should expect, after presenting the initial design to the client, to go through at least three rounds of revisions before the client approves the design. Two rounds are often sufficient, but given the fact that many designers now communicate with their clients exclusively through e-mail and voicemail, three rounds allows you to resolve any possible miscommunication that might naturally occur.

Whether you'll be designing one, two, or possibly more mockups for your client, be sure to limit the number of revisions the client can make to their preferred design. Some designers allow for unlimited changes until the client is satisfied. However, in my experience, limiting the number to under five helps keep the project moving forward.

If you include some kind of clause in your design contract that states the maximum number of revisions to the design before additional fees kick in, you can inform the client of his or her responsibilities and your expectations in advance. For example, you might want to state that the contract will allow a maximum of three rounds of revisions to the initial design and that any additional work beyond this maximum shall be automatically billed at $X/hour. This can also help prevent the more aggressive clients from asking more from you than they've agreed to pay for.

Working from the Site Map

Starting a design can sometimes be a daunting task when you're staring at an empty design canvas. To help you get started, I recommend that you go back to the visual site map you created in Chapter 3 and use it to guide you in the generation of the site mockup. Not only is it an agreed-upon, client-approved document about the site, but as you can see in Figure 7-1, it also contains at-a-glance information about all the navigation links, subnavigation elements, page order, and other data to be included on the mockup, such as copyright notice, footer links, and other branding or company details.

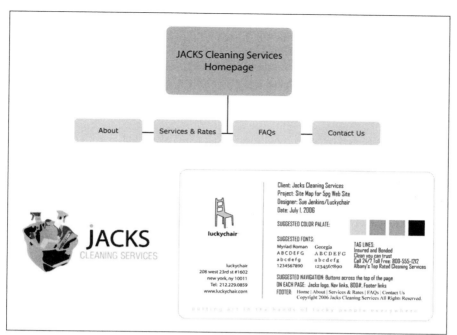

Figure 7-1: Use the site map like the one shown here as a starting point for your mockup.

Get all that information on the design canvas before you start thinking about the layout. Then you can combine the content with your design details from Chapter 6 (such as layout size and orientation, color values, and font selection) to create the design.

Creating the Mockup

This section describes in detail how to translate the information in the site map into a graphic mockup worthy of presentation to the client. A graphic mockup is the best way to show the client what the finished Web site will look like because it can demonstrate near-precise color, accurate representations of font sizes, and precision of placement of all the navigation and content elements on the site relative to one another. Furthermore, this precision assists with discussions between designer and client about revisions to the design should any need to be made.

Watch Your Step

If the idea appeals to you, feel free to sketch a mockup by hand before generating the graphical version of it in your preferred graphics program. I don't recommend, however, using a sketch in lieu of the graphical mockup. This is because sharing a sketch with a client creates too many opportunities for miscommunication.

Because the most important page of any Web site is the home page, you should plan to mock it up for the client (or for yourself, if you're designing your own site). If you and your client agree in advance that you, the designer, will mock up a different internal page (that is, any pages on the site other than the home page) instead of or in addition to the home page, doing so can be helpful if the budget and timeframe allow this. Generally, though, the home page sets the standards for the design, representing most or all of the graphical elements that will appear throughout the site.

Begin the mockup process by adding all the site elements to a blank, appropriately sized document in your graphics editor of choice. (Mine happens to be Photoshop.) Then position each element around the document window into a visually pleasing order consistent with the agreed-upon design directives. Expect to put in at least 8–12 hours for the initial design if you're an experienced designer — more if you're new or relatively new to the Web-design process.

As mentioned in this book's introduction, you can use any of several graphic applications to create the Web mockup, depending on your specific needs, budget, and personal preferences. In the following steps, you create an example mockup in Photoshop for an example client, Jacks Cleaning Services, but the following steps are focused enough for you to follow along with them when working in most other graphics programs, too:

1. **With Photoshop open, choose File → New to create a new document.**

   The New dialog box opens. Here you can enter the appropriate settings to set up your mockup.

2. **Enter 760 x 420 pixels for the Web page dimensions and 72 pixels/inch for the Resolution. For the Color Mode setting, choose RGB, 8 bit. (See Figure 7-2.)**

   These settings are typical, and you can use them for any Web page mockup.

   Pixels per inch refers to the number of pixels within a one inch space that are used to generate an image on-screen. A resolution of 72 PPI is recommended for creating low-resolution graphics for the Web.

3. **Click OK to close the dialog box and begin working in the new blank document.**

Information Kiosk

To better envision how the final Web site will look, some designers set their monitors to 800 x 600 or 1,024 x 768, take a screenshot of a maximized browser window, and then paste the screenshot into the new Photoshop document. Pasting the screenshot into Photoshop automatically creates a new layer in the document, which you can then toggle on and off during the design process. Not only will this method show approximate available design space when the design is complete, but seeing the design as it might appear in a browser will assist in selling the layout to the client when it comes time for client review and approval.

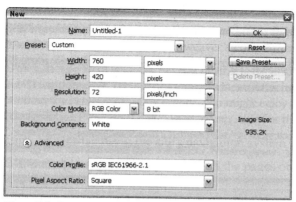

Figure 7-2: Set resolution, size, and color in the New dialog box.

4. Click the horizontal ruler and drag a guide to the point that's 150 pixels from the top of the page.

You'll use this guide to align the company logo (which is 150 pixels tall) along the top of the page and maintain alignment with other navigation elements that belong in the example mockup. If the rulers aren't visible, choose View → Rulers to display them. If the rulers are displaying a unit other than pixels, right-click (Windows) or Control+click (Mac) the ruler and choose Pixels from the resulting contextual menu.

5. Add any logo artwork and other company branding graphics to the document and position them roughly where they should appear on the Web page, as shown in Figure 7-3.

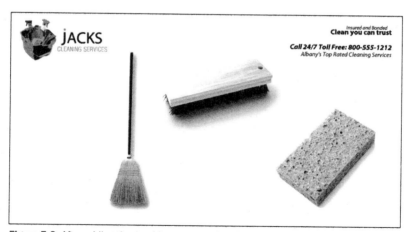

Figure 7-3: After adding the graphics, move each to its approximate location.

Art can be selected, copied, and pasted into Photoshop from another application, "placed" in the file through the Photoshop File menu, or dragged and dropped into the Photoshop document from another open file. Acceptable file formats include AI, EPS, PDF, TIFF, JPG, GIF, BMP, PNG, PSD, and PDF.

To follow along with these steps, you can find the graphics, text, and other specs for the Jacks Cleaning Services project on the companion Web site for this book. See the book's introduction for details about the Web site.

Information Kiosk

Smart Objects for Photoshop CS2 Users   Whenever you add logo artwork, illustrations, or graphical elements created with a vector program like Illustrator to a Photoshop file, which creates raster images, be sure to bring them into the Photoshop layout as Vector Smart Objects, which are containers inside which you can paste artwork that retains all its vector qualities and editability after pasting! Remember that vector images are images (usually line art) that rely on mathematical algorithms to determine their size, so you can alter their size without impacting the image quality. Raster images, however, are made of pixels, and altering the size of these images can impact the quality of the image.

To do this, you can either place the Illustrator file into the Photoshop document through the File menu or paste it into Photoshop by choosing Edit → Paste. Placing the file automatically converts the vector art into a Vector Smart Object, whereas pasting requires that you pay special attention to the dialog box, shown in Figure 7-4, that appears after pasting which prompts you to select a paste type.

When the dialog box appears, select the Smart Object option instead of Pixels to retain vector curves, scalability, and editability. Vector Smart Objects are easily identifiable in the Photoshop Layers panel by their peculiar thumbnail image. To learn more about Smart Objects and their capabilities, watch the Adobe QuickTime movie on Smart Objects at `www.adobe.com/products/photoshop/pop_smart.html`.

Figure 7-4: Use the Smart Object setting when pasting vector graphics into Photoshop CS2.

6. **Where applicable, add color to the mockup to delineate different areas of the layout.**

Use a primary color, as you learned in Chapter 6, to help identify different areas of the layout such as background page color and/or design background color when the design is fixed in width. Remember, as you learned in Chapter 4, for large flat areas of color, you might want to select a color from the Web-safe palette.

Color can be represented in bands, bars, lines, blocks, circles, squares, triangles, blobs, and other shapes. For instance, you might want to have a horizontal band of the primary color across the top where the company logo will reside, a band of a different secondary color just below that for a row of navigation buttons, and an accent-colored band off to the left or right below that for subnavigation page links, ads, and other information.

7. **Use the Horizontal Type tool to add the main navigation links to the mockup. Use the Character and Paragraph palettes to set the type to the desired font, size, leading, and alignment.**

You can add text to a document in Photoshop in two ways:

- *Use a "click and type" method.* Click once to set the insertion point from which point you can begin typing to create a line of text that won't wrap or break unless you press Enter or Return.

- *Use a "click, drag, and type" technique.* Click and drag to create a text area box in the document, and after releasing the mouse button, any typed text should automatically be contained inside the text area box. The boundaries of the text area box will determine when text will wrap from one line to the next, but you may also add manual line breaks by pressing Enter or Return. The benefit of the second way is that you can set the width of the text block to a specific size that will fit logically with the rest of the mockup before you start typing, or make adjustments to the area box dimensions after the type has been entered.

Each time you click and type or click, drag, and type with the Horizontal Type tool, Photoshop creates a new type layer. You can see three type layers in Figure 7-5.

I suggest you initially type the navigation links by using the click-and-type method to make one long list of links on a single Photoshop layer, adding an even amount of space between the text links for alignment purposes. It's much easier to format and move a single layer around the document window than it is to move and possibly reformat several layers. After the positioning is accurate and the design is approved, you could go back into the file and create individual text layers for any navigation elements that will need rollover graphics.

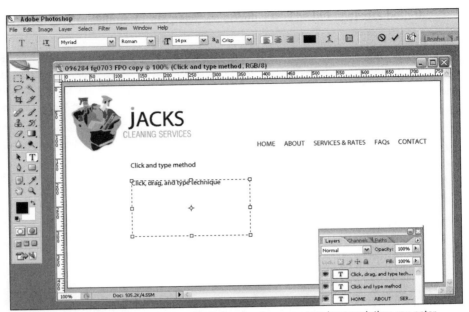

Figure 7-5: No matter how you enter text, Photoshop creates a new type layer each time you enter a new block of text.

As a general rule, navigation is often placed somewhere either near the top of the layout (below or to the right of the company identity) or along the left margin of the layout beneath the company identity. Each of the navigation text links should be clearly delineated either by designing button graphics behind, around, or to the sides of the link text, or by adding some kind of dividing symbol like a bullet (•) or vertical zero-width non-joiner (|) between them, like the examples shown in Figure 7-6.

		My Account | Login
About Us	Services	Contact

Figure 7-6: Separate navigation links with graphics or a dividing symbol.

8. **Again, using the Horizontal Type tool, type all the Footer navigation links as you'd like them to appear as HTML text at the bottom of each Web page.**

Footer links, as you'll recall from Chapter 1, are hypertext links representing all the main navigation links on the site that are placed at the bottom of each page to assist visually impaired visitors navigate the site using text readers. Footers are also handy as quick links to the main pages of a site, especially on pages that require scrolling.

As a shortcut, copy the main navigation links layer you just created and rename it something like "footer links" in the Layers palette. Then append the text on the new layer with any additional text links as needed, such as a link back to the home page and/or a site map page.

9. **Add another text layer to the layout for any copyright notice, company disclaimer, and other information that will also appear as HTML text in the footer area.**

Many Web sites add information about copyright, privacy, terms of service, site credits, and other information below the footer links. For example, a text line below the navigation links might read as follows:

Privacy Notice • © 2006, Company Name • All Rights Reserved

You worked on gathering the text in Chapter 3; refer to your notes for details about any content needed for the copyright or other text for your home page mockup.

10. **Add more text layers as needed for any text that will appear on the home page. Use the Character and Paragraph palettes to set the type to the desired font, size, leading, and alignment.**

As you learned in Chapter 6, text that represents the main content on the page should be mocked up in an acceptable cross-platform (PC and Mac) font at least 9 pixels in size with anti-aliasing set to None (so the text looks like HTML text). Acceptable cross-platform fonts include Verdana, Arial, Helvetica, Courier, Courier New, Times, Times New Roman, Georgia, Geneva, Trebuchet, Comic Sans, Impact, serif, and sans-serif.

Whenever possible, try to include examples in the text of any formatting styles that will be included on the site, such as headings, subheadings, bylines, paragraphs, and bulleted and/or numbered lists.

11. **On as many new layers as are needed, begin adding other page elements that will go on the mockup.**

Other elements might include pull quotes in special fonts, small flash movies, a toll-free number, a contact e-mail address, a search box and go button, dropdown menus, the date, links, advertisements, banners, certifications, logos, photographs, and other content.

At this stage, you should have all the content for the mockup in the Photoshop document. The next step is for you to begin strategically placing certain elements in visual high-traffic areas while arranging all the other elements in a visually pleasing way.

Strategically Placing Mockup Elements

A Web page, like the front page of a newspaper, has certain spots that visitors are more likely to see and where they're more likely to linger. The most popular real estate on a Web page, presuming that page is opened in a maximized browser window, is the area from the top of the window down to the bottom, before a visitor needs to scroll to see any hidden content. This part of a Web page, commonly referred to as the area *above the fold,* should include the following:

- Company name
- Logo
- Tag line (when applicable)
- Navigation
- Enough general information about the site to tell the visitors about the benefits (remember those from Chapter 1?) the site has to offer them

Including this information above the fold encourages the visitor to stay on the site and keep looking around and clicking through to other pages on the site. The reason this area is so valuable is that most visitors decide within five to ten seconds whether they've found what they were looking for when they typed the URL or clicked the link to visit the site.

If you don't believe this, think about your own browsing habits. How long does it take for you to decide whether any particular site has what you're looking for? Five seconds? Ten seconds? Thirty? The human brain processes so many calculations per second that, relatively speaking, ten seconds is a lot of time. Seasoned Internet users know exactly what they want, are an impatient bunch (when it comes to surfing the Internet), and will gladly keep searching until they find what they're looking for.

Watch Your Step

What should *not* be included above the fold? Typically, you should avoid including Flash intros and banners, advertisements, unnecessary text, and too many navigation links. Besides taking up valuable space, these unnecessary components can increase the size of the page, causing the page to load slower in the browser window. If each page on a site should take less than 15 seconds to load when using a 56K modem, you really can't afford to waste any space putting unnecessary information above the fold that could be just as easily placed elsewhere on the page.

When you're designing the area above the fold, the following tips are also helpful:

- Add headlines, subheadings, bylines, and other visual design elements that clearly communicate the site's benefits to visitors. Think of a newspaper: The name of the newspaper is the first thing you see, then the main story headline and text. You'll also find information about news items in different sections of the paper, a few bylines, and introductory text to three or four stories.

- Other good elements for the area above the fold (besides your navigation and key content) are links allowing visitors to sign up for a newsletter, contact the site, search the site, access a shopping cart, log in to an account, and bookmark the page.

- Certain elements should go on every page of the site for visual consistency and to encourage visitors to return.

- As you're arranging all the elements on the page, refer often to the words selected to identify the ideal site visitor as well as the identity for the site. Also keep the overall purpose for the site in mind because that concept can sometimes provide cues to positioning things in the layout.

To help you accurately determine the size of the area that is above the fold, take a look at Table 7-1. In general, you need to take into account the resolution the target audience uses, and within that resolution, allow space for scroll bars, navigation buttons, the status bar, and the address bar. Remember also that the width of a site needs to be manageable enough to navigate without having to scroll horizontally, so even with the wider monitor resolutions, the maximum width for the design should be in the 770–800 pixel range.

Table 7-1　　　Find the Design Area Above the Fold

Target Audience's Monitor Resolution	Design Space Above the Fold
800 x 600	720 x 420 pixels
1,024 x 768	1,000 x 600 pixels
1,280 x 1,024	1,260 x 800 pixels

Adding Design Elements to the Mockup

Next you should begin to add design elements to the mockup that will really make the design unique. This includes adding things like horizontal rules, vertical divider lines, custom bullets, rounded or specially angled corners, textures, drop shadows, special effects, buttons, borders, arrows, widgets, shapes to delineate the different areas of the layout, symbols, and other graphical embellishments.

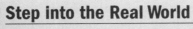

Step into the Real World

Making a New Mockup When the owner of English Lakeland Ramblers (www.ramblers.com) contracted me to redesign his Web site, so many changes needed to be made that we decided to treat the project as if it were a brand-new site and started the design process from scratch, following all the same steps you've learned in Chapters 1–6. For comparison, the following figure shows what the original Web site looked like before the project began.

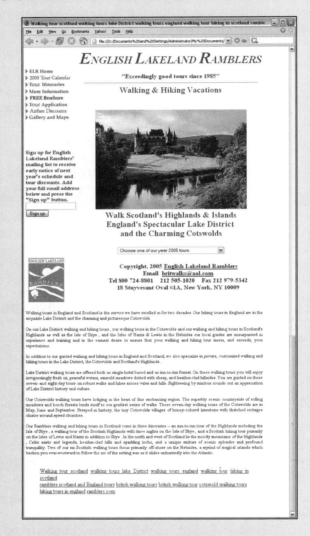

After creating a client site map, shown in the next figure, I combined that information with all the client's content and organized everything into a visually pleasing site mockup, as shown in the final figure.

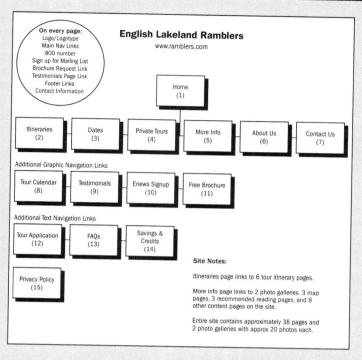

On every page:
Logo/Logotype
Main Nav Links
800 number
Sign up for Mailing List
Brochure Request Link
Testimonials Page Link
Footer Links
Contact Information

English Lakeland Ramblers
www.ramblers.com

Home
(1)

Itineraries (2) | Dates (3) | Private Tours (4) | More Info (5) | About Us (6) | Contact Us (7)

Additional Graphic Navigation Links

Tour Calendar (8) | Testimonials (9) | Enews Signup (10) | Free Brochure (11)

Additional Text Navigation Links

Tour Application (12) | FAQs (13) | Savings & Credits (14)

Privacy Policy (15)

Site Notes:

Itineraries page links to 6 tour itinerary pages.

More info page links to 2 photo galleries. 3 map pages, 3 recommended reading pages, and 8 other content pages on the site.

Entire site contains approximately 38 pages and 2 photo galleries with approx 20 photos each.

The design of the new English Lakeland Ramblers Web site is a vast improvement over the original site design. With the exception of a few additional links on the home page, the new site's navigation is consistent throughout the site, the look and feel of the design is more sophisticated and professional, and most importantly, the site projects a quality of excellence consistent with the reputation of the Ramblers' walking tours. To see the finished product, visit `www.ramblers.com`.

Take design risks. Repeating certain elements can provide instant unity to a design, but so can adding contrasting elements like using different sized fonts and contrasting colors. You might even want to try making several versions of the mockup to try out different text treatments or object alignment options. If you get stuck for ideas during the design process, spend time looking at other sites for inspiration.

Be thorough. Every element on the layout needs to seem like it was meant to be in the position it is, in the color it is, and in the size it is, relative to the other objects in the design. Above all, make the layout interesting, original, and creative. Here are some ideas that can help you generate the design:

- Have a single focal point.
- Use a maximum of three font faces.
- Organize the content so the site will be easy to navigate.
- Use consistent spacing between like objects such as bullet points, navigation links, and table rows.
- Add horizontal and vertical rules to create divisions between different areas on the layout.
- Use rounded edges, angles, and other shapes to break up the linear quality of the design.
- Make the text easy to read by using a single column no wider than 600 pixels or by breaking the layout into two or four columns.
- Use anti-aliased text for any text graphics, and text with anti-aliasing set to none for text that will be displayed in HTML.

Information Kiosk

Anti-Aliasing   When text is rendered on a Web page, the letter characters are rendered as low-resolution shapes with slightly jagged edges. By contrast, letter shapes in materials designed for print often have nice smooth edges. That smoothness comes from a digital rendering technique called *anti-aliasing,* which softens any blockiness by adding semitransparent pixels to the letter edges so that the shapes have a smoother appearance. The smoothness is further enhanced by the resolution setting of the graphic file. Web graphics should be set to 72 PPI, whereas print graphics should be at least 300 DPI.

In most graphic design programs, you should find a setting for text that allows you to control whether the text is rendered with or without anti-aliasing. Be sure to set anti-aliasing to None for any text in your mockup that will be rendered in HTML, and to choose one of the anti-aliasing options (crisp, strong, or smooth) for copy in your layout that will be used to generate Web graphics.

- Show hypertext links with underlines in the same color they will appear on the finished site.
- Leave white space in the layout to balance out the areas with content.
- Use photographs and illustrations to add visual appeal.
- Add headers, subheads, and pull quotes to break up large text areas.
- Use Web-safe colors whenever possible.

A simple design is usually more compelling than one that is overcrowded with bells and whistles. Try the squint test. If the page seems organized and balanced when you squint at it, you've done a good job. If parts seem too jumbled or too heavy on one side and too light on another, keep playing with the pieces of the layout until you can find a nice balance. Remember, too, to keep spacing and alignment between the elements consistent or deliberate throughout the layout. Good design allows the eye to flow from one area of the page to another, with areas of white space surrounding content so the eye has somewhere to rest as it moves among the important items in the layout. Figure 7-7 shows one example of a completed Jacks Cleaning Services mockup that incorporates all these design principles.

Figure 7-7: Good design is often balanced and organized, like this layout for Jacks Cleaning Services.

If you'd like to try your hand at creating a mockup for Jacks Cleaning Services, go to this book's companion Web site to get site specifications and graphics.

Finalizing a Mockup

When the design is complete to the best of your ability, put it away for a day or two and then return to it to be sure that it still looks finished to you. If you find any inconsistencies in spacing, alignment, coloration, or sizing, now is the time to make corrections and adjustments. The following questions can help you review your work:

- Does the layout look unified?
- Have you used too many fonts?
- Does the site have more than one focal point?
- Are the visitor benefit messages clear and easy to identify?
- Does the eye have any white space to rest upon?
- Are any design elements repeated throughout the design to give it a look of cohesiveness and professionalism?

In addition to this checklist, the following sections will help you finalize your mockup and present it to your client.

Showing the subnavigation (or rollover)

When I'm finished with a Web design, one of the secrets I use to help sell the finished mockup to my clients is to show at least one of the navigation buttons in the layout in its *rollover* state — that is, how the link will look when a visitor moves her mouse over one of the links on the main navigation, which is why this term is sometimes also call the *mouseover* state — complete with hand cursor pointing to the link, and including the look and feel of any subnavigation, when applicable. This allows the client to really get a feel for how the site's navigation will function when it's built in HTML. Figure 7-8 shows an example of a mockup that includes how the subnavigation menu will look when a visitor mouses over a navigation link.

Remember, clients are coming to you because A) you're the expert, the person who knows how to visualize a layout before it becomes a working Web site, and B) because they have no idea how to mentally conjure up this kind of design themselves. If you show them what they can expect to see in advance of the site-building phase, they will have little room for confusion about what they will see when the site actually gets built.

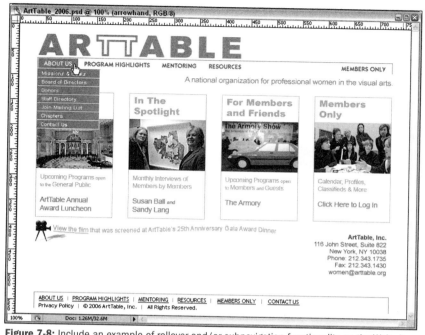

Figure 7-8: Include an example of rollover and/or subnavigation functionality on the Web site mockup.

Presenting a mockup to a client

After you add a sample of the rollover state to the mockup, you'll be ready to present the finished mockup to the client. Web mockup presentations can take many forms, including

- E-mailing a JPG, GIF, TIFF, or PDF file to the client for review

- Uploading a JPG, GIF, or PDF of the mockup to a test server and sending the client the URL to view it

- Meeting with the client in person to present the mockup on a laptop or computer screen in its native format, or as a JPG, GIF, or PDF

- Meeting with the client in person to show the mockup as a printout that's been mounted to an archival presentation board

Step into the Real World

Getting Written Client Approval   If I could share only one tip with you about working with clients, it would be "Get everything in writing." When communication is clear and both you and the client agree in writing about the steps of the design process, the project magically stays on track and within budget.

Start each project with a contract (and a deposit) and tell the client in advance that you will be obtaining her signature of approval at key points during the development process. Get approval on the site map, definitely get written approval on the completed mockup before you begin building the site in HTML, and be sure to also get a final signature at the end of the project when the site is finished before sending your final invoice. These signatures will be your insurance should the client change her mind about the site requirements while the project is underway. They also show her that you're committed to meeting your responsibilities as described in the contract.

In my experience, most people are lovely to work with and will treat the designer with respect. Nonetheless, clients occasionally will push for more but won't want to pay for any additional services. Don't be tempted to do any extra work for free, just to be nice, even when the client begs you to do something in a kind and gentle way. Your time is your livelihood, and you deserve to earn money for every minute you spend actively working on the project. Should additional changes beyond the scope of the project need to be made, the signatures allow you to feel confident about requesting more time, money, and/or materials to get the job done.

During your presentation, communicate to the client why the layout looks the way it does. Explain your reasons for selecting particular fonts, colors, and alignments. Point out all the key elements of the design, being sure to mention how it captures the identity of the site as well as caters directly to the target audience. Identify the focal point of the design and any other key elements you're particularly proud of.

Unless the client wants to confer with other members of her team, or with friends and family, she should be able to review the mockup in a reasonable amount of time, say one to five business days. After the review, she'll either provide you with feedback on what revisions she'd like you to make, or grant you written approval for you to begin building her new site in HTML.

Most clients will have at least one or more things to say about the mockup that require revision. If you disagree with anything a client wants changed, respectfully give reasons for why you believe the mockup works the way you've designed it. If she still disagrees and insists you make a particular change, say you'll try her suggestion, even if you're sure it won't work well or look right. With bad ideas, many clients will actually see how your version looks better than their suggestions when the two versions are compared side by side. Above all, however, remember that the client is paying you for the project and she needs to be happy with the results. Be willing to compromise, be open to making changes, and keep working until the design is approved.

Information Kiosk

Though not a practice I generally subscribe to, some designers intentionally add some kind of noticeable error to the layout before presenting the mockup to the client. The idea behind this technique is that by including something obviously wrong to the layout — like using the wrong font or color — the client will almost assuredly point out that error during the mockup review ("why is that blue?"), recommend a change of some kind ("make it red"), and come away from the process feeling valued for making a contribution to the design process. Sounds good in theory, but I've witnessed some clients say they actually liked the "bad" element, and removing something can be harder after the client has seen it. It's kind of like a Murphy's Law of Design: When given three options, the client will almost always choose the worst-looking design!

Designing Additional Web Site Graphics

After the client approves the Web mockup and provides you with written acceptance of the design, you still have a few more things to do with the mockup file *before* you begin optimizing graphics and building the site.

Namely, you need to create any additional graphics you intend to display on all the pages on the site. These additional graphics, for lack of a better term, include things like the over states of rollover buttons, bullets for customized lists, background images, navigation elements, curved corner graphics to make the hard corners on tables or layers look rounded, graphical horizontal rules or dividers, animated GIFs, page headers in special non-cross-platform fonts, illustrations, and photographs. For some of the additional graphics, like rollover graphics, you can create new layers in the existing mockup file. For most of the others, feel free to create new RGB, 8-bit, 72 PPI documents for them sized appropriately to match the graphics you need.

Header graphics

When your layout will use specialty font headers instead of headers styled with CSS, you should create and save them in a file separate from the mockup. That way, if any new pages are added to the site during the page-building process or sometime down the road after the site is launched, you can easily go back into the header graphic file and generate new headers quite easily.

Rollover graphics

Depending on the look of the rollover, you can actually create some rollover graphics by using Photoshop filters instead of having to create new layers in the mockup. For instance, if the rollover state of a navigation link is exactly the same as the normal state except for the color of the button text and the color of the button background, you can use Photoshop's Color Overlay Layer Style to modify the color of those layer attributes.

The following steps will walk you through the process of using the Photoshop Color Overlay Style in a Photoshop file:

1. **In Photoshop, choose File → New to create a new document.**

2. **In the dialog box that appears, set the page dimensions to 150 x 30, the resolution to 72 PPI, the color mode to RGB 8 bit, and the background contents to transparent. Click OK when you're done.**

3. **Choose Select → All.**

   This selects the entire area of the transparent canvas.

4. **Choose Edit → Fill to open the Fill dialog box and choose Color from the Use drop-down menu.**

   The Color Picker dialog box opens.

5. **Click the Only Web Colors option in the bottom-left corner of the dialog box to display only Web colors. Use your cursor to adjust the sliders along the center rainbow bar to point to orange. Select the color orange by clicking inside the large square area at the top-right edge.**

   You can tell you've selected the right color when the hexadecimal value field reads #ff9900, as shown in Figure 7-9.

6. **Click OK to close the Color Picker dialog box. Then click OK to close the Fill dialog box.**

   Photoshop should automatically fill your selected document with the chosen orange color.

7. **With the Horizontal Text tool, click inside the document and type the words** About Us.

   Photoshop automatically creates a separate layer for the text on top of the orange layer.

8. **With the text layer still actively selected in the Layers palette, click the Style button at the bottom of the Layers palette, as shown in Figure 7-10, and select the Color Overlay option.**

   The Layer Style dialog box opens, where you can select the desired hexadecimal color value for the rollover state style by clicking the red color field. When you've selected the color you'd like for the over-state graphic, click OK to close the dialog box.

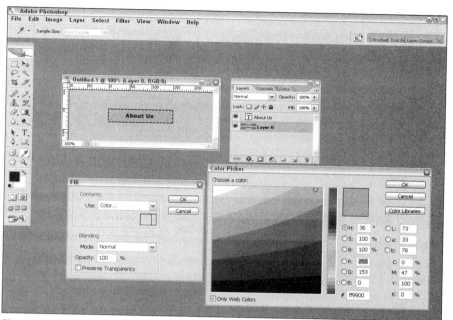

Figure 7-9: Choose a color for your graphics using Photoshop's Color Picker dialog box.

Figure 7-10: Add styles to the mockup text layers for creating rollover graphics.

The Layers palette will now display a small style icon and drop-down menu arrow on the right edge of the layer. To toggle the style on or off, click the style's drop-down menu arrow and click the eye icon next to the effect name to change the style's visibility status.

9. **To change the orange layer's color to another color for the rollover state, select the orange layer in the Layers palette, click the Style button at the bottom of the Layers palette, and select the Color Overlay option.**

The Layer Style dialog box opens.

10. **Select the desired hexadecimal color value by clicking the red color field for the rollover state style. Then click OK to close the Layer Style dialog box.**

A small style icon and drop-down menu arrow will appear on the right edge of the layer. Toggle the style on or off by clicking the eye icon next to the effect name in the layer's expanded style menu.

11. **Save your file.**

If the document requires additional style settings, select the appropriate layers, apply the desired styles, and then save your file upon completion.

When you go to optimize the graphics, as you'll learn in Chapter 8, you can toggle these layer styles on and off as needed for each of the button states.

Background images

With CSS, you can now set background images to repeat along the X axis, the Y axis, both the X and Y axes, or to not repeat at all. You can also position a background image precisely by using X/Y coordinates relative to the top-left corner of a browser window or an HTML container tag such as a table cell or layer. This means that background images no longer need be a million miles long or a zillion miles wide to tile seamlessly horizontally or vertically. You can use background images for the body of a Web page as well as for table backgrounds, table cell backgrounds, and layer backgrounds.

Other images

Look to the site map and continue creating all the graphics you need for the site. Most of the graphics you'll need to make will be obvious when referring to the content the client intends to use on the individual pages of the site. And if you happen to discover that you've missed some when you begin building the site, you can come back to your graphics program and create them later.

above the fold: Refers to the visible space in a maximized Web browser that a person sees without having to use the scroll bars. This is the most valuable space on a Web page and should contain branding, navigation, site benefit statements, and enough informative text to prompt a visitor to spend more time on the site.

cross-platform: In Web-speak, this term can mean either that a Web page can be easily viewed in a browser on any computer running any computer operating system (like Windows, Mac, Linux, or UNIX), or that a person knows how to use computers running the two most popular operating systems, Windows and Mac.

headers: Also sometimes called page headers, headings, or A-heads, headers refer to graphical renderings of page titles using specialized fonts that are placed at the top of the page content in lieu of creating headings using cross-platform compatible fonts styled with CSS.

internal pages: These are all the other pages on a site besides the home page. Visitors access internal pages by clicking links on the home page and on other pages throughout the site. (Also called a *subpage*.)

mockup: A graphical representation of the Web site layout used to communicate the look, feel, and functionality of a site before the graphics are optimized and the site gets constructed using HTML, CSS, and other development techniques.

navigation system: A Web menu system consistently placed on all the pages throughout a site whereby visitors can easily view a set of descriptive links and from that list, select links to access most, if not all, of the different pages of a Web site. Navigation systems range from the simple to the complex and can be created utilizing HTML, JavaScript, DHTML, Java, and/or other programming languages. The most popular systems are text based, list type, and JavaScript-enabled navigation.

PPI (pixels per inch): A consistent unit of measure referring to the number of pixels per inch that are viewable on a computer monitor. This should not be confused with DPI, or dots per inch, which refers to the measurements used to define the sharpness of a printed page.

raster: Graphics created in bitmap software programs (such as Photoshop) that use pixels to represent each part of the image. Raster programs are great for photographic retouching and building Web site mockups. However, these graphics don't look good when scaled larger than their original size.

continued

 *continued*

resolution: A computer monitor's resolution is determined by the number of lines running both horizontally and vertically across the screen. Common monitor ppi resolutions include 800 x 600; 1,024 x 768; and 1,280 x 1,024.

rollover state: This is the look of a navigation button or link when a visitor moves the cursor across a navigation link. Rollover graphics generally appear on the fly due to CSS or JavaScript in the page code that is activated when the user moves the cursor on top of the link. When the visitor moves the cursor away from the link, the link typically returns to its normal state immediately or after a predetermined delay measured in milliseconds.

vector: Graphics created in object-oriented software programs, like Illustrator, that use mathematical algorithms to construct the shapes and paths. These graphics often have smaller file sizes than their raster-based bitmap counterparts, and they will always retain their crispness and clarity regardless of their size after rescaling.

Last Stop

Practice Exam

1. **True or False:** Clients are just as happy approving a hand-drawn sketch of a mockup as they are approving a mockup created in a graphics program. Explain your answer.

2. The area of a browser window that gets the most attention from visitors is called _____.

3. How many focal points does a good mockup have?

   _____

4. Name two reasons why creating a graphical mockup for a Web site is beneficial.

   _____

   _____

5. List three tools learned in previous chapters that will help you begin creating the Web mockup.

   _____

   _____

6. How many changes to the mockup should you allow after the client's initial review? Why?

   _____

   _____

7. What makes a home page different from an internal page?

   _____

   _____

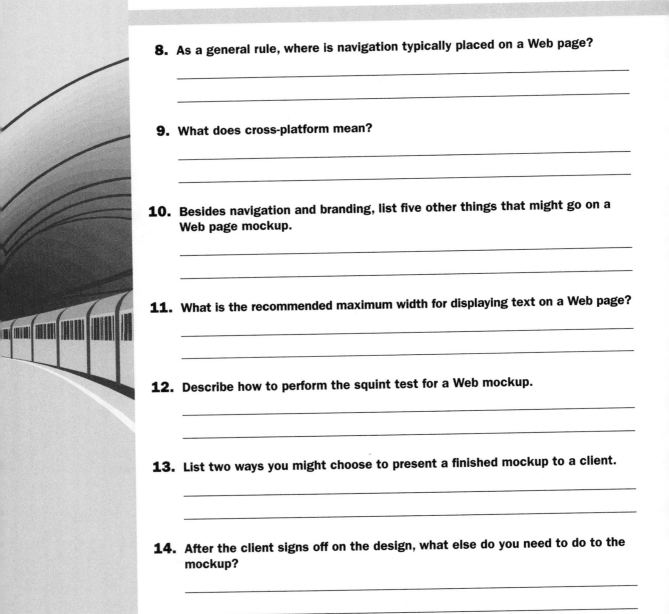

8. As a general rule, where is navigation typically placed on a Web page?

_____

_____

9. What does cross-platform mean?

_____

_____

10. Besides navigation and branding, list five other things that might go on a Web page mockup.

_____

_____

11. What is the recommended maximum width for displaying text on a Web page?

_____

_____

12. Describe how to perform the squint test for a Web mockup.

_____

_____

13. List two ways you might choose to present a finished mockup to a client.

_____

_____

14. After the client signs off on the design, what else do you need to do to the mockup?

_____

_____

EXIT

Optimizing Graphics

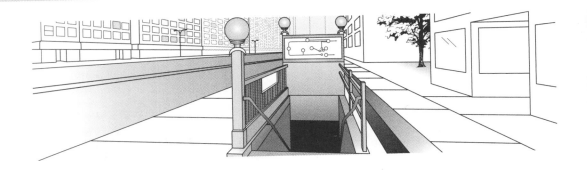

Enter the Station

Questions

1. Why would you want to choose different settings for a Web graphic than for a print graphic?

2. What are the benefits of using a Web image optimization program?

3. What type of image would you save in GIF format? What type of image is better optimized as a JPEG?

4. What do you need to consider when optimizing several graphics for a single Web page?

5. Why would you want to slice an image during the optimization process?

Express Line

If you're already familiar with Web graphics and optimization techniques, you might want to move ahead to learn about working with Web standards in Chapter 9.

The graphics and photos you use on a Web site differ in a variety of ways from the graphics and photos you might use for a print project. For one, print graphics are high resolution, whereas Web graphics must be set to a low resolution. Likewise, print graphics rely on the CMYK color mode, but any graphics used for on-screen presentation must use RGB color.

In this chapter, you'll learn what all those differences are and everything you'll need to know to create graphics that are ready for Web optimization. Without this preparation — and especially without optimization — the graphics and photos on your Web sites would simply be too large to transmit over the Web and display in a browser on a visitor's computer monitor.

In the following sections, you'll find an overview of Web graphics as compared to print graphics. You'll also discover information about choosing an optimization program. Following that, you learn about Web file formats, including how to select the right format for different graphic types. The last three parts of the chapter include the fine points about selecting different optimization settings, slicing up images before optimization, and finally, choosing the optimization output options that produce your desired results.

Understanding Web Graphics

When people talk about Web graphics, what exactly do they mean? To fully understand what it means to create a Web graphic, you should first understand graphics in general and evaluate the ways in which Web graphics differ from print graphics.

Graphics, whether for print or Web, can be created with a variety of software programs, the most popular among them being Illustrator, Photoshop, Fireworks, QuarkXPress, and InDesign. The finished graphics may be saved in a variety of file formats, depending on their intended usage.

Of all the applications you can choose from to create your graphic images, one primary consideration is whether the artwork needs to be developed and saved as either vector art or raster.

- **Vector:** A vector program uses mathematical equations to generate paths, lines, and shapes, which enables the image to be scaled up or down without any loss of resolution. Logos, for example, are best created in a vector program. When created as vector graphics, the logo artwork can be colored and scaled for any medium — online, newsprint, embroidered on a hat, printed on the side of a pen, and so on — and still look great no matter the size.

- **Raster:** Raster (or bitmap) programs represent images as a collection of tiny pixels or little squares of color, the number of which is determined by the file's resolution. The number of pixels in an image determines the image's quality; typically, the higher the number, the sharper the image; the lower the number, the fuzzier the image. An image set to 300 DPI (dots per inch), for instance, would have a high resolution and therefore be fine enough to use in a printed piece, whereas an image set to 72 PPI (pixels per inch) would have too few bits of information to print crisply, even though the image might look fine and clear on a computer monitor.

Table 8-1 shows a comparison of Web and print graphics based on a variety of key criteria. Because some features of graphics are so different from one another between Web and print, you must be sure to select the correct color mode for your graphic files *before* you create them. Choose RGB for all your Web projects and CMYK for print. In the section that follows, you'll find more details about each Web graphic feature listed in Table 8-1.

Table 8-1   Web and Print Graphic Comparison

	Web Graphics	Print Graphics
Color Mode	RGB	CMYK
Resolution	72 PPI	300 DPI
Unit of Measure	Pixels	Inches, Points, Picas
File Size	Lower file size will produce faster display on the Web.	Larger file size may produce sharper images in print.
Page Size	Images can be placed on an adjustable-size Web page.	Images are placed on layouts with fixed page size.
File Formats	GIF, JPG, or PNG	TIFF, EPS, PSD, PDF, BMP, AI, INDD, QXD, PPT, DOC

Color mode

There are two color modes, or *gamuts,* that graphic artists typically create and save their work in for Web and print design: RGB (Red, Green, and Blue, which are additive colors) and CMYK (Cyan, Magenta, Yellow, and Black, which are subtractive). You select the color mode for a graphic file when creating a new one, though the mode may also be changed at a later time if required.

Watch Your Step

If you forget to choose the correct color mode for your graphic files and you create some or most of the layout or image adjustments before realizing the mistake, be forewarned that converting a file from one color mode to another can cause noticeable shifts in color in the image that might render the image color inaccurate and possibly unusable. This is especially true for images created in RGB but intended for CMYK print.

Figure 8-1 shows how the different color modes achieve their color and what happens when all the colors in that mode are combined.

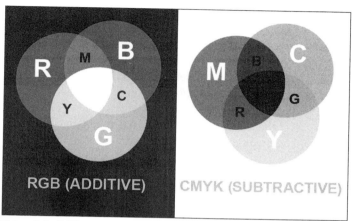

Figure 8-1: CMYK is used primarily for print, whereas RGB should be used for any on-screen presentation, including Web sites.

RGB colors are the additive colors of the visible spectrum, which means that when combined together, the resulting color is white light. RGB is used primarily for on-screen (computer monitor) presentations, such as Web pages and PowerPoint slide shows, because computer monitors use RGB technology to display color.

CMYK colors are the subtractive print colors used mainly for four-color reproductions. When cyan, magenta, and yellow are combined as inks, which are then printed on paper, the resulting color is technically black, which represents the absence of light.

Information Kiosk

I say "technically" because in reality, combining three inks creates a sort of muddy gray-black that isn't as rich and saturated a "color" as you're used to seeing when you think of black. To get a true rich black in any printed job, the printer must add a separate black ink to the printing process. That's where the K (for black) in CMYK comes from.

Color gamut warnings

Compared to the visible spectrum and the 16.7 million colors you can see on a 24-bit computer monitor, the CMYK color mode is somewhat limited. The current U.S. standard CMYK technology, or SWOP (standard Web offset press), simply can't reproduce on a printed page the same full range of color you can see on a monitor. Any color that can't be reproduced in print, therefore, is referred to as *out of gamut. Gamut* refers to the range of reproducible colors on any given device, such as a printing press or computer monitor.

In addition to colors that are out of gamut for print, another thing you might want to watch out for when creating graphics for the Web are colors that don't fall within the Web-safe palette. The Web-safe palette, as you'll recall from Chapter 4, refers to the 216 non-dithering (solid) colors that can be accurately displayed in browsers on both Mac and PC computers with 8-bit monitors set to display a maximum of 256 colors. (The reason the Web-safe palette has only 216 colors instead of 256 is because 40 of the 256 colors appear differently on a Mac than they do on a PC.) Following this same gamut logic, then, any color that can't be represented on-screen on an 8-bit monitor is considered non-Web-safe and would be called out of gamut for the Web.

Using the Web-safe palette is no longer as critical an issue in Web design as it once was because most newer computers have monitors capable of rendering millions of colors. Though it might still be good to use a color from this palette when coloring large flat areas of a Web page, such as a page or table cell background, or when speci- fying the color of styled text with CSS, it's no longer a general Web recommendation.

Fortunately, both Photoshop and Illustrator (the two programs used most by profes- sional designers) have a feature within the Color Picker dialog box that alerts designers when a selected color is either out of gamut for print or non-Web-safe. To demonstrate how this works, follow the steps outlined in the following Photoshop exercise:

1. **Launch Photoshop.**

You can access the Color Picker tool without opening a new document, but feel free to open a new document if desired.

2. **Click the Foreground Color box at the bottom of the Photoshop toolbar.**

This opens the Color Picker dialog box, which has several options for viewing color.

3. **In the R, G, and B text fields, enter** 0, 200, **and** 200, **respectively.**

After entering these numbers, the hollow circle icon within the large foreground color box moves to near the top-right edge of the square, thereby selecting a turquoise color.

To the left of the OK and Cancel buttons, you will see a rectangle with the new color on top and the previously selected color on bottom.

Directly to the right of those color swatches, you see four small warning icons, as shown in Figure 8-2. The top two indicate that the selected color is out of gamut for print and the bottom two indicate that the selected color is not Web-safe.

4. **Click the top triangular out-of-gamut warning icon.**

By clicking the warning icon, you're requesting that Photoshop find and sug- gest the nearest in-gamut print color that you could use instead.

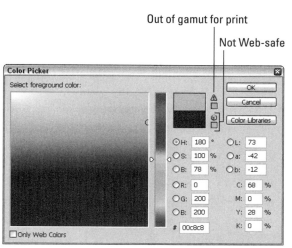

Out of gamut for print

Not Web-safe

Figure 8-2: Photoshop's Color Picker dialog box will show warnings for any selected color that is either out of gamut for print or non-Web-safe for a browser.

As you can see, the new selected color with the RGB values of 50/190/194 is now in gamut, but it isn't Web-safe.

5. **Click the bottom cubelike, non-Web-safe-color warning icon.**

You now have a color that is Web-safe (RGB values of 51/204/204) that is out of gamut for print!

Although you might not need to find a color that is both Web safe and printable, you have two ways to find such a color. First, you could click several times inside the large foreground color square until you find a color that is both in gamut and Web safe. The alternative is to select the Only Web Colors check box at the bottom of the dialog box. When this option is enabled, the nearest Web-safe color is automatically selected. Then try clicking one of the other Web-safe colors in the same color range and toggling on and off the Only Web Colors option until you find a value that is both Web-safe and in gamut, such as RGB 102/204/204.

That's it. Just pay attention to the warning icon area as you're selecting your colors for your print and Web projects. When you see an icon in the warning area, click it to ensure the selected color meets your needs for print and Web.

Resolution

When talking about creating Web graphics, *resolution* refers to the number of pixels per square inch (PPI) on-screen that are used to display an image. Though computer monitors can display different PPI settings, such as 640 x 480, 800 x 600, 1,280 x 1,024, and 1,600 x 1,200, Web browsers are capable of displaying images only at a maximum of 72 PPI.

Print graphics, by contrast, use dots per square inch (DPI) to determine the quality of the printed output. To print a graphic at a high quality, you must set graphics to at least 300 DPI (though in some cases, 150 DPI might be enough). Figure 8-3 illustrates the differences between DPI for print and PPI for Web.

Figure 8-3: Print graphics are displayed in dots per inch while Web graphics are displayed in pixels per inch.

Watch Your Step

In print, the more dots there are, the larger and clearer the image. On the Web, however, increasing the number of pixels per inch is unnecessary because browsers can't display images at resolutions larger than 72 PPI. Furthermore, a resolution greater than 72 PPI will not only increase the file size but may also increase the dimensions of the graphic, making the image more time consuming to download and potentially bigger than intended.

What do you do when you need a graphic for the Web but you also want it to print crisply when a Web visitor prints the Web page? Well, you can't do much about that after the graphics are created, but I can offer two suggestions that you might employ periodically before you begin your Web mockups:

Set the resolution to 96 PPI. When creating new graphics for the Web, set the resolution of the files to 96 PPI instead of 72 PPI. This tiny bump in resolution might make the Web graphic look crisper when printed without drastically increasing the size of the graphic; remember that the higher the resolution, the higher the file size, and the higher the file size, the slower the image will transmit and display on the Web. The bump in resolution may also affect the file's dimensions, so be sure to keep an eye on that, too.

Add a print media CSS. This technique presumes that you know CSS really well and have used CSS to add certain images to your page that will be printed, such as adding the image to the page as a background image to a table cell or layer. Then you'd create a second print media CSS that will replace the source (`images/sample.jpg`) of the Web graphic files with print graphic files (`images/print/sample.jpg`) when the visitor goes to print a Web page.

Because this book doesn't get into that level of detail with CSS, I highly recommend you begin your journey to learning more about advanced CSS techniques by reading Eric Meyer's article on *CSS Design: Going to Print* at `www.alistapart.com/stories/goingtoprint`.

Unit of measure

Print graphics can be measured in any unit you desire, though the most popular units for graphic designers tend to be inches, points, or picas. The unit you select to work in will determine the size of the image when printed. By contrast, everything on the Web is measured in pixels. For instance, instead of saying, "move that logo about a quarter inch to the right," you'd probably say something like, "move the logo 37 pixels to the right."

File and page size

The size of a graphic file is largely dependent on the DPI or PPI settings and the size of the image in inches or pixels. For example, a file set to 500 x 400 pixels at 72 PPI might only be around 6 x 5 inches in print size with a 585.9K file size, but an image set to 7 x 5 inches at 300 DPI might have a pixel dimension of 2,100 x 1,500 and a 12MB file size. On the Web, file sizes should be as small as possible while retaining the best possible quality image, whereas in print, file size is somewhat irrelevant as long as the printed output is sharp and clear.

Information Kiosk

If you're used to working in print, the only thing you really need to do differently for your graphics for the Web is to pay attention to the document settings whenever you create a new file. If you're new to both Web and print, as long as you select the appropriate color mode, resolution, file dimensions, and unit of measure in your new documents before you begin designing, you'll do just fine.

Selecting a Web Optimization Program

Regardless of which application(s) you choose to create your Web graphics in, such as Photoshop or Illustrator, you're going to need a special program that will optimize your graphics for display on a Web site. The two most popular optimization programs are ImageReady, which comes bundled with Photoshop when purchased alone or as part of the entire Adobe CS2 Suite, and Fireworks, which was specifically designed for the creation and optimization of Web graphics.

An optimization program applies a compression method to the digital information in an image in order to produce the smallest possible file size with the best possible quality. In other words, to be suitable for the Web, a graphic must be put through a compression process that takes the original image data and condenses it in such a way that the file size gets reduced to a point where the image quality is still acceptable. The smaller the file size, the faster the image can be transmitted over the Internet and displayed on a Web page. Even when the source file is set to 72 PPI, the graphic must still be optimized for Web use.

In the simplest terms, optimization means reducing file size while trying to retain quality. During the optimization process, you can control how much compression to apply to an image. Remember, the PPI of the file is a requirement of Web graphics, but a separate issue from the optimization process. Thus, when you create a new file at 72 PPI, that doesn't mean the file is already optimized. Rather, the file is at the correct size and resolution for optimization. If you need, therefore, to create a Web graphic from a high-resolution image, you must first reduce the resolution to 72 PPI and check the pixel dimensions to ensure the size of the graphic is suitable before you optimize the graphic.

The following overview of the optimization programs available can help you decide which one will work best for your needs:

- **ImageReady:** When it comes to optimizing graphics, I use ImageReady almost exclusively because it has an interface nearly identical to Photoshop, allows for the creation of simple rollover graphics and animation, has a special 4-Up panel for comparing optimization settings before selecting one, and offers several graphic output options, including saving optimized graphics along with a tables-based HTML page that includes prewritten JavaScript code for any rollover graphics you may have created.

- **Fireworks 8:** With this program, you can design, edit, and optimize graphics all at once by using a variety of tools similar to those found in ImageReady, but I find it a little cumbersome to work in because I'm so used to Photoshop and ImageReady. Fireworks graphics, which are created and saved in the PNG format, can be sliced, optimized, and exported. Fireworks even has a preview tool that shows any cross-platform differences in color display. As with ImageReady, Fireworks users can create graphics for JavaScript rollover buttons, pop-up menus, and other interactive features that Fireworks will generate with the optimized files. Output includes

HTML, images only, or both, just like ImageReady, but because Fireworks was developed by Macromedia, it also integrates seamlessly with Dreamweaver for round-trip editing.

Other, inexpensive options: Several other less expensive and freeware Web optimization tools exist, and I encourage you to use whichever ones you think will produce the best results. For instance, you might enjoy using the free GNU Image Manipulation Program (GIMP: `www.gimp.org`) or the inexpensive Graphic Converter X (`www.lemkesoft.com/en/graphcon.htm`) application. You can also try free online tools like the JPEG Wizard (`www.jpegwizard.com`) and GIFWorks (`www.gifworks.com`).

Optimizing Graphics with ImageReady

If you use Illustrator or Photoshop, your access to ImageReady is built right into the application. The following instructions show you how you can access the ImageReady compression "engine" when saving graphics for the Web from within Photoshop or Illustrator.

1. **To save a file for the Web, choose File → Save for Web.**

This opens the Save For Web - Powered By ImageReady dialog box, shown in Figure 8-4.

Figure 8-4: Use the Save For Web - Powered By ImageReady dialog box to optimize Web graphics while working in Photoshop or Illustrator.

2. Select either the 2-Up or 4-Up tab at the top of the dialog box to view your original image side by side with one or three versions of the image with specific optimized settings.

3. Set your optimization preferences on the right side of the panel.

   You'll find detailed descriptions of all the optimization settings, including output options, in the later sections, "Choosing Web Optimization Settings" and "Optimization Output Options."

4. Click the Save button to save the graphic to the specified file and folder on your computer.

   The dialog box automatically closes as the graphic is saved.

Information Kiosk

To preview any of your optimized graphics in a browser window before you add them to a Web page or upload them to a remote server, simply drag and drop the Web graphic from the location where you saved the optimized graphics (such as your desktop or a client folder) into any open browser window. The image will appear on a white background at its full size.

If you plan to use the other optimization tools that come with ImageReady (for instance, if you want to use the application to create rollover graphics or animation), launch the ImageReady application and optimize the Web graphics from there.

To work directly in ImageReady while already working in Photoshop, do any of the following:

- Choose File → Save for Web and click the Edit in ImageReady button in the bottom-right corner of the dialog box. This option also works in Illustrator.

- Launch the ImageReady application, and from within the application, open the file you'd like to optimize.

- Click the Edit in ImageReady button at the bottom of the Photoshop Tool palette, as shown in Figure 8-5. This method keeps Photoshop open in the background but closes and then reopens the graphic in ImageReady.

As you'll learn in the next few sections, ImageReady has settings that allow users to select the output file format and control the quality of the compression.

If you're looking to improve your Photoshop skills, check out *Photoshop: The L Line* by Gary Bouton.

Click to launch ImageReady
from the Photoshop Tool palette

Figure 8-5: Launch ImageReady quickly from the bottom of the Photoshop toolbar.

Picking the Right Web Format

The most common file formats for Web graphics are GIF, JPG, and PNG.

Information Kiosk

Web files that include additional information besides graphics or different data like video, sound, or other multimedia must be compressed by other means for transmission over the Web. File formats for those types of Web objects include PDF, MP3, MPEG, Flash SWF, and Shockwave.

After you create all the photos and graphics for your Web project (at 72 DPI in RGB 8 bit), saving them in the right Web file format is easy if you follow a few basic rules that will ultimately determine the final image's quality and file size. Take a look at Figure 8-6. The simplest way to decide is based on what the image contains:

- If the image is a photo or has a lot of gradient blends in it, choose JPG.
- If the image has larger areas of flat color or text, choose GIF or PNG.

Save as JPG

Save as GIF

Figure 8-6: Save files with photographs and gradients as JPG and all others as GIF or PNG.

Watch Your Step

Many browsers currently support these three types of optimized Web graphics: GIF, JPG, and PNG. Each type uses separate compression algorithms to reduce file size. Unfortunately, however, though the PNG-compressed images look better than GIF and have smaller file sizes, only the most popular browsers, version 4 and above, support them, so most designers still stick to creating GIFs and JPGs for all their Web graphics.

Table 8-2 shows a side-by-side graphics comparison chart of the three main Web formats so you can see at a glance which will work best for you.

Table 8-2   Web Graphics Optimization Formats

GIF	JPG	PNG
256 colors (8 bit) and grayscale (8 bit)	Millions of colors (24 bit) and grayscale (8 bit)	Millions of colors (24 bit) and grayscale (8 bit)
Supports transparency	No transparency	Supports transparency
Supports animation	No animation	No animation
Good for large flat areas of color and text	Good for photographs and images with large areas of gradient blends	Good for all image types, especially useful as graphics for Word, PowerPoint, and Excel applications
Lossless LZW compression	Lossy compression	Lossless LZW compression

Here's a more detailed description of each of these formats:

GIF (Graphic Interchange Format): This format created by the folks at CompuServe is officially pronounced "jif," like the peanut butter, but it's more commonly called "giff," with a hard *g,* as in *get.* It supports a maximum palette of 256 colors and is great for images with text and large flat areas of color.

Using a special LZW (Lempel-Ziv-Welch) lossless compression algorithm to shrink the file without removing detail, the GIF format can reduce file size up to around 60 percent of the original size during optimization. Colors in a GIF image that aren't part of the 256-color palette can be dithered (two colors alternated in a grid pattern) to approximate the missing colors. For more on dithering, see the section on optimization settings later in this chapter.

GIFs support transparency, which means parts of the image can be fully opaque while other parts allow you to see through to any objects or colors behind the image on a Web page.

GIFs also support animation through a rather crude optimization technique that saves multiple images into separate frames inside a single GIF file. The images for each frame of the animation can be saved onto individual layers in Photoshop, which can then be toggled to be either visible or hidden within each frame of the animation. When viewed in a browser window, each frame of the animated GIF plays consecutively (either with or without looping at the end), giving the illusion of a little movie.

JPG (Joint Photographic Experts Group): If your image is photographic and/or contains a lot of gradient color, choose the JPG/JPEG format, pronounced "jay-peg," because this file type supports a palette with millions of colors. Not only that, but saving photos for the Web in this format will result in smaller file sizes as compared to saving a photographic image as a GIF. This is because a GIF would be forced to use dithering to create any colors beyond the 256 palette. JPGs use a compression method called *lossy* whereby some digital information in the image is removed and becomes irretrievable (lost) after the compression.

JPGs do not support transparency or animation. Should you need either or both of these features, you must save the file as a GIF and potentially suffer some loss of image quality in lieu of the gain of transparency and/or animation.

PNG (Portable Network Graphics): This file extension, pronounced "ping," was created as a royalty-free raster alternative to GIFs, TIFFs, and occasionally JPGs, combining the best features of compression algorithms, such as lossless compression, and support for millions of colors and transparency. Unfortunately, browser support for this format remains inconsistent, so most designers continue to use GIF and JPG formats for all their Web graphics.

Probably the best way to really understand how Web graphics will look when compressed by one format or another is to see for yourself what each compression algorithm does to the image during the compression process. Figure 8-7 shows what happens to a graphic with flat color and text when saved as a GIF, JPG, and PNG. Figure 8-8 shows what happens to a photographic image when saved in the same three formats.

GIF 1.42 K   JPG 1.66 K   PNG 982 Bytes

Figure 8-7: Save images with large flat areas of color and text as a GIF for best results.

GIF 37.36 K   JPG 10.31 K   PNG 50.77 K

Figure 8-8: Photographic images and files containing gradients are best saved as JPGs.

As you can see, GIF is the better choice for the graphic with flat areas of color because JPGs and PNGs tend to pixelate the flat areas, especially around the edges of letter shapes. Likewise, JPG is the better choice for the photograph because it handles gradients and shadow areas better than GIF and PNG formats, which tend to display those areas as bands of color rather than a single smooth transition of color. PNGs are good replacements for GIFs, but if you decide to use them, pay attention to file size and be sure to test their display ability in all the browsers your target audience will be likely to use.

Choosing Web Optimization Settings

In most Web image optimization programs, you can choose from several optimization settings to create the optimized graphics to your specifications. The particular settings you select will determine several things about the output graphics, including the file format, size, number of colors, and quality.

When optimizing graphics, your main goal is to create the best quality image with the lowest possible file size. If you reduce the file size too much, the quality might suffer, and if you make the quality sharp, the file size might be too large. You must achieve a balancing point for each graphic, and you'll soon learn from experience which settings work best for different types of graphics.

Information Kiosk

One trick you can use when optimizing your graphics is to work within the 4-Up panel in ImageReady. That way, you can set each of the comparison boxes to different configurations by using options in the Preset optimization settings menu or by adjusting the controls in the optimization panel to reduce the file size. By comparing three different optimization settings side by side with the original image, you can easily select the one with the optimization settings that will create the best-quality image at the lowest possible file size.

Here are some additional optimization guidelines you should try to follow:

- **Size images as small as possible, and so that each image file does not exceed 30K, though 10K or less should be your target file size.**

- **Size images so that the download time for an entire Web page doesn't exceed 8 seconds on a 56K modem:** Even though about half of Internet users have cable, DSL, or T1 access, the other half are still visiting Web pages with 28.8 and 56K modems, which means pages will download at only about 4K per second. That's really slow. Therefore, because each image must be transferred to a visitor's computer, a 30K file will take about 7 seconds to load on a computer with a 56K modem. For a lot of visitors — especially the ones using older equipment with slower connection speeds — if the page takes longer than 8–10 seconds to load, the visitor might lose patience and leave the site before even seeing it! Unless you know for a fact that your target audience has a high-speed Internet connection, try your hardest to ensure that your pages (including HTML, images, CSS, JavaScript, and any other multimedia plug-ins or page enhancements) load within the 8- to 10-second timeframe.

Information Kiosk

To see how well your finished Web pages fare in a download speed optimization test, enter the URL of your completed Web page at www.websiteoptimization.com/services/analyze. For example, if you tested the Amazon.com Web site, the Optimization report would include a chart of download times that shows that the page takes 47.28 seconds to download on a 56K modem but only 1.65 seconds with a T1 connection. While fast enough for visitors with high-speed connections, that's kind of slow for the visitors with 56K or slower modems. At the bottom of the results page, you'll find an analysis and recommendations on how to improve the site.

GIF and PNG-8 Optimization

The following is an explanation of the optimization options you'll find in the Save For Web - Powered By ImageReady dialog box for creating GIFs and PNGs, as shown earlier in Figure 8-4. If you plan to use the ImageReady program as a standalone application, configure the optimization settings through the program's Optimize panel, as shown in Figure 8-9, which offers options similar to those in the Save For Web dialog box. When using any other optimization tools, feel free to refer to the following list when making optimization setting decisions.

Figure 8-9: The ImageReady Optimize panel has the same settings as the Save For Web - Powered By ImageReady dialog box when accessing optimization features through Photoshop and Illustrator.

Color Reduction Algorithm: The algorithm determines how the colors in the GIF file will be compressed. The algorithm is calculated by the color reduction type and the number of colors selected in the Colors field.

- **Adaptive:** Produces a color palette in the image by sampling colors from the image itself. By reducing the number of colors in the palette, the reduction algorithm produces a file with a smaller size.

- **Selective:** Produces a color palette like the Perceptual palette while preserving any Web-safe colors in the image and using only colors found in the graphic. This is the default option for GIF compression and tends to produce the most realistic color in the final output graphic.

- **Perceptual:** Produces a color palette that favors colors that the human eye is sensitive to.

Restrictive (Web): Produces a color palette in your image that favors the 216 colors in the Web-safe palette and prevents colors in the image from being dithered. This means your graphic's colors will be automatically converted to Web-safe colors. You can set the percentage of Web Snap in an adjacent slider. Unused colors will be discarded from the palette.

Lossy: A compression type that removes image data, reducing the file size by as much as 40 percent. The larger the lossy number, the more data will be removed. Typical lossy settings range between 0 and 10 with little noticeable image degradation. *Note:* You can't use this feature with Interlaced GIFs or when the Pattern or Noise Dither options are selected.

Colors: This setting allows you to change the total number of colors that will appear in the image and in the corresponding Color Table at the bottom of the panel. The maximum number of colors is 256, and the minimum is 2 (black and white). Web-safe colors in the Color Table will appear with a tiny white diamond in the center of the color square; non-Web-safe colors appear as solid color squares.

Dither: Dithering is a simulation technique whereby two colors are alternated in a checkered pattern that tricks the eye into seeing a new solid color based on the combination of the two colors used. A dithered green color, for example, could be created by tiling blue and yellow pixels together. This effect, while improving the image quality, does add to the overall file size.

Dithering is good for images with flat areas of color and for images containing gradient colors that need to be saved in GIF format because without it, the colors in the gradient tend to band out into stripes of color. This banding effect also occurs when viewing a Web page on a monitor with a resolution set to 256 colors.

The Dither option has four different settings:

No Dither: No dither will be applied to the image.

Diffusion: This dither type applies a more random dither pattern than the Pattern dither option. Set the percentage of the dither in the Amount field on the Optimize panel to control the amount of dithering in the image. The larger the percentage, the more dithered colors in the resulting image.

Pattern: This dither type creates dithered colors in a squarish pattern that might be more noticeable to the eye. Control the amount of dither by adjusting the dither percentage.

Noise: This dither type uses a more random pattern for the dither than Diffusion or Pattern. Set the dither percentage.

Transparency: Both the GIF and PNG formats allow you to save images containing transparent pixels. The transparent parts of the image will then appear invisible when placed on a Web page, and any underlying colors on the page (such as the page background color or a table cell or table background color) will show through those areas. The amount of transparency, on a scale of 0–100 percent, determines how many of the pixels will be transparent, semitransparent, or opaque. The transparency option has the following settings:

- **No Transparency:** In images containing transparency, any transparent and semitransparent pixels will appear as opaque or semi-opaque against the color selected in the Matte color field. For example, if the Matte color field is set to black, the transparent and semitransparent pixels in the image will appear as if they are sitting on a black background.

- **Diffusion:** This option controls the dithering pattern of semitransparent pixels. When selected, a random dither pattern is applied to semitransparent pixels.

- **Pattern:** With this option, semitransparent pixels will be dithered with the selected matte color in a square-like pattern.

- **Noise:** This option creates a more random dithering pattern than Pattern and Diffusion by blending semitransparent pixels with the selected matte color in an irregular, almost haphazard pattern.

Matte: If you know what color the image with transparency will be "sitting on" in a Web page, select a matching matte color to ensure that semitransparent pixels in the image blend smoothly with the background color. For example, if you know the background color of a page is a particular red with the hexadecimal value of #cc3333, set the matte color for your image with transparency to the same hexadecimal value for best results.

Interlaced: Selecting this option will cause the image to be downloaded in multiple passes, giving the viewer something to see as the image gets drawn in the browser window. This option is good for larger images but not so necessary for individual images under 10K.

Web Snap: The percentage number you choose here will determine how many of the colors in the color table will snap to the Web-safe palette. The higher the number, the more the colors in the resulting optimized image will be forced to snap to colors in the Web-safe palette.

JPG optimization

If you choose the Save for Web option in Photoshop and choose JPG as the file format you want to use, you'll see the following options, which differ from the GIF options:

Quality: The image quality controls the amount of compression in the resulting optimized image. You can select from five preset quality options (Low, Medium, High, Very High, and Maximum) in a drop-down menu, or you can use the Quality slider to manually shift the quality on a scale from 0 to 100 percent. The higher the percentage, the better the image quality and the larger the file size. Compare three different qualities by using the 4-Up panel to find the best quality with the lowest file size.

Progressive: Like the interlaced option for GIFs, the progressive setting creates JPG images that will display a low-resolution version of the file until the high-resolution version is finished downloading on the visitor's computer. Some older browsers might not support this feature, so be sure to test at least one progressive image in your target browsers before optimizing all your graphics with this setting.

Optimized: Select this option if you'd like the resulting image to be enhanced. Though this option may slightly reduce the image file size, optimized graphics might not display well, or at all, in some older browsers.

Blur: When images are set to use the lower-quality compression settings, you might begin to see jagged areas in the image, called *jaggies*. This is especially noticeable around the edges of contrasting colors, on flat areas of color, and on the edges of text. You can reduce these jaggies somewhat by applying a slight blur to the image. The more blur you add, the smaller the file size but the less crisp the resulting image. Therefore, if you do apply a blur, keep the setting below 0.5 for best results.

ICC Profile: Choose this option to preserve the image's ICC profile and have it embedded in the image to assist some browsers with color correction of the image. The ICC profile describes information about the graphic's RGB or CMYK color settings so that the color displays as intended.

Matte: When the original image has any areas that are blank (such as a transparent background layer), those pixels will be filled with the opaque color selected in this field. Try, if you can, to match the matte color to the background color the image will be placed on top of in the Web page. For instance, if the image will sit in a table cell with a black background, set the matte color to black before optimizing it.

Slicing Up Graphics

When I teach Photoshop and Dreamweaver classes, one of the questions I get asked constantly by students is, "How do I take my Web site mockup and turn it into optimized graphics?" Technically, because the slicing of images is really an ImageReady process and not a Photoshop or Dreamweaver technique, that skill doesn't get covered as part of the normal 18-hour class. However, as is often the case, when enough students clamor for it, I'll often stay late on the last day of class to give a quick demo of how to slice images in Photoshop before optimization in ImageReady.

Slicing graphics is a process of cutting a large rectangular image into several smaller rectangular pieces, which are then individually optimized and refitted together on a Web page, usually inside a container tag like a table cell (`<td>`) or a layer (`<div>`). Images are often sliced to help create rollover buttons and decorative graphics.

Further, when a large image is sliced, the individual pieces of the larger image will appear in a browser faster than the single large file.

Photoshop, Illustrator, Fireworks, and ImageReady all have a Slice tool that you can use to cut images into smaller pieces. The tool's icon typically looks like an Exacto blade, so it's easy to identify from the other tools on the toolbar.

To use the Slice tool in Photoshop, Illustrator, Fireworks, or ImageReady, do either of the following:

Drag and release: Select the Slice tool and drag the cursor through the image to create a rectangular marquee-like selection. When you release your mouse, the previously whole image will be sliced into pieces where you made the incision marks. For instance, if you were to drag the Slice tool to create a shape about 3 inches wide through the center of an image, when you released the tool, you'd end up with three slices, like the example shown in Figure 8-10.

Figure 8-10: Slice your image into pieces before you optimize your graphics.

Use guides to create slices: In Photoshop, Illustrator, or ImageReady, set your document to display rulers (View ➜ Rulers) so you can use guides as boundaries from which slices will be created. Drag guides from the ruler into the file to the places where you'd like the image to be sliced, as in the example shown in Figure 8-11. Use as many guides as you need to divide the larger image into smaller parts.

- **Illustrator CS2:** Choose Select ➜ Select All to select all the objects in your layout. Choose Object ➜ Slice ➜ Create from Guides.

- **Photoshop CS2:** Select the Slice tool and click the Slices from Guides button on the Options bar.

- **ImageReady CS2:** Choose Slices ➜ Create Slices from Guides.

Figure 8-11: Drag guides into your layout to assist with slicing images with precision.

If your guides create too many slices or in some places they slice your image not exactly as you intended, you can later combine slices horizontally and vertically to achieve the sliced layout you desire when you go to optimize the slices.

Now that you know what it means to slice an image, use the following steps to try slicing one so you can learn how to select the individual slices and choose all the different optimization settings you need. The following exercise uses a layout created in Photoshop that will be optimized with ImageReady. You can use a copy of the Photoshop PSD file of the Jacks Cleaning Services layout you saw in Chapter 7 by visiting this book's companion Web site or by going to www.luckychair.com/ 1-line/jacks.psd.

1. **Launch Photoshop and open the jacks.psd file found at www. luckychair.com/1-line/jacks.psd.**

   The image contains a Web layout for a cleaning service. Your job will be to add guides to the image, slice it, and optimize all the graphics.

2. **Choose View ➜ Rulers to see the rulers at the top and left edges of your open document.**

3. **The rulers should display in pixels. If your rulers are showing any other measure, such as inches or picas, right-click (Windows) or Control+click (Mac) anywhere on the top ruler and choose Pixels from the contextual menu that appears.**

4. **To create a guide, click on the top ruler, drag the cursor onto the layout to the top of the navigation bar, and then release your mouse.**

5. **Drag another guide from the top ruler to the bottom of the navigation bar.**

6. **Drag a third guide from the left ruler to the edge of the HOME button on the navigation bar.**

You could drag several additional guides onto the document to separate each of the navigation buttons. However, it might be faster to leave the entire navigation bar as it is and divide that piece into separate slices when you get into ImageReady.

In the Layers panel, notice that text layers exist for each of the navigation buttons on the navigation bar in this Photoshop file, and that each button has a special Color Overlay effect applied to it. (See Figure 8-12.) The Color Overlay effect for the Contact button is visible, as indicated by the visibility icon next to the effect name, but the effects for the remaining buttons are hidden from view.

Figure 8-12: The button text layers have Color Overlay effects that are either visible or hidden from view for the sliced image "normal" state.

Leave the effect turned off for now, but you'll access it in a later step to create an additional graphic for a rollover button when you optimize the images.

7. Launch ImageReady by clicking the Edit in ImageReady link at the bottom of the Photoshop Tool palette.

Clicking this button will open ImageReady, close the image in Photoshop while leaving Photoshop open and running in the background, and reopen the image in ImageReady.

8. Select the Slice tool and from the main menu, choose Slices → Create Slices from Guides.

ImageReady automatically slices the image into separate pieces based on the guides you added to your document. Now you'll combine a few slices and divide another.

9. With the Slice tool selected, click the slice containing the JACKS logo and Shift+click to also select the gray navbar slice and the slice below that containing the intro text.

You can tell when all three slices are selected by the yellow highlighting around the perimeter of the selected slices.

10. From the Slices menu, choose Combine Slices to join the three selected pieces into one larger slice.

You can also combine slices after selecting two or more adjacent slices by right-clicking (Windows) or Control+clicking (Mac) any of the selected slices. This pulls up the contextual menu from which you can choose the same Combine Slices option.

11. Next, you'll divide one larger slice into several smaller slices. Select the slice with the navigation buttons on it and choose Slices → Divide Slice.

This opens the Divide Slice dialog box, shown in Figure 8-13, where you can configure how the slice will be divided either horizontally, vertically, or both.

Figure 8-13: Use the settings in the Divide Slice dialog box to control how a selected slice will be carved up into smaller parts.

12. In the Divide Vertically Into area of the Divide Slice dialog box, enter 5 into the Slices Across, Evenly Spaced text box and click the OK button.

The slice should now have five vertical slice dividers, highlighted in yellow to indicate they're still selected. When the yellow highlights are showing, you can resize the divisions between the slices with the Slice tool.

13. Click the rightmost yellow divider line and drag it to the right just after the vertical black line dividing the button for CONTACT on the navigation bar. Then release your mouse button.

This is how you can resize the division between slices; as long as two adjacent slices are selected, you can resize the boundary between those two slices regardless of any previously drawn guides. When several slices (or all the slices) are selected, you can adjust any of the boundaries, including the entire horizontal or vertical division between a group of slices.

14. Continue adjusting the yellow dividers between each button so that each button will be its own graphic slice. If you accidentally deselect any of the slices, Shift+click the slice(s) to reselect them.

The next thing to do is to assign rollover functionality to each of the buttons. This involves the Layers panel and the Web panel in ImageReady. If the Web Content panel isn't visible, choose Window → Web Content to open it.

15. With the Slice tool, select the navigation button slice in your document that contains the word CONTACT. Then look to the Layers panel to find the corresponding text layer.

If the text layer's effects are collapsed, hiding the effects assigned to it, click the black expander arrow to the right of the T thumbnail on that text layer to expand the layer and reveal the Color Overlay effect.

16. In the Web Content panel, click the Options menu in the top-right corner and choose New Rollover State.

This creates a rollover state layer in the Web Content panel, which you can alter by adjusting the visibility effect to support the look of the graphic for the rollover state.

17. On the Layers panel, click the visibility icon box to the left of the hidden Color Overlay effect, which places a visibility eye icon next to the effect, thereby revealing the effect on the Rollover State layer in the Web Content panel.

Congratulations! You've just created a graphic effect that will be saved as a separate overstate graphic when you optimize your file.

18. For a challenge, select each of the remaining button slices and repeat Steps 16 and 17 to create rollover states for each button graphic.

Next, you'll select optimization settings for each of the slices. You can either select each slice and set optimization preferences for them one at a time or select all the slices in the file to make global slice optimization settings.

19. To select all the slices in the file, choose Slices ➔ Select All User Slices.

20. Using the Optimize panel, choose the preset called GIF 128 No Dither.

To fine-tune any of the other settings, expand the different sections of the Optimize panel and make the changes desired. For example, if you wanted to create interlaced GIFs, you would expand the Options section of the Optimize panel and select the Interlaced check box.

21. Choose File ➔ Save to save your work up to this point, before optimization.

22. Choose File ➔ Save Optimized As to open the Save Optimized As dialog box.

You'll use this dialog box to select your output options. If you'd like to see 2-Up or 4-Up comparisons, as you would when accessing the Powered By dialog box in Photoshop or Illustrator, click the 2-Up or 4-Up tab at the top of your document window. If you need more space to view the different optimization settings, expand the size of the document window by clicking and dragging the bottom-right corner.

23. Enter the following settings in the Save Optimized As dialog box and click OK:

- Save As: test.html
- Location: Desktop
- Format: HTML and Images
- Settings: Default Settings
- Slices: All Slices under Slices

ImageReady will automatically generate an HTML file containing all the images you just sliced and optimized, and put all the images, including any rollover graphics, into a folder called images. To learn more about the individual options in this dialog box, see the next section on "Optimization Output Options."

To view the sample HTML page (`test.html`) that ImageReady just created as part of the optimization process, double-click the HTML file to launch a browser window or drag and drop the file into any open browser window. Mouse over the CONTACT navigation button to see the rollover effect!

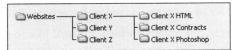

Figure 8-14: Use a uniform naming and filing convention like this to help keep track of all your projects and project files.

Optimization Output Options

Every optimization program is bound to have slightly different options when it comes to choosing what files and file formats to use for the output of your optimized graphics. The following settings are for ImageReady, whether you're using the application itself or the Powered By dialog box through Photoshop or Illustrator:

1. **Before you begin, whether you have a single unsliced graphic (which ImageReady treats as a single slice) or a file containing several slices, be sure to select all the slices you would like to optimize. If you want to optimize all the slices in a file, choose Slices → Select All User Slices. Otherwise, use the Slice tool and click and Shift+click to select only the graphics you want to save.**

2. **To access the optimization output options in the Save Optimized As dialog box, shown in Figure 8-15, choose one of the following options:**

   - From within the Save For Web - Powered By ImageReady dialog box, click the Save button.

   - From within ImageReady, choose File → Save Optimized As.

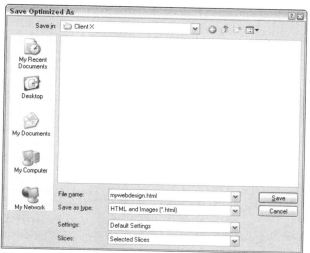

Figure 8-15: Choose a file type and format for your optimized graphic output.

3. In the File Name box, enter the name of the HTML file you'd like to save with the output.

The filename can be anything you want as long as it ends with the appropriate .html or .htm file extension, such as testpage.html or clientxyz.htm.

4. In the Save In drop-down list, choose a location on your local computer or network where the optimized files will be saved.

This can be your desktop or a folder on the computer where you intend to build the project's Web site.

5. In the Save As Type drop-down list, choose to save HTML and Images.

Other options include saving Images only or saving HTML only. Choosing HTML and Images will result in a sample Web page with JavaScript for any rollover buttons or animations, and all the optimized graphics saved to one images folder.

6. In the Settings drop-down list, choose Default Settings.

The settings determine specific information about the output, such as whether the output contains Meta data and what letter case (upper or lower) the output HTML code is written in. Unless using the default settings, you may customize options for Custom, Background Image, XHTML, and Other. Consult the ImageReady Help files to learn more about each of these settings.

7. If your optimized image contains more than one slice, from the Slices drop-down menu, choose whether to optimize All Slices, All User Slices, or only Selected Slices from this menu.

When in doubt, choose All Slices; you can always discard any unused optimized graphics later.

8. **After you've made all your choices, you can click the Save button to complete the Optimization output process.**

   The output files will be saved on your computer in the location specified in the Save In drop-down menu.

To view the HTML page containing the optimized graphics in a browser window before uploading the file to a Web server, double-click the HTML file or drag and drop the file into any open browser window.

dithered: Dithering occurs when two colors are alternately tiled in such a way that the eye is fooled into seeing a new solid color based on the combination of the two colors.

gamut: A range of colors that can be reproduced by any device, such as a color monitor or printer.

lossless: A type of compression algorithm for GIFs and PNGs that will shrink the file without removing detail.

lossy: A type of compression algorithm for JPGs with smaller file sizes, where the digital information in the image is removed and becomes irretrievable (lost) after the compression.

optimization: The process that converts a graphic into a format acceptable for viewing on the Web. Optimized graphics are smaller in file size than un-optimized graphics. For best results, the source file being optimized for the Web should be set to an RGB color mode with a resolution of 72 PPI.

out of gamut: When a color selected for on-screen display cannot be reproduced with color inks for print, that color is referred to as *out of gamut*. Likewise, any color that is not part of the Web-safe palette may be called out of gamut for the Web.

slicing: The process of cutting up a large graphic into smaller rectangular pieces prior to optimization, and the process of cutting up smaller graphics for the purposes of creating rollover effects. The sliced image can be reassembled on a Web page, usually within the confines of a table.

transparency: The blank areas in a graphic that will remain invisible in images optimized as GIFs and PNGs but will revert to the selected Matte color in images optimized as JPGs.

Last Stop

Practice Exam

1. True or False: GIF, JPG, and PNG files can be used for Web graphics and will display on a Web page in any version of any Web browser.

2. When setting up new graphic files, choose the _____ color mode for all your Web projects and _____ for all your print projects.

3. Name two acceptable file formats for Web graphics and two for print graphics.

   _____

4. Describe at least three ways Web graphics differ from print graphics.

   _____

   _____

5. If you need to create a logo for a Web page, would it be better to create the logo in a vector or raster program? Why?

   _____

   _____

6. What does it mean when a color you select for your artwork has a print color gamut warning icon next to it?

   _____

   _____

7. If you have a graphic that contains text, a gradient, and a swatch of transparent pixels, which file format would you use to get the best possible image and preserve the file's transparency?

   _____

   _____

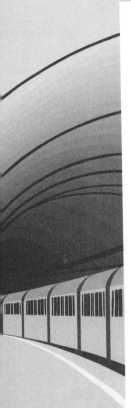

8. Name at least two goals you should try to meet when optimizing Web graphics.

_____

_____

9. Select the option to complete this sentence: The _____ the file size, the _____ the image can be transmitted over the Internet and displayed on a Web page.

A) Faster, bigger

B) Smaller, faster

C) Bigger, faster

D) Smaller, slower

10. What does dithering mean?

_____

_____

_____

_____

EXIT

Working with Web Standards (HTML/XHTML/ CSS/508)

STATIONS ALONG THE WAY

O Following the guidelines set by online Web standards organizations

O Visiting the World Wide Web Consortium online to learn about Web standards

O Adding a DOCTYPE to a Web page

O Understanding the differences between HTML and XHTML code

O Identifying ways CSS is better than HTML tags for styling Web pages

O Writing Section 508 Accessible code for visitors with disabilities

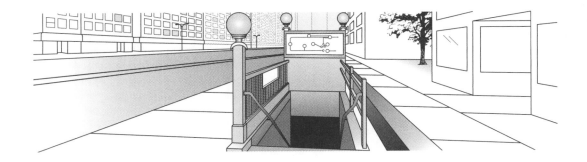

 # Enter the Station

Questions

1. What kinds of Web organizations exist to help create Web standards?

2. Why do standards for creating Web pages exist?

3. What are DTDs and why should designers use them in HTML code?

4. When should a page be written in XHTML instead of HTML?

5. What are the benefits of using CSS instead of HTML tags to style Web pages?

6. What are accessibility standards and how can you use them to improve a Web site?

Express Line

If you're already up to date on Web standards and eager to learn about using search engine optimization techniques, skip ahead to Chapter 10.

Web standards are an important part of the Web that every designer needs to understand and use. The standards generally focus on how a Web page works under the hood, but they can also have some important implications for a site's design. Most importantly, these standards help ensure that anyone or any device (such as a screen reader or search engine robot) using the Web — regardless of their browser or operating system — can view the content on a Web page.

Dreamweaver and GoLive do a respectable job of coding (particularly when certain preferences are set within the applications). However, it's up to the designer — especially if the designer intends to hand-code or use HTML coding programs like HomeSite and BBEdit — to ensure that the code is written in correct, valid, semantic HTML (code that uses tags to accurately define contents, such as <li> tags for list items) that follows the recommendations of the World Wide Web Consortium (W3C), the organization that helps develop these standards.

In addition to interoperability, designing Web sites that follow Web standards makes them easier to maintain and thus an even more cost-effective method for communicating with site visitors. The more all software and hardware manufacturers comply with these "W3C Recommendations," the better visitors' Web experiences can be. But that also means that as a designer or Web site builder, you need to do your part to follow the recommendations when writing the code for your pages.

In this chapter, you'll learn about the W3C and some of the goals it sets forth for Web design. You'll also find an introduction to following some of these standards, including using DOCTYPEs, styling page content with CSS instead of HTML tags, and writing valid semantic HTML and XHTML code. In addition to the standards that keep pages accessible and running smoothly across the Web, the federal government outlines standards for making Web pages accessible to people with disabilities. At the end of the chapter, you'll find a discussion about accessibility issues and how the federal government's Section 508 amendment to the Rehabilitation Act affects the way content should be coded in documents for the Web.

Following Web Standards

When the Web was a toddler (it was developed by Tim Berners-Lee at the European Organization for Nuclear Research [CERN] in 1989), it was much like the wild west. Anyone who was willing to take the time to explore its uncharted territories was welcome to do so, making up coding and presentation rules along the way to exist in the then largely unknown Internet world. Although this type of exploration lent itself to some amazing expressions of unbridled creativity, it also created an environment that had little in the way of standards, which meant that visitors to such Web sites wouldn't know what to expect upon arrival. Because there were no rules to follow, Web site navigation took on any and every form, making many Internet users feel frustrated and confused as to how they should go about finding the information they sought.

To be sure, the Internet was primarily a place for sharing information and not really a place for commerce or artistic expression. Yet as more and more businesses began using the Web space for advertising, the need for Web standards grew dramatically. This was especially true in the first few years of e-advertising and e-commerce, when the technically minded yet creatively challenged were the ones building all the early Web sites.

Fortunately for creative types, the Internet boom of the late '90s meant that designers, artists, and free-thinking Bohemian youth had a slew of new jobs to move into for which the main requirements were hard work, dedication, and out-of-the-box thinking to find new solutions to new problems. That's when chief information officers, site architects, webmasters, programmers, and Web designers were born and began making tons of money and sharing ideas that really worked.

Then, in 1994, Tim Berners-Lee founded the World Wide Web Consortium (W3C) as an international vendor-neutral group dedicated to bringing standards to the Web so that any software and any hardware could access the Web. The W3C's mission is "to lead the World Wide Web to its full potential by developing protocols and guidelines that ensure long-term growth for the Web." Since its founding, the W3C has published nearly 100 "W3C Recommendations" for Web standards, including the following:

- **The conformity to uniform methods of coding HTML and XHTML:** XHTML is an enhanced version of HTML with stricter coding rules that improve the accessibility of pages across browsers, operating systems, and other devices accessing the Internet.

- **The inclusion of DOCTYPEs in Web code:** This allows a browser to interpret a Web page as an application in the XML programming language. As a standard, this is important because XML allows programmers to create their own proprietary markup languages through which even more information can be exchanged on the Web. You'll find details about adding DOCTYPEs later in this chapter.

- **The use of Cascading Style Sheets to style markup:** As you'll find out later in this chapter, using CSS has a number of benefits.

 Transfer

Chapter 12 covers working with CSS in detail. In that chapter, you'll find an introduction to working with CSS from a Web standards perspective.

Learning about standards online

Today, the W3C Web site is the primary source for finding the latest information about anything Web related, from CSS to document formats to browser compatibility to graphics and many more complex issues that most designers have never even heard of!

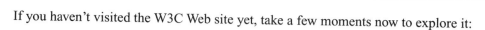

If you haven't visited the W3C Web site yet, take a few moments now to explore it:

1. **Point your browser to `www.w3.org`.**

2. **On the left side of the screen, under W3C A to Z, scroll down to and click the link for XHTML.**

   Your browser will jump to the new "MarkUp" page, which outlines all the HTML and XHTML resources on this site.

3. **To learn more about XHTML specifications, click the link called** specs (XHTML, HTML4, ...) **below the introductory paragraph near the top of the page.**

   Here you'll find a great explanation of XHTML 1.0 and a description of the three types of XHTML DTDs.

4. **Click your browser's Back button to return to the W3C home page.**

   You might need to click the Back button twice to get the browser to go back because the link you clicked in the last step might be counted by some browsers as a directional instruction.

5. **To learn more about how the W3C site is structured, click the New Visitors link at the top of the page.**

   This site contains a lot of information, which for some can be overwhelming. However, with an understanding of where to find the data you are seeking, the site will become much more useful to you.

6. **Click the Recommendations link in item #2 under the heading, "How is the W3C Web site organized?"**

   The Recommendations page lists all the W3C's recommended Web standards. New standards are added regularly as each new standard is approved.

7. **When you need to find information about a particular topic, return to the W3C home page and use the Google W3C Search feature on the right side of the page. To test the search feature, type** DTD **and click Go.**

   The search results will list pages on the W3C Web site that include the term *DTD*. For example, if you click the first link, titled HTML 4 Document Type Definition, you will find a page that defines what a DTD is and how it should be used in HTML files.

Spend time learning about the standards so you can learn how to build better Web sites. In addition to the W3C, several other organizations exist to provide recommendations for following standards on the Web, to fight for consistency and accessibility, and to offer suggestions and resources for compliance. In your browser, bookmark the URLs in Table 9-1 so that you can quickly return to them any time you have a question about Web standards and accessibility.

Table 9-1   **Web Standards Resources**

Resource	Web Address
W3C	www.w3.org
The Web Standards Project	www.webstandards.org
The Web Standards Group	www.webstandardsgroup.org
The Disability Rights Commission	www.drc-gb.org
Section 508	www.section508.gov
Web Accessibility In Mind	www.webaim.org

Most of these organizations have a bold commitment to creating standards that set precedents for structural markup languages (like HTML and XHTML), presentation languages (like CSS), scripting languages (like JavaScript), object models, and other additional markup languages, such as MathML and SVG.

Information Kiosk

As a point of pride, some site developers who take care to conform to the current standards will mention somewhere on their site (usually in the footer) that the site complies with the standards, like this one on HappyCog.com, a design, consulting, and publishing Web site, which shows by way of hypertext links that the site conforms to XHTML, CSS, and 508 standards:

Copyright © 1995–2006 Happy Cog™ Active ingredients: XHTML 1.0, CSS2, 508

Watch Your Step

Although this chapter offers an introduction to Web standards, you'll need to spend time on your own to research these standards in more depth. And although I've stated this already, it's worth repeating, because without an understanding of the problems and challenges that others have faced with code compliance, you can't truly understand your own responsibilities to conform with the new standards.

Layering Web site content

As far as other Web standards go, try your best to follow the latest recommendations. For example, in a presentation by Joseph Lindsay at the 2005 GOVIS Conference on Semantic HTML (courtesy of ERMA New Zealand, © Crown Copyright), he states that Web pages should be made up of layers, whereby each layer handles a different

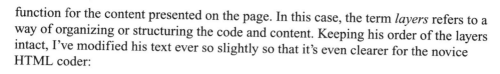

function for the content presented on the page. In this case, the term *layers* refers to a way of organizing or structuring the code and content. Keeping his order of the layers intact, I've modified his text ever so slightly so that it's even clearer for the novice HTML coder:

1. **Content:** The text, graphics, multimedia that appears in the body of the page
2. **Code semantics:** The tags, such as `<h1>`, `<ol>`, and `<p>`, that are used appropriately to match the content between them
3. **Code structure:** The page architecture that includes such tags as `<head>`, `<body>`, and `<div>`
4. **Content presentation:** Exclusively using CSS to style and position page content instead of the old font tags
5. **Behavior:** Adding interactive features to a page through the use of JavaScript and other programming

Watch Your Step

This layering concept, which can be seen as steps to follow when creating Web pages, might seem obvious and logical to anyone reading it for the first time, even for designers with a little HTML experience, but if you have a few years of coding under your belt, please agree only after examining and truly understanding what following these guidelines implies for your coding, because you might need to alter the way you've been coding Web pages to comply with them.

The preceding steps are very specific and propose that content is separated from presentation with CSS, that tags are used appropriately and accurately, and that the structure of the page is such that the page will still read logically without the CSS. If you learn the right way to do things, you'll be fine, but if you already know a way of coding that differs from these recommendations, you'll have to unlearn your old habits. That in itself won't be too difficult to do, but it will take a little extra care on your part.

Actually, if you use the order of the layers as a set of steps to follow when writing the code to build your Web pages, you might find that this new recommended way works even better than you've ever coded before:

1. **Get your content on the page.**
2. **Mark it up with the proper semantic HTML.**
3. **Ensure the structure is accurate and add `<div>` tags where needed.**
4. **Add CSS to style the presentation.**
5. **Add any JavaScript or other programming to create page interactivity.**

Remember this: The more you know about Web standards, the better you can create sites that conform to the standards, and the more likely you'll be perceived as an expert worthy of hiring for future Web projects.

Using DOCTYPEs (DTDs)

DOCTYPEs, although not necessarily new inventions (they've been around since about 1999), are only recently getting the kind of respect and attention they were intended to have. A DOCTYPE, also often referred to as a Document Type Definition (DTD) and sometimes called a Document Type Declaration (again, DTD), is a set of instructions to a browser that identifies the type of code that the page was written in as HTML, XHTML, or Frames. More importantly, a DOCTYPE informs the browser how the document should be interpreted as an application of the XML programming language.

Information Kiosk

Frames refers to a Web page presentation technique that uses `<frameset>` tags instead of `<body>` tags to make two or more pages display in a single browser window. This technique was frequently used in the early days of the Internet, when download times were slow, to help display new information faster. With the advent of broadband and faster connections, however, separating content into frames inside a browser window is no longer necessary. Designers today rarely, if ever, use frames for entire Web sites, but on occasion still use them to present data in certain sections or pages of a site. Framesets can be created with either HTML or XHTML code syntax and require the specification of an appropriate Frameset DTD to correctly display frame content in a browser.

By using a DTD on all your Web pages, you can improve the accessibility of your Web site to both human and non-human visitors alike while ensuring that your page code is valid.

Setting the DOCTYPE

The DOCTYPE itself is a line of code that gets added to each Web page, directly above the opening HTML tag (or opening XHTML tag in an XHTML file). The DOCTYPE associates an XML or SGML file with a DTD. Here's an example of the most common DTD, shown as it might typically be used in an HTML file:

```
<!DOCTYPE html PUBLIC "-//W3C//DTD HTML 4.01
Transitional//EN"
    "http://www.w3.org/TR/html4/loose.dtd">
<html>
<head>
<title>My Page Title</title>
</head>
```

```
<body>
Page content goes here
</body>
</html>
```

Each DTD is composed of two parts:

- The first half matches the DTD type to the type of code used in the Web document, such as this one, which identifies that the file is written in HTML 4.01 transitional code:

```
<!DOCTYPE html PUBLIC "-//W3C//DTD HTML 4.01
Transitional//EN"
```

- The other half of the DTD specifies the URL of a Web-accessible text file that contains more information about that DTD's usage:

```
"http://www.w3.org/TR/html4/loose.dtd">
```

The W3C recommends that all HTML, XHTML, and Frameset Web pages include a DOCTYPE specifying a DTD. The DTD identifies the type of code being used in the document so a Web browser knows how to interpret or process the information in the code and display the content on the page a little faster.

HTML DOCTYPEs

You can use three types of DTDs for HTML 4.01 on your pages. Use this first one for most, if not all, of your pages because it tells browsers to use the most accurate, standards-compliant page rendering. Keep in mind, however, that it does require that the HTML contain no coding errors or deprecated tags:

```
<!DOCTYPE html PUBLIC "-//W3C//DTD HTML 4.01//EN"
    "http://www.w3.org/TR/html4/strict.dtd">
```

This one is for pages that might contain legacy code, deprecated tags, and/or some minor coding mistakes, such as improper tag nesting, which don't or can't comply with strict DTD guidelines. The transitional loose setting tells browsers to be forgiving of any out-of-date tags and common code blunders:

```
<!DOCTYPE html PUBLIC "-//W3C//DTD HTML 4.01
Transitional//EN"
    "http://www.w3.org/TR/html4/loose.dtd">
```

And this last one is for pages using frameset tags to display two or more pages within a single browser window:

```
<!DOCTYPE html PUBLIC "-//W3C//DTD HTML 4.01 Frameset//EN"
    "http://www.w3.org/TR/html4/frameset.dtd">
```

XHTML DOCTYPEs

You have three kinds of DTDs for XHTML 1.0. Use this first one for most or all of your XHTML files that use CSS for page content presentation:

```
<!DOCTYPE html PUBLIC "-//W3C//DTD XHTML 1.0 Strict//EN"
    "http://www.w3.org/TR/xhtml1/DTD/xhtml1-strict.dtd">
```

This one, like its HTML counterpart, is for XHTML files that might still contain styling and presentation code within the file as well as certain tags and attributes that the strict DTD disallows:

```
<!DOCTYPE html PUBLIC "-//W3C//DTD XHTML 1.0
Transitional//EN"
    "http://www.w3.org/TR/xhtml1/DTD/xhtml1-transitional.
dtd">
```

And this last one is for frameset pages that use XHTML syntax rules:

```
<!DOCTYPE html PUBLIC "-//W3C//DTD XHTML 1.0 Frameset//EN"
    "http://www.w3.org/TR/xhtml1/DTD/xhtml1-frameset.dtd">
```

In addition to these DTDs, there's another for strict XHTML 1.1 and another for XHTML Mobile 1.0:

```
<!DOCTYPE html PUBLIC "-//W3C//DTD XHTML 1.1//EN"
"http://www.w3.org/TR/xhtml11/DTD/xhtml11.dtd"><html
xmlns="http://www.w3.org/1999/xhtml">
```

```
<!DOCTYPE html PUBLIC "-//WAPFORUM//DTD XHTML Mobile
1.0//EN" "http://www.wapforum.org/DTD/xhtml-mobile10.dtd">
<html xmlns="http://www.w3.org/1999/xhtml">
```

Information Kiosk

Strict XHTML 1.1 is a newer version of XHTML 1.0 Strict based upon the modularization of XHTML. Mobile 1.0 XHTML is a DTD used to describe code that's been developed for wireless display. Choose this form only if you're developing Web page content for wireless mobile devices.

Besides helping the browser recognize the code and parse it more quickly, when a DOCTYPE is specified in the head of an (X)HTML file, the file's code can be tested for accuracy by using an online markup validator like the one at http:// validator.w3.org. (You'll learn more about validation in Chapter 19.)

Adding a DOCTYPE in Dreamweaver

Web designers who use Dreamweaver can have the application automatically insert the right DTD appropriately into the code by choosing which DOCTYPE and DTD to use when creating new documents. After the DTD is specified, Dreamweaver will write DTD-specific code. For example, if you choose to build pages by using the XHTML 1.0 transitional DTD, Dreamweaver's code editor will automatically write XHTML-compliant code.

To select the appropriate DTD for your new documents in Dreamweaver, follow these instructions:

1. **Launch Dreamweaver and choose File → New to open the New Document dialog box shown in Figure 9-1.**

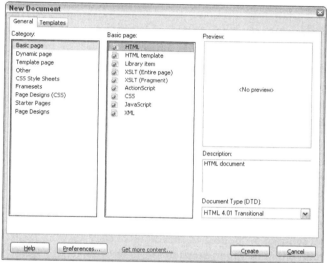

Figure 9-1: Use Dreamweaver's New Document dialog box to select the code and DTD type you'd like to work with.

2. **On the General tab, select Basic Page from the Category column and select HTML from the Basic Page column.**

   This will tell Dreamweaver to write and code a page with basic HTML.

3. **Use the Document Type (DTD) menu in the lower right to select a DOCTYPE.**

   Options in Dreamweaver 8 include HTML 4.01 Transitional, HTML 4.01 Strict, XHTML 1.0 Transitional, XHTML 1.0 Strict, XHTML 1.1, and XHTML Mobile. *Note:* The Frames HTML or Frames XHTML DTD will be automatically inserted into the page code when frames are used.

4. **Click the Create button to open the new page in the Dreamweaver workspace.**

   If you check the code in Code view, you will see the DTD at the top of the page, above the opening HTML tag.

Information Kiosk

Dreamweaver MX 2004 users can have a DTD inserted automatically in their pages but won't have as much control over which DTD gets added to a new page; the default HTML DTD is HTML 4.01 Transitional, and the default XHTML DTD is XHTML 1.0 Transitional. If you want any other DTD, you'll have to hand-code it into the document. Older versions of Dreamweaver, including MX and earlier, either didn't include the DTD at all or coded in only part of it automatically. If you're still using an old version of Dreamweaver, be sure to hand-code the appropriate DTD into your pages or upgrade your software to the latest version of Dreamweaver.

Writing HTML and XHTML Code

When you go to code your pages, regardless of whether you're using a code or WYSIWYG editor, the application you're using is probably writing code that conforms to HTML 4.01 standards, whether you realize it or not. With the advent of CSS, however, some older HTML tags have been deprecated (phased out) while some new HTML rules have been established, which means that if you're doing any hand-coding at all, with or without the help of an editor, you'll need to know the rules governing HTML 4.01 (and the rules of XHTML 1.0) to write valid semantic (X)HTML.

You can learn a lot about HTML from online tutorials, such as those found at W3Schools and WebMonkey, but you might find it even more useful to purchase a book on HTML. You'll find several titles available at www.wiley.com.

If you're not yet familiar with the differences between HTML and XHTML and you're wondering which markup language to use for your Web pages, you might want to start coding your projects with HTML and advance to XHTML when you feel confident about the structure and usage of HTML and what the differences are between the two. After you master using HTML, you can easily transition to XHTML code. Alternatively, you may choose to jump right into the world of XHTML right from the start, and that would be just as good.

The benefit of starting with HTML is that some tags and attributes are backward compatible with many older browsers, whereas XHTML isn't supported in part or in full by many of the older browsers. Programs like Dreamweaver and GoLive will code properly syntaxed semantic HTML and XHTML, but the programs aren't human, and you'll need to intervene occasionally to ensure that the code is properly formatted and remains that way any time you make alterations to your code by hand or need to make adjustments to the code for special code hacks and workarounds.

Table 9-2 shows a side-by-side comparison of writing HTML versus XHTML code. Review the rules for both and then use the markup that best meets your needs.

Table 9-2   HTML and XHTML Markup Comparison

HTML	XHTML

Code structure must be ordered correctly, but forgotten tags may be forgiven and cause a page to fail acceptably, such as forgetting to close the `<title>` or `<head>` tag. Failing in this context refers to how browsers interpret incorrect code and display the page, which in practice might look fine (failing acceptably) or terrible (failing unacceptably).	All code elements must be closed and placed in the proper location hierarchically within the opening and closing `<html>` tags, as in
	
	`<html>`
	`<head>...</head>`
	`<body>...</body>`
	`</html>`

HTML files should have, but aren't required to have, a DOCTYPE declaration.	All XHTML files must include a DOCTYPE declaration above the opening `<html>` tag, as in
	
	`<!DOCTYPE html`
	`PUBLIC "-//W3C//DTD XHTML 1.0`
	`Transitional//EN"`
	`"http://www.w3.org/TR/xhtml1/`
	`DTD/xhtml1-transitional.dtd">`
	`<head>`
	`  <title>Add your title`
	`here</title>`
	`</head>`
	`<body>`
	`...`
	`</body>`
	`</html>`

Tags can be written in upper- or lower-case, but lowercase is preferred, such as `<title>` instead of `<TITLE>`.	Tags must be written in lowercase, as in `<head>`, `<body>`, and `<p>`.
HTML cannot incorporate XML markup.	XHTML takes advantage of XML.
Tags and objects can be improperly nested with little consequence, so that `<b><i>cat</b></i>` would still be displayed in bold and italics.	Tags and objects must be properly nested, so `<strong><em>cat</strong></em>` would be incorrect, and `<strong><em>cat</em></strong>` would be correct.
Tags needn't always have closing tag elements, as with the `<p>`, `<hr>`, and ` ` tags.	All tags and objects must be properly closed. Tags that didn't typically need to be closed in HTML should now be closed by placing a space and backslash inside the tag, as in ` `, `<hr />`, and `<img />`. All other tags, such as `<p>` and `<li>`, must also be properly closed.

continued

Table 9-2 *continued*

HTML	XHTML
Values inside attributes of tags can be written either with or without quotes.	Values inside attributes of tags must be written inside quotes, as in `<div align="center">` and `<td width="145">`.
Attributes can use shorthand to minimize the code that needs to be written when the value matches the desired option, as with `<input disabled>`.	Attributes can no longer use shorthand and must now use the full syntax of the HTML code, as with `<input disabled="disabled" />`.
Objects use the name attribute, as in `<img src="becky.jpg" name="becky">`.	Objects must now use the id attribute instead of name, as in `<img src="becky.jpg" id="becky">`. During the transition from HTML to XHTML, consider using both `name` and `id` attributes so older browsers can still properly interpret and display HTML data, as in `<img src="becky.gif" id="becky" name="becky" />`.

Although XHTML appears to follow a much stricter set of rules than HTML, it's the current recommended standard for the Web and has many benefits that HTML lacks. For instance, because of all its standards, some say XHTML is easier to learn than HTML. Not only that, but it's easier to keep up and make changes to, and it's both XML- and XSL-ready. (XSL [eXtensible Stylesheet Language] is similar to CSS, but is used exclusively to define the presentation of content in XML files in a browser.)

Transfer

After your pages are coded, test the code for compliance to the W3C Recommended standards. You'll read more about code compliance and validation tools in Chapter 19. For now, as long as you tell your HTML editor to code in the desired markup language and pay attention to syntactical rules while making any code adjustments by hand, you should be able to code your pages properly, whether you choose to write in HTML or XHTML.

Using CSS Instead of HTML

Although you can format your text in HTML, the standards-compliant way is to format your pages using CSS. When you use CSS, you can define site-wide styles for the tags used to mark up your content and create custom tags to selectively style page elements, whereas in HTML, you have to apply a tag for every bit of formatting to every chunk of text or other content that requires the desired formatting.

Though you'll learn how to add formatting to your content with CSS in Chapter 12, I introduce you to the concept of styling with CSS (instead of using the old HTML font and other tags) here first, in the context of a chapter dedicated to following Web standards.

Because you might not be familiar with the old way of styling pages with HTML, let me give you an illustration of what it used to look like. When using the old font tags, each line or paragraph or block of text needed to be surrounded by <font> tags containing styling information about the font's face, size, and color:

```
<p align="center"><font color="#3e3d2d" size="1"
face="Verdana, Arial, Helvetica, sans-serif"><a
href="map.html"><i>If you're having trouble viewing this
page, click here</i></a></font></p>
```

Notice how much room the font tag and center alignment in the <p> tag take up, relative to the amount of content? Each character and space takes up a fraction of a byte in file size, and when you add it up, all the styling markup can dramatically increase the size of an HTML file, causing it to load slower in a browser window.

Now look at the code when styled using CSS where the <p> tag style is redefined in the CSS:

```
<div align="center"><p><a href="map.html"><em>If you're
having trouble viewing this page, click here</em></a>
</p></div>
```

Much simpler code. The alignment is now placed inside a wrapping <div> tag for more consistent rendering in different browsers, the old <i> tag gets replaced with new <em> tags, and the entire line of font styling is replaced automatically by the redefined style for <p> as described in the external CSS.

The benefits of styling your content with CSS are vast:

- **CSS is one of the W3C's core recommendations, so your site will comply with the current standards.** Furthermore, most HTML formatting tags are being deprecated by older browsers and aren't supported in XHTML code.

- **CSS helps separate form (how the page looks) from content (what's on the page) by moving all the page styling instructions into a centralized location.** That location can either be inline with the code, internal in the head area of the Web page, or on an external CSS document to which all the pages on a site are linked, the latter being the most useful method for working with CSS. The benefit of having an entire site's style information contained in a single external CSS file is that doing so allows for instant site-wide style updates.

- **CSS makes HTML pages smaller in file size, thereby speeding up page download times.**

- **CSS styles content semantically, so it requires fewer styles than the old HTML formatting tags.** For example, CSS allows designers to redefine the presentation of content contained inside particular tags, such as automatically adding a particular color and font face to any content marked up with H3 tags or applying the same background color and border attributes to any tables on the site.

- **CSS can be used to style the look of text, images, and objects as well as the positioning of objects on a Web page.** This feature alone drastically reduces the amount of code required to display objects on a page. For instance, objects contained in <div> tags can be absolutely positioned on a page with CSS. Before, to place something in an exact spot on a page required code hacks involving the use of tables with empty table cells and spacer gifs. All that code goes away with CSS.

- **CSS is infinitely editable,** meaning you can change the look of the page as often as you like without ever altering the content.

- **CSS is a more affordable solution for styling content because it takes less time to implement and update than the older styling techniques did.** With the old way, even simple changes might require the hand-editing of all the individual pages on a site. With CSS, one change there can update a style on a whole site.

- **CSS is easy to use and easy to learn.**

Step into the Real World

Retro-Formatting HTML E-Mails   Yes, CSS is better for formatting Web pages, but when it comes to formatting HTML e-mails, it's not. That's because a lot of older e-mail applications simply can't interpret and display e-mails using CSS yet. And, because the e-mail application used by an e-mail recipient can vary as drastically as the browser and browser version a person uses on the Web, e-mails (for the time being) need to use some old HTML formatting tags to get the job done.

To make matters even more confusing, currently, no HTML e-mail standards that I know of can assist you with the process of coding your HTML e-mails before you blast them out to the members on your list. There have been suggestions for recommendations to the W3C, but the W3C has made no official recommendations to the Web community yet. What I've found has been mostly conflicting information about what to do or not do. Therefore, I'm going to try to simplify and distill what I've found for you. If you follow these directions, you'll probably come up with a decently formatted HTML e-mail suitable for sending:

- Use a table with multiple rows and a maximum width of 500 pixels to hold the content of your e-mail.

- Try to avoid adding any styling information, such as margin size and background color attributes, to the <body> tag.

- Don't use <div> tags because they are often stripped by e-mail programs.

- If you want your e-mail to have a background color, nest your content table inside another table with a colored background attribute and a width set to 100%.

- Use `<font>` tags to style your content, or if you do decide to use CSS because you know your audience's e-mail programs can interpret CSS, embed your internal CSS text formatting styles (no CSS positioning styles, please) inside the body of the page rather than in the head. (What?! Yes, in the body, after the opening `<body>` tag.)

- Type the full address of all linkable URLs (`http://www.`*sitename*`.com/`*pagename*`.html`) somewhere in the body of the e-mail so that visitors with e-mail programs that automatically disable hyperlinks can copy the addresses and paste them into their browser.

- Use absolute links for all the images contained in your e-mail, such as `http://www.`*samplesite*`.com/images/sample.jpg`. Be sure to upload the images to the remotely accessible server hosting the site before the e-mail gets sent!

- Include a link to access the content on the e-mail in an alternative Web page, which must be uploaded to a remotely accessible server before the e-mail gets sent.

- Include contact information with e-mail, telephone number, and physical address, and a link to a Web-accessible privacy policy that explains how contact information from the recipient of the e-mail will be used.

- Include a link to subscribe and unsubscribe to your e-mail list.

- The e-mail should include the date sent, the author e-mail address or URL, and message ID from the sender's e-mail application. (This information should be included automatically when you send the mail, but you should still take a second to make sure it's there.)

- Try not to include any Flash, JavaScript, movies, plug-ins, or other media files; most e-mail programs strip those out or block them as spam anyway. Save the fancy stuff for your Web site.

- Create a plain text version to send along with the HTML-formatted version if your e-mail program allows for it. Doing so ensures that recipients with text-only e-mail applications and recipients who have disabled HTML capabilities will still be able to receive your missives.

When you're finished creating your HTML-formatted e-mail, test the e-mail by sending it to yourself on as many test e-mail applications as you can, such as AOL, Outlook, Gmail, Eudora, Yahoo!Mail, Lotus Notes, and so on. The more environments you can review the mail in, the better you can come up with ways to format the mail consistently before it goes out to everyone on your list.

You might also want to consider using an e-mail program or service that knows how to send HTML-formatted e-mails. From my own research and experience, I can highly recommend the following software programs and services:

- MailChimp, `www.mailchimp.com`
- ConstantContact, `www.constantcontact.com`
- VerticalResponse, `www.verticalresponse.com`
- Direct Mail, `www.ethreesoftware.com/directmail`
- MaxBulk Mailer, `www.maxprog.com`

If you're a Dreamweaver 8 user, you can configure your program in the Preferences dialog box to automatically write CSS instead of HTML tags. Then, if you ever need to revert to the old font tags for creating HTML e-mails, you can temporarily disable the CSS setting by choosing HTML and have Dreamweaver write the old font style tags for you. When you're finished, enable the CSS setting and go back to working with CSS.

After you begin styling your content with external CSS, you'll probably never want to go back to using the old font tags for styling. In fact, if you inherit someone else's site and are hired to do a redesign, you can create new CSS styles for the content and strip the old formatting tags from all the pages on the site as part of the redesign project. You might even use this "font tags–to–CSS conversion" as a selling point of your services by explaining all the aforementioned benefits to your client. Not only should the client be impressed by the scope of your knowledge on the matter, but he might even feel somewhat inclined to hire you for his next redesign project sometime down the road if he ultimately likes your design and enjoys working with you this time around.

Let me further illustrate how wonderful it is to use CSS for styling content by pointing you to some really amazing examples of how the same content can look completely different when styled with different CSS:

1. **Open your favorite browser window and go to www.csszengarden.com.**

   What you see here is the home page of the site as styled with the CSS developed by CSS mastermind, Dave Shea.

2. **On the right side of the page, under the red Japanese Torii gate where it says Select a Design, are several links to separate pages using the same page content but styled with different designers' CSS. Click any one of them.**

   I can't really tell you which to click, because that listing is regularly updated, but what you will see is the same content with a totally different look! Figure 9-2 shows the design I begin with on the left and the transformation of the page after I click a second link on the right. The tags in the code are the same on both pages; it's the CSS style definitions — which include font selection, colors, and graphics, among other things — that have been changed to achieve the new layout and look.

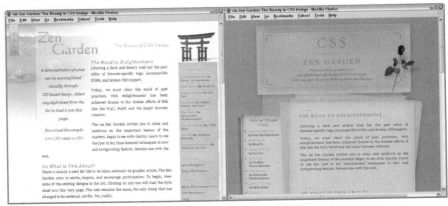

Figure 9-2: CSS magically transforms the appearance of the same content.

3. **Scroll down the page until you see a section titled Select a Design and click another link.**

Same content, different design!

At this point, you should be somewhat if not totally convinced of the amazing power of CSS!

4. **Click another link in the Select a Design column.**

What makes this particular site extremely brilliant is that any designer who submits his or her design to CSSZenGarden agrees to make the CSS open source, so you and I can go examine the CSS and learn how all the visual effects were created.

5. **To find the CSS for any particular page design on this site, look for a section called Resources and click the link called View This Design's CSS.**

When clicked, the CSS for that page will automatically open in your browser window. Figure 9-3 shows the CSS for the page on the right in Figure 9-2. In the CSS, you can see how the General Properties styles format the appearance of the page background and text links, and the Text Properties styles define the look of paragraphs and headers. Likewise, in the Div Properties section of the CSS, content contained in <div> tags with these named IDs (for example, #preamble) will be automatically styled by the style rules contained within them, such as the section on the page containing preamble text, where it says, "The Road to Enlightenment."

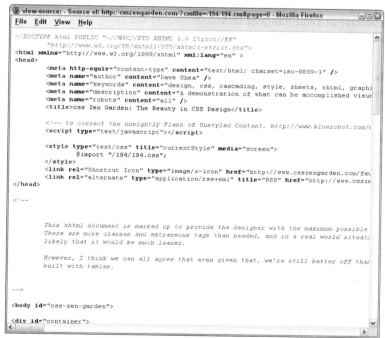

Figure 9-3: View the CSS code to find out how designers created different effects.

6. **To keep a copy of the opened CSS, choose File → Save or File → Save Page As to save the file to your local computer.**

The filename doesn't matter, so feel free to change it to whatever you want. What does matter is the extension; all CSS files must be saved with the `.css` file extension to work properly.

7. **To see even more designs using different CSS, click the link called View All Designs, which will take you to the CSS Zen Garden archive on Dave Shea's MezzoBlue site.**

From there you can click a link to View All Categories and see the designs sorted into different categories (which you might want to emulate in your own designs) such as 2 Column, 3 Column, Conceptual, Minimal, Themes, and more. It's a truly inspired idea with the ultimate goal of teaching you the benefits of styling with CSS.

Learning about Accessibility Standards

Did you know that people with disabilities make up nearly 10 percent of all the people using the Internet? It's true, according to the W3C, and because that's a larger percentage of potential visitors to the Web than the roughly 3.6 percent of all Internet consumers using the Mac OS (as opposed to Windows or Linux), people with disabilities make up a large enough group that you should definitely pay considerable attention to them when designing Web sites.

One of the Web standards organizations mentioned at the start of this chapter is the Section 508 government site. That particular organization is dedicated to compliance of Section 508 (29 U.S.C. 794d) of the Rehabilitation Act, especially with regard to the accessibility of Web sites to all people, whether employees of the federal government or not, especially those with disabilities. Although technically only legally applicable to federal agencies using, developing, maintaining, and procuring information technology, many Web designers and developers are now informally broadening the scope of Section 508 to include access to any and all information that is readily available on the Web to anyone, with or without disabilities.

Information Kiosk

The benefits of designing for accessibility don't stop with making sites more accessible to those with disabilities. By following accessibility guidelines, the content can be more easily accessed using a larger group of lesser known (but no less wonderful) Web browsers, such as Firefox, Safari, Opera, Mozilla, Lynx, and Amaya. And, the more devices that can access a Section 508–compliant site, the greater the likelihood of increased traffic and increased sales.

Understanding the HTML accessibility standards

The Section 508 amendment, which was passed in 1998, is often broken down into two parts: The first relates to HTML usage, and the second part deals specifically with JavaScripts, plug-ins, and other multimedia enhancements found on Web pages. Because you're more likely to focus your efforts on HTML compliance than on multimedia compliance, the following excerpt from `http://section508.gov` lists the standards from the HTML part (Web-based intranet and Internet information and applications) and briefly notes how you might meet each standard:

(a) **A text equivalent for every non-text element shall be provided (e.g., via "alt", "longdesc", or in element content).**

When building pages for the Web, each page must necessarily pass or fail each of the standards as set in Section 508. For example, a graphic on a Web page will fail Standard (a) when the image is missing its alt text description, as in `<img src="images/stevehayes.jpg">`, but will pass Standard (a) when the image contains a properly syntaxed alt description within the image tag, as in `<img src="images/508.gif" alt="Section 508 Government Seal">`.

(b) **Equivalent alternatives for any multimedia presentation shall be synchronized with the presentation.**

An example equivalent might include the specification of a long description in the HTML code that describes the content in a multimedia presentation.

(c) **Web pages shall be designed so that all information conveyed with color is also available without color, for example from context or markup.**

The page needs to make sense both with and without color style markup. Test your pages to see if the removal of color changes the experience of visiting the site.

(d) **Documents shall be organized so they are readable without requiring an associated style sheet.**

When using CSS, try toggling the CSS on and off to see if the ordering of the content makes sense without it because most assistive devices ignore CSS and strictly read content from top to bottom.

(e) **Redundant text links shall be provided for each active region of a server-side image map.**

Server-side image maps are rarely used compared to client-side image maps; however, if you must include these on your page, make sure you include text links for each region on the image map.

(f) **Client-side image maps shall be provided instead of server-side image maps except where the regions cannot be defined with an available geometric shape.**

Client-side image maps can usually accommodate any special active region shapes, so this shouldn't be too much of an issue.

(g) **Row and column headers shall be identified for data tables.**

When data is displayed in tables and header information is also included, the appropriate `<th>` tags must be used to define the header rows/columns.

(h) **Markup shall be used to associate data cells and header cells for data tables that have two or more logical levels of row or column headers.**

Use `<th>` tags instead of `<td>` tags to define table cells used as header cells.

(i) **Frames shall be titled with text that facilitates frame identification and navigation.**

Though using frames is highly discouraged from an accessibility standpoint, when they are used to present multiple pages in a single browser window, each page displaying in a frame must contain its own title tag, and each frame must have an appropriate frame name.

(j) **Pages shall be designed to avoid causing the screen to flicker with a frequency greater than 2 Hz and lower than 55 Hz.**

In layman's terms, don't add any animations to your pages with a super-fast flicker rate because certain frequencies can trigger seizures in visitors with a particular kind of epilepsy.

(k) **A text-only page, with equivalent information or functionality, shall be provided to make a Web site comply with the provisions of this part, when compliance cannot be accomplished in any other way. The content of the text-only page shall be updated whenever the primary page changes.**

Any time content cannot comply with accessibility guidelines, the URL to an alternate text-only page that contains instructions or information about the non-compliant content must be specified in the code.

(l) **When pages utilize scripting languages to display content, or to create interface elements, the information provided by the script shall be identified with functional (understandable) text that can be read by assistive technology.**

For instance, if your site uses JavaScript to create a rollover effect for all the main navigation links, the code should contain attending `<noscript>` tags that provide the visitor with information about the script's function as well as links to any pages that the script provides access to.

(m) **When a Web page requires that an applet, plug-in or other application be present on the client system to interpret page content, the page must provide a link to a plug-in or applet that complies with §1194.21(a) through (l).**

This you should do for all applications and devices that interpret content; always provide a link for your visitors to download any necessary plug-ins that are needed to view page content.

(n) When electronic forms are designed to be completed on-line, the form shall allow people using assistive technology to access the information, field elements, and functionality required for completion and submission of the form, including all directions and cues.

This means adding labels, coding access keys, tab order attributes, and other form accessibility tags and attributes to all the form fields.

(o) A method shall be provided that permits users to skip repetitive navigation links.

Use anchor links combined with a tab index to allow visitors to skip repeating navigation links. For example, you may want to make the first link in a nav bar called "Skip Navigation" combined with an anchor link that always takes the visitor to the first line of text on the page.

```
<a href="#start">Skip navigation</a>
<p><a name="start" tabindex="1">Welcome</a></p>
```

(p) When a timed response is required, the user shall be alerted and given sufficient time to indicate more time is required.

Don't use Meta tags, JavaScript, or any other kind of programming to make the page refresh or forward to another page without also providing visitors with alternate ways to adjust the timing and/or access the other information.

Information Kiosk

To view all the Section 508 Standards, including technical standards (§1194.21 Software applications and operating systems), visit

www.section508.gov/index.cfm?FuseAction=Content&ID=12#Web

For an informative and comprehensive look at what it means to pass or fail each standard, visit WebAim's 508 checklist:

www.webaim.org/standards/508/checklist.php

The W3C also offers accessibility checkpoints at

www.w3.org/TR/WAI-WEBCONTENT/full-checklist.html

You can find other extremely helpful information on the topic at the following Web sites:

www.diveintoaccessibility.org
www.joeclark.org/book/sashay/serialization
www.alistapart.com/articles/wiwa

Using Dreamweaver's accessibility tools

If you happen to use or plan to use Dreamweaver 8 to build your Web pages, you're in luck when it comes to coding for accessibility. To use the Dreamweaver 8 Accessibility prompts, you'll need to custom configure your copy of Dreamweaver. After you do this, Dreamweaver will automatically prompt you to add Accessibility attributes to your code when you insert certain objects into your Web pages.

Follow these steps to enable Dreamweaver 8's Accessibility prompts:

1. **Launch Dreamweaver 8 and choose Edit → Preferences (Windows) or Dreamweaver → Preferences (Mac) to open Dreamweaver's Preferences dialog box, shown in Figure 9-4.**

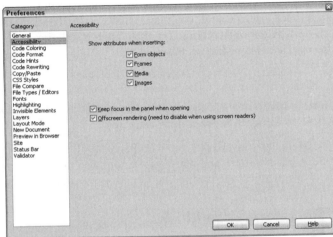

Figure 9-4: Get started with Dreamweaver's Accessibility tools by activating the option in the Preferences dialog box.

2. **Under Category, select Accessibility, and in the center of the dialog box, select each of the objects you'd like to be prompted to add Accessibility code for when inserting those objects on your Web page.**

3. **Enable the Keep Focus option to keep access to the Accessibility panel open rather than keeping the focus on the page in Design or Code view.**

   This option is a must for Web designers with disabilities who use screen readers.

4. **Disable the Offscreen Rendering option if you're using a screen reader and adding accessibility features to your Web pages in Dreamweaver is creating conflicts with it.**

5. **Click OK.**

   Changes to the Dreamweaver environment take effect immediately.

6. To test that the Accessibility prompts are working, open a new document and choose Insert → Image to open the Select Image Source dialog box.

7. Choose an image from somewhere on your computer and click the OK or Select button.

8. Before Dreamweaver drops the selected image onto your page, you should see the Image Tag Accessibility Attributes dialog box.

In the dialog box, you can enter alternate text in the Alternate text field and, if desired, add the Long description tag attribute by entering the URL to a Web page containing a text description of that image.

9. Click OK to close the Accessibility dialog box and see the image on your page.

accessibility: Any enhancement made to a Web site that can improve how visitors with disabilities and search engine robots/spiders access the information on the site's pages. Common coding enhancements include adding footer links, a site map page, alt text for images, page titles, Meta tags, object labels, titles for links, link tags to the home and site map pages in the head, access and tab index keys, and form input labels.

assistive technology: Any device, such as a screen reader, or non-human application, such as a search engine robot that accesses content on the Internet through means other than a Web browser.

client side: Any code, application, or code processing that is performed on the client's computer rather than on a server, such as image maps that specify areas on a graphic that link to other pages on the site.

code hacks: Unorthodox and creative use of HTML, CSS, JavaScript, and other code to manipulate objects on a Web page and/or work around existing limitations of the Web to achieve a desired visual effect.

CSS: Cascading Style Sheets. Special HTML code that describes the styling and positioning rules governing a Web document.

DOCTYPE: A line of code inserted above the opening HTML tag on a Web page that instructs a browser to interpret a Web page as an application of the XML programming language. There are different DOCTYPEs for HTML, XHTML, and Framesets, and it's up to the coder to insert the appropriate DTD (Document Type Definition) to match the style of coding used to write the document.

continued

 **continued**

frames/framesets: Framesets permit the viewing of two or more pages inside a single browser window using special frame and frameset tags in place of the traditional <body> tags of a regular Web page.

semantic HTML: Use of tags in HTML code that match either what the content is, like <p> for paragraph text, or what it is for, like the <label> tag used for form controls such as text fields and radio buttons, which don't have implicit labels.

server side: Any application or program that must run on a server rather than on a client machine to function properly, such as with Server-Side Includes (SSIs).

W3C: The World Wide Web Consortium is an international vendor-neutral organization that defines standards on the Web to improve Web accessibility and hardware/software interoperability.

Web standards: Guidelines that assist Web developers, programmers, and designers to create interoperable, accessible content for the Web.

XML: eXtensible Markup Language. An easily customizable programming language, like SGML (Standard Generalized Markup Language), for communication of information and application services between people and computers using structured and meaningful semantic code. Part of the W3C's recommendations for the Web.

XSL: eXtensible Stylesheet Language. Like an external CSS, an XSL document is used to define how content on an XML file should be visually presented in a Web browser.

Last
Stop

Practice Exam

1. True or False: A DOCTYPE goes inside the head area of a page.

2. According to the layering concept of a good Web page, proposed by Joseph Lindsay at the 2005 GOVIS conference, adding JavaScript behaviors should be the _____ of five steps in building a Web page.

3. "All tags must be written in lowercase letters" is one of the rules of _____ markup.

4. Name three Web standards organizations.

_____

_____

5. Why should you include a DOCTYPE in the code of all your Web pages?

_____

_____

6. List three benefits of styling content with CSS instead of with the old font tags.

_____

_____

7. Name at least one difference between coding for Web pages and coding for HTML e-mails.

_____

_____

_____

_____

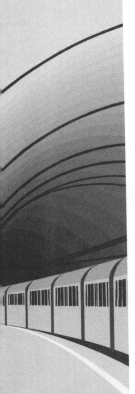

8. What are the benefits of designing an accessible Web site?

_____

_____

_____

_____

9. Give an example of proper nesting of tags around any word or phrase using the tags for bold `<strong>` and italics `<em>`.

10. To test your understanding of the differences between HTML and XHTML, see whether you can identify which language each of the following code examples were written in and whether the code is compliant or noncompliant:

Code Example 1:

```
<p>Welcome to planet Earth</p><hr />
```

Code Example 2:

```
<img src="images/kyle.jpg" alt="Kyle Jenkins"
width=150 height=150>
```

Code Example 3:

```
<TABLE>
    <tr>
        <TD><B><I>Pasta, Pizza, &
Calzones</B></I></td>
    </TR>
<TABLE>
```

Using Search Engine Optimization Techniques

STATIONS ALONG THE WAY

- O Understanding the ethics of search engine optimization (SEO)
- O Improving search engine rankings with HTML code
- O Increasing a site's visibility and accessibility with an HTML site map page

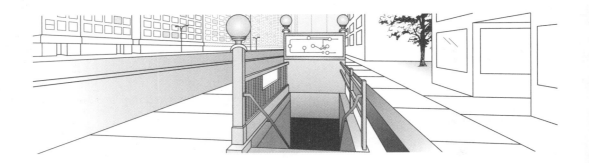

Enter the Station

Questions

1. Why is ethics an important consideration when optimizing a site's visibility to search tools?

2. What elements in a site, both on the page and in the HTML code, need to be a part of an SEO strategy?

3. Why would a site owner want to resubmit a site to a search engine?

4. How does an HTML site map differ from a visual site map?

5. How might an HTML site map help with search engine optimization?

6. How does an HTML site map make a site more accessible to visitors?

Express Line

If you're already familiar with SEO or are eager to begin building the site you designed, you can move along to Chapter 11, where you'll learn how to build basic pages in HTML.

B efore building a newly designed site, you need to put some time into planning which effective search engine optimization (SEO) techniques to use for the site. SEO is a combination of thinking strategically about the site's content, title tags, Meta tags, page structure, and accessibility coding — because the search engines rely largely on bots to develop their indexes — as well as submitting the site to search engines in order to help visitors find the site and improve the site's ranking within the search results.

Some clients will have a budget to spend on pay-per-click-type SEO services (an Internet advertising system, also known as *paid placement* and *cost-per-click advertisement,* whereby the advertiser bids on the keywords or keyphrases used by potential site visitors and pays a fee any time a visitor clicks a link that leads back to the advertiser's site). However, many more clients will have no money set aside for such marketing and will rely solely upon your knowledge and expertise to guide them through (or more likely, handle completely!) the process of getting their sites listed on search engines.

This chapter explains several SEO techniques you can put to use on your site or your clients' sites. In addition to specific ways you can improve rankings through your site's code, you learn why every site should include a site map page. In this chapter, you go about making that site map page accessible from all the other pages of the site to both improve search engine rankings and make the site more easily viewable to the widest possible audience.

Practicing Ethical SEO Techniques

As Web surfers began to rely more and more on search engines that use Web robots and spiders to build their databases, a whole cottage industry cropped up with the sole intent of tricking the bots. Search engines, in turn, improved the Web robots and spiders so that they automatically detect sites that use common scams. In fact, some of these sneaky practices got so out of control that the search engines have taken even more drastic measures to ensure their search results are as accurate as possible. (Otherwise, of course, the search engines wouldn't be useful.) One consequence of all this for Web designers is that they need to go into the field equipped with a clear understanding of both how to make a Web site visible to search engines *and* what search engines consider ethical and unethical practices.

Watch Your Step

To be sure, you or an "SEO service provider" can make some sneaky adjustments to your code to enhance site relevancy and improve rankings, but those things fall into the bucket of unethical practices and therefore won't be discussed in detail in this book. Be aware, too, that attempting these practices can put the home page URL and any additional pages listed on that domain at risk of being blacklisted by search engines. Trying to trick the system is counter-intuitive because in all likelihood most of the traffic coming to any site is generated through Google, Yahoo!, and other search engines. Just don't do it.

The next few sections go into detail about how you can design your Web pages with ethical SEO practices. In the following list, you find some unethical practices, just so you know what practices to avoid, and my strong entreaty for you to not use them:

- **Cheat:** Don't trick people into visiting a site by using inaccurate keywords, Meta tags, and content, or by false advertising or unethical page redirects. Please don't try to outsmart the search engines. The people who write the search programs are always on the lookout for cheaters, and if they find unethical SEO techniques on a submitted URL, they have the power to prevent the entire site from being indexed.

- **Tag padding:** Do not use multiple versions of the same tag, such as the Meta description or title tags, to try to get more information through to search engines than you can with one tag. This, too, will be viewed as spam by search engines and will put the URL at risk.

- **Image padding:** Don't use words in your alternative (`alt`) text attribute for images that have nothing to do with the image being described.

- **Keyword padding:** Do not engage in padding keywords into Web pages that have nothing to do with the Web site's specific business.

- **Keyword listing:** Avoid listing keywords in the body of your site content when their purpose is not clear. The only legitimate place for a list of keywords is inside the keywords Meta tag or when listing a site's products and services. If you list words in this capacity, do it carefully so that it doesn't appear to be a spam-like keyword listing. A safer method would be to write copy that logically includes all the products and services in paragraph form.

- **Hidden text:** Don't add keyword-stuffed text to a page where the font color matches the background color of the page or container holding the text. Search engines will detect such slimy practices and treat those pages, and possibly all pages at the offending Web address, as spam.

- **Oversubmit:** Never submit a URL to any search engine, index, directory, or listing more than once in any 24-hour period. Daily is also too often. Be realistic. Submit only when significant changes have been made to the layout or content of a site.

- **Duplicate page submissions:** Do not submit pages with identical content but different filenames. This will be viewed as spam and can put the Web address at risk.

Including Ethical SEO Techniques in Web Pages

Now that you know what *not* to do, you can learn about some good, effective SEO techniques. When it comes to effective and ethical SEO strategy, you can make several free and fee-based enhancements to the pages you design and code, which can improve how the content inside them gets indexed by the Web robots and spiders crawling the Web in search of new pages to add to their databases. I'll begin with an examination of what Web robots and spiders do and then talk about ways that you can improve search engine rankings for a home page and other destinations on a domain.

In general, *robots* and *spiders* are automated programs that perform specific tasks or "crawl the Web" on a mission to find new Web pages and index them in a large database. At minimum, when a new Web address and home page (typically named `index.html`) are found, that page will be automatically added to the robot/spider owner's indexing database. Any hypertext links on the home page might or might not be indexed automatically as part of the process, but because it's a possibility, it's important to pay special attention to both text content and hyperlinks.

By implementing some or all of the techniques you find in the following sections, you can greatly increase the ranking of your Web pages in search results listings for search engines such as Google, Yahoo!, MSN, and others.

Maximizing the impact of relevant keywords

This leads you to the first technique you'll employ as part of your personal ethical SEO campaign. Because robots and spiders search for meaningful content, the sites you design need to help the bots find that content through keywords that identify a company's products and services. By *keywords,* in this case, I mean the words or short phrases describing the product, service, or information your Web client wants to advertise to the world that a visitor might use in a search engine to find the client's site. These can be the same as the keywords in the `keywords` Meta tag, but because the content keywords and key phrases can be integrated into the text in the body of the page, there is much more latitude for including the most popular keywords the site's visitors are likely to use. As you begin evaluating the site content and considering the design, check the site as follows to make sure it's getting the most from keywords:

1. Make sure the body text for the site includes descriptive keyword phrases.

Say, for example, your client sells imported European wine. If one of the most popular items he currently sells is an imported Australian white merlot, then the words "Australian white merlot" would be a great key phrase to include in the page's text.

2. **It's critical that the keywords on every page of a site — especially the home page — are hyperlinked to other relevant pages on the site. Make a plan for including these links in your client's site, if they aren't already there.**

   For instance, if the copy on a page includes the phrase, "Learn more about our products and services, or contact us for more information," you can easily turn the words "products," "services," and "contact us" into hyperlinks that link directly to those pages on the site.

3. **To highlight certain words or phrases from the rest of the page content, mark up headings and other important text with bold (`<strong>`) and italic (`<em>`) styles and headings tags like `<h1>` and `<h2>`.**

   Using these heading and emphasis tags can alert search engine robots that the content contained inside them is likely to be more relevant to search engine users than other content on the page.

   Tell your client not to be too conservative with the content placed on every page. In fact, some SEO guidelines recommend having a minimum of 200 words of copy on every page so the spiders and robots have something to read and index.

Here's an example of a few paragraphs from a page of good, relevant home page content as it would appear in the code:

```
<h1>Welcome to SF Web Publishing<img
src="images/sfwplogo.gif" alt="Welcome to SF Web
Publishing" width="100" height="23" border="0"
id="logo"></h1>
<p><strong>SF Web Publishing</strong> is a web publishing
company specializing in <a href="webdesign.html" title="web
design" target="_self">web design</a> and development for
<em>nonprofit organizations</em> in the San Francisco Bay
area. Our mission is to offer beautiful, customized,
reduced-cost web design services for organizations
supporting education, the arts, wildlife and animal
welfare, human rights and civil liberties, energy
conservation, and the environment.</p>
<p>We welcome you to explore our site using our <a
href="sitemap.html" title="sitemap">site map</a>, learn
more about our web design and publishing <a href=
"services.html" title="services">services</a>, and review
our<a href="portfolio.html" title="portfolio">portfolio</a>.
Please <a href="contact.html" title="contact us"
target="_self">contact us</a> for more information or to
set up a free consultation.</p>
```

Content is marked up with heading, italic, and strong tags for emphasis, the copy includes plenty of descriptive keywords and key phrases, and text to other relevant pages on the site are hyperlinked.

Watch Your Step

Be sure the copy reads legibly and doesn't have keywords haphazardly thrown into it. Avoid at all costs the appearance of keyword spamming; rather than listing a bunch of keywords in a row, all the keywords need to be logically embedded in the page copy. For example, instead of listing shampoo, conditioner, deep conditioner, hairspray, hair products, hair treatments, hair accessories, and so on, write something like, "At X company, we sell only the best hair products and hair treatments on the market. You'll find high-quality shampoos, conditioners, and deep conditioners along with hairspray and hair accessories." Be sure to also include hyperlinks on the keywords to each of those product categories. If you feel stuck for different ways of presenting the content on the page, know that it is okay to reuse the content and wording placed elsewhere on the site. You could, for instance, say "X Company - Your Online Shop for the Finest Hair Products, Treatments, and Accessories" in the title tag and "X Company is your online shop for the finest hair products, treatments, and accessories. We sell shampoo, conditioner, deep conditioner, hairspray, and more!" in the description Meta tag.

Embedding object and image descriptions

Another ethical SEO technique involves using the `title` and `alt` attributes to describe certain page elements and images, respectively.

The `title` attribute can be added to several tags, such as links, tables, table cells, and table rows, to improve accessibility by describing the contents found within the structural element, like in the following line of code:

```
<table width="450" title="GymKids Fall Class Schedule">
```

The `alt` attribute describes generally what an image looks like or, when the image contains only copy, what that copy says:

```
<img src="images/recital.gif" alt="GymKids Spring Recital
Invitation" width="350" height="150" border="0" id="gala">
```

The inclusion of these tags in the code can increase search engine relevance with regard to targeted keywords while also improving how people using screen readers, text browsers, and other assistive technologies experience visiting the site.

Including description and keywords Meta tags

With regard to SEO, two Meta tags that you learned about in Chapter 3 can assist with site optimization:

- description: A brief description of the Web site's products and/or services in 250 characters or less, including spaces and punctuation. This description is often the text that gets displayed when the URL appears as part of a search engine's results listings, so if possible, use three or four keywords in the early part of the description.

- keywords: A list of the seven most important keywords and key phrases (1,024 characters, including spaces and punctuation) that visitors to the site might type into a search engine to find the Web site's products and services. These keywords should be listed in order of importance and include any plural versions of keywords if visitors might search for both the singular and plural instances, such as *teacher guides* and *teachers guides*. The same goes for common misspellings of important keywords for any site, like *pineapple, pinapple,* and *pinnaple* for a site that sells pineapples.

Information Kiosk

The keywords Meta tag has been so widely abused by unethical SEO practitioners that currently only one search engine, Inktomi (which is now part of Yahoo!), still uses keywords in factoring search engine rankings. Nonetheless, as long as one search engine uses them, that's enough to warrant having the keywords Meta tag in the code of your pages.

Though the same description and set of keywords are commonly used for all the pages on a single Web site, many SEO professionals suggest using customized descriptions and keyword lists for each page of the site to improve search engine rankings for individual pages.

Remember that these Meta tags don't appear in your actual site design. You simply place them in the head area of the page code. The syntax for these two Meta tags should be written as follows, where you'll fill in the specific content (shown in bold) for your particular Web site:

```
<head>
<title>My Page Title</title>
<meta name="keywords" content="OceanaSurf, surfing, surfing
classes, surf retreats, Santa Monica, CA">
<meta name="description" content="Sign up for surfing
classes and international surf retreats at OceanaSurf in
Santa Monica, CA. We welcome riders of all levels. Come
travel with us to surf the world's oceans.">
</head>
```

Transfer

Chapter 3 goes into more detail about writing effective description and keywords tags. I'll cover their exact placement, plus other meaningful Meta tags you can use on your pages, in Chapter 11.

Writing unique page titles

The next important free SEO technique you should use is adding unique titles to all the pages on your site, which will appear in the visitor's browser's title bar. Title tags can be used to both quickly identify the page contents to humans and target specific page content for spiders and robots with keywords and keyword phrases. For example, instead of using a simple description for the home page title, such as

```
<title>Janice Trimpe Sculptures</title>
```

use more relevant keywords in the title to improve the chances of people finding particular pages on the site when searching additional terms like *commissioned* and *bronze* and *sculptures:*

```
<title>Janice Trimpe: Art as Large as Life. Commissioned
and Monumental Bronze Sculptures</title>
```

Watch Your Step

In the titles, try to include a couple of keywords or key phrases near the front part, but be careful not to simply list keywords instead of identifying the content on the page. That could be misinterpreted as spamming and could blacklist the submitted URL from being indexed at all! The title needs to read like an enticing, informative sentence, not a laundry list.

Page titles can be any length up to about 70 characters. Bear in mind, though, that titles using the maximum number of characters or more might be truncated in the title bar of some browsers, reading as "Janice Trimpe: Art as Large as Life. Com . . ." instead of the full title as listed in the code. Still, for the extra bump that having well-written, keyword-rich, descriptive titles can do for your site rankings, seeing shortened titles in a browser's title bar might not be a critical issue.

Submitting a Web address to search tools

When your site is complete, be sure to try having it listed on as many search tools as you think will assist the target audience in finding the site. You do this by submitting the site's URL to the most popular, important search tools that the target audience is likely to use. These tools include search engines (which use robots and spiders to crawl the Web in search of new listings) and search directories (a categorized list of sites, sometimes compiled or edited by people instead of bots).

Watch Your Step

This does not, in my opinion, necessitate the use of search engine submission tools that will blast the URL of a site, spam-like, to any and every search engine around the globe. In fact, the results of these types of submissions often create mountains of e-mail spam for the submitting e-mail address, and the inclusion of the URL on those search engines will rarely, if ever, increase sales. What's more, some SEO submission tools submit the URL directly to spam sites (which are just pages of site listings that clog up the Internet and have no purpose what-soever), which can jeopardize the integrity of the domain when it comes to listing the site legitimately on the major search engines. The best way to get a site listed, then, is to hand-submit the URL to the major search engines and directories and/or pay a reputable listing service like Google AdWords and Yahoo! SearchMarketing for pay-per-click advertising.

Most search engines and directories (and the occasional search listing, which uses search engines and directories) will charge you a fee for submitting a URL with them, but a couple are free. Table 10-1 shows a listing of the most popular tools for search engine submissions.

Table 10-1   Search Engines, Directories, and Search Listings

Service Name	URL	Service Type	$$ or Free
Google	www.google.com/addurl/ ?continue=/addurl	Search Engine	Free
Open Directory Project	http://dmoz.org/add.html	Search Directory	Free
Yahoo!	http://submit.search. yahoo.com/free/request	Search Directory	Free (requires registration with Yahoo!)
AOL Search	Submit URL to Google and your listing should appear in AOL's search listings	Search Listing	Free
MSN Search	http://submitit.bcentral. com/msnsubmit.htm	Search Listing	Free
Google AdWords	http://adwords.google.com	Search Engine	$$
Yahoo! Search Marketing	http://searchmarketing. yahoo.com/index.php Yahoo! is now a hybrid of purchased indexes: Inktomi, AltaVista, & AlltheWeb	Search Directory	$$

Some SEO professionals might encourage you to resubmit your URL to search engines, listings, directories, and indexes any time you update even a single page on a site. To me, however, that appears to be more like a form of computerized Internet harassment than a smart business practice. What seems more logical and respectful is to make regular quarterly resubmissions to each of the tools listed in Table 10-1 or to make resubmissions at slightly more frequent intervals if the content on the site is updated more regularly. You could even create a folder of bookmarks to these search engine submission service sites to help streamline the resubmission process. Figure 10-1 shows, for example, how you'd submit a site to Google.

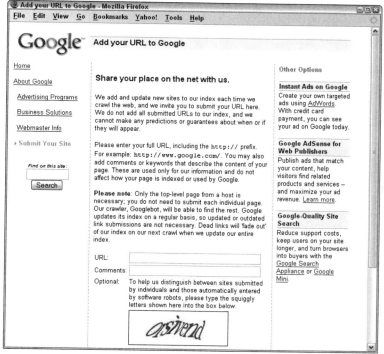

Figure 10-1: To submit a site to Google, simply enter the complete home page URL.

After you make a submission, each search engine, listing, index, and directory can take anywhere from a day to two months to get listed. For instance, Google claims listings will occur within four weeks of submission, but listings can just as likely occur within a day or two. Tell your client to be patient while waiting for the listing to appear after the home page URL has been submitted. Just because a site gets published doesn't automatically mean it will be found instantly by any and every search engine. All publishing a site means, really, is that the content on the domain is publicly accessible to anyone with an Internet connection. To be listed, a URL must be submitted to a search engine, listing, directory, or index. Tell your client that as long as the submitted URL directs Web surfers to a totally complete Web site, the listing should happen within a reasonable timeframe, typically between one and eight weeks.

Information Kiosk

After a site gets indexed on Google, you can quickly find out how many of the site's pages Google has indexed by typing **site: mywebsite.com** into Google's Web search field. For example, to see how many instances there are for Wiley.com, the publisher of this book, type **site:wiley. com** into the Google search field. Astoundingly, the results are 13,500,000!

Step into the Real World

Creating a Favicon   Ever notice that when you bookmark a favorite Web site or view a page in your browser that sometimes a little icon shows up to the left of the Web address in the address bar?

That's called a *favicon*. Though it won't necessarily improve search engine rankings for a site, it's a really nice detail to add to a site to help it stand out from the pack.

To create your own favicon, you'll need Photoshop and a special plug-in for Photoshop (or a good icon editor like Microangelo or the free online icon editor at `www.favicon.co.uk`) to save the file with the proper `.ico` file extension. The rest is pretty simple.

You'll take three steps to add a favicon to a site: create the icon, add it to the Web site, and make it easy for visitors to bookmark the page:

1. **Create the icon in Photoshop as a 16-x-16-pixel, 8-bit RGB file.**

   That's really tiny, so you might want to create the icon at a slightly larger size, like a factor of 16 such as 80 x 80 or 64 x 64, and then scale it down to 16 x 16.

To save the image as an icon, you'll need the Windows Icon (ICO) file format plug-in for Photoshop. To download the plug-in, go to `www.telegraphics.com.au/sw`.

2. **Associate the icon with the Web page by adding code to all the pages on the site. You can do so in two ways.**

The first way is to name the icon `favicon.ico` and upload it to the root level of the site's remote server. When the icon is named `favicon.ico`, any time a visitor using Internet Explorer bookmarks a page on that site, the favicon will automatically be associated with the Web address that was saved. This method, as you can guess, won't work 100 percent of the time because not all site visitors will be using IE to access the Internet.

The second way is to name the icon whatever you want and add a special line of code to all the pages on the site you'd like to have the icon associated with. The line of code contains a link that needs to be customized to your site and added between the `<head>` tags of the code for each page that you want it to work with:

```
<link rel="Shortcut Icon" href="http://www.mywebsite.com/myicon.ico">
```

Or if using site root relative links,

```
<link rel="Shortcut Icon" href="/favicon.ico">
```

You need to save the favicon to the root level of the site to work properly, so please don't save it into your images folder. For more information on root levels and site structure, see Chapter 15.

3. **Prompt visitors to add the URL to their browser favorites menu by adding a JavaScript link or button to your site. You can use the following code, courtesy of Microsoft, to create the link:**

```
<script>
<!--
if ((navigator.appVersion.indexOf("MSIE") > 0)
  && (parseInt(navigator.appVersion) >= 4)) {
    var sText = "<U><SPAN STYLE='color:blue;cursor:hand;'";
    sText += "onclick='window.external.AddFavorite(location.href,";
    sText += "document.title);'>Add this page to your
        bookmarks</SPAN></U>";
    document.write(sText);
}
//-->
</script>
```

The text inside the script shown in italics can be customized to say anything suitable for individual Web sites, such as "Click here to bookmark this site."

Using an HTML Site Map

In Chapter 3, you learned about one type of site map — the visual site map, which is a visual representation of the virtual architecture of a site before the design gets created. The visual site map, if you'll recall, diagrams all the pages on a site, including the interconnectivity of the main pages through navigation and subnavigation. In addition to helping the client gather and define site content, a visual site map is extremely useful for the creation of the design, as you saw in Chapter 7. At this stage, now that you've designed the site and it's ready to be built, you can use the visual site map again as a resource for another type of site map, the HTML site map, which will become part of the Web site itself.

In its most basic form, the HTML site map is a list of standard hypertext links to all the pages on a Web site. The list should include the home page and all the main categories and subcategories (and further subcategories when necessary) of the site, plus any other pages on the site that might not be accessible through the main navigation, such as a Privacy or Terms of Service page.

In the content area of the site map page (typically saved as `sitemap.html`), all the pages on the site should be laid out in a simple list format, like the one shown in Figure 10-2.

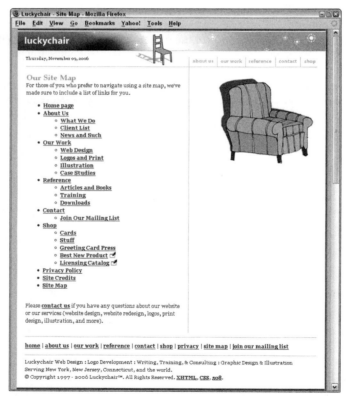

Figure 10-2: Here's an example of the site map page I use on my own Web site, Luckychair.com.

You add a link to the HTML site map — both in the footer and in the header — to all the pages of a site in order to make the site accessible to

- Visitors with disabilities using screen-reading programs or other devices
- Visitors with other browsing preferences, such as text-only browsers and browsers with JavaScript disabled
- Visitors who want to be able to go directly to any page on the site with a single click, rather than using the site's navigation system
- Visitors who want to see at a glance all the pages on a given site and how they're virtually organized

Beyond the human good, the mere existence of a site map helps search engines find and index all the pages of a site. Later, when the site gets indexed by a search engine, the contents of that site (and typically some, if not all, the pages on the domain) become more readily accessible to visitors, which in turn can increase business. That's partially due to the fact that many search engine robots and spiders completely ignore images and other graphics on a page and instead look only at Meta tags and marked-up text and hyperlinks when indexing individual pages. Because the site map page contains hyperlinks to all the pages on a site, all the pages should be indexed and therefore accessible to a wider audience.

If you're still not convinced about the benefits of having an HTML site map page, ask yourself this: If my site has a page for services, and the services page links to six additional pages that have further information about each of those six specific services, wouldn't I want visitors to be able to find those specific pages from a search engine rather than have to navigate to those pages from the home page? For example, a site for a company that creates artsy journals, custom stationery, and greeting cards might sell more journals overall when visitors searching just for journals can click a link from a search engine that takes them directly to the journals page of the site; a much more efficient way of shopping than having to begin the journal search from the company's home page.

Creating the HTML site map

To practice your skills at converting a virtual site map into an HTML site map Web page, use the site map from Jacks Cleaning Services, shown in Figure 10-3, and follow these steps:

1. **Create a new HTML page in your preferred HTML or WYSIWYG editor.**

The new page should contain the basic HTML code structure, including DTD, `<html>`, `<head>`, and `<body>` tags. If it doesn't, type in that code.

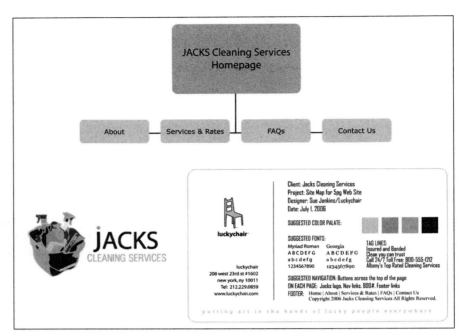

Figure 10-3: Use the architectural site map diagram to build the HTML site map page.

2. **In the body of the page, using the unordered list (`<ol>`) and list item (`<li>`) tags, type in the names of all the pages on the site as they appear on the virtual site map from top to bottom, left to right.**

In other words, create a list from the words: Home, About, Services & Rates, FAQs, Contact Us, and Site Map.

The HTML code for the site map page should use the unordered list tags, like the following one, which can specify different bullet types such as disc, square, and circle for each tier in the list (though you can also control the look of the list with CSS):

```
<ul type="disc">
<li>Home</li>
<li>About</li>
<li>Services & Rates</li>
<li>FAQs</li>
<li>Contact Us</li>
<li>Site Map</li>
</ul>
```

Note: When the site also contains pages that are not linked to the main navigation, such as a Privacy Policy or Customer Support, add those pages to the bottom of the list, right above the site map.

3. **In this example, the Jacks site does not have any subpages below the main navigation. However, if there were subpages, those pages would be added to**

the list as a subset of the main page they should be listed under, as shown in this example:

Job Opportunities

- Internships
- Jobs

4. **If desired, write out a descriptive sentence beneath each bulleted item to tell visitors what they can expect to find on each page.**

The description not only helps visitors viewing the page, but it also helps search engines locate and index the page.

Because the Jacks site is rather small, this would be a particularly good idea. Using your imagination, write out a brief description (directly below each page name) of what visitors will find when they visit each of the pages on this site.

5. **Turn each of the linkable pages in the list into hyperlinks with title attributes by adding link tags to the code.**

Make up each filename as you create each hyperlink, such as about.html for the About page:

```
<li><a href="http://www.jackscleaningservices.com/
about.html" title="Jacks Cleaning Services - About Our
Services">About</a><br>Learn how Jacks Cleaning
Services can tackle all your cleaning needs, from
rented apartments to large corporate offices.</li>
```

6. **Save the file as sitemap.html.**

When creating a site map for a client's site, save the file to the same location as the site's index.html home page.

To preview and test the page, double-click the file to launch a browser and view it or drag and drop the file into any open browser.

Making the site map accessible

The completed site map page needs to be easy to get to from all the other pages on the site. The site map should be linked in two key areas of a Web page. The first place to add the link is in the footer area of every page, along with the footer links to all the main pages of the site, as shown in Figure 10-4.

Home | About Us | Our Services | Contact | Privacy | Site Map

Figure 10-4: Include a site map link in the footer of every page.

The second place to put a link to the site map page is in the head of the HTML code of every page. This will also make the site map accessible to people using methods other than browsers to access pages on a Web site. The link includes both the `rel` tag attribute, which defines the link as a site map link, and the `href` attribute, where you can supply the filename of the site map if it's different than the one shown here. The link must be placed in the code between the page's opening and closing `<head>` tags:

```
<html>
<head>
<title>my page title</title>
<link rel="Site Map" href="sitemap.html">
</head>
```

Site maps are also especially useful for larger sites that might rely on graphics-heavy JavaScript, DHTML, or Flash navigation menus, which can't be easily accessed by certain screen-reading programs, text-only browsers, other assistive technologies, or Web robots or spiders. This isn't to say that you should never use JavaScript or other methods for navigation; on the contrary, they might all be fine solutions for navigation. When you do use them, however, you should at the very least include a link to the site map page in the footer of every page, and when you use JavaScript, be sure to also include `<noscript>` tags for visitors who have JavaScript disabled or use devices that can't read JavaScript. The following example shows how you might add a `<noscript>` tag to your code:

```
<noscript>
<p>This site uses JavaScript for the main navigation. To
access the pages without JavaScript, please use the links
on the <a href="sitemap.html">Site Map</a> page.</p>
</noscript>
```

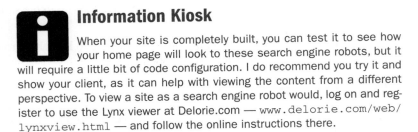

Information Kiosk

When your site is completely built, you can test it to see how your home page will look to these search engine robots, but it will require a little bit of code configuration. I do recommend you try it and show your client, as it can help with viewing the content from a different perspective. To view a site as a search engine robot would, log on and register to use the Lynx viewer at Delorie.com — `www.delorie.com/web/lynxview.html` — and follow the online instructions there.

To make the most of your site map Web pages, do any or all of the following enhancements in addition to the techniques I've already described:

- Below each main category of the site map, include a sentence to describe the contents to be found on that page and/or in that section.

- Use the `tabindex` tag attribute (normally used for form fields, but they can also be used to add a tab index number to image maps and links) inside each hypertext link to help visitors with disabilities access those links with a single keystroke, such as

```
<li><a href="washcloths.html" title="100% cotton wash
cloths" tabindex="4">
Wash Cloths</a></li>
```

Include the `title` attribute in every hypertext link on the site map. (See "Embedding object and image descriptions," earlier in this chapter, for a refresher on adding this attribute.)

Consider creating context-specific navigational hypertext breadcrumb links, such as *Home* ➔ *About* ➔ *Staff Directory,* to the tops of the content areas on all your pages to show visitors where they are in the hierarchical position within the site. You can see an example in Figure 10-5.

Consider adding a Search feature to your site to further assist visitors in finding exactly what they're seeking. Google has a nice free search tool you can use (www.google.com/searchcode.html), or you can find several other free and fee scripts online that will add search functionality.

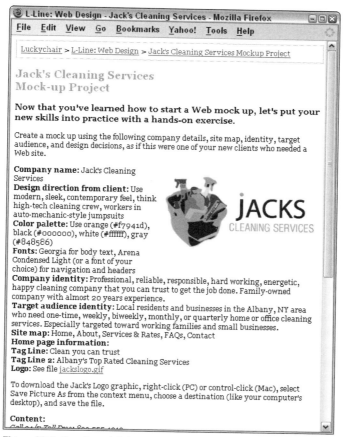

Figure 10-5: Breadcrumb links show visitors what page they are on relative to other pages and sections on a site.

alt attribute: An attribute of image tags that allows designers to provide a text description of the image to visitors using assistive devices to access the Web.

description Meta tag: A short description about a site that is placed in the head area of a Web page's code and is used by some search engines to appropriately index the page.

favicon: A custom icon created for a Web site that will be associated with the site inside a browser's bookmarks menu. In some browsers, the icon will also appear next to the Web address in the browser's address bar. To create the icon with the appropriate .ico file extension, you need a special plug-in for Photoshop; otherwise, the file needs to be created with an icon editor.

HTML site map: A Web page that includes links to all the pages on the site and is typically accessible through a link in a site's footer.

keywords: Words, or sometimes phrases, used in the keywords Meta tag and/or embedded in the copy in the body of a Web page, that describe the specific information to be found on a particular Web site or page and are used by search engines to help visitors find information on the Internet. For example, a company that sells pet food would help generate more traffic to its site by using keywords to describe its products in the kind of detail potential visitors might use to find its products, like "diet cat food," "all natural dry dog food," and "100 percent corn, wheat, and oat hamster pellets."

<noscript> tags: When a site uses JavaScript, it should also include <noscript> tags directly following any instance of <script> tags so that visitors using browsers and other devices that ignore or don't use JavaScript can view additional content.

padding: The unethical practice of including extra, redundant, unnecessary, and/or irrelevant keywords in alt text for images, in keywords and description Meta tags, in title tags, and in the body text of a Web page in an effort to improve a site's search engine ranking.

pay-per-click: An advertising service that lets the advertiser bid on search keywords to improve search engine rankings and that requires the advertiser to pay a fee to the service provider each time a visitor clicks a link that leads back to the advertiser's site.

robots/spiders: Automated software programs that "crawl the Web" in search of new pages to index and add to a database that is accessed when visitors use the search engine to find information.

search engine: A service that provides links to Web sites based on keyword search terms used by the site visitor. Links to the pages in the search engine database are typically gathered through the use of robots and spiders.

search index: Also sometimes called a *search directory,* this type of link repository contains a categorized list of links to Web sites that has been compiled and/or edited by humans rather than by computers.

search listing: A search service that uses data from both search engines and directories when providing link information to site visitors using the service.

SEO: Search Engine Optimization. Any techniques employed in the code and/or content of a Web page to assist with the indexing of a site by search engines and the improvement of ranking order within them.

spam: Most often used to refer to unsolicited, unwanted e-mail, but also sometimes used in reference to Web sites that practice unethical techniques in an effort to garner higher search engine rankings.

`tabindex` attribute: A tag attribute typically used with form fields that can also be used with image maps and hyperlinks to provide visitors with disabilities one-key access to the pages contained in the hyperlink code.

`title` attribute: This tag attribute describes the content in the tag element, such as links, tables, and table cells, and improves accessibility to visitors with disabilities.

Last Stop

Practice Exam

1. True or False: Each page on a Web site should have a unique page title.

2. List three ethical SEO techniques you can use to improve search engine rankings for a domain.

_____

_____

3. Why shouldn't you engage in unethical SEO practices?

_____

_____

4. Name three locations on a page where using keywords or key phrases is appropriate.

_____

_____

5. How often should a completed site be submitted to search engines to improve search engine rankings?

_____

_____

6. What is the difference between a visual site map and an HTML site map?

_____

_____

7. Name the two places on a Web site where links to the HTML site map page should go.

_____

_____

8. In what ways can having a site map page on a Web site improve the site?

_____

_____

_____

_____

9. Insert appropriate `alt` and `title` attributes in the following line of code:

```
<a href="bookreview.html"><img src="images/bookcover.gif"
width="150" height="70" border="0" id="book"></a>
```

Building Basic Pages

STATIONS ALONG THE WAY

- Structuring your HTML pages to include all the necessary elements
- Adding text, graphics, navigation, lists, tables, and other media to a page
- Linking text and graphics to other Web pages
- Using semantic HTML to identify different structural content elements
- Labeling objects on a page in preparation for styling with CSS
- Making content accessible with HTML

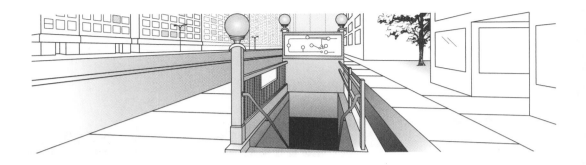

 # Enter the Station

Questions

1. What's the proper order in the code for the page title, Meta data, and DOCTYPE?

2. Why do you need to include Meta tags in the code?

3. How many different types of links can you create with HTML?

4. What are link targets and how can they best be used?

5. How can you use HTML to mark up content semantically?

6. What are tag labels and how can you use them with CSS and JavaScript?

7. How can you use HTML to improve page accessibility?

Express Line

Building semantic Web pages might be something you're already familiar with. If that's the case, skim over the chapter headings here to see whether there's anything you might be interested in learning that you didn't already know. If not, you can move past the information here and go to Chapter 12, where you'll learn about using CSS for page formatting.

So far, you've learned a bit about HTML coding, syntax, and structure. You've also made important decisions about the look and feel of the design and even mocked up the home page in a graphics editor for the client to review and approve. In this chapter, you begin to put all that knowledge together into one HTML document.

You begin with an overview of a bare-bones HTML page. Beyond the bones, the rest is up to you! This can be a daunting task, to say the least, especially for the novice designer. The feeling of building a Web site from scratch can be similar to the feeling a painter has when looking at a new, blank canvas. Where should you begin when you can do so many different things? The solution is to not let the options overwhelm you; you just need to get the first page built, and then building the rest of the site is fairly straightforward.

In this chapter, you'll learn about using Meta tags; adding page content like text, lists, tables, and graphics to the body of the page; creating hyperlinks; properly marking up content and labeling objects in preparation for using CSS and JavaScript; and improving page accessibility for all Web visitors, both human and machine.

Setting Up the Basic HTML Skeleton

Several components need to be in the code of a Web page to ensure the page will render properly in a browser. Not only do the parts need to be present, but they also need to be placed in the right order; if the order is incorrect, or if any of the parts of the code are missing or misspelled, the page might not display well (or at all) when viewed in different browsers. In fact, as you learn more about building Web pages, you'll quickly discover that a single page can look very different in different browsers, even when all the code is correct!

Transfer

If you've skipped ahead to this chapter in anticipation of being able to build a Web site before you know any HTML at all, please jump back to Chapter 4, which introduces HTML, and to Chapter 9, which introduces Web standards. There, you'll learn what HTML is, what it does, and how it needs to be written. Then, after you've read and digested that (and hopefully practiced with it for a while), you can come back and continue learning here.

A well-structured Web page has six core parts. As long as your page has all these parts in the proper order, the page will have a solid foundation upon which the content can rest:

1. DOCTYPE

2. HTML tags

3. Head tags

4. Title tags

5. Meta tags

6. Body tags

Information Kiosk

When Dreamweaver or any of the newer versions of HTML code or visual editors are being used, those programs should automatically drop in what I call the "bones" of a Web page anytime you create a new HTML document. You should also be able, while creating the new document, to choose which DOCTYPE DTD to include in the page, such as HTML 4.01 Transitional or XHTML 1.0 Strict. (Chapter 9 introduces the basics of choosing a DOCTYPE.) As part of the bones, Dreamweaver drops the Content-Type Meta tag into the page, which identifies the type of characters being used in the code. But, as you'll notice in the following example, that tag is inserted above the <title> tag, even though the steps above suggest you should add Meta tags after the <title> tag. The truth is that either order is fine, so long as both are present; however, most designers tend to place Meta tags after <title> tags.

Here's an example of the HTML bones you'd see if you created a new HTML document in Dreamweaver 8 with the HTML 4.01 Transitional DTD:

```
<!DOCTYPE html PUBLIC "-//W3C//DTD HTML 4.01 Transitional//
EN" "http://www.w3.org/TR/html4/loose.dtd">
<html>
<head>
<meta http-equiv="Content-Type" content="text/html;
charset=iso-8859-1">
<title>Untitled Document</title>
</head>

<body>
</body>
</html>
```

As you can see, all the key elements are there, accurately nested and in their proper place within the code.

The easiest place to begin building your first page is at the top:

1. **Refer back to Chapter 9 and choose the right DOCTYPE for your page.**

The DOCTYPE (DTD) needs to go at the very top of the code, as shown in the preceding example.

2. **Add the <html> tags if your editor hasn't done so already.**

When creating XHTML files with Dreamweaver, the program should automatically add the xmlns attribute with the opening <html> tag when it drops in the DTD, as shown in the preceding example. If you're hand-coding an XHTML page, therefore, be sure to also type in that attribute.

```
<!DOCTYPE html PUBLIC "-//W3C//DTD XHTML 1.0
Transitional//EN" "http://www.w3.org/TR/
xhtml1/DTD/xhtml1-transitional.dtd">
<html xmlns="http://www.w3.org/1999/xhtml">
<head>
<meta http-quiv="Content-Type" content="text/html;
charset=iso-8859-1">
<title>Untitled Document</title>
</head>

<body>
</body>
</html>
```

3. Enter the **<head>** tags.

Meta data that gives information about the site to machines (such as search engine robots) will be placed between the opening and closing <head> tags. Typical Meta data includes page titles and Meta tags. Furthermore, the head section of the code may also contain links to external files required for the processing of the data on the page, such as CSS style information and links to external CSS and JavaScript files.

4. Between the opening and closing **<head>** tags, enter opening and closing **<title>** tags, and between those, insert the text that will appear in the browser title bar.

 Transfer

For the title, be sure to give every page on a site a unique, descriptive title. The titles can be up to 70 characters long, including spaces and punctuation, and should include descriptive keywords to help visitors find the information on the page. (Refer back to Chapter 10 for more information.)

5. Beneath the **<title>** tags but before the closing **<head>** tag, add the **description** and **keywords** Meta **tags, as well as any other <meta> tags the page needs to include.**

I introduce the description and keywords Meta tags in Chapter 3, but also review them in the next section. The next section in this chapter explains the remaining Meta tags you might want to include in the page's HTML.

6. And last but not least, the content for the site goes between the **<body>** tags, which should be coded between the closing **</head>** tag and the closing **</html>** tag.

The details of this step are what the bulk of this chapter is about — making sure the text, images, tables, links, and more are all added to your HTML page. By the end of this chapter, you should have a Web page with code that is valid and ready to be formatted in CSS.

Understanding Meta Tags

Meta tags are special lines of code in the HTML of a Web page that don't appear in a browser window but are instead used to communicate important information about the site to Web browsers and search engine robots and spiders. The information contained in the various Meta tags can be useful for the process of indexing a single page or an entire site in a search engine's database, as well as informative to any visitors clever enough to view the page's source code.

The Meta tags themselves need to be placed in the code somewhere between the opening and closing <head> tags. More often than not, they're inserted in the code directly after the closing </title> tag but before the closing </head> tag, like the example that follows. However, from time to time, you might see the Content-Type Meta tag (described later in this section) above the <title> tag, which is fine too:

```
<head>
<meta http-equiv="Content-Type" content="text/html;
charset=iso-8859-1">
<title>Snorkeling and Diving Adventures of Southern
Florida</title>
<meta name="Keywords" content="Snorkeling, scuba diving,
scuba divers, snorkelers, glass bottom boats">
<meta name="Description" content="Plan your aquatic
vacation with SDASF. We offer snorkeling and diving
adventures throughout southern Florida. Private charters
and passenger vessels available.">
</head>
```

Transfer

The two most important Meta tags to include on every page to improve search engine indexing and ranking are Description and Keywords, as shown in the preceding example code. To be sure, Keywords will no longer do much, if anything, when it comes to improving search engine rankings, but I think they're still worth including because they provide at least one search engine, Inktomi, with keywords to help visitors find your site.

Description contains a readable sentence or two using a maximum of 250 characters to describe what can be found on the Web site. The Description appears in the search engine results when the URL is listed after a visitor performs a keyword or key phrase search. Keywords includes a list of words separated by commas that visitors might use to find the Web site's products or services with a search engine. Refer to Chapter 10 for details about supplying content for these tags.

Beyond the Description and Keywords tags, you can use several other Meta tags for communicating information to visitors and search engine robots and spiders:

Robots: Tells search engine spiders/robots whether the site should be indexed and whether links on pages should be followed when indexing is allowed. The default option is to "index, follow", which will both index the submitted URL and follow any hyperlinks to internal pages and external site links. The tag can also be specified in the code and written in any of the following ways, depending on your preferences:

```
<meta name="robots" content="All">
<meta name="robots" content="index,follow">
<meta name="robots" content="noindex,follow">
<meta name="robots" content="index,nofollow">
<meta name="robots" content="noindex,nofollow">
```

Language declaration: Determines which written language is used for the content presented on the page, such as English, French, or German.

```
<meta http-equiv="Content-Language" content="en">
```

Get further information about language declarations from the W3C site: www.w3.org/TR/i18n-html-tech-lang/#ri20050208.091505539.

Character encoding: Informs browsers of the type of character encoding, or set of letters, being used on the Web page, such as the A–Z alphabet or Chinese characters. Dreamweaver automatically includes this Meta tag as part of the bones of a new Web document.

```
<meta http-equiv="Content-Type" content="text/html;
charset=iso-8859-1">
```

To learn more about character encoding, visit the W3C site at www.w3.org/TR/REC-html40/charset.html#doc-char-set.

Refresh: Forces the page to reload in the browser window at the specified number of seconds, such as 120 seconds for 2 minutes. Refreshing the page used to be a useful tool for sites providing up-to-the-minute data or sites that needed to redirect visitors to a different URL. In the following example, the page would refresh after 30 seconds:

```
<meta http-equiv="refresh" content="30">
```

In recent years, however, this Meta tag has been used nefariously, and some search engines have begun penalizing sites that use it. If the purpose of the refresh is to redirect visitors to a new permanent page address, a 301 redirect would be a smarter solution.

Revised: Displays the date the site was last revised. You must update this Meta tag manually unless you use some kind of programming or scripting language to automatically recognize and update the date for you.

```
<meta name="revised" content="Ryan West, Indigo
Interiors, 7/07/06">
```

You can use other Meta tags, like `Publisher`, `Copyright`, `Author`, and `Reply-to`, to provide information about the publisher and author of a Web page:

```
<meta name="Publisher" content="Florida Sea Vacations">
<meta name="Copyright" content="Copyright 2006, Florida Sea
Vacations. All rights reserved.">
<meta name="Author" content="Martin Strickstein for Florida
Sea Vacations">
<meta name="Reply-to"
content="info@floridaseavacations.com">
```

Meta tags must be hand-coded unless your code editor has some kind of Meta tag insert tool or you plan to use any of the freely available online Meta tag generators. I like the one at SubmitCorner (`www.submitcorner.com/Tools/Meta`) because it gives you the option of generating more than just descriptions and keywords, and it also displays maximum character hints next to many of the tag form fields that can be generated on the site.

To see how the Meta tag generation tool works, follow these directions to create a set of Meta tags for an imaginary company that rents mopeds in San Diego, California:

1. **Open your favorite Web browser and go to the Submit Corner Web site at** `www.submitcorner.com/Tools/Meta`.

   In the center of the page is an area called META Generator with a list of check boxes for Recommended and Suggested Tags.

2. **Select the Enable/Disable All the Above META Tags check box.**

   This should select all the options under both Recommended and Suggested Tag categories by adding a check mark inside each of the boxes.

3. **Click the Proceed button.**

   The META Tag Generator form will then appear, as shown in Figure 11-1.

4. **Type the following words into the Keywords text field on the form:**

   Moped rentals, scooter rentals, mopeds, bicycles, scooters, ScootCoupes, Segway human transporters, one-seaters, two-seaters, San Diego, CA, guided tours, MZ, Peugeot, TGB, Binetto, Mondial, Adly

5. **Enter the following information in the Description text field:**

   San Diego Mopeds and Scooters rents hundreds of scooters, mopeds, Segways, bicycles, and fun cars to locals and vacationers each week. Rentals are available by the hour, daily, and longer. Come try our new two-seater ScootCoupes and Segway Human Transporters.

6. **In the Abstract text field, enter the following:**

   Hourly, daily, and weekly scooter, Moped, Segway, and fun car rentals in San Diego, California

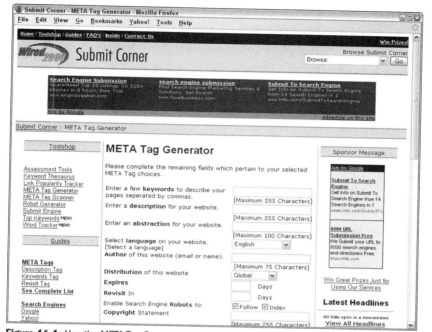

Figure 11-1: Use the META Tag Generator form at SubmitCorner.com to write your meta tag code.

Like the `Description` tag, the `Abstract` Meta tag provides information about the site. It should read like a simple one-line description of what can be found on the entire page.

7. Leave the Language menu set to English, but you can click the Language menu to see all the different languages that you can select, such as English, English (US), and English (UK).

8. In the Author field, type San Diego Mopeds and Scooters.

The author is the person or company taking credit for writing the content on the site.

9. Click the Distribution menu to reveal the options for this Meta tag, but leave the menu on the Global option.

You can select one of three levels of distribution, depending on how the author specified in the Author field would like the page to be distributed on the Internet. Choose Global if a worldwide audience is desired, Local for U.S. publishing only if in the U.S., or Internal Use for pages that shouldn't be made available to the public.

10. (Optional) To set an expiration date for a page, which will notify browsers when that page's content will no longer be relevant and the page can be deleted from the search engine database, specify the number of days that the page should be valid for.

The tag generator form converts the number of days you enter in the Expires field into the appropriate tag format:

```
<meta http-equiv="Expires" content="Fri, 23 Feb 2007
20:26:14 GMT">
```

11. Enter 7 in the Revisit field.

The number entered here tells search engine robots/spiders how often to visit the site and re-index the pages.

```
<meta name="revisit-after" content ="7 days">
```

12. Leave the Follow and Index check boxes enabled in the Robots field.

13. Type the following sentence into the Copyright field:

Copyright 2006, San Diego Mopeds and Scooters. All Rights Reserved.

14. Click the Generate My META Tags button.

The form gathers up all the information you just entered and formats it into Meta tags with proper syntax.

15. Then all you'll need to do is copy the code and paste it into your Web page, right before the closing </head> tag.

Your results should look like this:

```
<META NAME="keywords" CONTENT="Moped rentals, Scooter
rentals, Mopeds, bicycles, scooters, ScootCoupes,
Segway human transporters, one-seaters, two seaters,
San Diego, CA, guided tours, MZ, Peugeot, TGB, Binetto,
Mondial, Adly">
<META NAME="description" CONTENT="San Diego Mopeds and
Scooters rents hundreds of scooters, Mopeds, Segways,
bicycles, and fun cars to locals and vacationers each
week. Rentals are available by the hour, daily, and
longer. Come try our new two-seater ScootCoupes and
Segway Human Transporters.">
<META NAME="abstract" CONTENT="Hourly, daily, and
weekly scooter, Moped, Segway, and fun car rentals in
San Diego, California">
<META HTTP-EQUIV="Content-Language" CONTENT="EN">
<META NAME="author" CONTENT="San Diego Mopeds and
Scooters">
<META NAME="distribution" CONTENT="Global">
<META HTTP-EQUIV="Expires" CONTENT="Fri, 23 Feb 2007
20:26:14 GMT">
<META NAME="revisit-after" CONTENT="7 days">
<META NAME="copyright" CONTENT="Copyright 2006, San
Diego Mopeds and Scooters. All Rights Reserved.">
<META NAME="robots" CONTENT="FOLLOW,INDEX">
```

Watch Your Step

Please note that this generator creates Meta tags in all capitals. Although capital letters in tags aren't detrimental to HTML files, you can't use them in XHTML files, which is fast becoming the new Internet standard. Therefore, before using these form-generated tags in a page you intend to publish, regardless of whether the DTD is for HTML or XHTML, convert all the tags into lowercase text, like the following example: `<meta name="robots" content="Follow,Index">`. To quickly replace all instances of "META NAME" with "meta name" in Dreamweaver, use the Find and Replace tool.

Adding Content to Pages

Content refers to any text, images, navigation, Flash movies, QuickTime movies, and other media files and plug-ins that can be viewed on a Web page. As long as the content is properly coded and placed between the opening and closing `<body>` tags, it should appear in the body of the page in a browser window.

In this section, you'll learn all the basics about how to add text, graphics, lists, and tables to a Web page:

- **If you plan on hand-coding your pages, be extra careful about entering all the code correctly.** You'd be wise to invest in an HTML book and/or spend as much time as you can learning HTML from an online tutorial to ensure your HTML markup is compliant with the latest rules for HTML 4.01 (or XHTML 1.0). To code an image into a page by hand, for example, you'll need to insert the HTML tag for the image as well as include any attributes for it, such as `width`, `height`, and `alt` text.

- **If you use an editor, be it a WYSIWYG code editor or an HTML-only editor, the application does some of the work for you.** For example, when inserting an image with an editor, all you'll probably need to do is select the desired graphic file from a dialog box and, once inserted, add any attributes desired for the graphic in a special panel (like the Properties Inspector in Dreamweaver), which will then add those attributes automatically to the code.

Either way you intend to code, you'll quickly find that any tiny mistake can have a significant impact on how the page renders in different browsers. An extra space or a missing quotation mark can drastically change how the page is viewed!

Transfer

Movies and other plug-ins must include the proper coding so that visitors can see them in a browser, and thus are a bit more complex to add to your pages, especially when hand-coding. When you get to Chapter 17, you'll learn about more advanced content adding, such as embedding Flash movies and other multimedia plug-ins in a page.

Text

Text is the easiest thing to add to a page because you can quickly transform it into paragraph text and headings, organize it into a list, or place it into rows and columns within the structure of a table or layer.

Try not to be too concerned about how the text looks (font face, size, color, and so on) while you're adding it to the page. Here's the overall process I recommend:

1. Get text onto the page first before you do any formatting.

It will be easier and faster to do all the formatting at once after the content is in place, especially if you plan on formatting content with CSS and other markup. The same goes for adding any dynamic functionality like JavaScript rollover buttons to the page. Get the content on the page first and then add the dynamic functionality.

Take the following sample text, for example:

```
Creating Custom History Panel Commands
The History Panel is one of those tools in Dreamweaver
that many users don't take full advantage of. When the
panel is open, it records all the actions you make in
an open document, up to a certain number of steps (as
specified in the General category of Dreamweaver's
Preferences), and lets you take multiple steps backward
with the use of the panel's slider.
```

2. Mark up the text with the appropriate HTML tags to define what the different parts of the content are.

I've added tags to the sample text to identify both the main heading (<h1>) and the general paragraph (<p>) text:

```
<h1>Creating Custom History Panel Commands</h1>
<p>The History Panel is one of those tools in
Dreamweaver that many users don't take full advantage
of. When the panel is open, it records all the actions
you make in an open document, up to a certain number of
steps (as specified in the General category of
Dreamweaver's Preferences), and lets you take multiple
steps backward with the use of the panel's slider.</p>
```

The following sections explain the different types of markup you can add to the text.

Headings

Heading tags are preformatted tags that identify parts of text that are different from the regular content, such as headlines, subheadings, and bylines, by making them bold and either slightly larger or slightly smaller than regular paragraph text. Heading tags range from `<h1>` through `<h6>`, with `<h1>` being the largest preformatted text and `<h6>` being the smallest. Figure 11-2 shows how each of the following tags transforms the content in a browser:

```
<p>This is normal paragraph text</p>
<h1>This is heading 1</h1>
<h2>This is heading 2</h2>
<h3>This is heading 3</h3>
<h4>This is heading 4</h4>
<h5>This is heading 5</h5>
<h6>This is heading 6</h6>
```

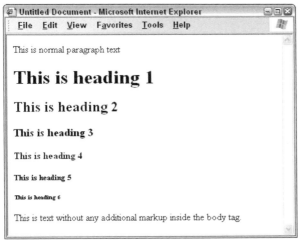

Figure 11-2: HTML tags for text are used to identify the different parts of the content, like headings and paragraphs.

Bold and italic emphasis

When your content contains a word or phrase that needs to stand out from the rest of the content, use bold or italic tags. Though in previous versions of HTML `<b>` and `<i>` tags were used, you should now exclusively use `<strong>` for bold and `<em>` (which stands for *emphasis*) for italics. The old `<b>` and `<i>` tags will be backward-compatible in HTML, but they won't be viewable in XHTML. The new `<strong>` and `<em>` tags, then, should be used for all new Web pages, and you should convert any old bold and italic tags to the new ones when inheriting an old site for maintenance or redesign.

When you need to make something both bold and italic, be sure to use proper tag nesting in the code, where the closing tags mirror the order of the opening tags:

```
<h1>Creating Custom History Panel Commands</h1>
<p>The <strong>History Panel</strong> is one of those tools
in Dreamweaver that many users don't take full advantage
of. When the panel is open <em>it records all the actions
you make</em> in an open document, up to a certain number
of steps (as specified in the General category of
Dreamweaver's Preferences), and lets you take
<strong><em>multiple steps backwards</em></strong> with the
use of the panel's slider.</p>
```

Text alignment

Text can be aligned left, center, right, or justified, relative to the browser window or container tag (such as paragraphs, headings, table cells, and <div> tags) inside which the content sits. For best results, add the align attribute to the opening container tag:

```
<p align="left">Take a few minutes to explore our site.</p>
```

Text can also be indented from the left and right margins with the use of the <blockquote> tag, which is primarily meant for use with quotes:

```
<blockquote>Bookmark this site so you can easily return
here when you're ready to make a purchase.</blockquote>
```

Transfer

The font face, size, and color of text on a Web page can be decided upon when styling your content with Cascading Style Sheets, which you'll learn about in Chapter 12. So for now I'll move on to adding other page content.

Graphics

In Chapter 8, you learned about the differences between GIF, JPG, and PNG file formats, so at this stage you should have all your graphics optimized and ready to add to your Web pages.

To help keep track of the images that will go on a site, keep all the graphics in a folder called "images" or "img" at the root level of the folder on your local computer containing your client's site. That way it will be much easier to locate and insert them into pages. When several categories of images need to remain separated, organize them in subfolders within the main images folder, such as images/skylines/memphis.jpg or images/buttons/contact.gif.

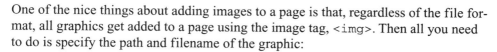

One of the nice things about adding images to a page is that, regardless of the file format, all graphics get added to a page using the image tag, `<img>`. Then all you need to do is specify the path and filename of the graphic:

```
<img src="images/filename.gif">
```

Watch Your Step

The filename and extension of each graphic should be spelled in all lowercase letters whenever possible. Be sure, too, that the filename in the code exactly matches the filename as it is written in the images folder. This is rather important because some servers won't display an image on a page if the filename is written one way in the code on the Web page (`MyMom.JPG`) and another way as the name of the file in the images folder (`mymom.jpg`).

Step into the Real World

When Not to Use Alternate Text for Images   When adding images to your pages, be sure to list the alternate (`alt`) text attribute for each image. Alternate text, if you'll recall from Chapters 9 and 10, refers to the text that screen readers and other devices will use to identify the contents of the graphic for people with disabilities viewing your pages with assistive devices.

```
<img src="filename" width="100" height="100" alt="Alternate text
  here" border="1">
```

As an added treat, the `alt` text also appears as pop-up text in some browsers (like IE 6 on a PC) when a visitor moves the cursor over an image.

Understandably, however, some images on a page are used solely for decorative purposes. For those types of images, include the `alt` attribute but leave its contents blank to keep the tag HTML 4.01– and XHTML 1.0–compliant, as in this example:

```
<img src="filename" width="100" height="100" alt="" border="0">
```

If you forget to add the blank `alt=""` attribute, your image code won't be compliant with the recommended standards set forth by the W3C. To add the blank `alt` attribute to an image in Dreamweaver, select the graphic on your page in Design view and type **<enter>**, including the brackets, in the Alt text field in the Properties Inspector. Or, when Accessibility features are enabled for graphics, simply enter the `alt` text (and a long description link, if desired) into the Image Tag Accessibility Attributes dialog box when it appears before the image gets inserted on the page.

Decorative images include, but are not limited to, corner graphics for tables (to create a curved corner effect), horizontal and vertical dividing lines, spacer GIFs (transparent 1 x 1 pixels often stretched out to hold open empty table cells to specific sizes), bullets, and nontextual ornamental borders and graphics.

With the tag in place, you can add the following attributes:

- **Size:** After listing the location and name of the image in the image tag, include the `width` and `height` attributes of the graphic in pixels:

  ```
  <img src="images/filename.gif" width="100" height="100">
  ```

  Image sizes can also be noted in percentages so that if you wanted to stretch out a 1-x-1-pixel image, say, to span the entire width of the page or a smaller area like a table cell, you could use

  ```
  <img src="images/line.gif" width="100%" height="1">
  ```

- **Border:** By using the `border` attribute, you can display images with or without a black border. Borders can be of any thickness by changing the number of pixels in quotes:

  ```
  <img src="images/filename.jpg" width="100" height="100" border="1">
  ```

  The border attribute might need to be set to `"0"` in some instances to remove any unnecessary padding around the image when placed next to another image.

  ```
  <img src="images/filename.png" width="100" height="100" border="0">
  ```

  Unfortunately, `border` attributes in HTML are limited to black, so if you want to create a border in another color, use CSS, where you can also specify the border's thickness and style (solid, double, grooved, dashed, and so on).

- **Image padding:** Padding is extra space around the outer edges of an image to help keep text and other objects from butting right up against it. Though you'd probably do better to style any needed padding on your images by using CSS, which offers more precise control, you can add uniform padding on both the left and right sides of an image as well as on both the top and bottom of an image by using the `hspace` (as in horizontal space) and `vspace` (as in vertical space) tag attributes. This can be useful when trying to separate an image from any text that wraps too closely around the image edges.

  To add even spacing around the entire image, use the same number of pixels for both tag attributes:

  ```
  <img src="images/chickens.jpg" alt="Baby Chicks at
  PawPaw Farm" width="200" height="125" hspace="5"
  vspace="5" border="0">
  ```

Text wrapping: To make text wrap to the left or right around an image, as shown in Figure 11-3, you must add the `align` attribute to the inside of the image tag:

```
<p><img src="images/team.jpg" alt="Our Team"
width="216" height="143" hspace="5" border="0"
align="left">Our team is committed to providing you
with the best possible service. For that reason, we
make all our e-mail addresses and telephone numbers
available to the public.</p>
```

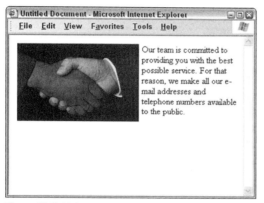

Figure 11-3: Make text wrap around an image by adding the left or right align attribute to the <img> tag.

Watch Your Step

Should you accidentally add the `align` attribute to the container tag, in this case the `<p>` tag as shown here, the image won't wrap and will instead be treated like another word within the paragraph. Try it yourself to see the difference:

```
<p align="left"><img src="images/team.jpg" alt="Our Team"
width="216" height="143" hspace="5" border="0">Our team is
committed to providing you with the best possible service.
For that reason, we make all our e-mail addresses and
telephone numbers available to the public.</p>
```

Using the graphic file information in the following table, write or type the lines of code that would add each of the images to a page. For this exercise, you can presume that all the images are in a folder called images. For instance, the first graphic in the table could be added to a Web page with the following line of code:

```
<img src="images/airplane.gif" width="270" height="230"
alt="Airplane">
```

Filename	Width	Height	Border	Alt Text
airplane.gif	270	230	0	Airplane
cliftonbridge.jpg	450	350	1	The Clifton Suspension Bridge in Bristol, England
sculpture.jpg	200	165	2	Marilyn May Figure
enews.gif	100	75	0	Newsletter Sign Up
getinvolved.gif	465	20	0	Get Involved Now!
photos/brochure.jpg	125	100	1	Brochure Request

Lists

Lists are a great way to organize content in a Web page. To make text content display in list format, you'll need to add two different kinds of tags to the code:

1. **First, the entire list must be surrounded by list tags.**
2. **Then, each item in the list must be surrounded with list item tags.**

You can create two kinds of lists with HTML: unordered lists and ordered lists. Unordered lists display each item in the list with one of three types of bullets next to it, whereas ordered lists display each item in the list with an Arabic or Roman numeral or letter next to it. In both instances, the type of bullet or number is an attribute of the ordered or unordered list tag.

Unordered lists, which use the <ul> list tags, can have three different bullet types: disc, circle, or square, as shown in Figure 11-4. You mark up unordered lists as follows and specify the type of bullet in the opening list tag:

```
<ul type="circle">
  <li>Pizza</li>
  <li>Calzones</li>
  <li>Pasta</li>
</ul>
```

Designers who'd prefer to use custom bullet graphics instead of the three HTML bullet types can do so by creating special CSS styles. You'll learn how to do this in Chapter 12.

Ordered lists, by contrast, use <ol> list tags and can have five different appearance types: numbered (1, 2, 3), lowercase lettered (a, b, c), uppercase lettered (A, B, C), lowercase Roman (i, ii, iii), and uppercase Roman (I, II, III). To specify the list type for ordered lists, enter 1, a, A, i, or I in the type attribute:

```
<ol type="1">
  <li>Corned Beef, Sauerkraut &amp; Swiss</li>
  <li>Cajun Chicken Club</li>
  <li>Crab Cake Hoagie with Spicy Mayo</li>
</ol>
```

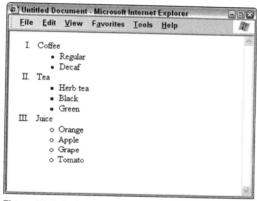

Figure 11-4: In the markup, you can specify three types of bullets for an unordered list.

Information Kiosk

Should you happen to leave off the list `type` attribute on either unordered or ordered lists, the default list type will be disc and numbered, respectively.

To create a list that contains a sublist, simply add another list to the code in line with any of the primary list items. In the following example, an unordered list is nested inside an ordered list:

```
<ol type="A">
  <li>Coffee
    <ul type="disc">
      <li>Regular</li>
      <li>Decaf</li>
    </ul>
  </li>
  <li>Tea </li>
  <li>Juice</li>
</ol>
```

Nested lists can be created, ad infinitum, when lists containing subcategories are desired. To see how simple it is to create a list, try this example:

1. Enter the following content into a blank Web page in your favorite code editor.

```
Digital Cameras
  Canon
    3 megapixel
    4 megapixel
  Sony
  Kodak
Printers
  Inkjet
  Laser
    Black & White
    Color
  Multifunction
```

2. **Decide what type of list you'd like for the main list (or start with the most nested lists instead) and add the markup for the list type and list items. Repeat for the other two list levels.**

For instance, make Digital Cameras and Printers a numbered list and make Canon, Sony, and Kodak and Inkjet, Laser, and Multifunction both bulleted lists.

3. **Save your file with the `.html` extension and select the Preview in Browser option in your editor to view your markup in a browser.**

Most editors provide the option of viewing the code in a browser of your choice. For example, in Dreamweaver, you'd choose File ➜ Preview in Browser and then select one of the browsers from the editable list of installed browsers on your computer.

Tables

Tables are the perfect way to organize data and other content on a Web page, particularly because anything that can go on a page can be placed inside a table cell, and you have more control over the alignment of content in a table than outside a table. Tables can have any number of rows and columns, be any width and height, have any colored border, and have any background color or tiling background image. What's more, the cells of the tables can also have unique widths, heights, and background colors and/or background images that sit on top of whatever styling attributes happen to be applied to the table.

Similar to the code to create lists, tables also require a few different code parts:

1. **The first part is the `<table>` tag, which defines the size of the table.**

2. **Then come table row tag pairs (`<tr>` and `</tr>`) for each row within the table.**

3. **In between each table row tag pair should go the table data tags (`<td>` and `</td>`), one for each of the cells that will create columns within each row.**

The minimum number of rows and columns you can have is one each, which creates a one-celled table:

```
<table>
  <tr>
    <td> cell contents </td>
  </tr>
</table>
```

4. **With this basic structure in place, you have a number of attributes to choose from so that the table will appear in the browser just as you envisioned.**

With the advent of HTML editors, coding tables by hand is no longer a necessary evil. Dreamweaver, for example, allows you to quickly and quite painlessly split and merge cells, set widths and heights, and add color to borders and backgrounds with just a few clicks. To be sure, it is very important that you understand how tables are constructed with code when you use them, but if you can, use a code editor to create them!

The following sections walk you through the important table attribute options (as well as options you might learn about elsewhere but are better off avoiding) regardless of how you plan to enter them.

 Information Kiosk

As for styling your tables, do as much as you can with Cascading Style Sheets. Within the code, you can still set table and cell alignment, cell padding, and cell spacing, but use CSS to specify any of the other table and cell attributes that have to do with how the table looks.

Table widths and heights

Tables can have widths and heights specified in the code in the opening `<table>` tag. The following bullets explain how the sizing works:

- **The size can be notated in pixels or in a percentage that's relative to the size of the viewing browser window (or other container tag).** For example, a table can be fixed at 500 pixels wide or have a width of 80 percent of the browser window. Any time a percentage is specified, that number will maintain the same aspect ratio to the browser as the browser gets resized larger and/or smaller by the user.

  ```
  <table width="80%">
  ```

- **When the width of the table isn't specified, the size of all the table cells will collapse to fit the contents inside them, whatever the contents might be.** The largest contents in any one cell will determine the width of the entire column and/or the height of an entire row.

- **If, however, you specify the size of the table cell, the contents of a cell will have no effect on the width and height of its respective column or row.** The exception is when the contents of the cell exceed the preset cell size.

The code for a 400-pixel-wide, two-row, two-column table with set cell sizes and a 1-pixel border looks like this:

```
<table width="400" border="1">
  <tr>
    <td width="300" height="200"> Account Number </td>
    <td width="100" height="200"> Account Balance </td>
  </tr>
  <tr>
    <td> 612345612345643122 </td>
    <td> $423.00 </td>
  </tr>
</table>
```

Nesting tables

Like lists, tables can be nested inside table cells to create truly unique layouts for content. For example, you might need to create a layout for displaying products that requires a place for a product image, product name, description, details, stock number, and price. With a single table, you might not be able to size all the cells exactly as you'd like, but with a table nested inside another table cell, you could, as shown in Figure 11-5.

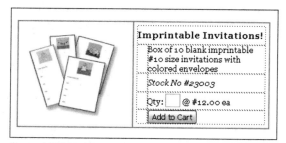

Figure 11-5: Use nested tables to create precise, unique content layouts.

Splitting and merging table cells

If desired, you can split any single cell into two or more columns or rows. Likewise, you can merge any two or more contiguous table cells that create a rectangular shape.

To merge cells, one of two special attributes, colspan or rowspan, must be added to the <td> tag that initiates the merge. Essentially, both attributes define a region that spans across *n* number of rows or columns. As shown in the following example, when the colspan attribute is used, only one <td> tag is needed for the part of the row being spanned. Alternatively, when the rowspan attribute is used, any row or rows after the first cell in the rows being spanned does not need a <td> tag:

```
<table width="234" border="1">
  <tr>
```

```
      <td height="23" colspan="3">Lunch Menu:</td>
   </tr>
   <tr>
      <td width="68" rowspan="2">Lite Fare</td>
      <td width="93">Garden Salad</td>
      <td width="51">$8.00</td>
   </tr>
   <tr>
      <td>Soup</td>
      <td>$4.00</td>
   </tr>
</table>
```

Table borders

When adding a border to a table, the size refers only to the thickness of the outer table edge. Any border width larger than 1 pixel will create a beveled table edge, as shown in Figure 11-6.

Transfer

If you hate the bevel (which is very old school and will make your table look awkwardly retro), you can create a nonbeveled border of any thickness and color by using CSS. See Chapter 12 for details on formatting with CSS.

Figure 11-6: Adding a border larger than 1 pixel on a table using HTML code produces a border with a beveled edge.

The cellpadding and cellspacing attributes

Two other unique attributes you have control over in a table are `cellpadding` and `cellspacing`, both of which, when added, uniformly apply to all the cells and cell walls in a table:

- `cellpadding`: This is the pixel space between the contents of the table cells and the cell walls. The larger the number of pixels, the more padding is added between the cell walls and the cell contents.

- `cellspacing`: This refers to the thickness of the cell walls between the cells.

Information Kiosk

By default, all tables have 1 pixel of `cellpadding` and `cellspacing`, even when these attributes are not specified in the code. This means that when you apply a 1-pixel border to a table with the HTML `border` attribute, the border will look like a double line instead of a solid line. To remove this default spacing and create a solid 1-pixel border with the HTML `border` attribute, include both `cellpadding` and `cellspacing` attributes in the opening `<table>` tag. Set the `cellpadding` to the desired amount and set the `cellspacing` to 0:

```
<table width="500" border="1" cellpadding="10"
cellspacing="0">
```

Alternatively, you can zero out the `cellpadding` and `cellspacing` in the HTML and apply a border and padding to the table with CSS.

Background and border colors

You can apply the background color (`bgcolor`) attribute both to the entire table in the opening `<table>` tag and selectively to individual table cells in opening cell tags. You can apply border colors (`bordercolor`) to the entire table as well as to table cells, but the `bordercolor` attribute for individual table cells is inconsistently supported in browsers and isn't a recommended practice.

To illustrate, you might have an overall background color on the entire table, specify a border color for the table, and have one of the table cells display with a different background color:

```
<table width="324" border="1" cellpadding="2" cellspacing=
"0" bordercolor="#000066" bgcolor="#99ccff">
  <tr>
    <td height="23" colspan="3"
bgcolor="#ff9966"><strong>Lunch Menu</strong></td>
  </tr>
  <tr>
    <td width="120" rowspan="2">Blue Plate Specials:</td>
    <td width="136">Meat Loaf</td>
    <td width="48">$7.95</td>
  </tr>
  <tr>
    <td>Macaroni &amp; Cheese</td>
    <td>$6.95</td>
  </tr>
</table>
```

To keep your code clean and to separate form from content, I strongly recommend you use CSS for background and border color attributes instead of using the `bgcolor` and `bordercolor` attributes described here.

Tiling background images

Adding a tiling background image to a table or table cell with HTML makes the image repeat endlessly both horizontally and vertically. This is typically done when a designer doesn't know CSS and wants to add a background image to the table. You tile a background image by adding the `background` attribute, which specifies the location and filename of a graphic to tile in the background, to the opening `<table>` tag and/or any opening table cell (`<td>`) tag:

```
<td height="23" colspan="2" background="images/dots.gif"
bgcolor="#ff9966">Breakfast</td>
```

A better solution for background images, however, is to use CSS.

Table and cell alignment

As for the alignment of tables, you can align them within the page or within any other container tag by using the `align` attribute inside the opening `<table>` tag. Alignment options are `left`, `right`, and `center`:

```
<table width="300" align="center" cellpadding="2"
cellspacing="0"  bgcolor="#99ccff">
```

Information Kiosk

Occasionally, you might find that adding the `align` attribute to the `<table>` tag produces uneven results in certain browsers. Should that happen during your testing, before publishing a site, wrap your entire table with `<div>` tags and add the `align` attribute to it:

```
<div align="center">
<table width="200" border="1" cellspacing="0"
bgcolor="#ccccff">
  <tr>
    <td height="23" colspan="3"
bgcolor="#cc66ff">Beverages</td>
  </tr>
  <tr>
    <td width="120" rowspan="2">Sodas:</td>
    <td width="136">Large Coke</td>
    <td width="48">$1.95</td>
  </tr>
  <tr>
    <td>Small Coke</td>
    <td>$.95</td>
  </tr>
</table>
</div>
```

Figure 11-7 shows how the preceding code looks inside a browser.

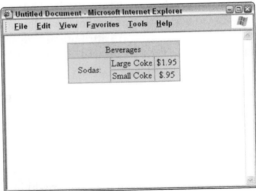

Figure 11-7: The <div> tags ensure that this centered table aligns properly.

To set the alignment of the contents inside any table cell, use the `align` and `valign` (vertical alignment) attributes in the opening `<td>` tag of the cell requiring alignment:

```
<td width="120" rowspan="2" align="left"
valign="top">Desserts</td>
```

Horizontal alignment options are `left`, `center`, and `right`, and vertical alignment options are `top`, `middle`, `bottom`, and `baseline` (which aligns the image bottom to the baseline of text within the table cell and at times looks no different than the `bottom` attribute).

Table headers

If table content needs to have a header row and/or header column, you could use the `<th>` tag instead of `<td>` tags where needed. Table header tags are preformatted to display any text in boldface without the need of bold tags:

```
<tr>
    <th width="100" rowspan="2" align="left"
valign="top">Hot Drinks:</th>
    <td width="136">Cappuccino</td>
    <td width="48">$3.95</td>
  </tr>
```

Information Kiosk

In truth, however, you'd be better off creating and applying custom CSS styles to any cell that needs special formatting instead of using the <th> tag because several of its attributes (including width, height, bgcolor, and nowrap) are being deprecated in XHTML 1.0 Strict DTD.

The nowrap attribute

To force the contents of a cell to display in one complete line, without any line breaks or wrapping when the content hits the right cell edge, add the nowrap attribute to the table cell tag (`<td>`):

```
<td width="120" rowspan="2" nowrap="nowrap">Store Location,
Address, and Telephone Number</td>
```

Adding the nowrap attribute will override the specified column width, but it'll keep the contents of the cell all on one line. Nonetheless, because this attribute is deprecated in XHTML 1.0 Strict, a better solution is to ensure that the cell widths are set to the proper size.

The id attribute

Lastly, when you plan on styling your tables and/or table cells with CSS, be sure to add an id attribute to each of your tables. This will help make your tables easier to identify from one another as well as allow you to more quickly apply CSS and JavaScript to them. The id attribute should be added to the opening `<table>` tag:

```
<table width="200" border="1" cellspacing="0" id="Menu">
```

Creating Hyperlinks

A *hyperlink* is a link in a file to any other file on the Web, whether it's located on the same site as the linking page or on another site out on the Internet. Links are typically created by pairing the href attribute (hypertext reference), which defines the destination, with the `<a>` anchor tag, which converts the contents between the opening and closing `<a>` tags into a link:

```
<a href="url">Link to another page</a>
```

Local and global links

Depending on the location of the linked file, the URL can be written as a link to another page on the same site (local) or to a page or file on another site (global). When the linked file is local, only the filename (and relative location when other than at the root level) needs to be listed:

```
<a href="contact.html">Contact Us</a>
```

```
<a href="about/history.html">Company History</a>
```

When the link is external to the site of the referring page, the entire Web address needs to be included in the hypertext reference:

```
<a href="http://www.weather.com">Weather</a>
```

```
<a href="http://www.google.com/maphp?hl=en&tab=wl&q=">
Google Maps</a>
```

Link targets

By default, the file specified in the link will open in the same browser window, and no extra code is necessary to make this happen. This is referred to as "targeting the same window." To make the linked file open in a new browser window, you need to specify the target location by using the `target` attribute of `"_blank"` within the referring `<a>` tag:

```
<a href="http://www.weather.com"
target="_blank">Weather</a>
```

The other options for the `target` attribute are `"_self"` for the same browser window; `"name"` to target an already named and opened browser window (such as `popup`) or named frame if frames are used (such as `leftnav`); `"_top"` to target the entire browser window and break any preexisting frames; and `"_parent"` to target the master frame of a nested frameset.

As a practice, it's a good idea to inform visitors any time you intend to open a new browser window from a link, especially when the linked file is a PDF or non-HTML file, because some visitors might view new windows opening as a nuisance. You can make an indicator by adding some kind of graphic next to the link or by adding text in parentheses next to the link.

Linking images

You can turn images and other objects into hyperlinks as long as the HTML code properly surrounds the object. Follow these steps to insert an image on a page and convert it into a hyperlink:

1. **Create a folder on your desktop called Image Link Demo.**

2. **Inside this folder, create another folder called images and place inside it a copy of the image you intend to use for this exercise.**

   If you don't have an optimized graphic ready to use for this exercise, visit this book's companion Web site (see the Preface for details) or www.luckychair.com/1-line and save a copy of the Joe's Tiny Diner GIF into this new images folder. Right-click (Windows) or Control+click (Mac) the image to open the contextual menu, from which you can choose an option to save a copy of the file.

3. Open your favorite HTML editor, create a new document, and save it into the Image Link Demo folder with the filename `imagedemo.html`.

Most editors should automatically generate the structural HTML tags (the bones) for the page so you can begin adding content right to the body of the page. If your editor doesn't do this or if you're using a simple text editor, add the following code to your empty page:

```
<!DOCTYPE HTML PUBLIC "-//W3C//DTD HTML 4.01
Transitional//EN"
"http://www.w3.org/TR/html4/loose.dtd">
<html>
<head>
<meta http-equiv="Content-Type" content="text/html;
charset=iso-8859-1">
<title>Untitled Document</title>
</head>
<body>
</body>
</html>
```

4. Between the opening and closing <body> tags, insert a copy of the image you saved in the images folder by adding the following line of code:

```
<img src="images/filename.gif" alt="alternate text">
```

Be sure to replace `filename`, the file extension, and `alternate text` in the code of your page to match your selected image. If you happen to know the width and height of the image, add that too. For example, if you're using the Joe's Tiny Diner GIF, the code should look like this:

```
<img src="images/joestinydiner.gif" alt="Joe's Tiny
Diner" width="212" height="115">
```

5. Convert the image into a hyperlink by adding more code around the image tag.

For testing purposes, use Google for the "link to" address:

```
<a href="http://www.google.com"><img
src="images/joestinydiner.gif" alt="Joe's Tiny Diner"
width="212" height="115"></a>
```

6. Save the file and launch a copy of it in a browser window.

If you're in Dreamweaver, BBEdit, or HomeSite, there should be a shortcut key (like F12) you can press to launch a primary browser for local testing purposes. Alternatively, you can drag and drop the HTML file by its icon into any open browser window, and the page should display.

7. In the browser window, click the graphic. When your browser switches over to Google, you've done it perfectly!

If the hyperlink didn't work, go back and check the spelling and syntax in your code. Something as small as a missing bracket or quotation mark can make all the difference in the functionality of your page!

At times, you might need to add a border around your images. When the image is also a link, the border takes on the attributes of a hyperlink.

8. **Add a border to the image so you can see what this looks like. Back in your code, add the `border="1"` attribute to your image.**

Your code should look something like this:

```
<a href="http://www.google.com"><img src="images/
joestinydiner.gif" alt="Joe's Tiny Diner" width="212"
height="115" border="1"></a>
```

9. **Relaunch your test page in a browser now to see how the image looks with the border.**

Your image will appear with either a blue (default link color) or purple (default visited-link color) 1-pixel border.

If you like the look of the border around your linked image but don't want it to take on the coloration of a hyperlink, change the border attribute to `border="1"`, create a border style using CSS, and apply that style to the image with the `class` attribute.

Other link types

Besides regular hyperlinks, you can create three other kinds of links in HTML:

 E-mail links: These links will open a blank e-mail message in the visitor's computer's default e-mail application with the Mail To address already filled in. If desired, you can also make the e-mail link automatically populate the Subject line by appending the e-mail address with a question mark, the word `subject`, and the actual line of text to be used as the subject line:

```
<a href="mailto:info@url.com?subject=My Subject
Line">Email us</a>
```

Watch Your Step

E-mail links are very vulnerable to spambots, and you really shouldn't use them anymore. Instead, encrypt your e-mail addresses by using any of the widely available encryption methods. If you haven't done so already, read the sidebar about protecting e-mail addresses in Chapter 5, which recommends three Web sites that provide free e-mail encryption.

Image map links: *Image maps* are specified hotspots on part of a graphic that have an associated hyperlink to another file. Images can have multiple image map hotspots as long as each hotspot coordinate is specified. For example, a site could have a group photograph of all the team members with the outline of each member hotspotted with an e-mail link.

Image maps are fairly complex to create by hand but are a snap to make when using a program like Dreamweaver. In Dreamweaver, you can use either the Rectangular or Oval Hotspot tool to draw a simple hotspot shape on an image, or create a more unique hotspot shape by using the Polygon Hotspot tool. After the coordinates for the hotspot are defined, the link to the chosen file will be specified along with a target destination for the link, if needed. The following HTML code shows how a rectangular hotspot can be mapped to a graphic:

```
<img src="images/logo.gif" alt="ABC Company"
width="300" height="72" border="0" usemap="#Home">
<map name="Home">
<area shape="rect" coords="73,73,156,85"
href="index.html" target="_self" alt="ABC Company -
click to return to the home page">
</map>
```

Named anchor links: These links, often called simply *anchor links,* will jump a visitor from one part of a Web page to another part of that same page when clicked. Anchor links are especially useful as quick links to sections referred to in a Table of Contents or answers in a list of FAQs, as well as jumps back to the top of the page after long passages of text.

Named anchors require two parts in the code to function properly: the anchor (or destination the link goes to on the page) and the link to the destination.

All anchors need to be given a specific name for the anchor link to work, so try to name your anchors after their functionality or purpose. For example, if your table of contents is listed numerically, name the anchor after the section, such as 325019 or faq6. Anchor names may include any combination of numbers and letters but can't contain any spaces or funny characters (such as / or *).

In the next exercise, you'll add an anchor link to a Table of Contents.

1. **Open your favorite HTML editor, create a new document, and save it with the filename `anchor.html` into the Image Link Demo folder you created in the last exercise.**

If you have deleted the folder, just create a new one.

2. In the code of the new `anchor.html` file, type the following content between the opening and closing `<body>` tags:

```
Apples

Bananas

Pineapples
```

APPLES: *Random text. Random text. Random text. Random text. Random text. Random text. Random text. Random text. Random text. Random text. Random text. Random text. Random text. Random text. Random text.*

BANANAS: *Random text. Random text. Random text. Random text. Random text. Random text. Random text. Random text. Random text. Random text. Random text. Random text. Random text.*

PINEAPPLES: *Random text. Random text. Random text. Random text. Random text. Random text. Random text. Random text. Random text. Random text. Random text.*

3. Place your cursor in the code right before the word *PINEAPPLES* (next to the words *Random text*) and type `<a name="pineapples"></a>`.

If you're using a code editor, you might have a way to quickly insert the named anchor rather than hand-coding it in. Dreamweaver, for instance, has a button on the Common tab shaped like a golden anchor, which will quickly insert the appropriate code for the named anchor after providing the program with the anchor name.

Information Kiosk

Note that the `<a>` tag for this part of the anchor link doesn't surround any content. This is because you don't want to create a link from anything; you merely want to create a destination hotspot on the page.

The pineapples section of your code should now look like this:

```
<p><a name="pineapples"></a>
<strong>PINEAPPLES:</strong> Random text. Random text.
Random text. Random text. Random text. Random text.
Random text. Random text. Random text. Random text.
Random text. Random text.</p>
```

4. To create the link to the named anchor, add a hyperlink around the text or other asset that will link to the anchor, but rather than adding a filename to the **href** attribute, you'll add a number symbol (#) and the name of the anchor.

In this example, add the link to the word *Pineapples* in the Table of Contents:

```
<a href="#pineapples">Pineapples</a>
```

5. Save the file and launch the page in a browser window to test the named anchor. The word *Pineapples* at the top of the content should appear as an underlined hyperlink that, when clicked, should jump the page to the section on Pineapples containing the random text.

To get this test to function in a way that you can see the jump occur, you might need to reduce the width and height of the browser window so that the random text of the pineapple area is hidden from view before you click the link.

In addition to being used as links from one spot in a page to another, anchor links can be used in conjunction with jumping to a specific spot on another page. You might, for example, want to let visitors click a link on one page that takes them right to a course description in the middle of another page. To do that, simply add a number symbol and the anchor name after the filename extension in the href attribute:

```
<a href="coursedescriptions.html#2319">Course Description
for Astronomy, Class #2319</a>
```

Now that you see how easy it is to create an anchor link, you might never create a long page without them. And, as long as each named anchor has a unique name, you can have as many of them as you like on a page.

Semantic HTML Coding

When it comes to coding pages, the more you use semantic HTML, the easier it will be for you to identify the different parts of your content and use that content for a variety of purposes, such as applying CSS styles, pulling collected data from visitors into a database, and adding JavaScript to objects to make the page more interactive.

Semantics, simply put, refers to the proper usage of HTML 4.01 and XHTML 1.0 tags based on those tags' contents. In other words, use the right tags for the job. So, when adding a paragraph of text, surround it with <p> tags; when creating a page header, use the tags for headings 1–6; when creating lists, use <ol> or <ul> and <li> tags; and so on. What semantics does not refer to is how the contents of an HTML page will appear in a browser; the presentation of the page should, as much as possible, be defined with Cascading Style Sheets.

In addition to proper usage, semantics also refers to the avoidance of using any deprecated tags such as the old <center> tag for center alignment and <font> tags for text styling. Most tutorials will not even cover these deprecated tags anymore, but they're important to know about because you might, in the course of doing business, inherit an old site from a client for either site maintenance or redesign. Table 11-1 lists all the deprecated HTML tags along with suggestions for replacement methods.

Table 11-1   Deprecated HTML Tags and Suggested Alternatives

Deprecated Tag	Usage	Suggested Alternative
<center>	Centers objects	Use <div> tag with the alignment attribute, as in <div align="center">
<font>	Applies font styles to fonts	Style using CSS
<basefont>	Sets default font style	Style using CSS
<menu>	Creates menu lists	Use <ol> or <ul>
<dir>	Creates directory lists	Use <ol> or <ul>
<s> and <strike>	Strikethrough	Style using CSS
<u>	Underline	Style using CSS
<applet>	Inserts applets	Use <object>
<isindex>	Adds search fields to a page	Use <form>

Watch Your Step

Besides these deprecated HTML tags, several HTML tag attributes, such as using vlink as an attribute of the <body> tag, have also been deprecated in favor of using CSS for styling text and other elements on a page. As long as you do most of the content presentation in CSS rather than in the HTML code, you needn't be concerned about which exact HTML attributes are deprecated. However, even if you do accidentally use them, as part of your prelaunch testing process, you'll verify the accuracy of your HTML/XHTML code with some online compliance tools to ensure that the code meets the minimum standard requirements to be compliant with the DTD you selected for your pages. Should any deprecated tags be identified at that time, you can change them.

Labeling Objects

Get in the habit now of labeling, or assigning a name to, all the objects on your pages by using the id attribute, especially for objects you plan on styling with CSS and making dynamic with JavaScript. The W3C refers to objects as *elements,* which really just means anything, including text surrounded by paragraph or header tags, that can be added to a Web page.

To label an object, the id attribute should be added to the object's opening tag as you insert each object onto a page, in the syntax id="*name*". The only real rules to follow when using the id attribute are to remember that

- No two objects can use the same id value in a single HTML file.

- The id is case sensitive and must begin with a letter but may contain any combination of letters and numbers as well as periods, underscores, hyphens, or colons.

- Although technically, the preceding two points mean that you can call IDs whatever you want, you should nevertheless try to name your IDs after their purpose as much as possible, such as sidebar1 or Sale_Items. This practice is in keeping with the theme of using semantic HTML.

IDs, in addition to being used as CSS selectors and script elements, can also be used as anchors for hypertext links, names of objects, and identifiers for other applications that might be parsing data from your pages, such as when a script extracts data from a form field into a database.

The id attribute can be added to text blocks, tables, images, <div> tags, plug-ins, media files, form fields, and any other objects you plan to style with CSS and/or make dynamic with JavaScript or other programming languages. The following examples show how and where to add the labels to different tags:

```
<table width="200" border="1" cellspacing="0"  id="menu">

<div align="right" id="specials">

<p id="specialparagraph">This sentence has a unique id
attribute.</p>
```

In some instances, the id attribute is used to replace the old name attribute, but in other instances, the name attribute still pertains. The situation can get even more confusing when you begin dealing with form fields because the id and name attributes function differently, depending on which browser the visitor is using to view the form. To avoid confusion and reduce troubleshooting time, you might in certain circumstances want to include both attributes within particular tags, like with images and form fields:

```
<img src="images/invitations.gif" alt="Invitations" name=
"invitations" id="invitations" width="175" height="140">

<input type="text" name="textfield" id="textfield">

<frame src="main.html" name="mainFrame" id="mainFrame"
title="mainFrame">
```

Fortunately, when you use a code editor like Dreamweaver, the program will automatically know which tags to add both attributes to.

Improving Page Accessibility

Though some designers might prefer to get all their content on the page and then go back and improve it for accessibility, it's a much better practice to add accessibility features during the page-building process. That way, you're assured of including all the different tag attributes and other accessibility enhancements as you add each element, rather than having to second guess and do double the work checking for objects that do or don't include them.

In previous chapters, you've learned about some of the must-have site accessibility features, such as footer links, a site map page, alternate text for images, page titles, and description Meta tags. You can further improve page accessibility by including additional accessibility tags and tag attributes in the code.

Table 11-2 lists the most common accessibility coding enhancements. Try to use them as often as possible.

Table 11-2   **Accessibility Improvement Tags**

Name	Description	Sample Usage
alt attribute in an image tag	Provides descriptive text for images for visitors using alternative methods of viewing or experiencing Web pages as well as for non-human visitors like search engine robots.	`<img src="images/go.gif" alt="Go Button" width="20" height="20" border="0">`
`<title>` tag	A unique descriptive title can be applied to each page on a site. `<title>` tags are searched by search engine robots and can improve search engine rankings when peppered with descriptive, relevant keywords.	`<title>Waterloo Design, Book Covers, CD Covers, Ontario, Canada</title>`

Name	Description	Sample Usage
Object labels (id and name)	Use the id attribute to label any objects you intend to style with CSS or add JavaScript to. When labeling images for JavaScript, be sure to also include an identical name attribute.	`<img src="cat.jpg" id="jack" border="0" alt="My cat, Jack">` or `<img src="img/access.gif" alt="Access Online" name="Access" id="Access" width="160" height="50" border="0">`
Long description (longdesc)	The alt text attribute can handle only about 70 characters. For times you'd like to provide a longer description for any image, add the long description attribute (longdesc) to link to a separate text-only Web page that contains the longer description. Use as many long description links with attending pages as desired.	`<img src="images/pugetsound.jpg" alt="The Puget Sound" width="500" height="115" longdesc="pugetsound.html">`
title attribute for links	Add the title attribute to all hyperlink tags.	`<a href="waiver.pdf" title="Waiver Form (PDF)">PDF</a>`
Table title attributes	Similar in function to alt text for an image, the title attribute goes in the opening `<table>` tag and provides a title and description for the contents of a table.	`<table width="300" border="1" cellspacing="0" id="perennials" title="Perennials" summary="Top 10 Perennials for 2007">`
`<link>` tags in the `<head>` of the page to the home and site map pages	These links improve accessibility for visitors using assisted viewing devices and enable search engine robots and spiders to more readily index pages in a database.	`<link rel="Index" href="index.html">` `<link rel="Site Map" href="sitemap.html">`
Footer links	Add navigational hyperlinks at the foot of each page to mirror any graphic-only links to the main pages on a site.	Home - <u>About Us</u> - <u>Contact</u> Each word will be hyperlinked to its respective page, as in `<a href="contact.html">Contact</a>`

continued

Table 11-2 *continued*

Name	Description	Sample Usage

A site map page	This page lists the hyperlinks to all the accessible pages on a site, with any subpages listed under the main category page.	Home
		About Us
		  Company History
		  Board of Directors
		  Our Mission
		Contact
		Each word or phrase will by hyper-linked to its respective page, as in
		`<a href="mission.html">`
		`Our Mission</a>`

Contrasting foreground and back-ground colors	One of the most common disabilities for visitors on the Internet is color blindness. Try to use colors with a strong enough color contrast that the difference can be detected by people with this disability.	Check out the accessibility color wheel by Giacomo Mazzocato at `http://gmazzocato.altervista.org//colorwheelwheel.php` Use this tool to assist with choosing color combinations that can improve page readability for those with partial or full color blindness.

Access keys	Add keyboard shortcuts, by using the `accesskey` attribute, that visitors can use (typically in combination with the Alt or Option key, as in Alt+C) to quickly jump to links, form fields, and other accessible objects on a page.	`<a href="contact.html"`
		`accesskey="c" title=`
		`"Contact Us page">`
		`Contact Us</a>`

Tab index (tabindex)	Often used in conjunction with the `accesskey` attribute, the `tabindex` attribute allows visitors to use the Tab key to advance from one link, form field, or other accessible object on a page to another. If desired, the order of the tab index need not follow a direct top-to-bottom, left-to-right progression.	`<a href="contact.html"`
		`title="Contact Us page"`
		`tabindex="2">Contact Us`
		`</a>`

Form input tag labels	When the `<label>` tag is used in conjunction with a label and form field, visitors can click anywhere in the vicinity of the radio button, check box, or label text to select that option.	`<label for="checkbox">`
		`Soup</label>`
		
		`<input type="checkbox"`
		`name="soup" value="soup"`
		`accesskey="s" tabindex=`
		`"10" id="soup">`

anchor: A tag used to specify a target destination within the same file containing the hyperlink to it. Anchor links are good for tasks such as linking to the answers in a list of FAQs or term definitions in a glossary.

attribute: A special characteristic of a tag using the syntax `attribute="x"`, such as the width and height of an image, the alignment of a table cell, and the style of a bullet in an ordered list.

deprecated: Any HTML tag or tag attribute that has been phased out of usage in favor of better coding and styling methods and will no longer be supported in HTML 4.01 and XHTML 1.0 markup, and thus might not work in newer browsers.

global link: Any hyperlink that requires the specification of the full path of the file being linked to, as in `http://www.wiley.com/WileyCDA/WileyTitle/productCd-0470096284.html`.

heading: A headline, subheading, or other important text that can be separated visually from the rest of the text on a page by marking up the text with any of the preformatted `<h1>` through `<h6>` HTML tags.

hotspot: On an image map, an area defined by rectangular, circular, or polygonal coordinates. See *image map.*

id/label: A tag attribute that identifies the tag with a unique word that can then be used to apply CSS or to assign JavaScript to the tag or contents inside the tag.

image map: A graphic with one or more *hotspot* regions defined with coordinates in the HTML code that can have behaviors attached to them, like calling a JavaScript to display another image or a link that opens another Web page.

indexing: The process by which a URL is automatically (and in some cases, manually) added to a database by a search engine robot or spider, which crawls the Web in search of new information.

link target: The browser window a linked file will display in. Default options include `_self` and `_blank` for normal Web pages and `_top` and `_parent` for pages displaying in Framesets. Links may also target already open browser windows by specifying the id of the open window in the target attribute, such as `target="closeup"`.

local link: A hyperlink that links to a file on the same domain and does not require the full path of the URL, as in `about.html` or `services/landscaping.html`.

continued

 *continued*

Meta tags: Tags containing Meta data that are placed between the opening and closing <head> tags on a Web page, the contents of which are used to communicate information about the page/site to browsers, search engine robots and spiders, visitors using assistive devices to view the pages, and visitors savvy enough to view the file's source code.

object: Any element that can be added to a Web page, such as a block of text, an image, a Flash movie, an MP3 file, or a plug-in.

semantic HTML: Using tags appropriately to define the information contained within them, such as using <p> tags for paragraphs and <li> tags for items in a list.

syntax: Correct grammatical structure of HTML, CSS, JavaScript, and other markup and programming languages. Checking the syntax includes ensuring that quotes, brackets, equal signs, back slashes, periods, and other characters are in the proper order and location within the code.

Last Stop

Practice Exam

1. True or False: Some of the data in Meta tags will appear in the body of the page when viewed in a browser window.

2. In a table, to increase the space between the contents of a table cell and the cell walls, you add _____, and to increase the thickness of the walls between the table cells, you add _____.

3. If you wanted a page to be indexed but you didn't want any of the internal and external hyperlinks on the page to be followed by search engine robots or spiders, which `robots` Meta tag content option would you select?

A) `<meta name="robots" content="All">`

B) `<meta name="robots" content="index,follow">`

C) `<meta name="robots" content="noindex,follow">`

D) `<meta name="robots" content="index,nofollow">`

E) `<meta name="robots" content="noindex,nofollow">`

4. Besides hyperlinks, name two other kinds of HTML links.

_____

_____

5. What are the six core parts of a well-structured Web page and what order should they be in?

_____

_____

6. List three examples of Web page content and define where in the code they should be placed.

_____

_____

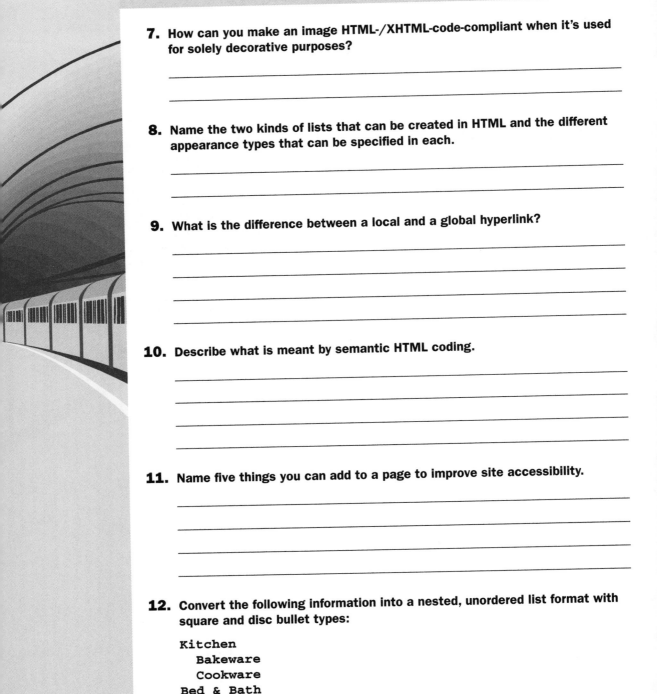

7. How can you make an image HTML-/XHTML-code-compliant when it's used for solely decorative purposes?

_____

_____

8. Name the two kinds of lists that can be created in HTML and the different appearance types that can be specified in each.

_____

_____

9. What is the difference between a local and a global hyperlink?

_____

_____

_____

_____

10. Describe what is meant by semantic HTML coding.

_____

_____

_____

_____

11. Name five things you can add to a page to improve site accessibility.

_____

_____

_____

_____

12. Convert the following information into a nested, unordered list format with square and disc bullet types:

```
Kitchen
   Bakeware
   Cookware
Bed & Bath
   Pillows
   Blankets
```

Page Formatting with CSS

STATIONS ALONG THE WAY

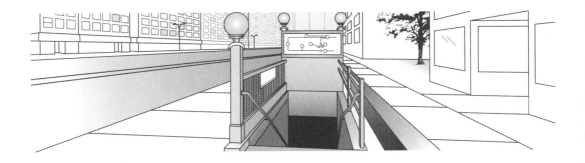

Enter the Station

Questions

1. Where in the code can you place CSS?

2. How many CSS files can you associate with a single document or Web site?

3. How might you use CSS and media types to format content for different devices used to view or interpret a Web page?

4. What kinds of style attributes can you apply to a CSS style?

5. What types of objects on a page can you style with CSS?

6. How can you use CSS to save time designing Web pages?

Express Line

If you're already familiar with CSS and feel comfortable creating your own CSS styles, skip ahead to learning about navigation systems in Chapter 13.

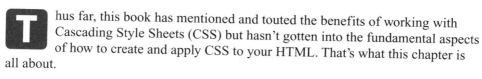

Thus far, this book has mentioned and touted the benefits of working with Cascading Style Sheets (CSS) but hasn't gotten into the fundamental aspects of how to create and apply CSS to your HTML. That's what this chapter is all about.

The World Wide Web Consortium (W3C) has strongly recommended CSS for several years now because it gives designers and programmers the highest degree of control over how Web content is presented in a browser window. Much like a word processor or page-layout program's style sheets, CSS for the Web enables you to set default formatting options so that all the text within a certain tag follows the design specifications of the mockup. CSS also enables you to set customized styles and positioning attributes that you can selectively apply to text, images, lists, tables, and other objects on a page.

When you use CSS to control a site's presentation, you can apply detailed settings to pretty much any page element, including the following:

- Font face, size, style, and color
- Margins, padding, and indenting
- Line and letter spacing
- Background colors and images
- Border colors
- Table and list formatting
- Layer size, style, and positioning
- Hyperlink formatting

CSS is fairly easy to write and implement, and if you read the text and follow along with the exercises in this chapter, you'll be up and running pages with CSS in no time.

To make the task of learning about styling pages with CSS smoother, this chapter breaks CSS down into several digestible parts. First you'll learn about CSS style syntax. Then you'll discover the difference between inline, internal, and external style sheets and how to link an external CSS to an HTML file. After that, you learn the basics of creating custom styles, redefining default tag styles, and using CSS to set several tag styles at once or link styles to IDs that you set in the HTML. You'll find an overview of the eight different CSS style categories, which will help you find the attributes you need when you create your own style sheets. (You can find a full listing of all the CSS style attributes in each of the eight CSS style categories in Appendix A.) The chapter ends with instruction on formatting with CSS and a helpful list of the best on- and offline CSS resources.

Learning about CSS

In the late 1990s, Cascading Style Sheets were developed as an enhancement to HTML so that styling information for an entire Web site could be centralized into a single external document, thereby reducing the amount of code required for styling in every page of a Web site.

Besides keeping HTML code less cluttered than it would be using the old <font> tags for text formatting, using CSS provides other benefits, including the following:

- **Faster page download times**
- **Improved access for visitors with disabilities**
- **Improved management of presentation:** A single external CSS file for a site also means you can quickly make modifications to an entire site, much faster than you could using the old <font> tags. For example, if you were using old HTML tags for styling, you'd have to specify the font face, size, and color every time a new paragraph required a different font appearance:

```
<p><font color="#993300" size="2"
face="Georgia,Times,serif"><a
href="contact.html"><b>Contact Us</b></a></font></p>
```

    By contrast, when all the font attributes are transferred to the default styling for paragraphs (the <p> tag) in an external Cascading Style Sheet, the HTML code becomes much simpler:

```
<p><a href="contact.html"><strong>If you're having
trouble viewing this page, click here</strong></a></p>
```

- **Easier site maintenance after the site is published:** With the old <font> tags, anytime the site's look needed changing, all the files would need to be modified and uploaded to the server before the changes would take effect for site visitors. With CSS, only the updated CSS file needs to be uploaded to the remote server before everyone can see the changes.

Anatomy of a style

A CSS style uses *selectors* and *declarations* to make up the instructions for the style, which instruct a browser how to modify the display of content. Figure 12-1 diagrams the anatomy of a CSS style to help you understand how styles are written.

The syntax of a style runs generally as follows, including all the funny punctuation and spacing:

```
selector { property: value; }
```

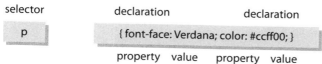

Figure 12-1: Each style in a Cascading Style Sheet has a selector and declaration.

In the actual CSS, a style looks something like the following example, where the style selector is h1 and the declaration defines the desired color of any content placed between h1 tags:

```
h1 { color: #0099cc; }
```

In more detailed terms, the selector and declaration work together as follows:

Selector: The selector, or name, of the style can reflect a tag name, like p or h1, or have a custom name like .mystyle, or the ID of an object preceded by the number symbol (#), such as #sidebar. The selector tells the browser which tag(s) in the HTML to select and apply the style to, such as all content on the page/site surrounded by <h1> tags. As you'll learn later in this chapter, three different types of selectors exist in CSS. Typically, selectors identify a single element to be styled. However, for efficiency of code, you can group selectors together, separated with commas, when the selectors share certain style attributes, as in the following example, which will set the default font to Verdana for all paragraphs, heading 1s, and heading 2s:

```
p,h1,h2   {font-family: Verdana, Arial, Helvetica,
sans-serif; }
```

Declaration: The declaration can contain a single style definition or a block of definitions separated by semicolons, and is listed between opening and closing curly braces { }. The declaration provides the details of the style, including what should be changed and to what degree, like the color of an element being changed to a particular blue. Although only three types of selectors exist, declarations can include an unlimited number of property-value pairs (style attributes) from any of the eight different style categories.

As you'll quickly learn, after you set certain style attributes in the CSS for particular tags, only attributes that differ need to be specified for subsequent styles. For example, if you wanted, you could make Georgia the default font for the entire site by setting that as a style attribute for the body. When set, all fonts would display in Georgia unless specified differently in subsequent style definitions.

Inline, internal, and external CSS

You can place CSS style sheet definitions in three different locations relative to the HTML code they'll be styling:

- **Inline** styles lie right next to the HTML code, often surrounding the content they'll be styling. This type of CSS code is hardly ever used anymore. (Designers use either internal or external styles instead.) The following example shows inline CSS with the <p> tag of HTML code:

```
<p style="color: #009999; font-size: 14px;">The
Hawaiian Islands</p>
```

- **Internal** style definitions (sometimes called *embedded* styles) must be placed in the <head> of a Web page's HTML code before the styles themselves can be applied to the content. When placed internally, CSS styles must be wrapped with special <style> tags so that the browser can identify the content as CSS styles. Within the <style> tags, the styles must further be surrounded by special comment tags (<!-- and -->) to prevent older browsers from displaying the style definitions in the body of the Web page. For example, in the following code, the CSS for the <p> tag appears between the <head> tags so that all instances of text within <p> tags in the body of the HTML are formatted as 14px with the hexadecimal color of #009999:

```
<!DOCTYPE HTML PUBLIC "-//W3C//DTD HTML 4.01
Transitional//EN"
"http://www.w3.org/TR/html4/loose.dtd">
<html>
<head>
<meta http-equiv="Content-Type" content="text/html;
charset=iso-8859-1">
<title>L-Line: Web Design</title>
<style type="text/css">
<!--
p {font-size: 14px; color: #009999;}
-->
</style>
</head>
<body>
<p class="state">The Hawaiian Islands</p>
</body>
</html>
```

Although better than the old HTML <font> tags for styling, when CSS is internal, the definitions can be applied only to that single page, which isn't very useful or economical when dealing with multipage Web sites.

External style sheets are the gold standard for CSS. Even for sites as small as one to five pages, external CSS files, which some refer to as *linked* styles, keep all the styling in one centralized file for easy access and easy maintenance. After you create the external style sheet, you can link it to as many HTML files as desired.

When you style the CSS in the external style sheet (a .css file), you create the style definitions following the syntax discussed earlier in this chapter but leave out the opening and closing style and comment tags around all the style definitions. In other words, the only things in the external CSS file are the style definitions, such as:

```
p {font-size: 14px; color: #009999;}
```

In the HTML, you add a link to the external file between the <head> tags, as shown in the following example:

```
<!DOCTYPE HTML PUBLIC "-//W3C//DTD HTML 4.01
Transitional//EN"
"http://www.w3.org/TR/html4/loose.dtd">
<html>
<head>
<meta http-equiv="Content-Type" content="text/html;
charset=iso-8859-1">
<title>L-Line: Web Design</title>
<link href="usamaps.css" rel="stylesheet"
type="text/css">
</head>
<body>
<p class="state">The Hawaiian Islands</p>
</body>
</html>
```

You find more details about linking external CSS to HTML pages in the next section and later in this chapter.

You can use all three CSS types in any combination to achieve the desired results. For example, you can have one master external CSS file, a few internal CSS styles on a couple of pages, and a few instances of inline styles on a particular page of a site. More likely, however, you'll have one master external CSS file for an entire site.

If you combine different types of CSS, keep in mind that style definitions are hierarchical in nature. This means that whichever style definitions lie closest to the content (your text, graphics, and so on) take precedence. External CSS is overridden by internal CSS, which is overridden by inline CSS or any other inline styling tags and attributes, including any old <font> tags.

This hierarchical rule also applies to redundant or conflicting CSS within the same document. Should a file contain something like two <body> tags with conflicting <font> tags, the style definition that sits lower in the list of styles (in the following example, the one specifying "Courier New" as the default font) will be the one style the page will display in:

```
body {
  font-family: Georgia, "Times New Roman", Times, serif;
}
body {
  font-family: "Courier New", Courier, mono;
}
```

Linking external CSS to a page

Linking to an external CSS requires only one line of code, which references the name and location of the external CSS file, relative to the root level of the server on which the site resides. The line of code needs to be placed somewhere between the opening and closing <head> tags of every HTML page on a site that will be using it. As long as the filename of the CSS is accurately entered in the HTML file, the link provides instructions to the browser on how to interpret the CSS style information and render the page in the browser.

Here's an example of a link to an external CSS file:

```
<link href="global.css" rel="stylesheet" type="text/css">
```

The other attributes in the <link> tag besides the href are required to help the browser interpret the data on the linked CSS file. The rel attribute identifies the linked file as a style sheet, and the type attribute specifies that the linked file is written in text/css format.

When placing the CSS link in your Web page code, try to keep the link's location consistent from page to page. For instance, you might want to add it directly following the last Meta tag, or place it right above the closing <head> tag.

When using external CSS files, you also need to think about where they belong in the file organization of the site:

ONE FARE ⊙ CSS files typically sit at the root level, which should be in the same place as the index.html home page.

Information Kiosk

The *root level*, as you'll recall from previous chapters, refers to the ground floor of your site on the remote host server. Typically, the home page (index.html) sits at the root level along with an images folder and other main pages. Additionally, some sites create subfolders at the root level to house JavaScripts, CSS files, or pages that fall into a similar category, such as all the pages relating to a company's service.

If, however, you have two or more Cascading Style Sheets for the same Web site, you can save all the CSS files into a folder at the root level, perhaps called css, and access them from there just as easily, as long as the href indicates the location of the folder and the filename:

```
<link href="css/global.css" rel="stylesheet"
type="text/css">
```

Setting CSS media types

In Web speak, the *media type* is the specification within a Cascading Style Sheet that identifies the device that will be used to access the HTML file being styled. Examples of a media type include a computer screen, a printer, a hand-held gadget, Braille translator, speech synthesizer, or other type of assistive device. Table 12-1 identifies all the media types currently in use.

Table 12-1   **CSS Media Types**

Media Type	Definition
all	Good for all devices, recommended as the default catch-all type when multiple CSS are specified.
aural	Used with text-to-speech devices.
Braille	For Braille tactile feedback devices.
embossed	For paged Braille devices.
handheld	Used for small screened devices with limited bandwidth capabilities and often monochromatic or limited color displays, such as the Blackberry or Web-enabled cell phone.
print	Best for files intended for print, whether actually printed or viewed only in Print Preview mode.
projection	For overhead projectors or documents turned into transparencies for projection.
screen	Best for color monitors.
tty	Good for teletype machines, special text terminals, and other "fixed-pitch character grid" devices. Note: When creating CSS for this type, avoid specifying sizes of any objects on the page in pixels.
tv	Used for TV-type devices that might have less robust features than a regular color computer monitor.

Step into the Real World

Multiple Media Types at Work   Though a lot of the style attributes in CSS work across all media types, some are to be used only with specific media, like the speech-rate property that can be used only with aural devices. More often, though, some attributes that are shared by two devices might need adjusting in the secondary CSS so that those attributes look good on both devices. In cases like this, creating two CSS files, one for each device, might be necessary to improve the experience of the HTML document on both devices.

Take, for example, the case where a Web page looks good on-screen, but when the content is printed, some of the graphics take up so much room that they force the printer to cut off some text and push any remaining text onto another page. You can easily solve this problem by creating two style sheets: one for all media types and the other for printers.

To illustrate this point, follow these steps:

1. **Launch your favorite browser and open the sample media types demo file at `www.luckychair.com/1-line/cssmediatypes.html`.**

   This page contains a `<link>` tag with an `all` media type attribute that specifies a particular external CSS.

2. **Choose View → Source to take a look at the code. Right before the closing `</head>` tag, you'll also see another link to an external CSS file, but this second CSS link uses the `print` media type:**

   ```
   <link href="cssdemo.css" rel="stylesheet" type="text/css" media="all" />
   <link href="cssmediatypes.css" rel="stylesheet" type="text/css" media="print" />
   ```

   The `cssmediatypes.css` style sheet contains a few attributes that are different than the `cssdemo.css` style sheet. Namely, in the `cssmediatypes.css` file, the entire list at the bottom of the page has been styled as a hidden block with the `block: none;` attribute, and the contents on the entire page have been placed inside a layer that has the fixed width of 500 pixels for print.

3. **To see how the content on the page looks differently when you go to print it, choose File → Print Preview from your Browser's main menu to open the Print Preview dialog box.**

You can add media-dependent style sheets to a file in two ways:

One method uses the @media or @import at-rules surrounded by <style> and comment tags (to hide the style specification from displaying in the body of the page when the page is viewed in old browsers). The syntax is slightly different for @media or @import, but they do essentially the same thing:

```
<style type="text/css">
<!--
@media print {
   /* dragyyn.css */
}
-->
</style>
```

or

```
<style type="text/css" media="print,handheld">
<!--
@import url("surface.css");
-->
</style>
```

The other uses a `<link>` tag that specifies the location and filename of the external CSS and includes the media attribute defining the media type:

```
<link rel="stylesheet" type="text/css"
    media="print" href="eceon.css">
```

If you'll be using internal CSS as opposed to an external CSS file, the @media method is nice for indicating the media type because you can specify multiple media types and contain the style definitions internal to the HTML page, as in this example:

```
<style type="text/css">
<!--
@media screen, print {
  body { font-family: Georgia, "Times New Roman", Times,
serif; }
}
-->
</style>
```

Or you can stack the style definitions on top of one another when the attributes differ, as shown here:

```
<style type="text/css" media="all">
<!--
@media screen {
  body { font-size: 14px; }
}
@media print {
  body { font-size: 12px; }
}
-->
</style>
```

When the CSS files will be external to the pages on the site, the @import at-rules or `<link>` method are more useful. My preference is to use the `<link>` method listing the all media type on top and any specific media type CSS below:

```
<link rel="stylesheet" type="text/css"
    media="all" href="surface.css">
<link rel="stylesheet" type="text/css"
    media="print" href="eceon.css">
```

Linking external CSS and setting media types in Dreamweaver

Dreamweaver users can easily insert the link to an external CSS without having to remember all the code or the proper syntax. What's more, when creating links to an external CSS in Dreamweaver, you can also choose the desired CSS media type.

The following steps will show you how to link an external CSS to an open HTML file in Dreamweaver with the all media type. You'll need a sample HTML file and a sample CSS file to do this exercise. If you don't have sample files, feel free to download the Sample HTML File for Chapter 12 Exercise files from this book's companion Web site (see the Preface for details) or the Luckychair L-Line support page (www.luckychair.com/l-line).

1. **In Dreamweaver, open the HTML file you'd like to add a CSS link to and click the Attach Style Sheet icon at the bottom of the CSS Styles panel.**

   Clicking the icon opens the Attach External Style Sheet dialog box. If you don't see the CSS Styles panel, choose Window → CSS Styles to open it.

2. **Type the name of the CSS you'd like to link to the file in the File/URL text field or click the Browse button to find and select the desired CSS.**

   If you're using the sample files you just downloaded from the Web, click the Browse button to navigate to the location where you saved the sample files, and select the cssdemo.css file.

3. **Next to the Add As option, select either the Link or Import radio button.**

   The Link option adds the CSS as an external file using the <link> tag:

   ```
   <head>
   <link href="cssdemo.css" rel="stylesheet"
   type="text/css">
   </head>
   ```

   The Import option, by contrast, specifies the external CSS within a style link inside the head of the page by using the @import at-rule:

   ```
   <head>
   <style type="text/css">
   <!--
   @import url("cssdemo.css");
   -->
   </style>
   </head>
   ```

4. **Click the Media drop-down menu and select the ALL media type.**

   To specify multiple media types, type the names of the media types desired, separated by commas and no spaces, such as screen,print,tty.

5. If desired, click the dialog box's Preview button to see how the newly linked CSS file styles your sample HTML file.

6. Click OK to complete the link.

Dreamweaver's CSS Styles panel now displays the newly attached CSS file, and the sample HTML file is styled with the attributes on the linked CSS.

CSS Style Selectors

Now that you have an understanding of the differences between internal, inline, and external CSS style definitions, I'll talk about the different style selectors. You can use any of three style selector types to create a CSS style: custom class styles, tag redefines, and advanced CSS selectors. Though they all use roughly the same syntax for the style declarations, each type determines which parts of the HTML will be modified.

Applying styles selectively with custom class

Custom class styles, or simply *custom styles,* are for times when you want to create a style and then selectively apply it to text or objects on a Web page. For example, in the sentence "Our customized Content Management System (CMS) makes it possible for you to control and maintain your online publications," you could create a custom class style to modify the words *Content Management System (CMS).* Here's how the CSS style declaration would look for that custom style with a selector named .cms:

```
.cms {
  font-family: Georgia, "Times New Roman", Times, serif;
  font-size: 23px;
  font-weight: bold;
  color: #990000;
}
```

You can name custom class styles anything you like, but in keeping with the concept of semantic HTML, try to name your custom styles after the function they'll be performing, such as .highlight or .imageborder.

Watch Your Step

When writing the custom class styles in the CSS file, be sure to include a period (.) directly before the style name, as shown in the preceding code. The presence of the period performs two functions. First, it helps you quickly identify custom styles from other types of styles when reviewing your CSS code. Secondly, and perhaps more importantly, the period informs browsers that the style is a custom class that will be selectively applied to content on the page.

After you specify the style declaration in the CSS, you can apply it to any object in the HTML document by appending the `class` attribute to the opening container tag of the object or content being styled. Note that when specifying the custom style in the HTML code with the `class` attribute, the period doesn't go before the style name; the period is required only in the style definition part of the CSS. In the following example, because the style is being selectively applied to the text *Content Management System (CMS)*, the class is applied to the content using the `<span>` tag rather than the `<p>` tag:

```
<p>Our customized <span class="cms">Content Management
System (CMS)</span> makes it possible for you to control
and maintain your online publications.</p>
```

Information Kiosk

The `<span>` tag, by the way, is an empty container tag that does nothing until you tell it to do something, such as apply a style to content or align the contents to the left, center, or right.

Redefining tag defaults

Without the use of any CSS, all HTML tags are preformatted to look a particular way and perform specific functions. Take the `<h1>` tag, for example. This tag is preformatted to be big, black, and bold, and its intended use is to identify the headline(s) in the content.

The *tag redefine* style selector type changes the preformatted look of any existing HTML tag like `<p>` and `<h1>`. With CSS, you can redefine the preformatted style to be anything you like. As long as the redefine is specified in the CSS, you can style `<h1>` to match the design and color scheme of your site, such as Geneva, 36 pixels, bold, and indigo blue:

```
h1 {
   font-family: Geneva, Arial, Helvetica, sans-serif;
   font-size: 36px;
   font-weight: bold;
   color: #6666cc;
}
```

Redefining existing tags is one of the best ways to globally style content on a site without having to selectively apply the styles as you must with custom class styles. In fact, most designers at a minimum define styles for the `<body>`, `<p>`, `<h1>`, and `<td>` tags. A redefined `<body>` tag, for instance, can take on many of the attributes that were formerly applied to the opening `<body>` tag in HTML code, such as removing default page margin spacing and changing the page background color. Here's a typical example of how a `<body>` tag might be redefined in the CSS:

```
body {
  margin-left: 0px;
  margin-top: 0px;
  margin-right: 0px;
  margin-bottom: 0px;
  background-color: #bbc6c2;
}
```

Other HTML tags that designers often redefine in CSS include `<html>`, `<h1>` through `<h6>`, `<td>`, `<li>`, `<img>`, and `<hr>`.

Morphing other page elements with advanced selectors

The *advanced selector* type is where a lot of the fancy footwork in CSS occurs because the selector can be written in a variety of ways:

- When used to modify the look of hyperlinks, for example, the advanced selector is written in two parts separated by a colon — `a:link`, `a:visited`, `a:hover`, and `a:active`.

- When used to apply the same styles to several tags, the advanced selector is divided by commas, as in `body, th, td`.

- When an advanced selector is used with `id` attributes in the HTML, the selector is simply labeled with a number sign and the attribute name.

- When styles need to be applied only to specific content areas, the advanced selector can be written with any combination of tags, punctuation, and custom class names, as in `p.cms`, `#content img`, and `#tablistmenu span`.

The most common usage of the advanced selector is to modify the default color and attributes of hyperlinks. By default, all hyperlinks use a royal blue for unvisited links and a purple color for visited links. Because these colors, in all likelihood, won't match the colors in your site's design, you can change them with CSS. What's more, you have the benefit of adding two additional style states to all hyperlinks; in addition to normal link and visited link states, with CSS you can style the *hover* state, which occurs when a visitor mouses over links, and the *active* state, which appears when a visitor clicks a link.

To change just the color of a hyperlink for all four link states, you would add the following style definitions to your CSS, replacing the hexadecimal values in this example with your desired color values for each of the link styles:

```
a:link {
    color: #6666cc;
}
a:visited {
    color: #009999;
}
a:hover {
    color: #0099cc;
}
a:active {
    color: #990000;
}
```

 Watch Your Step

When creating the link styles, take care that they're created in the order they will be experienced, because if the link styles are out of order, they may not work properly when viewed in a browser. Create the normal link state first, then the visited state, then the hover state, and lastly the active state as shown in the preceding example.

You can also use the advanced selector to create styles for any combination of tags all at once as well as tags with specific id attributes. To style multiple tags at once, list all the tags separated by commas and no spaces in the selector half of the style definition:

```
body,th,td {
    font-family: Georgia, "Georgia Ref", Tahoma, "Palatino
Linotype", Palatino, serif;
    font-size: 12px;
    color: #26506c;
}
```

To style an object with an id attribute, set the selector by writing a number symbol (#) followed by the ID name, as in this example where the object is a <div> layer with the attribute id="border":

```
#border {
    border: 1px dashed #cad0d6;
    margin: 0px 1px 0px 0px;
    padding: 10px;
}
```

Like a tag redefine selector, which automatically changes how contents surrounded by a particular tag appear, anytime a style name uses the #ID syntax, the style definition will automatically be applied to the object with the matching ID.

Transfer

To refresh your memory about setting `id` attributes for elements within the HTML, see Chapter 11.

The Eight Style Categories

In some of the preceding examples, you've seen a few of the attributes that you can add to a style definition, such as the border attribute, font size, and background color.

To help make choosing the right style attributes a little easier, you just need to remember that there are eight different style categories to choose from. Once you know the category you need, choosing the attributes within it makes much more sense.

Transfer

This section is your introduction to the different types of CSS attributes. You can find specific details about all the CSS attributes in each category in Appendix A. Use this appendix as your guide, as you begin using CSS to make your design ideas come to life on the page.

The eight style categories in CSS are

- **Type:** The type properties include attributes that can modify the way text appears on a Web page. Attributes include font face, font size, font style, font color, font decoration, font weight, font variant, font case, and line height.

- **Background:** You can apply background properties like color or a background image to a number of different objects on a Web page including the page, a layer, a table, a table cell, and even text.

Transfer

Layers are like tableless table cells that can be absolutely or relatively placed anywhere on a Web page using the `<div>` tag and CSS style definitions. You'll learn more about layers in detail in Chapter 14.

- **Block:** Block properties control the alignment and spacing of objects on a page through their tags and attributes. Blocks include text, content inside `<div>` tags (with and without positions specified), tags using the `display:block` style, and images or paragraphs set with absolute or relative positions. For example, use a block attribute to specify that a particular block of text has text alignment set to justify.

Box: When the box properties are used, styled objects can be positioned anywhere in a browser window. The padding and margin box style rules can be applied selectively to any or all of the four sides of the styled object (such as left and bottom or top, left, and right). However, if you're styling less than all four sides, remember to add 0 values to the sides that should not contain values, rather than leaving them blank. Use the box styles for things like adjusting the margins on a page or adding padding to content inside a table cell.

Information Kiosk

Though not all attributes apply styles to all four sides of an object, word, or block of text, as a general rule, try when entering individual values to rules with top, bottom, left, and right fields to enter 0 or None for any sides that should not contain values. This should improve the way the page is rendered in a variety of browsers. For example, the `padding` attribute in the box properties category can take on values for top, bottom, left, and right. If you want padding only on the top and left sides of an object, be sure to enter 0 as the unit for the right and bottom sides of the style definition:

```
.mystyle {
    padding-top: 5px;
    padding-right: 0px;
    padding-bottom: 0px;
    padding-left: 5px;
}
```

Border: Border properties define the color, style, and width of borders around any styled object. Because borders can go on all four sides of an object, each side can have different border attributes. As with margins and padding, be sure to add a 0 or None to any side not being styled for best results.

List: When styling lists with CSS, you can easily select the list type for both numbered and bulleted lists, the bullet position relative to the contents of the list, and if desired, whether to use your own graphic for the bullet image.

Positioning: The positioning attributes are used primarily to style layers using the `<div>` tag, but you can also use them to style an image or block's position within the browser. For layers, you can style the contents as well as the container with attributes in this category.

Extensions: With extension properties, you can change the cursor, create page breaks, and add special effects filters (like a shadow or blur effect) to the page. Unfortunately, few of them are supported by the most popular browsers. If you'd like to use any of these attributes, test them in as many browsers as you can on both Mac and PC platforms.

Formatting with CSS

As you build more and more Web sites, some styles will become a regular part of your standard design practice. For instance, you might always want to set your page margins to zero, specify a page background color, choose a default font for all text content, create redefine styles for paragraphs and headings, specify style attributes for at least two (link and visited) of the four link states, and make a custom bullet style for styling lists.

To help you with your first project, follow the steps in the next exercise to create your own sample starter master CSS file.

1. **You will need to create a sample HTML file to apply your new CSS to. Open your favorite HTML editor to create and save a new HTML page. Save the file with any filename you like to any accessible location on your computer. The sample HTML file will need paragraph text, a heading 1, an unordered list, and at least one hyperlink. Enter any content you like.**

If you don't feel like creating your own sample HTML file, use the `cssdemo.html` file from this book's companion Web site or find it at `www.luckychair.com/1-line`.

2. **Create another blank file, but this time delete any HTML code from it and save it with the `.css` file extension into the same location on your computer as your sample HTML file.**

Name the file something like `master.css` or `my.css`.

3. **Add the following code, which includes a media type set to *all*, to the `<head>` area of your sample HTML file:**

```
<link href="master.css" rel="stylesheet"
type="text/css" media="all">
```

If you named your CSS file something besides `master.css`, change the sample code accordingly.

This link, if you'll recall from earlier in the chapter, will tell the sample HTML file to use the style definitions in the linked external CSS.

4. **Create a redefine style in your CSS file for the `<body>` tag that sets the top, left, bottom, and right page margins to 0px, the padding on all four sides of the page to 20px, and the background color to a pale seafoam green with the hexadecimal value of #d0d9cc.**

Your style code for this page should look like this:

```
body {
    margin: 0px;
    padding: 20px;
    background-color: #d0d9cc;
}
```

When all four sides of an object use the same value, you need to specify the value only once. However, when the value is different on one or more sides, you must specify each of the sides, such as `padding: 20px 0px 0px 20px;`

5. **Create a redefine style in your CSS file for the `<p>` and `<h1>` tags by specifying the font, font size, and font color for each.**

Here's an example of the code you might use:

```
p {
    font-family: Georgia, "Times New Roman", Times,
serif;
    font-size: 14px;
    color: #000066;
}
h1 {
    font-family: Georgia, "Times New Roman", Times,
serif;
    font-size: 36px;
    color: #990000;
}
```

6. **If your sample page doesn't include any hyperlinks yet, add a link to Google.com and another to Yahoo.com somewhere within the body of the page:**

```
<a href="http://www.google.com/">Google</a><br>
<a href="http://www.yahoo.com/">Yahoo!</a>
```

7. **To change the default coloration of your new hyperlinks, you'll need to create styles for the four hyperlink states. You can specify any attributes you like for each of the four states, from changing the font or font weight, to modifying the text color or background color, to altering the default text decoration.**

I covered hyperlink states earlier, in the section "Morphing other page elements with advanced selectors."

Here's an example of the code you might use for the four link states:

```
a:link {
    font-weight: bold;
    text-decoration: underline;
    color: #0099cc;
    }
a:visited {
    font-weight: bold;
    text-decoration: underline;
    color: #990000;
```

```
        }
a:hover {
    font-weight: normal;
    text-decoration: none;
    color: #ffffff;
    background: #ff9933;
    }
a:active {
    font-weight: normal;
    text-decoration: none;
    color: #ffffff;
    background: #cc0000;
    }
```

8. To style the unordered list, you can either redefine the `<li>` tag or create a custom style that can be selectively applied to any `<li>` tag with the `class` attribute. If desired, specify an image to replace the default bullets.

The style definition will look the same whether you redefine the `<li>` tag or create your own custom class style; only the selector will be written differently, as either li { or .bullet {.

Your code for the bullet style should look something like this:

```
li {
    list-style-position: outside;
    list-style-image: url(images/bullet.gif);
}
```

9. Save your HTML and CSS files and launch your HTML file in a browser window.

To view the page in a browser, you can either double-click the HTML file or drag and drop the file icon into any open browser window.

The file should display with all the style attributes you just created in your master CSS file. If it doesn't, reopen the files and check the accuracy of all your code, fix any errors you find, and retest.

10. Test your new hyperlink styles in the browser window by

   a. Mousing over the Google link to see the hover style.

   b. Clicking and holding the mouse over the Google link to see the active style.

   c. Clicking the Google link and returning to your sample page by clicking the browser's Back button to see how the Google link changes to the visited link state.

Now that you have your first master CSS file, rather than re-create the wheel each time you start a new Web project, you can use this file as the starting point. Of course, for some projects, building the CSS from scratch might be easier or more practical, but if having a master CSS file will save you time, by all means use it as a design technique.

Information Kiosk

When you're first learning CSS, you have so much to understand that the application of styles to a Web page probably gets limited to styling text. Hopefully, the preceding exercise helped get you started working with CSS. But remember that you can do much more with CSS than make your fonts look prettier. With CSS, you can style page attributes like margins and a background color; text like paragraphs and headings; tables and table cells including color, border, and background images; the four link states for all hyperlinks; lists and bullets; and even the style and positioning of a `<div>` tag layer. And that's only the tip of the iceberg!

Finding Additional CSS Help

One of the best ways to learn more about CSS is to look at the code developed by others. By reverse-engineering the CSS and HTML code, you can really get an in-depth understanding of how positioning and styling of content with CSS work. Then you can implement the same or similar methods into your own Web pages.

Several sites showcase innovative and unique CSS styling, some of which also allow you to view the source code behind the work. My favorite resource is Dave Shea's `www.csszengarden.com`, but you can easily find many others by searching for CSS, CSS tutorials, CSS tips, and so on. Table 12-2 lists some great sites you should definitely visit and bookmark.

Table 12-2   CSS Online Resources

CSS Resource Name	CSS Resource Web Address
W3Schools Tutorial	www.w3schools.com/css/default.asp
W3C Tutorial	www.w3.org/MarkUp/Guide/Style
W3C's CSS	www.w3.org/Style/CSS
CSS Zen Garden	www.csszengarden.com
CSS Vault	http://cssvault.com
CSS Beauty	www.cssbeauty.com
Glish	www.glish.com/css
Max Design	http://css.maxdesign.com.au

Having a reference guide at your fingertips is also extremely useful. You can find a number of CSS references by searching for titles at www.wiley.com.

Lastly, for a really nice listing of CSS resources and access to a CSS blog where you can share your ideas and ask questions of other CSS designers, visit www.mezzoblue.com/zengarden/resources.

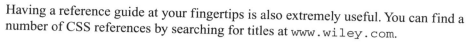

advanced selector: One of three selector types in CSS that allows for creating styles using peculiar selector syntax, such as a:link for styling hyperlinks, #sidebar for styling a <div> layer with the id of sidebar, and body,th,td for styling multiple tags under a single declaration.

at-rule: A set of rules that allow the embedding of one file in another file. For CSS, either the @import or the @media at-rule may be used to embed an external CSS into a Web page.

comment: Any content in the body of an HTML file that's surrounded by <!-- and --> is considered comment text and won't appear in the body of a page when viewed in a browser window. Comment tags are often used to label different parts of the HTML code as well as communicate information to visitors who might be looking at the HTML code.

custom class selector: One of three CSS selector types that lets designers create custom styles that can be selectively applied to objects on a Web page through the class attribute, as in <p><span class="highlight">Bears</span> are the number one threat.</p>.

declaration: In CSS, the definition of the style, made up of one or more lines of properties and values such as color: #ffffff.

external css: CSS style information saved to a file with the .css file extension. External CSS, which are sometimes simply called *linked* CSS, may be linked to any number of Web pages using the <link> tag or embedded in a Web page using either of the two at-rules.

continued

 *continued*

hyperlink state: The appearance of a hyperlink in one of four states as determined by a visitor's interactivity with it. Normal links are unvisited links, visited links are links that the visitor has already clicked, hover links are how the links look when a visitor hovers the cursor over the link, and active links are how the links look when a visitor clicks them. By default, all HTML hyperlinks display in either blue underlined text (unvisited link) or purple underlined text (visited links). These default style attributes may be redefined using an advanced selector.

inline css: CSS style definitions that are coded in the body of a Web page right next to the content they are styling, the way old `<font>` tags used to be used to style text.

internal css: CSS style definitions coded between opening and closing `<style>` and comment (`<!--` and `-->`) tags in the head of a Web page. Such styles will only modify the page they are embedded on.

layer: A tableless container created with the `<div>` tag. Layers may be absolutely or relatively positioned and styled with CSS using the `id` attribute and may contain any content found elsewhere on a Web page.

leading: The space between lines of type from the baseline of letters on one line to the baseline of letters on another line. The term comes from old printing press days when strips of lead were used to create the spacing between blocks of metal type.

media type: An attribute of a CSS file being linked or embedded in an HTML file that specifies a target media type with which the Web page will be viewed. The most common media types are `all` (for any device), `screen` (for monitors), and `print` (for printers), though the list also includes several for the various kinds of assistive devices used to access the Internet.

selector: In CSS, the name of the tag or object to be styled, such as `p`, `.highlight`, or `#layer8`.

<span> tag: An HTML tag that is essentially an empty container that will perform any function assigned to it by an attribute, such as applying a custom style to selected content with the `class` attribute or aligning the contents of a particular tag with the `align` attribute.

tag redefine selector: One of three CSS selector types that allows designers to redefine the default look of content marked up with a particular tag. For instance, the `<h1>` tag by default looks large, bold, and black but can be redefined in the CSS to use a specific font, font size, font color, and more.

Last
Stop

Practice Exam

1. True or False: Tag redefine styles and advanced selector styles using the #*ID* naming convention will automatically be applied to the tag or object containing the same ID.

2. A _____ is the name of the style, and the _____ is the definition of the style, made up of one or several properties and _____.

3. Name the three locations where CSS styles can be placed and state which of them is the most useful, even for small sites.

   _____

   _____

4. If your page uses an external CSS to style most of the content but also uses a few conflicting internal CSS styles, which styles will the page display with in a browser window, internal or external? Why?

   _____

   _____

5. How many ways can a CSS media type be indicated in HTML? Name them.

   _____

   _____

6. Name the three different CSS selector types.

   _____

   _____

7. List three benefits of styling HTML pages with CSS.

_____

_____

8. What can you do to improve the way an object appears in a browser when only two of the object's four sides need styling, such as padding?

_____

_____

9. What are the four hyperlink states and how or when are each of them activated?

_____

_____

_____

_____

10. Write a tag redefine style for p that includes font, font size, and font color attributes.

_____

_____

_____

_____

Creating Navigation Systems

STATIONS ALONG THE WAY

- O Matching a navigation system to a site's organization
- O Learning the basic principles of Web navigation systems
- O Developing text-only menus to make sites accessible to visitors with disabilities
- O Determining how submenus will function and be displayed
- O Creating the four most common types of navigation systems

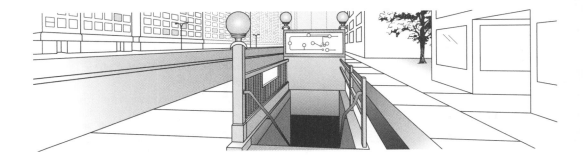

Enter the Station

Questions

1. How do navigation systems help improve a visitor's experience of a Web site?

2. Is it better to develop a wide or a deep navigation system?

3. What are the differences between text-only, rollover button, tiered JavaScript, and CSS list navigation systems?

4. What other types of navigation systems exist?

Express Line

You can organize navigation menus inside table cells or inside layers using the `<div>` tag. Chapter 14 will teach you about the differences between layers-based and tables-based page layouts. Traditionally HTML layouts have used tables. However, with the advent of CSS, more and more designers have begun migrating toward a totally layers-based layout. If you'd prefer to read up on the differences between the two layout techniques before you create some sample navigation menus in this chapter, skip ahead to Chapter 14.

W hen visitors go to a Web site, they expect to find exactly what they're looking for in three clicks or less. If they don't find what they're looking for or if the links they click are misleading in any way, they'll quickly leave the site and search elsewhere — unless they know for a fact that the site is the only source online that has what they're looking for. Therefore, when it comes to navigation, not only should the site look good, but it must be intuitively easy to understand and simple to navigate.

In this chapter, you build upon the work you've done in previous chapters to select and create the right navigation system for a Web site. First you'll learn basics about matching a site to the right system. Then you'll have the opportunity to create four of the most popular navigation menu systems; text, rollover button graphic, JavaScript multi-tier, and CSS list.

Considering the Site's Organization and Audience

Before selecting the navigation system for any site, refer to the site architecture that you created with the client. (This site structure is what you used to create the site map diagram in Chapter 3.) Having a good idea of the organization and structure of all the pages provides you with the best understanding of the type of navigation that is needed for any particular site. The architecture will help you determine the naming and order of all the main navigation links and subpages (if any) of the site. With the site architecture in hand, you should be able to classify pages into one of three categories:

- **Main pages** that should be accessible from any other page on the site
- **Subpages** that fall logically into a category of one of the main pages and are accessible through some kind of submenu
- **Additional pages** that aren't part of the main navigation but are accessible through hyperlinks located in various spots throughout the site, such as in the footer or in the body text area of a page

In addition to the site organization, other variables might further influence which type of navigation works best for a Web site:

- **General usability:** You need to consider the general usability of the navigation. For example, the menu needs to be easy to find, use, read, and interpret; be concisely written and meaningful; and be in the same location on every page of the site so that visitors don't need to go searching on the page to find it.

- **Audience:** Also consider the audience when choosing a navigation menu type. An audience of mostly seniors and visitors with disabilities might require larger fonts for menu buttons than an audience made up primarily of college students.

- **Expandability of the navigation system:** Be sure to ask your Web client whether he has plans to grow the site with additional main pages and/or subcategory pages. If he does, you'll most likely be tasked with regularly updating the navigation system, which might make some navigation system types more appealing from a design standpoint than others. For example, text and CSS-styled list menus might be more easily expandable than menus that use precisely fitting rollover graphics with JavaScript.

Learning about Navigation Systems

When a Web site contains two or more pages, it must provide a way for visitors to get to all the other pages on the site. The simplest form of navigation is the hypertext link. This type of navigation requires only that the destination filename be specified in the link. Although extremely functional and accessible, a text-only navigation menu can tend to look kind of boring. As an alternative, the site can have a more complex-looking menu that uses graphics, CSS, and possibly JavaScript or some other programming language to handle its dynamic functionality.

Ideally, the menu needs to provide a simple route to all the information available on the main pages of a site. How that route appears and works is the function of the navigation system. Determine with your client where the navigation will be placed on the page relative to the other content, and when applicable, how and where to display any subnavigation menu items.

An important principle in Web design navigation can also guide your navigation design. This principle states that the visitor should be able to find what they're looking for in the fewest number of clicks. To help realize that principle, the menu can be either *deep* or *wide*, depending on the number of main navigation links in the menu.

- **A wide menu** refers to a navigation system that lists links to all the main pages on a site in a single horizontal row, as shown in Figure 13-1. If the site is rather small, having six links across the page might be a suitable solution. On the other hand, for a site that has 14 main pages, there is probably no visually appealing way to list all 14 links in a single horizontal row. You could try breaking the links into two rows of seven, but that might confuse the heck out of site visitors. Alternatively, you could present the wide menu to visitors as a single vertical list of navigation buttons. If, however, the large number of main pages is simply the result of the client's failure to organize content, try to help your client rethink the architecture in terms of a deep navigation menu system.

In a deep menu, pages are grouped into like categories to reduce the total number of main navigation links. Each group has a main page (About Us), and the subsequent pages in the group (Our History, Our Team, Our Mission) become the accessible subnavigation menu of some kind, as shown in Figure 13-2. The subnavigation menu can be a pop-up or fly-out type of menu from the main navigation link, a second row of links that appears below the first row of links when activated by the main navigation link for that group, or a sidebar area that appears somewhere on the page when activated by the main navigation link of that group.

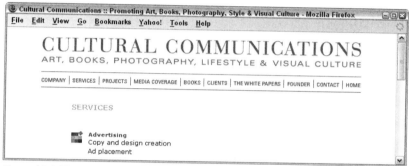

Figure 13-1: Wide navigation menus are perfect for sites with a small number of main pages and no subpages.

Figure 13-2: Build deep navigation menus for sites with multiple subpages.

To build a deep or wide navigation system, you can choose from several kinds of coding solutions, depending on the site's specific needs:

Text only: A simple horizontal or vertical navigation menu made up of hyperlinks, typically separated by some kind of character or small graphic.

Rollover buttons: Navigation menus that use JavaScript to alternate normal-state button graphics with over-state button graphics when a visitor interacts with the buttons using her mouse.

- **JavaScript multi-tier:** Like the text-only menu, but employs JavaScript to create multiple tiers for subnavigation menu display. Though typically using only HTML links, you can also use rollover menu buttons in a JavaScript multi-tier navigation system.

- **CSS list:** The most user-friendly navigation system to date. CSS list menus use simple HTML links in list format to which CSS styles are applied.

- **Tree-style:** This menu type is similar to the Explore feature on computers running the Windows OS, which lists directories and subdirectories using tiny icons for folders and files along with little plus or minus symbols to indicate whether any of the items in the menu are expanded or collapsed.

- **DHTML:** (Dynamic HyperText Markup Language) These menus use hypertext and or graphic hyperlinks embedded inside `<div>` layers, which are hidden or revealed through the use of JavaScript.

- **Java applets:** A special menu application created in the Java programming language (not to be confused with JavaScript, a markup language) that is totally OS independent. Though currently not the most accessible-friendly type of menu system, new features within the programming language are being developed to improve that.

- **PHP/Perl:** Navigation menus created with the Perl programming language that typically use simple graphics for the links.

- **Forms (jump menu):** Jump menus allow visitors to select a destination from a predetermined set of options and either have the browser automatically redirect them to the selected page after the selection, or redirect after the visitor clicks a Go or Submit button.

- **Flash:** Flash menus are built in the Flash application using actionscript, and can contain text, graphics, rollover effects, sound, and other types of animation and special effects. Such menus are saved as `.swf` files, which are then inserted into a Web page as a multimedia file that plays when the page loads in a browser.

How do you know which navigation system (or blend of them) to choose? You can draw your answer from a combination of reasons. After creating a few of the different types yourself, you're likely to develop a personal preference for one or two menu styles over the others. Likewise, your clients might come to you with particular preferences, such as "I want to have a fly-out menu that sits along the left margin of the page," that simply must be catered to. As long as the menu is easy to find, easy to read, easy to use, and always in the same place on every page, it can be the right choice for a site.

Creating a Text Navigation Menu

A text-based navigation menu is the simplest and easiest kind of navigation system you can create because it generally consists of a series of hyperlinks to the main pages of the site. You can present this type of menu in either of two ways:

- First, similar to a footer menu, it can have all the hyperlinks in a row or column with each link separated by a line break or character of some kind, such as a bullet, dash, or vertical line. See Figure 13-3 for an example.

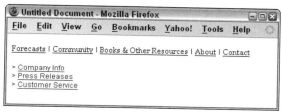

Figure 13-3: Text navigation menus can be presented vertically or horizontally either with or without special character separators.

- The second way to display a text menu is to separate each of the links by placing them inside table cells. This technique allows for a little more styling pizzazz with CSS. Figure 13-4 shows an example of how navigation links can be organized inside a table.

Figure 13-4: Place links inside table cells to help visitors more easily identify each link and to create more of a button appearance.

With simple text hyperlinks and CSS styling, you can change the normal, visited, hover, and active states of the text. However, if you add a little JavaScript to the mix, you can do more interesting mouseover states for simple text links inside a table cell.

In the following exercise, you'll create a text-based navigation bar in a table format, and then add CSS and JavaScript.

1. **In your favorite HTML editor, open a new blank HTML file and save it on your computer with the name `tablenav.html`.**

   Where you save the file is entirely up to you.

2. **Insert a 500-pixel-wide table on your page that contains 1 row and 5 columns, has 3 pixels cell padding, and 0 pixels cell spacing. In each of the five table cells, type the following words from left to right:** Company, Services, Quality, Resources, Contact.

Each table cell should be 100 pixels wide. You can set the width in the code if you like by adding the `width="100"` attribute to each opening `<td>` tag.

Next you'll style the table cells and links with CSS. Because you'll be creating only two styles for the rollover effect, and this is a demo, the CSS can be internal to the page.

3. Before the closing `<head>` tag in the code, type the following code for an internal CSS, but don't write any style declarations yet:

```
<style type="text/CSS">
<!--

-->
</style>
```

4. Launch the page in a browser right now so you can see how the table looks before you style it with CSS.

In fact, to get an idea of what's happening each time you add new code to your page, launch your favorite browser after each of the remaining steps.

5. Create a custom class style in the internal CSS called `.tableborders` with a 1-pixel solid border with the hexadecimal value of #003366. Your CSS code should look like this:

```
<style type="text/CSS">
<!--
.tableborders {
  border: 1px solid #003366;
}
-->
</style>
```

Custom styles, if you'll recall from Chapter 12, must be hand-applied to tags that need to be styled before the styles will be rendered in a browser window. Therefore, you must go back into your code and add the `class="tableborders"` attribute to all the `<td>` tags in your table.

6. Add the `tableborders` custom style to all five of your table's opening `<td>` tags, as shown in the following line of code:

```
<td width="100" class="tableborders">
```

Launch the page in a browser now to see how adding the `tableborders` style improved the look of the navigation table.

7. Convert all your navigation text into hyperlinks. To do this, you can either enter filenames for each hyperlink `href` attribute, such as `<a href="company.html">`, or add the a null link to the `href` attribute, like `<a href="#">`:

```
<td width="100" class="tableborders"><a
href="#">Company</a></td>
```

Launch the page in a browser again to see how all the links look. By default, all hyperlinks are royal blue and have an underline. In this exercise, you want to remove the underline because by virtue of the words being in a table, they'll seem like navigation links and visitors will likely mouse over them.

8. **Create another custom class style and call it `.tablelinks`. This style will have an attribute that removes any text decoration, like the default link underline. The CSS code should now look like this:**

```
<style type="text/CSS">
<!--
.tableborders {
    border: 1px solid #003366;
}
.tablelinks {
    text-decoration: none;
}
-->
</style>
```

You could also create CSS styles for all the link states, but for this exercise that's unnecessary because you'll be changing the background color of the table cells with JavaScript.

9. **Add the `tablelinks` custom style to all five of the table's `href` tag attributes, as shown in the following line of code:**

```
<a href="#" class="tablelinks">
```

Relaunch the page in a browser. The blue underlines are gone!

10. **To change the background color of the table cells, you'll need to insert some simple JavaScript in each opening `<td>` tag. The JavaScript contains CSS style instructions that tell the browser how to style the links for the mouseover and mouseout states:**

```
<td width="100" class="tableborders"
onmouseover="style.backgroundColor='#ccccff';"
onmouseout="style.backgroundColor='#84c1df'">
```

Apply the JavaScript to each opening `<td>` tag in the table. If desired, substitute the hexadecimal colors in this example with any other hex values of your choice.

11. **Launch the page in a browser to test the table hyperlinks.**

The background color of each table cell changes when you mouse your cursor over any part of the desired table cell (refer to Figure 13-4).

To see a color version of these three text-based navigation systems, go to this book's companion Web site or www.luckychair.com/1-line.

Creating a Rollover Button Graphic Navigation Menu

Rollover button graphic navigation menus consist of a series of hyperlinks that use JavaScript to control the visibility of two same-sized button graphics: One graphic shows the button's normal state, and the other the `mouseover` link state. When both button graphics have the same width and height, the JavaScript rollover effect displays both graphics smoothly.

 Watch Your Step

If one of the graphics is different in size than the other, the over-state graphic will be stretched or squished to match the same dimensions as the normal-state graphic, giving the over-state graphic a skewed effect.

JavaScript for rollovers usually requires up to three different script parts to function (depending on how the script was written), and those parts must be placed at specific points within the HTML code. One of the parts is called a *preload script,* which is placed in the `<head>` area of the code and preloads the rollover-state graphics into the visitor's browser's cache so that by the time the visitor mouses over a button, the over-state button graphic is ready to appear. Without the preload script, there would be a delay in the rollover functionality. The other two parts are the *event handler,* which gets placed in the `<body>` tag and tells the browser when to process a preload script when present, and the rollover script itself, which gets written inline with the button image(s) and contains the rollover instructions to the browser.

 Information Kiosk

When placed between `<script>` tags in the body of the page, JavaScript code executes immediately as the page loads in a browser. To have the script load at other times, you must place the script elsewhere in the code and then call upon it to execute when a visitor's mouse movement triggers a particular event.

In the case of rollover buttons, the JavaScript must be added to all three locations:

- **Between the opening and closing `<head>` tags:** These *function* scripts must be placed between two `<script>` tags somewhere inside the head of the code. For rollovers, this script contains parameters for a preload function.

```
<head>
<script type="text/JavaScript">
...
</script>
</head>
```

Inside the opening <body> tag: This *event* part of the script instructs the browser how and when to execute any scripts in the <head> of the page, often using the onload attribute, such as

```
<body onload="preloadImages();">
```

or

```
<body onload="MM_preloadImages('images/button_1-
over.gif')">
```

In the code, between the <body> tags: Script placed inline with the rest of the code will be executed in the browser based on the parameters and instructions contained within the script. For example, a script for a rollover button contains instructions for swapping two images based on two mouse events, onmouseover and onmouseout:

```
<a href="florals.html" onmouseout="MM_swapImgRestore()"
onmouseover="MM_swapImage('Image1','','images/button_1-
over.gif',1)"><img src="images/button_1.gif" alt=
"Florals" name="Image1" width="112" height="23"
border="0" id="Image1"></a>
```

The actual JavaScript used for the rollover functionality, which identifies the graphics to be swapped for each button, can be written in several different ways even though they all essentially function the same. To find the code you'd like to use, you can search the Internet for free JavaScript that will handle the rollover effect.

Information Kiosk

Free JavaScript is everywhere on the Net, and I encourage you to spend time browsing through all the free JavaScript sites like http://javascript.internet.com and www.javascript.com to see how much you can do with JavaScript, in addition to adding rollover scripts.

Alternatively, if you're using an image optimization program like ImageReady or a code editor like Dreamweaver, those programs write a version of workable JavaScript code for you.

Outputting rollovers in ImageReady

With ImageReady you can choose to output images and html when you go to save optimized graphics. The resulting HTML file will contain all the necessary JavaScript code to make any specified rollover graphics function as rollover buttons. What's more, the code contains parameters for inserting a total of four graphics for the mouseover, mouseout, mousedown, and mouseup link states:

```
<a href="filename.html"
    onmouseover="changeImages('button_01',
    'images/button_01-over.gif'); return true;"
    onmouseout="changeImages('button_01',
    'images/button_01.gif'); return true;"
    onmousedown="changeImages('button_01', 'images/
    button_01-down.gif'); return true;"
    onmouseup="changeImages('button_01', 'images/
    button_01-up.gif'); return true;"><img
    src="images/button.gif"></a>
```

Information Kiosk

The four link states for JavaScript rollover buttons exactly match the four link states for regular hypertext links. The normal link state is associated with the onmouseout event handler and displays the default button graphic before a visitor interacts with it. The hover state is controlled by the onmouseover event handler and displays the mouseover graphic when a visitor hovers the mouse over the button. The third link state, like the active link state in CSS, uses the onmousedown event handler to display a graphic for the button during the mouse click. The final button state uses the onmouseup event handler and is used to display a fourth graphic that appears after the clicked button is released, like a visited link, as the browser follows the button's hyperlink to the destination page.

To create a simple rollover button with four link states in ImageReady, follow these steps:

1. Open a new document in ImageReady. When the New Document window appears, set the Image Size to 100 x 30 pixels and the Contents of First Layer to Transparent. Then click OK.

A new untitled ImageReady document window will appear.

2. Click the Set foreground color box on the ImageReady toolbar to open the Color Picker dialog box. Enter 99cc66 in the hexadecimal color field and click OK.

This sets the foreground color to a Web-safe green.

3. Choose Edit → Fill to open the Fill dialog box. Make sure the Use field is set to Foreground Color and click OK.

This tells ImageReady to use the green color you just selected with the Color Picker to fill the transparent layer in the Layers panel. If the Layers panel isn't visible, choose Window ➜ Layers.

Since you're creating four link states, you'll need add three more layers to your document.

4. **At the bottom of the Layers panel, click the Create New Layer button three times.**

Three new layers will appear in the Layers panel above Layer 1, named Layer 2, Layer 3, and Layer 4.

5. **Repeat Steps 2 and 3 to add the following fill colors to the new layers: Layer 2: #ff9933, Layer 3: #339999, Layer 4: #66ccff.**

Now all the layers contain unique colors, making them easy to identify for each of the rollover link states.

If desired, also add a text layer above Layer 4 that says "Button" and another layer above that (Layer 5) with a 1-pixel black stroke along the edge of the button and apply a *pillow emboss* Bevel and Emboss layer style to it.

6. **In the Layers panel, click the eye visibility icon next to Layers 2, 3, and 4 to hide them, leaving only Layer 1 visible in the document window.**

This sets the default look of the normal-state button by hiding any layer that shouldn't be visible when the button first appears in the browser window.

7. **To create the "over" button layer state, click Layer 1 in the Layers panel to select it. Then click the options menu button in the Web Content panel and choose New Rollover State from the options menu.**

The Web Content layer should now display two layers: one that's titled Untitled-1_01 and, below that, Rollover States, Over.

8. **Click the options menu button in the Web Content panel and choose New Rollover State from the options menu again.**

This time, a second rollover-state layer appears, titled Down.

9. **Choose the New Rollover State option from the options menu two more times to create the remaining two rollover-state layers in the Web Content panel.**

The next two rollover-state layers will be titled Selected and Out.

10. **In the Web Content panel, select the Down rollover layer to activate it, and then back in the Layers panel, click the eye visibility icon next to Layer 1 to hide it and click the eye visibility box next to Layer 2 to show it.**

The Down state in the Web Content panel is now orange.

11. **Click the Selected rollover layer in the Web Content panel to activate it, and using the visibility eye icons in the Layers panel again, hide Layer 1 and show Layer 3.**

The Selected state in the Web Content panel is now teal.

12. Click the Out layer in the Web Content panel to select it, and in the Layers panel, hide Layer 1 and show Layer 4.

The Out state in the Web Content panel is now blue, and you've successfully configured a look for each of the button's link states, as shown in Figure 13-5.

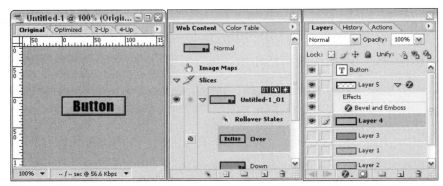

Figure 13-5: Hide and show different layers in the Layers panel when configuring the Rollover States in the Web Content panel.

13. To add a hyperlink to this graphic, select the Untitled-1_01 layer in the Web Content panel, and in the URL field of the Slice panel, enter the filename and extension of the destination Web page.

For testing purposes, enter the full path to the Google home page in the URL field: `http://www.google.com/`. In the Slice panel, you may also enter a link target (such as **_blank**) and alternate text for the button to match any text appearing on the button face, though you could configure this information later in a code editor, such as Dreamweaver.

If the Slice panel isn't showing, choose Window ➜ Slice

14. Save your file as a Photoshop `.psd` file with the filename `fourlinks.psd`.

Save the file before optimizing the button graphics for best results.

15. Choose File ➜ Save Optimized As to open the Save Optimized As dialog box. Set the File Name to `fourlinks.html`, the Save As type to HTML and Images, the Settings to Default Settings, and the Slices to All Slices. Set the destination for the files in the Save In field to your computer's desktop and click Save.

ImageReady will generate an images folder filled with all four button state graphics and an HTML file containing the JavaScript necessary to make the button work when it appears in a browser.

16. Launch the `fourlinks.html` file in a browser window to view your new four-link-state button.

You can launch the file by double-clicking the file icon or by dragging and dropping the file into any open browser.

17. **Test your new button.**

Move your mouse over and off the button a few times (without clicking yet) to view the hover state. Then click to view the active state and release to view the up state. When you release your mouse, the button remains in the up state with the up-state graphic showing.

Creating rollovers in Dreamweaver

Dreamweaver users can create rollover buttons by two methods, both of which use different JavaScript scripts. One method involves attaching the "Swap Image" and "Go to URL" behaviors to already inserted normal-state graphics on the page. The other method, described in the following steps, allows you to choose the original and rollover graphics, select the page the button will hyperlink to, and enter alternate text for the button link, all using the Insert Rollover Button option.

Information Kiosk

A *behavior,* in this context, is any interactive JavaScript that Dreamweaver can insert into the code of your page. Behaviors pair an event with an action that is triggered by the event, such as changing the normal-state button graphic to the over-state button graphic (the action) when a visitor hovers the mouse above it (the event). Dreamweaver comes preinstalled with about 22 behaviors to help designers quickly configure interactive features on their pages.

Before you begin the next exercise in Dreamweaver, you'll need two optimized button graphics of the same width and height for the normal and mouseover states of the rollover button. The button graphics can be any color and size. For example, you might create a graphic that is 100 x 20 pixels in size, includes the text CONTACT in the center, and has a blue background for the normal state and a green background for the mouseover state.

Follow these steps to have Dreamweaver insert a rollover button on a page and automatically write all the necessary JavaScript:

1. **Choose File → New to open a new document in the Dreamweaver workspace. Save the file as `rollover.html` into the folder of your choice on your computer. Within that folder, create another folder called *images* and place a copy of your two optimized button graphics inside it.**

For best results, define a managed site in Dreamweaver with the root level directory set to the folder you just saved the `rollover.html` file in.

2. **In Design view, place the insertion point inside the `rollover.html` file where you'd like the rollover button to be inserted.**

You must specify the location before adding the graphics, so that Dreamweaver knows where to insert the JavaScript and images.

3. **Choose Insert → Image Objects → Rollover Image.**

This opens the Insert Rollover Image dialog box, as shown in Figure 13-6.

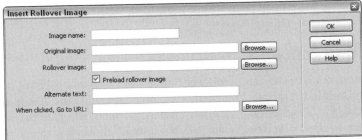

Figure 13-6: Enter rollover button details using Dreamweaver's Insert Rollover Image dialog box.

4. **In the appropriate fields in the dialog box, type a name for the rollover button, browse to and select the graphics to use for both the original and rollover image states, and add alternate text to mirror any text on the button graphic. Then add a filename, URL, or null link for the hyperlink.**

The image name you provide acts as an `id` for the image that the JavaScript attaches to. The Preload Rollover Image option is enabled by default to add the preload script to the HTML. Leave that option enabled.

5. **Click OK to close the dialog box.**

Upon closing the dialog box, Dreamweaver inserts the rollover button normal-state graphic and JavaScript on the page at the insertion point.

If you take a peek at the code, you'll see that JavaScript has been placed between the `<head>` tags and in the opening `<body>` tag, as well as at the insertion point in the body of the page inside the `<img>` tag containing the normal-state button graphic.

6. **Save the page and preview it in a browser by selecting any of the browsers listed under the File → Preview in Browser menu.**

7. **Test the rollover button in the browser window by moving your cursor over the button graphic.**

Information Kiosk

To make an entire navigation menu using this Dreamweaver JavaScript rollover button technique, create a table with the appropriate number of cells across a single row or column, and follow Steps 1–6 to insert a rollover button in each table cell.

Creating a Tiered Text-Based JavaScript Navigation Menu

JavaScript menus can look and function well even without the use of button graphics. In fact, you can create an entire menu with any number of fly-out submenus, all with the use of JavaScript and a little CSS styling. Like any JavaScript function, you can write the code in a variety of ways — or simply use scripts that are free or for sale. Some free scripts come with code editors like Dreamweaver, and others are shared online. Specialty scripts that are for sale often incorporate interesting effects like fades, swipes, and other unusual DHTML transitions.

One of my favorite JavaScript navigation menus is Dreamweaver's Show Pop-Up Menu, which you can easily configure using a dialog box accessible through the Behaviors panel. What's great about this menu script is that you can use either text or graphics for your main navigation links and simple HTML text for any subnavigation (and sub-subnavigation) pop-up menus.

To use the script, all you'll need to do (after optimizing all your main navigation link rollover button graphics, if you choose to use graphics) is use the dialog box to specify the name and order of each link in the pop-up menu for each main navigation link and then customize presentation features such as font face, font color, and position in a dialog box. Dreamweaver handles all the writing of the code for you.

 ## Watch Your Step

Unlike the JavaScript menus you've created earlier in this chapter, this pop-up menu behavior automatically creates and uses an external JavaScript file called mm_menu.js in addition to adding scripts to the <head> area and <body> tag of the page with the menu. You must upload this external JavaScript file to the server hosting the published site along with the page(s) on the site containing the pop-up menu; without this file, the menu won't function.

Follow these steps to insert a Dreamweaver pop-up menu on your page:

1. **Choose File → New to open a new document in the Dreamweaver workspace. Save the file as popupmenu.html into the folder of your choice on your computer.**

   For best results, define a managed site to the folder in which you saved the popupmen.html file.

2. **In the open popupmenu.html file, select an object (like an already inserted rollover button with a hyperlink) or text link to which you'll attach the menu.**

You'll use the linked rollover button graphic or text link to trigger the JavaScript that makes the pop-up menu appear. If you don't have an inserted hyperlinked button graphic or hypertext link yet, create one now and select the object in Design view before continuing.

3. **On the Dreamweaver Behaviors panel (which is paired with the Attributes panel inside the Tag Inspector panel), click the Actions (+) button and choose Show Pop-Up Menu.**

   This opens the Show Pop-Up Menu dialog box shown in Figure 13-7. The dialog box has four tabbed sections that help you customize the menu's appearance.

   If the Behaviors panel isn't showing, choose Window ➜ Behaviors.

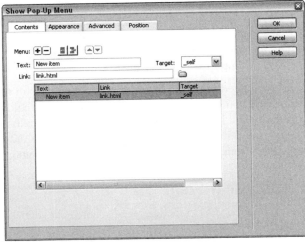

Figure 13-7: The Show Pop-Up Menu dialog box allows you to customize each pop-up menu specific to your site's design.

4. **The first tab, Contents, is where you'll create links for the pop-up menu. Create separate links for About Us, Our Mission, Historic Timeline, and Board of Directors. Menu items can be sorted, edited, and removed:**

   - *Text:* Type a text label for each menu item, such as **Contact Us**.

   - *Add Item:* Click the Menu (+) button to add another menu item. You can tell when an item has been added successfully because it will list the link label, hypertext link, and target.

   - *Remove Item:* To delete an item from the menu, select the list item and click the Minus (–) button.

   - *Link:* Type the filename with extension or the entire URL of the target destination. If desired, use the folder icon to browse for and select a file on your computer.

- *Target:* If desired, select a target name or frame for the link. Unnamed frames won't appear in the list.

- *Indent/Outdent:* To create another tier in the submenu with any selected menu item, click the Indent Item button. To undo an indented menu item, select it and click the Outdent Item button.

- *Move Item Up/Down:* Adjust the order of any menu items by selecting the item that needs to be moved and clicking the up or down arrow until the item is in the desired spot.

5. **Select the Appearance tab to define the look and feel of the pop-up menu's normal and over states. Choose Vertical, Verdana, 11px, Bold, Left Align, #66666 (text) and #dbdbd0 (cell) for the Up State colors and #ffffff (text) and #993400 (cell) for the Over State colors:**

- *Orientation:* Choose either a Vertical or Horizontal menu.

- *Font:* Select a font set from the Font menu, or if desired, create a new font set by selecting the Edit Font List option at the bottom of the menu.

- *Size:* Enter the menu's font size in pixels.

- *Bold/Italic:* Click the B and I style buttons to apply bold and italic to the menu fonts. The buttons toggle the styles on and off.

- *Text Align:* Choose a text alignment option for the pop-up menu list items. Click the Left, Center, or Right Align button to toggle the alignment on and off.

- *Up State/Over State:* Click all four Up and Over State Text and Cell color picker buttons to select the colors the menu text and cell background will display in.

6. **Next click the Advanced tab to make modifications to the default menu cell formatting. Set the menu delay to 800 ms, the text indent to 4, and turn off borders. Leave all the other options at their default settings:**

- *Cell Width/Height:* By default, both the width and height are set automatically to match the size of the widest menu item. To change this attribute, select Pixels from the Automatic drop-down list. This activates the Cell Width/Height box so that you can enter a precise pixel value.

- *Cell Padding:* This attribute is just like the cell padding on a table cell, which adds space between the contents of a cell and the cell walls. Enter the desired value, if any, in pixels. To completely remove space, enter **0**.

- *Cell Spacing:* Use this attribute to adjust the space between the menu's cell walls. Enter a value in pixels or enter **0** to remove the space completely.

- *Text Indent:* To add an indent uniformly to all the menu items, enter a value in pixels. To remove space completely, enter **0**.

- *Menu Delay:* The delay controls how long it takes the menu to disappear after a mouseout event. The default menu delay is set to 1000 ms or 1 second, however you can adjust the delay time if desired.

- *Pop-Up Borders:* To view the pop-up menu with borders, select this check box. Click again to remove the check mark and view the menu without borders.

- *Border Width:* When borders are enabled, you may enter a value in pixels for the border's width.

- *Border Color/Shadow/Highlight:* Click the color picker buttons to select the colors for the menu's border, border shadow, and border highlight.

7. The last tab on the dialog box sets the Position of the pop-up menu relative to the object or hyperlink that menu is attached to. Select the Below and at Left Edge of Trigger option for the menu position:

- *Menu Position:* The pop-up menu can pop up in one of four positions relative to the trigger object: Bottom Right Corner of Trigger, Below and at Left Edge of Trigger, Above and at Left Edge of Trigger, or Top Right Edge of Trigger.

- *X/Y Coordinates:* To fine-tune the positioning, enter a pixel value in either or both of the X/Y coordinate fields. The values are calculated from the top-left corner of the trigger object.

- *Hide Menu on onMouseOut Event:* This option is enabled by default and makes the pop-up menu disappear when the visitor moves the mouse away from the menu. Only disable this feature if you want to have the menu remain visible.

8. To insert the menu on the page, click OK.

9. Save the page and preview it in a browser by selecting any of the browsers listed under the File → Preview in Browser menu.

To view the pop-up menu, move your mouse over the trigger object on the page. Figure 13-8 shows an example of what the menu might look like.

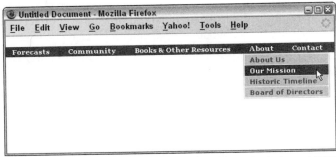

Figure 13-8: Dreamweaver's pop-up menus use simple JavaScript and HTML.

Information Kiosk

From time to time, depending on the computer platform and version of Dreamweaver you're using, this behavior can exhibit a bug that prevents you from adjusting the menu's cell width and height pixel sizes on the Advanced tab of the Show Pop-Up Menu dialog box. If this should happen to you, you'll need to manually adjust the cell size in the JavaScript code.

The menu cell width and height are displayed in the JavaScript code in red text (shown in bold in the following code) in the `mmLoadMenus` JavaScript that's inside the `<head>` area of the code. The following example shows roughly where you'll need to look in the JavaScript to make the manual adjustments to the width (**85**) and height (**23**) of the cells:

```
<script type="text/JavaScript">
<!--
function mmLoadMenus() {
   if (window.mm_menu_0105144808_0) return;
          window.mm_menu_0105144808_0 = new
Menu("root",85,23,"Georgia, Times New Roman, Times,
serif",14,"#ffffff","#ffffff","#00c3b2","#d45201","le
ft","middle",3,0,100,-
5,7,true,true,true,6,false,false);
```

If after seeing the menu in your browser, you decide you want to make further adjustments to it, reselect the trigger object on the page in Design view and click the yellow spiked gear icon for the Show Pop-Up Menu behavior in the Behaviors panel. This will reopen the Show Pop-Up Menu dialog box, where you can make any desired changes and save them.

Creating a CSS List Navigation Menu

One of the newest ways of creating a navigation menu is to combine HTML list formatting with CSS. This method allows you to use graphics while keeping the code uncluttered. It also produces the fastest loading and most accessible type of Web pages when compared to any of the JavaScript navigation methods.

You can style lists with CSS in several ways, and depending on your needs, one way might be more suitable for a particular site than another. The simplest method is to nest an unordered list inside a `<div>` container tag with an `id` attribute and then create CSS styles for that `id` as well as for the `<ul>` and `<li>` tags and all the hyperlinks in the menu. You then style each hyperlink with two graphics: one that forms the left and one that forms the right side of each button. However, rather than creating two sets of graphics for the normal and over states, you'll simply stack the normal and over shapes in a single graphic file. In other words, in the left side button graphic, you'll stack the normal-state left button edge directly on top of the over-state left button edge. Then you'll do the same thing for the right button, as shown in Figure 13-9.

Figure 13-9: Stack the normal- and over-state button layers inside a single optimized graphic.

You're now going to build your own list navigation menu with CSS, like the one shown in Figure 13-10. To assist you with the process, I've already created the two graphics you'll need, available for downloading from this book's companion Web site or at www.luckychair.com/1-line. Before you begin the exercise, set up a folder on your computer called CSS List Demo, set up another folder inside it called images, and inside the images folder save a copy of the two downloaded graphics.

Figure 13-10: CSS list navigation menus can use any kind of graphic and any length of button text.

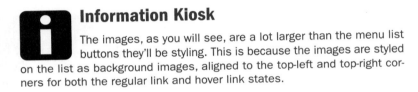

Information Kiosk

The images, as you will see, are a lot larger than the menu list buttons they'll be styling. This is because the images are styled on the list as background images, aligned to the top-left and top-right corners for both the regular link and hover link states.

Follow these instructions to build a CSS-styled list navigation menu:

1. In your favorite HTML editor, open a new blank HTML page and save it into your CSS List Demo folder with the name **csslistmenu.html**.

2. Create an unordered list with five list items: About Us, Services, Partners, In the News, Employment Opportunities, and Contact Us.

A list type attribute that specifies which bullet to use for this particular unordered list is unnecessary because you'll be styling the list with graphics in the CSS.

3. Wrap the entire list inside a **<div>** tag with the **id** of **tablistmenu**.

Your code should look like this:

```
<div id="tablistmenu">
  <ul>
    <li>About Us</li>
    <li>Services</li>
    <li>Partners</li>
    <li>In the News</li>
    <li>Employment Opportunities</li>
    <li>Contact Us</li>
```

```
    </ul>
  </div>
```

4. Turn each of the list items into null hypertext links using the number symbol (#) instead of the filename and add a matching `title` attribute to the `<a>` tag, as in the following example:

```
<li><a href="#" title="About Us">About Us</a></li>
```

Null links are great to use as stand-ins for links when building components of a page like navigation menus. Later, when the component is complete, you can replace the null links with the real link filenames.

5. Add a pair of `<span>` tags around each link item, as in the following sample line of code:

```
<li><a href="#" title="About Us"><span>About
Us</span></a></li>
```

Each button in the menu needs a background image with curved corners, but the size of each menu item is determined by the length of the text. To solve this issue, you'll create a second style for the left edge of each menu item that will wrap around each link to give the illusion of a single background image. This second style will be applied to these `<span>` tags.

6. To style the page, create an internal CSS and define a tag redefine style for the `<body>` with a 0 margin, 0 padding, and the font set to Trebuchet, bold, 11px, with a 1.5em line height:

```
<style type="text/CSS">
<!--
body {
    margin:0;
    padding:0;
    font-family: "Trebuchet MS", Verdana, Arial;
    font-size: 11px;
    line-height: 1.5em;
}
-->
</style>
```

7. Add a Menu Styles comment in the internal CSS after the `<body>` tag redefine style definition.

```
<style type="text/CSS">
<!--
body {
    margin:0;
    padding:0;
    font-family: "Trebuchet MS", Verdana, Arial;
    font-size: 11px;
    line-height: 1.5em;
}
```

```
/* :::MENU STYLES::: */
-->
</style>
```

8. Create a new advanced selector style in the internal CSS for the `<div>` tag with the **id** of **tablistmenu** with the following style attributes:

```
#tablistmenu {
    float:left;
    width:100%;
    background:#cae4ef;
    border-bottom:1px solid #0e5d7e;
    font-size:95%;
    line-height:normal;
}
```

This style spans the full width of the browser window, has a blue background color, includes a 1-pixel navy blue border along the bottom edge of the `<div>` container, and slightly reduces the font size of the text in the menu list.

9. To style the list, you'll create a tag redefine style for the `<ul>`. However, rather than simply list `<ul>` as the selector, you'll use advanced CSS syntax to write a descendent selector that identifies the `<div>` with the **id** of **tablistmenu** as the sole location for the `<ul>` styles:

```
#tablistmenu ul {
    margin:0;
    padding:10px 10px 0 50px;
    list-style:none;
}
```

The `<ul>` style sets the margin for the entire list to 0; adds padding on the top, right, and left sides of the list; and sets the list style (where a customized bullet graphic might go) to none.

10. You also need to create a style for the `<li>` tags so that each item will display inline (in a row) without any margin or padding:

```
#tablistmenu li {
    margin:0;
    padding:0;
    display:inline;
}
```

If you're using a code editor like Dreamweaver, you might now notice in Design view that the list shifts from a vertical orientation, with one item stacked atop another, to a horizontal set of items displaying side by side. If, on the other hand, your code editor doesn't have a preview or design pane, launch your page in a browser to see the list displaying inline.

11. To add the background image to each list item, you must create a style that's applied automatically to each link inside the list. This style will specify the background image, among other CSS attributes:

```
#tablistmenu a {
    float:left;
    background:url("images/cssmenuleft.gif")
    no-repeat left top;
    margin:0;
    padding:0 0 0 4px;
    text-decoration:none;
}
```

Note that the background image is set to no-repeat with an orientation relative to the top-left corner of the list item link.

This image, however, does only half the work of creating the look of a button for the navigation menu. The other half, as described earlier, must be accomplished with a second style that wraps around the link text using the <span> tag.

12. **Create a new style that will be applied automatically to the <span> tags surrounding each link in the list to set the background image and other CSS attributes on the right side of each button:**

```
#tablistmenu a span {
    float:left;
    display:block;
    background:url("images/cssmenuright.gif")
    no-repeat right top;
    padding: 5px 15px 4px 6px;
    color:#ffffff;
}
```

This background image is set to no-repeat with an orientation relative to the top-right corner of the list item link. It further specifies what color each link becomes — in this case, white.

Watch Your Step

Internet Explorer 5 for the Mac has a bug that prevents the list from displaying correctly. You must add the following #tablistmenu a span style information to your CSS to fix that bug, either with or without the special comments and comment tags:

```
/* ::: This hack fixes a bug in MAC IE5 ::: */
#tablistmenu a span {float:none;}
/* ::: End of hack for MAC IE5 ::: */
```

13. **The last piece of the puzzle is to control the hover style for the menu items. This requires three styles, which works as follows:**

First, set the color that the text will change to for the hover state of each link. Then, to get the hover state of each background graphic to display (which in this case begins exactly –42 pixels down from the top-left edge of each graphic), you must adjust the horizontal and vertical background positioning attributes of both the list link and link span hover states:

```
#tablistmenu a:hover span {
    color:#0e5d7e;
}
#tablistmenu a:hover {
    background-position:0% -42px;
}
#tablistmenu a:hover span {
    background-position:100% -42px;
}
```

14. **Save the page and preview it in a browser by selecting any of the browsers listed under the File → Preview in Browser menu.**

Move your cursor over the list items to see how the graphics change on mouseover.

Step into the Real World

Adding Special Comments to CSS Files   To help you keep track of where certain styles begin and end in the CSS, add special comments between CSS comment tags whenever different style sets, like the menu list styles or link states, are introduced. In addition to being helpful to anyone else viewing your CSS, comments also give your CSS a more organized, polished look.

Comment tags within a CSS use the /* *text* */ syntax, where the *text* part can contain any text you like, spanning as many lines in the code as needed.

To illustrate, you might add the following comment and comment tags to the CSS code in this exercise, directly following the closing curly brace of the <body> tag style:

```
/* :::MENU STYLES::: */
```

The semicolons (:) in this example help the eye identify the comment tag more readily. Certainly, however, you can add other special characters or use none, leaving only descriptive text between the comment tags, in normal upper- and lowercase lettering (Menu Styles) or in all caps, as shown here.

When any section of styles is fairly long, you might also want to include ending comments and comment tags for the section, such as:

```
/* :::END MENU STYLES::: */
```

In external CSS files, these CSS comment tags (and the contents of them) can stand alone between the style definitions. However when including CSS comment tags on an internal CSS, you must make sure that the special CSS comment tags fall between the regular HTML comment tags (<!-- and -->) in the code. If you forget to include the regular HTML tags, both the style declarations and the comments will appear in the body of the page!

```
<!-- /* .....MENU STYLES..... */ -->
```

The beauty of this type of CSS styling is its simplicity. Each button uses HTML list item text, styled with CSS, and only two graphics for the button background. Moreover, the same two graphics are used over and over again for each button. And, with any graphic, after it's loaded into the visitor's browser cache, the reuse of that image no longer requires downloading and re-caching. It also saves tons of file space, which translates into much faster page download times. Even better, when visitors using assistive devices come to the page, as well as any visitors who have turned off their browser's CSS functionality, the links will still be organized and accessible.

behavior: JavaScript inserted into the code of a Web page that performs an action in the browser window when triggered by an event, such as preloading a set of images for a rollover button appearing on the page and changing a rollover button's graphics when a visitor interacts with it.

comments: Any descriptive text that can be added to the head or body of a Web page between comment tags, as in `<!-- this is a comment -->`, to help identify parts of the code or make comments about them without fear of those comments being displayed in the browser. When adding comments to CSS between the style declarations, each comment should be on its own line in the code and include `/*...*/` syntax, such as `/* this is a comment */`.

CSS list navigation menu: These navigation menus use HTML list tags to build all the items in the menu, which are then styled with CSS. Because the list items generally use HTML text instead of graphics, this type of menu is most accessible to visitors with disabilities.

deep navigation system: A navigation scheme that includes submenus off the main navigation menu that provide access to each of the pages on a site with a single click.

event: A message of sorts that a browser generates automatically when either the page loads in the browser or a visitor interacts in certain ways with the content on the page. The message is generated by specifying the appropriate event handler in the JavaScript. Event handlers include `onmouseover`, `onclick`, and `onload`.

inline: In CSS, this attribute converts a vertical list into a horizontal list.

onmousedown: A link state that is activated when a visitor clicks a text link or linked object.

continued

onmouseout: A link state that is activated when a visitor moves the cursor off a text link or linked object after having just moved the cursor over the text link or linked object.

onmouseover: A link state that is activated when a visitor moves the cursor over a text link or linked object.

onmouseup: A link state that is activated when a visitor releases the mouse button after clicking a text link or linked object.

preload script: A type of JavaScript script that runs automatically when the page loads in a browser window and instructs the browser to preload files specified in the script (typically graphics for rollover buttons) into the visitor's browser cache so that those files are ready to use when the page is finished loading.

subnavigation: Any part of a navigation menu that is secondary from the main menu, such as links to the Bio, Awards, and Press pages that fall under the link to the main About page. A subnavigation menu can be a pop-up menu from the main navigation link, a second row of links that appears below the first row when activated by the main navigation link for that group, or a sidebar area that appears somewhere on the page when activated by the main navigation link of that group.

tiered navigation menu: This type of menu uses links with submenus to create tiers of navigation. Each tier may include additional submenus, and every link, no matter where it lies within the tiered navigation scheme, provides visitors access to any page in the menu with a single click.

wide navigation system: A navigation scheme that provides links to all the pages on the site through a single horizontal (though sometimes vertical) set of navigation links. Although this type of navigation provides single-click access to all the pages on a site, it isn't suitable for sites with more than, say, ten main navigation pages because it might reveal a lack of organization inherent in the site architecture.

Last Stop

Practice Exam

1. True or False: JavaScript works only when placed in the body of a page.

2. With JavaScript, you can create buttons for up to ___ different link states.

3. List three variables of a good Web site navigation system.

_____

4. Over ten types of coding solutions can be used to create navigation menus. List five or more.

_____

5. What happens when the two graphics used for a rollover button aren't the same exact size?

_____

_____

6. What does a preload script do?

_____

_____

7. What is the purpose of adding comment tags inside CSS, and what is the proper syntax for them?

_____

_____

_____

_____

8. Describe the difference between deep and wide navigation menus.

_____

_____

_____

_____

Layers- versus Tables-based Layouts

STATIONS ALONG THE WAY

- O Understanding how tables and layers impact standards compliance and accessibility
- O Learning the pros and cons of creating layouts with tables and layers
- O Creating a sample tables-only layout
- O Creating a sample layers-only layout
- O Finding free, preformatted, layers-based layouts online

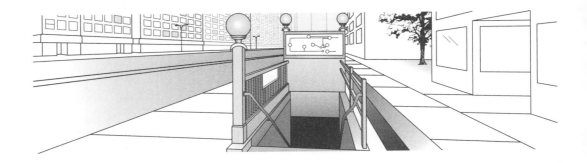

 # Enter the Station

Questions

1. What are the benefits of creating a layout with tables?

2. What are the benefits of creating a layout with layers?

3. How can you determine whether to build a site using tables or layers?

4. Is it okay to create hybrid layouts that utilize both tables and layers?

Express Line

If you already understand how to build Web site layouts by using layers, pass over this chapter and go to Chapter 15, where you'll learn how to create and work with Dreamweaver templates and how to build and use Server-Side Includes.

Before designers got involved in the world of Web design, Web sites mostly consisted of text, some lists, a couple of images, and a table or two. Pages of this kind were certainly easy to "design" because not much forethought was required to make pages like that look good. When more decorative graphics, color, and precise font selections entered the mix — essentially an effort to add the creativity and visual appeal common in print layouts in the new online format — creating a Web page layout required a lot more planning, and the HTML coding became more time-consuming, too.

To work around the challenges of making a Web design look more like a print design, designers first tried designing layouts with large graphics instead of HTML text and a few images. This method allowed designers to use any font they liked with any images in any configuration. But as you might remember, the pages weren't at all accessible, and the large images often took too long to download.

The next best solution was to still use graphics but use a lot less of them combined with other text and content and organize everything inside of a table so that it had a sense of order to it. When precisely measured and aligned, having a design held together in this way seemed a perfect solution, albeit a code heavy one. To assist with more images being loaded into a browser, larger images were sliced and placed inside individual table cells with the idea that a handful of smaller images would load faster than a single larger image. To make the pages load even faster, any graphic that was simply a large flat area of color could be replaced by adding background color attributes to the tags for the body of the page, a table, or a table cell.

The tables-based layout had a long healthy run until Web standard developers came up with better ideas to help make Web pages more accessible to the widest possible audience. Their solution involves using semantic HTML and CSS, with content laid out using layers instead of tables. Tables can still be used, and in fact are the best solution for organizing some content, like form content and tabular data, inside a Web page. However, layers for the layout part of a Web site design are simply the more efficient way to design and format accessible HTML markup — that is, if you can figure out how to code the CSS to do it! CSS can sometimes be very tricky to understand and manipulate, but just like tables, you can learn special code *hacks* (unconventional use of code, scripts, programming language, and CSS to make the page look and/or function the way you want it to) from others' experiences that can fix some of the common problems certain browsers have with displaying some CSS attributes.

In this chapter, you'll start with an examination of the differences between creating a tables-based and layers-based layout for a site. You'll have two exercises for creating sample layouts in both tables and layers styles, and the chapter will end with a list of resources for free CSS layers-based layouts.

Tables versus Layers

If you're brand-new to the world of Web design, learning to build layers-based layouts from the start will be easy enough to do. However, if you've already learned a little bit about making layouts with tables and want to learn how to work with layers, you'll probably need to unlearn a few habits you might have developed from working with tables.

Before I launch into how wonderful layers are, let me assure you that using tables is *not* a bad thing and that if you choose to continue using tables for laying out your pages, no layers police will come in the dead of night and take you to table user's prison. Layers are simply more flexible than tables because when combined with CSS, they can be positioned relatively or absolutely anywhere on a Web page. Tables, by contrast, can be aligned only to the left, center, or right of a page.

Transfer

In Chapter 9, you learned about the things you can do to conform with the current set of W3C recommended HTML Web standards. Besides all the tag changes and code additions, standards compliancy also means migrating from using tables-based layouts to exclusively (or near exclusively!) using layers-based layouts. The main reason behind creating standards-compliant Web design is to make Web pages accessible to the widest possible audience. The audience might be using a variety of devices or software to access those pages, including all the different browsers and browser versions, hand-held devices like cell phones and Blackberries, speech synthesizers, Web spiders or robots, and the like. Unfortunately, most pages today barely comply with Web standards, but that's certainly not the fault of anyone in particular, because the issue of standards compliancy is relatively new. What you can do as a designer today, however, is try to follow the HTML standards recommendations of the W3C when building any new site or redesigning any existing site. Using layers fits right into the overall mission of standards by allowing designers to precisely position and style content using CSS instead of HTML, which means code is lighter, pages load faster, and more visitors (whether they're humans using a browser or other device or nonhuman such as search engine robots) can access that content.

Take a look at some of the pros and cons of both layout methods.

The benefits of creating layouts with tables are

- They're easy to use.
- You can easily nest tables inside other tables.
- Tables can contain any content that can be placed elsewhere on a page.
- You can style tables, table cells, and cell contents with CSS.

- They stay on the page exactly where you put them.
- You can size them precisely or with percentages relative to the browser size.
- Although tables use a lot of code, there is a logic to how you can construct and style them.

The benefits of creating layouts with layers are

- The code is cleaner because it uses less HTML markup.
- Layers free you from having to design within traditional rows and columns.
- You can stack layers on top of other layers (z-index).
- You can control layer visibility with JavaScript.
- You can position layers anywhere on a page.
- Layers can nest inside other layers.
- You can style and position layers with CSS using the #layerID as the selector name.
- Layers can contain any content, just like tables, that can be further styled with CSS.
- Without touching the HTML layer markup, you can completely change the look and position of the layer's contents by modifying the CSS.

As you can see, there are good reasons for using both layout methods. Purists will tell you to create layers-only layouts, but old-school designers might say hybrid layouts are fine. I say that if you're unsure of whether you should build a layout using tables or layers, you should opt for layers. Nonetheless, some parts of layouts simply call for tables, so use them if you need to and don't feel guilty about it. You shouldn't feel pressured into creating perfect layers-only layouts; creating hybrid layouts or mostly layers layouts is really fine.

Tables, as you learned briefly in Chapter 11, are gridlike containers that can have any number of rows and columns. Each section in the grid, defined by a set of <td> tags, is a table cell. Take a look at the code of a typical two-row, two-column table:

```
<table width="300" border="1" cellspacing="3"
cellpadding="3">
  <tr>
    <td>....</td>
    <td>....</td>
  </tr>
  <tr>
    <td>....</td>
    <td>....</td>
  </tr>
</table>
```

When you need more unusual layouts, you can merge rectangular-shaped contiguous table cells to create a larger cell using the `rowspan` or `colspan` attribute. Alternatively, should you need further subdivisions in any single cell, you can split it into any number of rows or columns.

Tables and table cells can be precisely sized or sized relative to the browser window or other containing tag. You can nest them inside other table cells, as often as needed, to create meticulous layouts that accommodate even the most complex designs and presentation requirements. If you want to alter the appearance of the table and its contents, you can easily style them with CSS by either making Tag Redefine styles for the `<table>`, `<tr>`, `<th>`, and/or `<td>` tags or by creating custom class styles that are selectively applied to any of those tags as well as to the contents of any table cell.

Although definitely competent, tables on their own simply can't do everything a designer might want them to do. You'll often need to use special code hacks to get the contents of the tables to line up just the right way, with the desired margins and spacing and alignment. Using spacer GIFs, for example, is one hacky way of forcing a table cell to stay open to a desired width and height without collapsing due to lack of contents.

Information Kiosk

A *spacer GIF* is typically a 1-x-1-pixel transparent GIF that is inserted onto a Web page with false width and height measurements to hold open a space with those dimensions, such as `<img src="images/spacer.gif" width="100" height="100">`. Spacer GIFs are also often used to hold table cells open to precise sizes as well as create false margins to the left or right of text, giving a page more of a desktop publishing or print layout feel.

Layers, on the other hand, are like single-celled tables that can be placed anywhere on a Web page, including alongside, above, below, and nested inside other layers. Look at how simple the code is for a single layer:

```
<div id="Layer1">Text inside a DIV tag.</div>
```

When a layer (the `<div>` tag) contains an `id` attribute, only an advanced selector CSS style needs to be created to style and position it, such as

```
<style type="text/css">
<!--
#Layer1 {
    position:absolute;
    left:100px;
    top:100px;
    width:200px;
    height:200px;
    z-index:1;
    font-family: Geneva, Arial, Helvetica, sans-serif;
    font-size: 12px;
```

```
      color: #336699;
      background-color: #99ccff;
      margin: 0px;
      padding: 20px;
      border: 1px solid #ff6600;
}
-->
</style>
```

You can style and position layers with any CSS attributes, and layers can contain any content that might appear elsewhere on a Web page. You can further style that content — including tables and any contents inside the table cells — with CSS. Though definitely not as intuitive to use as working with tables, layers have become the new teacher's pet of the Web classroom.

As you'll see in the layers layout exercise later in this chapter, with the knowledge of a few simple techniques, you can soon be creating your own simple layouts with layers.

Creating a Layout with Tables

A tables-based layout can take on many different forms, depending on the look of the design before the site is built. Because you can stack tables above and below one another as well as nest them inside each other, you can achieve amazing layouts if you have the knowledge and patience to try to create them!

A typical site design includes an area for branding, navigation, and body content, often-times with the design of the page going right up to the edges of the browser window. These parts can be composed of stacked and nested tables, as shown in the diagram in Figure 14-1, to help improve the alignment and positioning of the cell contents.

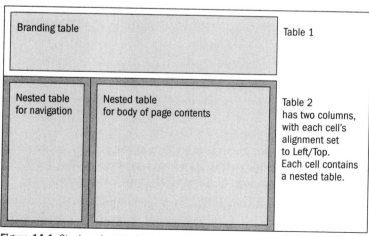

Figure 14-1: Stack and nest tables to achieve a layout that matches your design.

Follow these steps to build a tables-based layout that matches Figure 14-1:

1. **Create a folder on your computer called Layouts. Then, in your favorite HTML editor, open a new blank HTML with the HTML 4.01 Transitional DTD and save it into the Layouts folder with the name** `tablelayout.html`.

   If you're using Dreamweaver, define a managed site to the new Layouts folder.

2. **Insert a table on the page with the following specifications: Width=100%, Height=150, Rows=1, Columns=1, Border=0, Cellpadding=0, and Cellspacing=0.**

   This will create a single-celled table that spans the entire width of a browser window, inside which you can place branding information for the client, either directly inside the cell or nested inside another table in that cell.

3. **Place your cursor in the code of your page directly following the closing** `</table>` **tag and add a line break tag,** `<br>`.

   Adding the break will put the cursor in position to add another table to the page, stacked directly underneath the first one.

4. **Insert a second table on the page with the following specifications: Width=760, Rows=1, Columns=2, Border=0, Cellpadding=0, and Cellspacing=0.**

   This second table has two columns. The left side will be for navigation, which you can achieve with a nested table when using rollover button graphics or a CSS-styled list. The right column will be for the main content on the page, either right in the cell or inside another nested table.

Information Kiosk

The contents inside of table cells sometimes don't align properly in some browsers when the alignment attributes aren't specified in the HTML. Whenever you're working with tables, therefore, set the alignment (`align`) and vertical alignment (`valign`) attributes for every table cell in the code, such as

```
<td align="left" valign="top">Contents of cell</td>
```

Table cell horizontal alignment options include `left`, `center`, and `right`, and vertical alignment options include `top`, `middle`, `bottom`, and `baseline`.

5. **Add a nested table inside the left table cell of the bottom table with the following attributes: Width=150, Rows=6, Columns=1, Border=0, Cellpadding=5, Cellspacing=0, Align=Left, and Valign=Top.**

   Each cell in this table can contain the site's navigation links or rollover buttons.

6. **Now, with your insertion point inside the right table cell of the bottom table, add another nested table with these attributes: Width=610, Rows=1,**

Columns=1, Border=0, Cellpadding=5, Cellspacing=0, Align=Left, and Valign=Top.

This table will be for holding the main content on the page.

Watch Your Step

If the main copy for the page doesn't need to be broken up or ordered with table cells, why place it inside a nested table? The answer has to do with cell alignment. Sometimes, when content is added directly to a table cell like this, the content won't align itself to the top-left corner of the cell, even when the alignment attributes are specified. The code hack, or workaround, is to place the content inside a nested table, itself having the `left` and `top` alignment attributes.

The last task of creating this tables-based layout is to add styling and content. For the purposes of this exercise, you'll create an internal CSS. However, were this a real client's site, creating an external CSS would be more beneficial.

7. Add an internal CSS to the head area of your page and set the **body** tag redefine style attributes to the following: margins=0, padding=0, and background=#ffffff. Your internal CSS should look like this:

```
<head>
<style type="text/css">
<!--
body {
    background-color: #ffffff;
    margin: 0px;
    padding: 0px;
}
-->
</style>
</head>
```

Upon saving the document, notice how the margins on the page shift from the default 9 pixels of margin spacing to 0 pixels of margin spacing. The top table should now extend to the very top, left, and right edges of the page when viewed in a browser.

8. Create a custom class style called **.toptable** that sets the background color to #66ccff for the top table in the layout.

```
.toptable {
    background-color: #66ccff;
}
```

Remember, you must manually apply custom styles to the tag that needs styling before you can see the effect created by the style in the browser.

9. To apply the new **.toptable** style to the top table in your layout, add it to the opening **<table>** tag using the **class** attribute.

```
<table width="100%" height="150" border="0"
cellpadding="0" cellspacing="0" class="toptable">
```

Save and launch your page in a browser to view the effect.

10. **Create another custom style, this time called `.navigation`, and add the following style attributes to it:**

```
.navigation {
    font-family: Georgia, "Times New Roman",
    Times, serif;
    font-size: 14px;
    color: #ffffff;
    background-color: #ff9900;
    font-weight: bold;
    border-top-width: 0px;
    border-right-width: 1px;
    border-bottom-width: 1px;
    border-left-width: 0px;
    border-top-style: none;
    border-right-style: solid;
    border-bottom-style: solid;
    border-left-style: none;
    border-bottom-color: #000000;
    border-right-color: #000000;
}
```

This style will be applied to the navigation part of the page, but before you do that you need to add some content to those table cells.

11. **Enter text in each of the six table cells of the nested table on the left of the page to create mock navigation links.**

Type **Link One**, **Link Two**, and so forth, or enter your own text in each cell.

12. **To apply the new navigation style to the nested table, add the `class="navigation"` code to each of the opening `<td>` tags in the nested table.**

```
<td class="navigation">Link One</td>
```

Save and launch the page in a browser again to see how the navigation style looks now.

13. **Place your cursor inside the nested table on the right side of the page and enter a headline and some random text inside it.**

Create a headline that says *This is the Headline* and two or three sample paragraphs. Style the headline with the `<h1>` tag. The paragraphs should each be enclosed between opening and closing `<p>` tags.

14. **Create a tag redefine style for `<p>` and `<h1>` in the internal CSS with the following attributes, which will automatically be applied to those tags when the page is saved and viewed in a browser:**

```
p {
    font-family: Georgia, "Times New Roman",
    Times, serif;
    font-size: 12px;
    padding: 0px 0px 0px 20px;
}
h1 {
    font-family: Georgia, "Times New Roman",
    Times, serif;
    font-size: 30px;
    font-weight: bold;
    padding-top: 10px;
    padding-right: 0px;
    padding-bottom: 0px;
    padding-left: 10px;
}
```

You can create other styles to control the look of the rest of the page. If you inserted a logo into the top table on the left side, you could create a style to control how far the image sits relative to the top-left corner of that space. Figure 14-2 shows a screenshot of this exercise with a little more content and a few additional styles.

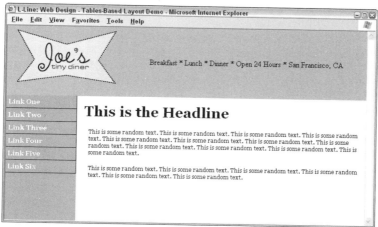

Figure 14-2: Tables-based layouts can include text and graphics and are easy to style with CSS.

If desired, use your imagination and creativity to continue styling the rest of the page with new CSS styles. You can apply a background image to any of the tags, such as the <body> tag or the master <table> tag. You can apply a background color or image to the left column of the bottom table so the area beneath the navigation buttons continues in the same color down the left margin. You can style all four link states for hyperlinks. Check out the code on the samplelayout2.html page at www.luckychair.com/l-line to see examples of these styles in action.

Creating a Layout with Layers

Layers are like free-spirited table cells. They're container tags that can hold any content and can be positioned anywhere on a Web page, including nested inside another layer. Using CSS for positioning, you can place them alongside, inside, above, below, and on top of each other. Furthermore, with CSS, you can style them to look similar to tables without all the extraneous code that tables require.

Adding a layer to a page is quite simple, for it requires only the `<div>` tag with an id attribute for attaching a CSS style:

```
<div id="header"><img src="images/logo.gif" width="200"
height="72" alt="ABC Company"></div>
```

When the `<div>` tag is assigned an id attribute, you can create the style for the layer, such as the example shown in the following code, in a style sheet in the `<head>` area of the page or on an external CSS:

```
<style type="text/css">
<!--
#header {
    position:absolute;
    left:0px;
    top:0px;
    width:10px;
    height:200px;
    z-index:1;
    font-family: Geneva, Arial, Helvetica, sans-serif;
    font-size: 12px;
    color: #336699;
    background-color: #99ccff;
    margin: 0px;
    padding: 20px;
    border: 1px solid #ff6600;
}
-->
</style>
```

What's so amazing about layers is that when combined with CSS styling, you can create unlimited variation with essentially the same HTML markup. (www.csszengarden.com is a perfect example of flexible layers styled and positioned with CSS.)

To illustrate how, with just a few minor changes to the CSS, a page layout can be completely transformed, you'll now create a two-column page layout with layers and CSS and then adjust the CSS at the end to change the look of the page. For demonstration purposes, the CSS will go inside the page rather than on an external style sheet. Were this layout to be used for a real site, however, you could begin either by creating an external CSS for the page or by creating the CSS internally to build this page and then transfer all the styles to an external CSS file before building any other pages for the site.

Step into the Real World

Using Descendant Selectors   If you've ever looked at another designer's CSS code and couldn't quite figure out why the syntax was written in a particular way or where exactly it was being applied on the page, you might have been looking at a *descendant selector style*. Descendent selector styles will be applied only to a specific tag that happens to be contained in another tag or series of other tags, such as an image inside a table cell inside a particular layer.

Descendent selector styles can be used for all kinds of styling tasks, including creating custom link states for different parts of a Web page. Here's an example of a selector for the hover state of a hypertext link that will apply only to links in a layer called `footer`:

```
#footer a:hover {
    padding: 5px;
    border: 1px solid #993300;
    background-color: #d94904;
    color: #fff;
}
```

Here's another example that will apply only to the hover state of any list item inside an unordered list in a layer called `linklist`:

```
#linklist ul li a:hover {
    color: #94ab36;
}
```

Descendant selector styles can help you to control how an image and/or text sits inside a layer. In the case of the exercise for creating a layers-based layout, for instance, you could control how the content in the `identity` layer is positioned relative to the layer's edges either by adding padding to the layer's style itself, or by creating a special descendant selector style that will only apply to other tags nested inside the layer, such as a <p> tag or <h1> tag.

To see what I mean, follow these steps to create your own descendant selector style:

1. **Wrap <h1> tags around the logo image you add to the `identity` layer in Step 3 of the layers layout exercise, like this,**

   ```
   <div id="identity"><h1><img src="images/joestinydiner.gif" alt="Joe's Tiny
     Diner" width="212" height="115" border="0"></h1>
   </div>
   ```

2. **Create a descendant selector style for <h1> in the CSS, like this,**

   ```
   #identity h1 {
       margin: 0;
       padding: .75em;
   }
   ```

The new style will be automatically applied to the <h1> tag inside that layer, but not to any other <h1> tags on the page.

You can create descendant selectors for any set of tags and preexisting styles such as links in a footer or images in a navigation (nav) bar. Create as many of them as you like!

To create a CSS layers-based layout, follow these steps:

1. In your favorite HTML editor, open a new blank HTML with the HTML 4.01 Transitional DTD and save it with the name `layerslayout.html` into the Layouts folder you created in the last exercise.

The page you're about to build will have a two-column layout with an area for the header above the two columns and a footer below them. The left column will be fixed in width, and the right column will have a liquid width that grows and shrinks proportionate to the size of the browser window.

For this layout to function properly, you must add a series of layers to the page in the proper order. The id attributes of the layers are named semantically to match the function they'll perform, such as *navigation* and *footer*.

2. Directly following the opening `<body>` tag, create five layers using the `<div>` tag and give each one its own id attribute:

```
<div id="container">
    <div id="identity">
    </div>
    <div id="navigation">
    </div>
    <div id="main">
    </div>
    <div id="footer">
    </div>
</div>
```

To better see the different layers (which are also sometimes called *containers*) and how they're organized on the page, you'll next add some placeholder content to identify each part. Then, after the page is styled, you can go back into each section and add other content. When inserting copy, be sure to use semantic HTML by wrapping the correct tags around the content, like `<p>` tags for paragraph text and `<h1>` to `<h6>` tags for headings.

3. Inside the `identity` layer, add a logo and/or a site name.

If desired, use the Joe's logo from this book's companion Web site (or visit www.luckychair.com/1-line to make a copy) or just type the name **Joe's Tiny Diner** wrapped in `<h1>` tags. If you use an image, the markup looks something like this:

```
<div id="identity"><img src="images/joestinydiner.gif"
alt="Joe's Tiny Diner" width="212" height="115"
border="0">
</div>
```

If you use text for the site name instead, the markup looks like this:

```
<div id="identity"><h1>Joe's Tiny Diner</h1>
</div>
```

4. In the **main** layer, type a header and a few paragraphs of text. Wrap the header in **<h1>** tags and the paragraph text in **<p>** tags:

```
<h1>This is the Page Name</h1>
<p>This is some random text. This is some random text.
This is some random text. This is some random text.
This is some random text. This is some random text.</p>
<p>This is some random text. This is some random text.
This is some random text. This is some random text.
This is some random text. This is some random text.</p>
<p>This is some random text. This is some random text.
This is some random text. This is some random text.
This is some random text. This is some random text.</p>
```

5. In the **navigation** layer, drop in another **<div>** tag with the **id** of **links** and inside it create an unordered list with six null hyperlinked list items:

```
<div id="navigation">
    <div id="links">
    <ul>
      <li><a href="#">Link One</a></li>
      <li><a href="#">Link Two</a></li>
      <li><a href="#">Link Three</a></li>
      <li><a href="#">Link Four</a></li>
      <li><a href="#">Link Five</a></li>
      <li><a href="#">Link Six</a></li>
    </ul>
    </div>
</div>
```

Transfer

You can style all the links in this section to look like navigation buttons by creating a style for #links. Refer to the navigation systems exercises in Chapter 13 for specific instruction on styling list items.

6. In the **footer** layer, enter some typical footer copy with null links, such as

```
<div id="footer">Copyright &copy;  2006 Joe's Tiny
Diner | <a href="#">Home</a> | <a href="#">Site
    Map</a> | <a href="#">Privacy Policy</a> | <a
href="#">Contact</a></div>
```

Note: The © is a special HTML entity for the copyright symbol. Use the entity instead of the regular copyright symbol (©) to ensure that it will display more accurately in multiple browsers and can be read properly by screen readers and other assistive devices.

This step completes the structural part of the layout. Next you'll create CSS styles to control how the page content will be presented in a browser.

Information Kiosk

As a practice, try to begin styling the page from the outside in. In other words, begin by redefining the `<body>` tag, then style the `<p>` and `<h1>` through `<h6>` tags, then style the `<div>` tags, and then the `<div>` contents.

7. Create a tag redefine style for the **`<body>`** tag to set the margins and padding on the page to 0 which will make the site layout begin at the very top-left edge of the browser. If desired, add a font style, color, and size for the entire page as well as a page background color.

```
body {
    margin: 0px;
    padding: 0px;
    background-color: #ffffff;
    font-family: Georgia, "Times New Roman",
    Times, serif;
    font-size: 12px;
    color: #000000;
}
```

Information Kiosk

The `<body>` tag deals with the body attributes for the entire page. However, not all containers will inherit the `font` attributes specified when the `<body>` attributes are redefined in the CSS. To ensure all containers use the same font and other global attributes within the redefined body style declaration, remove the font styles from the main `<body>` style and move them to a secondary advanced selector style that specifies the `<body>` and other subcontainer tags:

```
body {
    margin: 0px;
    padding: 0px;
    background-color: #ffffff;
}
body,th,td {
    font-family: Georgia, "Times New Roman",
    Times, serif;
    font-size: 12px;
    color: #000000;
}
```

Next you must create styles for each of the `<div>` tags so that the layers are positioned accurately on the page.

8. Create an advanced selector style for the `container` layer by using the `#layerid` syntax. Set the margins to 0 and the background color to white. In addition, to give the illusion of a column effect down the entire left column of the page, behind the `navigation` layer, you can add a background image that repeats only along the Y axis (down).

```
#container {
    margin: 0;
    background-color: #ffffff;
    background-image: url(images/leftbg.gif);
    background-repeat: repeat-y;
}
```

You can download a sample 195-pixel-wide background image for this exercise from this book's companion Web site or at www.luckychair.com/l-line.

9. Using the same advanced selector style technique, create a style for the `identity` layer. Set the background color to #ff9999 and add a 2-pixel-wide dotted black line to the layer's bottom border.

```
#identity {
    background-color: #ff9999;
    border-bottom: 2px dotted #000;
}
```

Information Kiosk

When a hexadecimal value uses the same number for each pair of the three-pair number, only the first number or letter of the pair needs to be specified, such as #000 for #000000 or #f36 for #ff3366.

10. Make a style for the `navigation` layer that includes a fixed width of 160 pixels and the `float:left` attribute.

```
#navigation {
    float: left;
    width: 160px;
    margin-left: 12px;
    padding-top: 1em;
}
```

The `float` attribute tells the browser to keep that layer positioned always on the left side of the page.

11. Because some browsers are buggy about the way contents inside a layer get displayed, and presumably you'd want everything inside the layer to line up properly, create a descendant selector for the `<p>` tag inside the `navigation` layer that sets the top margin to 0:

```
#navigation p {
    margin-top: 0;
}
```

The next step in styling this page involves creating styles for both the `main` and `navigation` layers. Specifically, you'll need to set the margin for the `main` layer slightly wider than the `navigation` layer size so that it doesn't fall below the navigation layer.

12. **Create a style for the `main` layer with 1em of padding on the top, and the top margin=0, right margin=2em, bottom margin=0, and left margin=200px:**

```
#main {
    padding-top: 1em;
    margin: 0 2em 0 200px;
}
```

Because the `navigation` layer width is set to 160, the left margin on the `main` layer needs to be slightly wider, around 200 pixels, more or less.

Information Kiosk

An em is one of the units of measure acceptable on the Web that also make pages more accessible to a wider audience. What makes the em different from pixels and percentages, however, is that each em unit varies because its size is equal to the point size of the specified font face. If the font for a page is set to 10px, for example, one em will be exactly 10px.

13. **Next make a style for the `footer` layer with the `clear:both` attribute, a background color of #ff9999, a little padding on all sides, the text aligned to the center, and a 2-pixel dotted black border along the layer's top edge:**

```
#footer {
    clear: both;
    background-color: #ff9999;
    padding: 1em;
    text-align: center;
    border-top: 2px dotted #000;
}
```

Adding the `clear:both` attribute to this style tells the browser that the `footer` layer must not appear alongside the other layers but should instead appear below them.

14. **Save the page and preview the layers-based layout in a browser.**

The page margins are set to extend all the way to the four edges of the browser window.

15. **To make the page set apart from the browser's edges, go back into the `container` layer style and change the margin from 0 to 2em on the top and bottom and 10% on the left and right:**

```
#container {
    margin: 2em 10%;
    background-color: #ffffff;
    background-image: url(images/leftbg.gif);
    background-repeat: repeat-y;
}
```

Play around with changing some of the other attributes in the CSS to see how you can modify the look of the HTML markup. To see a live example of this layout, go to www.luckychair.com/l-line.

Using Layout Resources for CSS and Layers

An easy way to begin designing with CSS and layers is to use CSS layers-based design templates. You can choose from many good resources for free, clean, standards-compliant templates, which you can modify to match your site design by tweaking and adding your own CSS styles.

A good starting place for Dreamweaver users is to use any of the six CSS layers-based page layouts that come built into Dreamweaver. These page design guides are accessible from the New Document dialog box in the Page Designs category under the General tab, as shown in Figure 14-3.

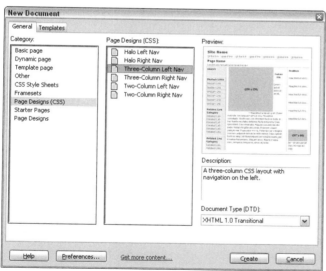

Figure 14-3: Dreamweaver 8 includes six prewritten CSS layers-based layouts you can use as a starting point to building your own Web site.

The Halo Right Nav layout shown in Figure 14-4, for example, comes with its own CSS file and has a liquid two-column design with an area for the site's branding, a main navigation bar across the top that includes subnavigation links when applicable, utility links, a site search box, a page title and breadcrumbs, content for main text, an area for capsule stories in other areas of the site, a sidebar for related links and advertising, and a footer area, all of which you can restyle with CSS.

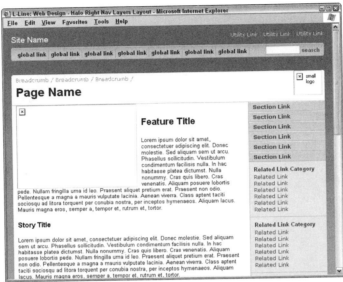

Figure 14-4: Dreamweaver's Halo Right Nav layout includes an area for the logo, top navigation bar with subnavigation, page title, breadcrumbs, and sidebar section links.

Another good source for free CSS layout pages is the Glish site (www.glish.com/css/home.asp), where you'll find free sample layouts for two, three, and four columns. In my opinion, the more you explore what can be done with CSS, the more it will start to make sense to you. Visit as many of the sites listed (in no particular order) in Table 14-1 as you can, and be sure to also do a search for CSS layouts in your favorite search engine.

Table 14-1   Free CSS Page Layout Templates

Site Address	Freebies, Tips, and More
http://webdesign.about.com/od/ websitetemplates/a/bl_layouts.htm	A comprehensive list of links to sites offering free CSS layouts
www.ssi-developer.net/main/ templates/index.shtml	Five free CSS page-layout templates

Site Address	Freebies, Tips, and More
www.bluerobot.com/web/layouts	Free two- and three-column CSS page layout templates
http://websitetips.com/css/templates/#csstemplates	A great list of links to sites offering free CSS layouts
http://webhost.bridgew.edu/etribou/layouts	Free CSS layouts with special features like styleswitchers and a very nice free CSS menu
www.oswd.org	Free blog templates
www.cssfill.com	Free CSS/XHTML layouts and templates for Web sites and blogs
http://blog.html.it/layoutgala	40 different CSS layouts based on the same markup
www.thenoodleincident.com/tutorials/box_lesson/boxes.html	16 free CSS layouts
www.csscreator.com/version2/pagelayout.php	An online CSS page-layout generator. *Note:* You must create a free account to use the tools on this site
www.maxdesign.com.au/presentation/page_layouts	Over 20 free CSS page layouts with tutorials
http://24ways.org/advent/css-layout-starting-points	CSS Page Layout basics tutorial by Rachel Andrew

code hacks: Unorthodox and creative use of HTML, CSS, JavaScript, and other code to manipulate objects on a Web page and/or work around existing limitations of the Web to achieve a desired visual effect.

descendant selector: A special type of style declaration that will be applied only to the set of tags specified in the style's selector, such as a hover link on a styled list inside a <div> layer using a particular ID, such as #footer ul li a: hover.

div: The tag used in (X)HTML to specify a layer in the code. See also *layer*.

continued

em: One of several relative units of measure in Web design (the others being en, ex, or percentages) that is supposed to be the equivalent of the font size specified in a parent element elsewhere in the code. Thus if the font for a page is set to 12 pixels (px), 1 em will be exactly 12 pixels. Relative units make Web pages more accessible.

inherit: In CSS, to automatically take on the properties of a parent class. For instance, if the font is specified in a redefined style for the body (parent), all paragraph tags (child) will automatically inherit the same font unless otherwise specified in the CSS.

layer: A tableless container using the `<div>` tag that, with CSS, can be styled and positioned anywhere on the page, including nested inside or stacked above or below other layers, and inside which any content may be placed and styled.

nesting: Embedding one object inside another object, as with tables inside the cell of another table or a layer inside another layer.

spacer GIF: Typically a 1 x 1 transparent GIF that is inserted on a Web page with false width and height measurements to help keep a table cell open to a desired size and to help bump content around on a page to give the illusion of more print-like layouts on the Web.

stack: Placing objects above or below other objects on a Web page, such as tables and images, oftentimes with the `<br>` tag between each object.

table: A type of HTML container that uses `<table>`, `<tr>`, and `<td>` tags to create a gridlike structure, inside which any content that would appear elsewhere on a Web page may be placed and styled. To be more standards compliant, however, there has been a recent shift away from tables-based layouts to layouts using layers.

z-index: The style attribute that specifies the stacking order of layers and other absolutely positioned objects on a Web page. The larger the z-index number, the closer the object appears to the viewer in the browser window.

Last
Stop

Practice Exam

1. True or False: Web layouts using tables are just as standards compliant as layouts using layers.

2. Name five benefits to using tables and five for using layers for page layout.

_____

_____

3. Describe how layers get styled with CSS.

_____

_____

4. Tables and layers are very similar in that they both can contain any content that can go elsewhere on a Web page. Where they differ is in how you can place them on a Web page (such as above, below, or next to other tables or layers). Name the two placement locations that layers can use that tables cannot.

_____

_____

5. What is a descendant selector?

_____

_____

6. What are spacer GIFs and why are they sometimes used with tables?

_____

_____

_____

_____

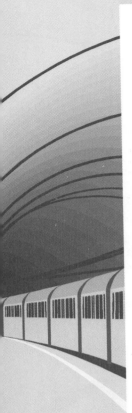

7. Why is it sometimes necessary to nest a table inside another table cell?

_____

_____

_____

_____

_____

Using Templates and Server-Side Includes (SSIs)

Stations Along the Way

- Understanding the benefits of a master template
- Using and creating Dreamweaver templates
- Making Web page content modular with Server-Side Includes
- Differentiating between site-root and document relative paths
- Choosing the right solution: Templates versus Server-Side Includes

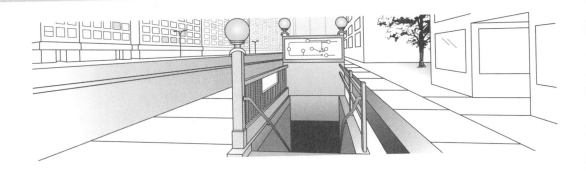

Enter the Station

Questions

1. What is a Dreamweaver template?

2. How might you use templates to manage site updates?

3. What are Server-Side Includes (SSIs)?

4. How do you create and use an SSI?

5. What is the difference between document relative and site-root relative paths?

6. When using SSIs, what special rules do you need to follow?

7. How can you determine whether to use templates or SSIs to build a site?

Express Line

If you already know which method you'll be using to build your site pages — whether it be template, SSIs, or some other time-saving process — you can advance to Chapter 16 to learn about creating forms and processing form data.

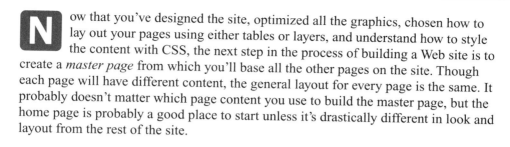

Now that you've designed the site, optimized all the graphics, chosen how to lay out your pages using either tables or layers, and understand how to style the content with CSS, the next step in the process of building a Web site is to create a *master page* from which you'll base all the other pages on the site. Though each page will have different content, the general layout for every page is the same. It probably doesn't matter which page content you use to build the master page, but the home page is probably a good place to start unless it's drastically different in look and layout from the rest of the site.

Information Kiosk

What I like to do, because my clients often enjoy seeing the progress I make on their sites as I build them, is build the master page based on the Web site's home page. This gives the clients a peek into the site-building process and gets them excited about seeing the finished product. It also gives them an opportunity to review the sample page for layout accuracy and functionality. At this stage, should the clients raise any issues regarding the layout or navigation, I can correct those concerns before generating any of the other pages.

To build this master page, you have tools at your disposal so that starting a new page with the master requires the least amount of redundant work. You also want a master that enables you to quickly and efficiently make updates to the pages at a later time. You might not think you need to consider site updates until after you build the site, but in fact, the projected frequency of the updates can be a major determinant for how you create the site's pages.

To minimize redundant work, the master includes features that are common to all pages on the site. If a navigation bar appears across the top of the layout on all the pages of a site, for instance, you don't need to rebuild that navigation bar on all the individual pages of that site as you build each page. For that matter, even copying and pasting code from one page to another is too much work.

When it comes to managing future site updates, two site construction solutions for the nondynamic Web site work beautifully: Dreamweaver's templates and a nonproprietary solution called Server-Side Includes, or simply SSIs. Basically, these tools enable you to change every page on a site simply by making the changes once to your master page.

Watch Your Step

You can create a master in other ways, but these methods generally won't be as effective as Dreamweaver templates or SSIs. For example, you could create a nontemplate master file and then every time you need another page you'd just open the master file, do a Save As to save it with a new filename, and then modify the content that's different on the newly saved file, repeating this process until all the pages were done. But such a method still doesn't address how to make site-wide changes to the navigation bar without having to individually go into the code of every page on the site to do it.

This chapter will provide you with an overview of working with Dreamweaver templates and SSIs. Both methods assist you with making global updates to a site with the least amount of effort. Both work in markedly different ways and are suited for different purposes. You'll find explanations and exercises on working with both methods here and a comparison chart at the end of the chapter to assist you with determining which solution will work best for any site you happen to create.

Using Dreamweaver Templates

Depending on which code editing application you use to build your site, you might have the option of creating a template or stationery page for the site, from which you can generate all the other pages on the site. This not only establishes visual consistency between the pages, but can also significantly reduce the time it takes to build the rest of the pages on the site and make changes to those pages anytime the site needs global modifications.

Dreamweaver's templates and GoLive's stationeries are good examples of this type of master page technique. Templates are a really good solution for most small- to medium-sized Web sites (under 30 pages) that use little to no dynamic capabilities, because template-based pages can be updated rather quickly with minimal effort on the part of the designer.

My preference for smaller sites is to work with Dreamweaver's templates. After a template file is created, you can specify which areas on that master page will be editable in any template-based pages. For example, you might want to create an editable area for the main content on the page and another area for the page header graphic. With the editable areas established, anytime a new template-based page is created, only the content in those editable areas can be altered, whereas the rest of the content is locked down and remains uneditable.

Create as many templates for a site as you need to; there is no limit to the number or complexity of the templates you create for each Web project. Templates can have more than editable regions, too. Designers can create nested templates, optional editable regions, and repeating regions within the template.

Nested templates: A template embedded inside another template, such as when one section of the site uses a special layout requiring its own set of editable regions and that layout falls within the editable area of the parent template, as with a product details page on an e-commerce site.

Optional editable regions: An editable area specified on a template that can either be shown or hidden in a template-based page, such as a link back to the top of a page on pages with lots of content.

Repeating regions: A section of a layout that can be repeated as often as needed inside a template-based page, such as an entire table row containing a set of editable regions.

Transfer

This chapter only skims the surface of the things you can do with Dreamweaver templates. As your skills grow, you can experiment more with advanced techniques, such as nested templates and so on. To find a book to guide you, you can search for Dreamweaver titles at www.wiley.com.

The true beauty of a template-based Web design is that, should any part of the locked, uneditable part of the template need altering (like a navigation button that is no longer needed on the site), rather than having to individually update all the pages, only the template would need adjustment. The code editor then automatically updates the changed, locked code on all the template-based pages.

Information Kiosk

Another really useful aspect of working with Dreamweaver's templates is the fact that you can integrate them with Contribute software. Sites built with templates can be managed by the designer through Dreamweaver, and Contribute users (like the client) can be authorized to modify the editable regions of that site without needing to know anything about Web design. Contribute is extremely easy to learn and use and puts the client in control of some of his or her site's editability. To see how easy it is to use Contribute with Dreamweaver, check out other books about Dreamweaver and Contribute at www.wiley.com and download a free trial version of Contribute from Adobe.com.

Preparing a page to become a template

You can build Dreamweaver templates from scratch with a blank HTML template page or convert any existing HTML/XHTML page into a Dreamweaver template by choosing File ➜ Save as Template. My suggestion is for you to create a complete sample page in HTML or XHTML first and then convert it into a template. This way, you have a chance to work out the kinks in the regular (X)HTML document before it becomes the master template you use to create all the other pages on your site.

To get the page ready to become a template, the process works as follows:

- Start as you normally would by creating a new HTML/XHTML page and inserting the desired DTD (Document Type Definition).

- Get all the parts of the layout in their proper places by adding the content and inserting the graphics with `alt` text attributes.

- Add footer links at the bottom of the page.

- Include `<meta>` tags in the `<head>` of the code and any of the other accessibility attributes to the code you can think of to make the page as accessible as possible.

- Add dynamic functionality (like rollover buttons or initial layer visibility) and assign hyperlinks where desired.

- Style all the content with CSS.

- When all that is done, run a spell check and read through the code looking for errors.

- Test the page in as many browsers and browser versions as possible on both Mac and PC platforms and on any other devices you can test. Fix anything that needs fixing.

- Show the page to your client to get feedback and input.

- Make any adjustments to the site's layout if needed and get the client's approval again, in writing, before you build more pages.

Information Kiosk

In the last item in the preceding list, I say "get the client's approval again, in writing" because clients sometimes have "brilliant ideas" at this stage. They might think of another page to squeeze in, want to move something over (even though they've already seen the design and approved it), or add a whole new section to the layout. If your contract states that no modifications can be made at this stage without an addendum to the contract (and it should!), remind your client of this clause and tell him you'd be delighted to make any changes he'd like for an additional fee. If the client is serious about the change, he'll agree to the addendum. But if his brilliant idea was just whimsy or, more often than not, just a natural inclination to want to feel a part of this process, he'll change his mind about wanting to make any modifications to the design and give you his signed approval to continue.

Converting an HTML/XHTML file into a template

When you and your client are confident in the layout and styling of your sample Web page, you'll be ready to convert that page into a Dreamweaver template.

Follow the steps in this section to convert any regular HTML/XHTML file into a Dreamweaver template. You may use your own file or the sample file called `templatedemo.html` available from this book's companion Web site or `www.luckychair.com/l-line`:

1. **Save the sample page you'll be working with into a new folder on your desktop called TemplateDemo. Then create a new site managed in Dreamweaver in that folder.**

   Managing a site provides access to Dreamweaver's advanced site management features, and it must be done when working with templates so that Dreamweaver can appropriately write code to manage template-based file updates.

   To create a managed site, choose Site → New Site. When the Site Definition dialog box opens, click the Advanced tab. In the Local Info category, enter a name for the site in the Site Name field (such as Template Demo), and in the Local Root Folder field browse to and select the TemplateDemo folder you just created on your desktop.

2. **With the sample page open in the Dreamweaver's workspace, choose File → Save as Template.**

   The Save As Template dialog box opens, as seen in Figure 15-1.

   Figure 15-1: Enter details about the new template in the Save As Template dialog box.

3. **The Site drop-down menu in this dialog box should now list the name of this managed site. If you've defined a site but that site name isn't showing on the drop-down menu, click the menu's down arrow to select the name of the site for this project.**

   The Existing Templates field shouldn't have any templates listed, unless you or someone else has already created a template for this managed site.

4. **In the Description text field, type a short description for the template you're about to create. This can be a sentence describing the client or a short phrase about what this template will be used for.**

   For example, if the template is for an Artist's portfolio Web site, the description might read something like **Karen Marker's Portfolio Web Site**. If you're using the sample page provided for this exercise, you might enter **East Side Auto Body Site**.

5. **In the Save As field, enter a name for the template.**

A good naming convention for templates is to use the client's name or something similar. For instance, if the client's company is called Telephone Mates, Inc., you might name the template *telmates* or *TMI*.

6. **Click Save, and when the "Update Links?" dialog box appears, click Yes.**

When Dreamweaver converts the HTML file into a template with the .dwt file extension, the program also creates a new Templates folder in the root directory of the managed site and saves the new template file inside it.

Clicking Yes in the Update Links dialog box lets Dreamweaver automatically update links to graphics and other files with appropriate *document relative path* syntax (which you'll learn about in a later section of this chapter titled "Editing paths to work with SSIs") to match the new location of the template file. This ensures that any template-based files created from the template will use accurately syntaxed paths. For example, a link to contact.html in the original HTML file will be updated to ../contact.html inside the new template file. Likewise, a link to an image such as <img src="images/cat.jpg"> would be changed to <img src="../images/cat.jpg">. The dot-dot-slash (../) before the link location tells a browser to go up a level in the server's directory to find the specified file.

Watch Your Step

If you accidentally click No in the Update Links dialog box, the links in the template won't function properly. Should that happen, close the new template file, delete it from the new Templates folder, and begin again at Step 1. Then make sure you click Yes when the Update Links dialog box appears again.

By default, the entire template is locked, which means that any pages generated from it at this point can't be edited, unless you want to make global changes to all the pages by editing the template itself or unless you specify one or more editable regions. In the next steps, you'll create an editable region in the template.

7. **With the template file open in the Dreamweaver workspace, place your insertion point inside the document, preferably in Design view, and select all the text in the main content area of the page.**

If you're using the templatedemo.html file, select the contents from "Making Your Car Great . . ." to ". . . tortor dolor ac dui."

The selected content will demark the area that will be converted into an editable region.

8. **Choose Insert → Template Objects → Editable Region; enter a name for the selection, such as Content, into the New Editable Region dialog box; and click OK.**

This name, as shown in Figure 15-2, now identifies the region inside the template as well as inside any template-based pages you create.

Name of editable region

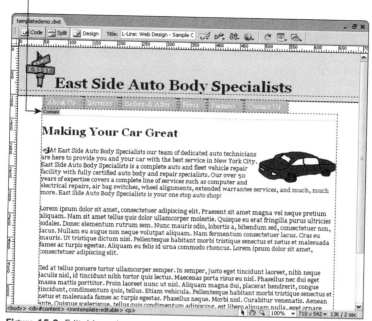

Figure 15-2: Editable regions appear outlined in blue and have a tab with the region's name at the top-left corner of the outlined space.

9. (Optional) **Continue creating editable regions on the template as needed by selecting content, choosing Insert → Template Objects → Editable Region, and giving each new region a unique name.**

Templates may contain an unlimited number of editable regions, but editable regions may not be nested inside other editable regions.

10. **When you're finished creating editable regions, save and close the Template file.**

You'll learn how to create a template-based page in the following section.

11. **To modify the template, and thereby update any locked areas on any template-based files, reopen the template file, make the changes to the code, and save the page.**

Upon saving any changes to a template, Dreamweaver asks whether you want to automatically update all the template-based pages. As long as you're in a managed Dreamweaver site and you say Yes, Dreamweaver will handle rewriting all the changed code to any template-based file within that managed site.

Template files contain special Dreamweaver template comment tags that identify the beginning and end of each editable region within the file. Don't modify these comment tags; without them, Dreamweaver won't understand how and where to make global modifications to template-based page code.

Here's an example of what these special comment tags might look like:

```
<!-- #BeginEditable "Content" --><IMG
SRC="../images/about.gif" alt="About Our Services"
WIDTH=340 HEIGHT=30><!-- #EndEditable -->
```

In addition to the beginnings and ends of editable regions, the templates also include an editable area in the <head> of the code, in case JavaScript, CSS, or other <head> code elements need to be placed inside the head of a template-based file. These tags have the name attribute of "head":

```
<!-- InstanceBeginEditable name="head" --> ... <!--
InstanceEndEditable -->
```

Creating and editing template-based files

Template-based files are easy to create and use because the pages behave just like any other HTML page except that they have locked-down, uneditable regions that are controlled by the template.

To create a template-based page in Dreamweaver, follow these steps:

1. Choose File → New.

When the New Document dialog box opens, click the Templates tab.

2. From the left column of the dialog box, select the name of the managed site that contains the template you'd like to use. In the middle column, select a template from the list of available templates for that site. A preview of the selected template will appear in the Preview pane. Click the Create button to continue.

A new, untitled, template-based page will appear in the Dreamweaver workspace window.

3. The untitled file must be saved before you begin adding code to the editable regions. Choose File → Save to save the new template-based file with a filename and extension of your choice (like contact.html for a contact page) into the same managed site.

Editable regions in the template-based file are outlined in blue and have a tab with the region name at the top-left corner of each editable area.

4. Make modifications to the content in the editable regions of the template-based file as desired.

5. Save the page after making changes. Repeat Steps 1–3 to create additional template-based files.

Step into the Real World

Dreamweaver Template Workarounds   When working with Dreamweaver templates, you'll quickly notice that, in a template-based file, all the uneditable code — the locked parts of the template that you haven't made into editable regions — will be grayed out in Code view and unselectable in Design view.

The preferred way to make changes to an uneditable area on a template-based page is to go back into the original template and make the changes there, but those changes will be global and will automatically update all the template-based pages on a site.

What, then, should you do when you need to make a change to a locked part of a page in just one or two of the site's pages? You have several choices, depending on your specific needs.

First, you could edit the code on the pages in question by using a simple text editor, outside of Dreamweaver. This would permanently change the code, unless or until the next time you made changes to the template and had Dreamweaver do a global update. In that case, saved changes to the template will overwrite your hand-coded changes.

A second option to modifying parts of a page or two would be to convert those parts into editable regions on the master template. The drawbacks to this method, however, are

- You might be working in a team and *not* want that new editable area to be editable on the rest of the site.

- If you've created the pages of the site before you add the new editable area, you might need to reapply the updated template to all the pages on your site. (Dreamweaver has a tool that allows you to manually apply templates. Choose Modify ➔ Templates ➔ Apply Template to Page to open the Select Templates dialog box, select the template you'd like to use, and click the Select button.)

A third option is to build a separate template, based on the master template, for just those one or two pages that need a special editable area. This solution will require that any changes you want to globally apply to all the template-based pages must be made to both templates, but at least it keeps the locked areas locked where you need them to be.

The last and perhaps most useful option is to create an optional editable region in the original master template. This type of region can be on or off by default and then be shown or hidden from within a template-based page when needed. You can insert optional editable regions through the Insert ➔ Template Objects ➔ Optional Editable Region command. To hide or show an optional editable region from within a template-based page, choose Modify ➔ Template Properties. A dialog box will open, listing any optional editable regions for that page, from which you can select the regions and enable or disable them as needed.

Working with Server-Side Includes

For larger sites, sites that use programming to control dynamic content, and sites that will need frequent updating, Server-Side Includes (SSIs) might be a better solution than using Dreamweaver templates. Unlike templates, which hard-code all the pages on a site and require the user to set editable regions for template-based pages, SSIs break Web pages into components, kind of like pieces of a puzzle. You have the main page and the pieces. The main page contains the HTML structure and perhaps a few layout elements on the page that never change. The pieces, composed of HTML, are actually external HTML files that are plugged into the main page with a single line of code where the content should appear. The browser displaying the page seamlessly integrates any SSI content by grabbing the information inside the SSI files from the server and displaying that content as if it were hard-coded into the main page.

Elements that might make good SSI files are navigation bars, footer links, or other components or content on pages that require frequent updating. SSI files can be composed of text, graphics, JavaScript, Flash movies, and anything else that might go on a regular Web page. The only code that the SSI files shouldn't contain are the bones of the Web page, namely any <html>, <head>, <meta>, <title>, or <body> tags. The reason the SSI files don't need those structural code elements is because they're already provided by the main HTML page where the SSI content is included.

For example, say you wanted to put all the site's footer information into an SSI file called footer.html because you know the site will be growing and you'll be adding more links to it every month. The footer page content might include links to all the current main pages on the site, copyright information with the year, and Web address, as shown in Figure 15-3.

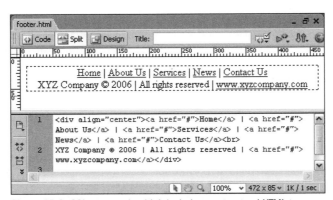

Figure 15-3: SSI content shouldn't include any structural HTML tags.

To include the footer.html SSI file's content inside another page, simply add a special link tag specifying the name and location of the external SSI in the spot on the main page where the SSI's content should appear. The line of code you need to include will look something like this:

```
<!--#include file="footer.html"-->
```

Using that same link line of code, presumably in the same location on every page, you can include the footer.html SSI content on as many pages of a site as desired. A site visitor never knows the difference between actual hard-coded content and content parsed in an SSI file. In fact, if visitors were to view the source code of a page that had an SSI link, they wouldn't see the `include` link tag in the code; instead, they'd see the actual content from the SSI file, inline with the code, as if you had written the page without SSIs. The server and the browser do all the work to ensure that visitors see the SSI content presented seamlessly as part of the page in the browser.

With the SSI `include` link inserted on a page, you don't need to do anything else to ensure that content displays in the insertion location. And when the SSI content needs updating (like changing the year from 2006 to 2007 or adding another hypertext link), you need to edit and reupload only the external HTML SSI file (in this example, the `footer.html` file) to the remote server hosting the Web site. When that's complete, all the pages on the site automatically display the updated version of the external SSI file's content.

Making changes to an external SSI file is just like making changes to any other HTML file. Open the SSI file in your favorite HTML code editor, make the changes, and resave the file. As long as you remember to upload the changed SSI file to the remote server, the changes will appear on any page that includes a link to that particular SSI file.

Though SSIs might seem like the best solution for creating easily updatable Web sites, there are hurdles to using them:

- **The server has to be capable of parsing the data.** Check with your host provider or system administrator to find out whether the server is capable of this function. Some servers can do the work but must have special software installed to do it, but other servers simply can't be configured to perform the task.

- **The link code must be accurate.** The link can contain a couple of variables, and if they're incorrect, the server hosting the pages won't understand how to parse the data contained in the SSI file. The syntax of an SSI link is also slightly peculiar and must be accurate to ensure the SSI file is parsed.

- **The extension on files including SSIs might need to be modified** from `.html` to `.shtml`. This means that visitors trying to reach a particular page, such as `www.yoursite.com/about.shtml`, will not be able to access that page if they directly type in the address as `www.yoursite.com/about.html`.

- **You must alter the paths to any graphics and links** inside the SSI file. SSI files require site-root relative paths to function properly.

- **Files requiring parsing place greater demands on the server,** which can translate into slightly longer download times. The delay might be only a fraction of a second, but it's there, and in some cases might be very noticeable. That could affect visitor loyalty.

Creating, including, and testing SSIs

If the host server does process SSIs, you begin the process of adding SSIs by finding out whether you'll need to change the file extension on pages containing SSIs. The change would require you to add an *s* before the normal file extension, such as from `.html` to `.shtml` (or from `.htm` to `.shtm`). The *s* in front of the `.html` or `.htm` extension tells the server that SSIs are included in the file and that the server will need to do a little extra work to parse the SSI content.

The next step is to ensure that the SSI include code is accurate. Depending on the host server's type, you'll either use the word *file,* as in the example in the preceding section, or the word *virtual,* as in this example:

```
<!--#include virtual="footer.html"-->
```

 Watch Your Step

The `include` link must be typed accurately for this feature to work. Pay particular attention to the lack of space between the opening comment tag, the number symbol, and the word `include`.

The name of the file you include can be in any location on the host server as long as that path is referenced in the link to it. For instance, the SSI needn't be at the root level of your site. It could be in a subdirectory, like in a folder called ssi:

```
<!--#include file="ssi/footer.html"-->
```

Or in a folder on a completely different URL on a different server:

```
<!--#include
file="http://www.myotherco.com/ssi/footer.html"-->
```

The last thing you'll need to do to successfully use SSIs is change any paths to graphics or other files in the include HTML files from *document relative* to *site-root relative.* In other words, any hypertext links or references to objects appearing on the page must use the site-root relative paths, which will be explained in the "Editing paths to work with SSIs" section later in this chapter.

In the next exercise, you'll convert part of a Web page into an external SSI and then include it as an SSI back into the page it was removed from. Before you begin, download a copy of the sample SSI demo files (which include an `.html` file and an images folder) from this book's companion Web site or from www.luckychair.com/l-line and save it into a folder on your computer. Dreamweaver users should manage a site to a new project folder called SSI Demo and save the demo files inside it.

1. **Open the `ssidemo.html` file in your favorite HTML editor.**

   This page contains a header with a graphic, a navigation bar styled with CSS, a page title, body text, and a footer.

2. **In the code, select and cut all the footer content, from the empty `<p>` tag right below the `<div>` tag with the `id` of footer to the closing `</p>` tag right before the closing `</div>` tag.**

The footer code you select and cut from the page should look like this:

```
<p> </p>
<p><a href="home.html">Home</a> |
    <a href="about.html">About Us</a> |
    <a href="services.html">Services</a> |
    <a href="before.html">Before &amp; After</a> |
    <a href="press.html">Press</a> |
    <a href="partners.html">Partners</a> |
    <a href="contact.html">Contact</a><br>
    Copyright (c) 2006 East Side Auto Body Specialists |
    <a href="sitemap.html">Site Map</a> |
    <a href="privacy.html">Privacy Policy</a>
</p>
```

The only tags remaining in that part of the code on the page after you select and cut the code should be the opening and closing <div> tags for the footer.

The cursor should now be flashing in the code in the space between the footer <div> tags. Leave your cursor there.

3. **Open a new, blank HTML file and delete any HTML code that your code editor might have automatically placed in the file, such as a <dtd>, <html>, <head>, <meta>, <title>, and <body> tags.**

The document should be completely blank, with no HTML tags, markup, or other content inside it.

4. **With your cursor at the top of the code view area of this blank file, paste the footer content you cut from the ssidemo.html file.**

The code should be exactly the same as what you cut from the other file, as shown in the code example. If the code has any extra line spaces, you may remove them. Figure 15-4 shows how the code should look, without any of the structural HTML tags.

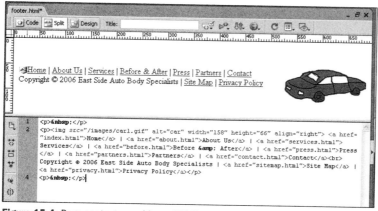

Figure 15-4: Page content saved in an SSI file doesn't need to include any tags.

5. Save this new file with the pasted code as `footer.html` into a new folder called ssi inside the same folder where you saved the `ssidemo.html` file. Then close the file.

The root level of the folder you're working in should now contain three items: the `ssidemo.html` file, a folder called ssi, and inside the new ssi folder, the new `footer.html` file.

6. Back inside the `ssidemo.html` file, your insertion point should still be between the footer `<div>` tags. At this spot, type the link to the new external SSI file inside the new ssi folder:

```
<div id="footer">
<!--#include file="ssi/footer.html" -->
</div>
```

Dreamweaver users might suddenly see the SSI content magically appear in Design view, inline with the rest of the page content, while still only seeing the include link in Code view.

7. Launch the page in a browser to view the results.

You should see the SSI content at the bottom of the page. If you don't see it, you might need to enable your browser to view files as if it were a server. Dreamweaver users can quickly turn on a feature to do this by selecting the Preview Using Temporary File option in the Preview in Browser category of the Preferences panel. Non-Dreamweaver users, unfortunately, might need to upload the sample file to a live server that can parse SSI files to see the SSI in action.

To get the test file working, you might also need to change the file extension on the page that has the SSI link in it from .html to .shtml, and possibly modify the include type attribute from file to virtual.

In this exercise, you used file as the type of SSI. In some servers, the type must be changed to virtual. You have a 50/50 chance of being right, so if file doesn't make the SSI appear on the page when viewed in a browser and the server is SSI capable, virtual should.

Even if you do see the SSI file on your page, you're not quite done with the SSI configuration yet. You must still ensure that any links inside the SSI file use site-root relative paths. In the next section, you'll modify the paths to work properly and test them in a continuation of the last exercise.

Editing paths to work with SSIs

Two types of paths can be used in HTML when referring to files and other objects, document relative paths and site-root relative paths. For SSIs to work, the links inside any SSI files must use site-root relative paths. To better understand the differences between them, in this section, you look at the structure of each.

Document relative paths are the default type of path system in Web pages, whereby the code used to link pages together and reference objects included in the pages is relative to the point at which each file is located and the full URL or path to the Web site is omitted from the page reference. For example, a document relative path from the home page to a particular subpage of an About section called About Our Projects might look like this, where the `href` specifies a file (`aboutprojects.html`) sitting inside a folder (`about`) that resides at the root level of the Web site's server:

```
<a href="about/aboutprojects.html"><img
src="images/bullet.gif">About Our Projects</a>
```

Because the About Our Project page sits in a directory (folder) called `about`, both the directory and filename are needed in the path. If you were to turn the path into a sentence, you might say, "Starting from here, go to and open a page in the `about` folder called `aboutprojects.html`." When that page is displaying in the browser window, a link on that page back to the home page would need a path that tells the server how to get to the home page from its present location by using a `../` before the filename, which tells the browser to look for the named file one level below the current level on the server:

```
<a href="../index.html"><img
src="../images/bullet.gif">Home</a>
```

Site-root relative paths, by contrast, tell the server to always look for the named file or object relative to the site's root. This means the path on the home page to the `aboutprojects.html` page would need to look like this:

```
<a href="/about/aboutprojects.html"><img
src="/images/bullet.gif">About Our Projects</a>
```

And the path back to the home page from the `aboutprojects.html` page would look like this:

```
<a href="/index.html"><img
src="/images/bullet.gif">Home</a>
```

Information Kiosk

The backslash before any link or sourced object, like the image in the preceding sample code, tells the browser to start looking for the path to the specified file at the root of the site. In the case of the `footer.html` SSI example, all the links in the SSI file to the main navigation pages would need to use site-root relative paths for the server to parse the included data properly on all the pages of the site.

A good analogy to remember the difference between document relative and site-root relative paths is to think about giving directions. Document relative directions would tell you how to get to New York City from your current location, wherever in the world you might be. Site-root relative linking, by contrast, gives you directions to New York City, or any other destination for that matter, always starting from the same place in Los Angeles.

To illustrate, adjust the paths in the `footer.html` page from the last exercise:

1. **Open the SSI file that you just created (`footer.html`) in your favorite HTML editor.**

   The footer has simple text and hyperlinks to other pages. As you can see in the code, each hyperlink lists just the filename and file extension, such as `index.html`.

2. **Add a backslash before each linked filename, such as `<a href="/index.html">`, and then save and close the file.**

   Adding the backslash makes the path to each of the hyperlinks site-root relative so the server and browser can properly parse the SSI file data.

   This file doesn't contain any graphics, and because you'd also need to modify the paths to graphics where they are part of the SSI code, in the next steps you'll add a graphic to the footer and then modify the path to be site-root relative.

3. **In the code of the `footer.html` file, insert a copy of the `car1.gif` graphic (that you downloaded in the ZIP or SIT file for the last exercise) between the second `<p>` tag and the first hyperlink:**

   ```
   <p><img src="../images/car1.gif" alt="car" width="158"
   height="66" align="right"><a
   href="/index.html">Home</a>
   ```

   When an image is located in an images folder, the link to it would normally use a document relative path for the source of the image. However, because this image is now inside an external SSI file, the path must be converted to one that is site-root relative.

4. **Change the path to the image from document to site-root relative by placing a single backslash before the image folder name:**

   ```
   <p><img src="/images/car1.gif" alt="car" width="158"
   height="66" align="right"><a
   href="/index.html">Home</a>
   ```

Watch Your Step

If you forget this step, you'll quickly discover the omission when testing the page prior to publishing. The same goes for regular hyperlinks: Although the links themselves might look normal in the browser, when clicked, their paths won't bring a visitor to the correct page until you convert the paths into site-root relative paths.

As a final reminder, here are all the questions you'll need to remember to ask yourself when working with SSIs:

- Can my server handle SSIs?
- Does the SSI link specify the proper type, file or virtual, for my server?
- Is the SSI include code properly syntaxed?
- Do I need to change file extensions on pages containing SSI links from `.html` to `.shtml`?
- Are all the paths to documents and images in the external SSI file site-root relative?

Comparing Templates and SSIs

Both Dreamweaver templates and Server-Side Includes are great solutions to building sites that need regular updating, but both have different benefits and drawbacks. Templates are good for smaller sites managed by a single person, whereas SSIs are good for large sites that plan on making regular updates to certain pages.

Choosing a site construction method is simple based on the answers to a few questions about the site's size, functionality, server type, and future management plans. If you're unsure whether to use templates or SSIs on your site, use the suggestions in Table 15-1 to help you decide.

Table 15-1   Site Construction: Templates versus SSIs

Use Templates if . . .	Use SSIs if . . .
The site is small (under 30 pages).	The site is large (over 30 pages).
The site will be managed by only one person.	The site will be managed by two or more people.
Updates to the site will be performed infrequently.	The site will require regular or frequent updates.
The site administrator understands that anytime changes to the template are made, all the updated template-based pages must be uploaded to the site's server before visitors can see the changes.	The site administrator understands that only updated SSI files need to be uploaded to the site's server before visitors can see the changes.
	The host server supports SSIs.
	The site is database driven (ASP, JSP, PHP, CFML).

document relative path: A path that provides directions to a server for accessing linked pages and other site content relative to the current page.

editable region: A specified part of a locked template file that can be edited in any template-based file.

hard code: Code that must be written directly into a file, as opposed to code that is contained in an external file. Dreamweaver templates rely on hard-coding when making global updates to template-based files. SSIs, by contrast, use only a link to an external file with the included content. When the content inside an SSI file is modified, the link to the external file remains the same.

locked area: Any part of a template-based file that isn't part of an editable region.

managed site: In Dreamweaver, a managed site means that you've created a project account of sorts for a particular site that you'll develop. Managing a site requires, at minimum, the input of a project name and the specification of a local root folder on your computer. When Dreamweaver knows where the files for your project will be housed, it can successfully save new files to the same directory and perform site management functions within that location.

master page: Any page, whether a special template, stationery, or regular Web page, that is used as the starting point for creating other pages on a site.

optional editable region: A region on a template-based file that can be made visible or hidden, depending on the page's needs.

parse: To extract information from one file and apply it to another file. When referring to SSIs, this process involves the browser requesting information from the server and then embedding the returned data into the page displaying in the browser at the specified location in the code.

site-root relative path: A path that provides directions to a server for accessing linked pages and other site content relative to the root directory of the site. In other words, all paths must originate from the same location on the host server as the home page.

SSI link: The link code that identifies the external file containing HTML code that should appear on that page in place of the link when viewed in a browser.

template-based page: Any Web page that has been generated from a master template file. These pages will have locked and editable regions based on the specifications within the template.

Last
Stop

Practice Exam

1. True or False: You can have a maximum of five editable regions on a Dreamweaver template.

2. What does (. . /) represent when placed at the start of a path to a file or graphic?

_____

_____

3. Name one way that you could modify part of a template on just 2 out of 20 template-based pages.

_____

_____

4. If two files contain the same amount of text and graphics, which type will typically load faster in a browser, a template-based file or file containing SSIs? Why?

_____

_____

5. Describe the steps involved in making a change to a locked area of a template that will alter all the template-based pages.

_____

_____

_____

_____

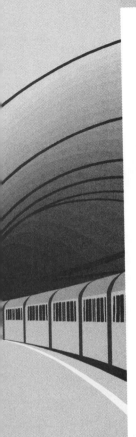

6. When converting a normal file into a template, what happens if you accidentally click No when prompted to update links?

_____

_____

_____

_____

7. List at least three considerations you should take into account when using SSIs.

_____

_____

_____

_____

8. Explain the difference between document relative and site-root relative paths.

_____

_____

_____

_____

9. Write two lines of code: one that sources an image using document relative paths and another that uses site-root relative paths.

Creating Forms

STATIONS ALONG THE WAY

- O Determining what information to request from visitors
- O Encrypting data collected from a form
- O Building a Web page form with a validation script
- O Testing a validated script

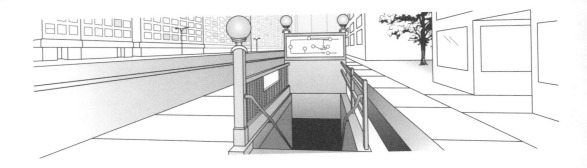

 **Enter the Station**

Questions

1. What kinds of information should you collect from visitors on a form?

2. How many different form-processing methods are there, and which are the best to use?

3. What kinds of tags can you use to build a Web form?

4. In what ways is validating forms useful?

5. How do you test forms prior to publishing?

6. What measures should you take to make forms secure?

Express Line

Although as a designer, you need to understand what forms are and how they work, not every Web site includes a form. If your current project doesn't require forms, you might want to skip this chapter and move to adding interactivity, the focus of Chapter 17, or cleaning up your code and beginning to test, which you learn in Chapters 18 and 19.

If you've spent any time on the Internet at all, you've encountered at least one or two online forms. Forms are Web-enabled tools that allow sites to collect information from visitors for a variety of reasons, including to sign up for services, request information, join a mailing list, purchase products, register for events, pay bills, handle online banking, and much more.

Building a form page in HTML is rather simple because you can use only a handful of tags for creating the form fields. After you determine what information to collect from visitors, you can organize the form contents into a neat table format with form labels on one side and form fields for user input on the other.

Where forms get tricky, however, is in the processing of the collected data because forms, by default, are unsecure files. This means that any data collected could be easily pilfered — unless you take security measures. You might think that security shouldn't matter much unless you're collecting personal information like an address or credit card number, but e-mail addresses need protecting, too.

In this chapter, you'll learn how to construct a Web form, add a JavaScript validation script to it to assist visitors in completing the form accurately, and submit a valid completed form to a remote location for processing. In addition, you'll briefly learn about form encryption and other security measures you can take to help keep collected information safe.

Transfer

Because creating the form is rather simple, if after reading that section and doing the accompanying exercise you think you'll be more likely to hire a programmer or other specialist to configure, validate, and test your form than do it yourself, move ahead in the book to Chapter 17, where you'll learn about ways to make Web sites interactive.

Organizing Visitor Information

The kind of information you collect from visitors on a Web form depends on what you'll use the information for. Forms can ask for anything you need, including

- **General personal information** like name, address, phone number, and e-mail address

- **Purchasing information** like credit card, billing address, and shipping address

- **Account information** like username, password, and password hint question

- **Miscellaneous information** like what the visitor is interested in finding out, feedback and opinions, or even something silly, like a favorite pop song

You gather the information by including check boxes, radio buttons, and comments or questions fields on your form. Figure 16-1 shows an example of some typical form fields.

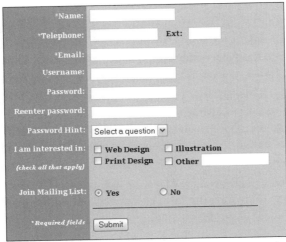

Figure 16-1: Forms collect all kinds of data including personal, purchasing, and account information.

In this age of information, collecting data from site visitors has legal and ethical aspects. For instance, a site may not legally collect information from minors. Further, each site has a moral and sometimes a legal obligation to inform visitors how collected data may be used. Many sites include a link to a privacy statement or similar policy that outlines what data the site owner is collecting and how the owner may use that data or disclose it to other parties, affiliates, and subsidiaries.

Ideally, when collecting information from visitors, you'll make the forms as user friendly as possible. Forms should be easy to navigate with a mouse or with the Tab key, be easy to read, not be too long, and be easy to understand what information you're asking for and how that information should be formatted in the input fields, such as omitting dashes and spaces (2125551212) from a phone number or making sure to include them (212-555-1212). Hints as to how to fill in fields or indications as to which fields are required are great additions to enhance form usability.

Watch Your Step

Try not to be too intrusive in your request for visitor information; collect only what you (or your client) really need. For instance, if the site plans to send regular scheduled e-newsletters to registered visitors, is it really necessary to collect the visitor's complete name, mailing address, phone number, fax number, and cell phone number along with the e-mail address? Maybe, but maybe not. Collect only the information that has relevant usage for the site, because requesting too much information might deter people from submitting any personal information at all. Some clients get around the issue of wanting and needing information by including all the desired fields in the form but making only certain form fields required, rather than all the fields, for the form to be successfully submitted.

To organize the fields of information you intend to collect, use tables and other simple formatting code (like paragraph and line breaks) plus CSS styling to make the form match the look of the rest of the site. For unusual layouts, because you can't nest forms, use nested tables. As long as all the form fields reside inside a single set of `<form>` tags, whether or not those fields sit inside tables or nested table cells won't affect form functionality.

Information Kiosk

One technique I like to use when building forms is to set up all the form labels first. Most forms can fit nicely inside a multirow, two-column table. Add the form labels, like Name, Address, and Telephone number, to individual table cells along the left side of a two-column table and then go back along the right side of the table to add the form fields next to each label. When those steps are complete, you can add any field input hints (enter 6- to 8-digit passcode) and required field indicators (* required). Then style the form with CSS. Your main goal is to keep the information neat and organized, so the visitor knows intuitively how to navigate through the form.

Encrypting and Processing Form Data

Because forms are unsecure documents, you must take measures to protect the information you're collecting, especially when that information is private and confidential such as a password, credit card number, or other personal information that a visitor might feel uneasy about sharing with the site. Your visitors need to feel confident that an unscrupulous outsider can't hack the information they're sharing with the site, resulting in any kind of identity theft. That security is the full responsibility of the Web owner.

The ultimate type of site security is the SSL (Secure Sockets Layer) digital security certificate. The SSL helps provide secure connections between the visitor and host computers by encrypting all the collected and transmitted data. Internet Explorer indicates to the visitor that a site uses SSL with a small lock icon that appears in the bottom-right corner of the browser. Likewise, when viewing secure pages in Firefox, you'll see a lock icon in the address bar, and the entire address bar field will change color. Other browsers provide additional proof to indicate SSL certificates are present on a site, such as generating a special pop-up window that notifies the visitor when they've entered and exited a secure area on the site. All these visual indicators provide the visitor with a sense of security about submitting personal information to a site.

You can purchase SSL certificates from several agencies, but check with your site host provider first to see whether it supports the SSL company you'd like to use. The most popular (and most expensive) SSL providers are VeriSign (www.verisign.com), Thawte (www.thawte.com), and GeoTrust (www.geotrust.com), but a few others exist, too. SSL certificates range in price from affordable to hefty. Expect to pay an annual rate between $250 and $1,800 for the certificate. Your host provider can often handle the procurement of the certificate for you, either with or without an added installation fee.

Watch Your Step

If you aren't purchasing an SSL certificate, take measures to make collected form data as secure as possible. Some solutions include using log-in JavaScript and browser cookies as well as more advanced prepackaged and customized programming techniques that fall beyond the scope of this book. At a minimum, use simple data encryption at the host end.

Data encryption is a process by which information submitted to a server from a completed Web form is encrypted during the data transfer by using an application or server-side script written in PHP, CGI, ASP, JSP, ColdFusion, or Perl. In addition to transmitting the data securely, most scripts also include instructions for returning information to the visitor, like forwarding the visitor to a Thank You page, replacing the form with a Thank You message within the same page, and/or sending notification of the completed submission to a specified e-mail recipient, like the Webmaster.

Step into the Real World

Forwarding Visitors to a Thank You Page   When I submit a form online, I like to see some kind of acknowledgment of my submission, such as a sentence appearing automatically on the page that says something like "We received your submission" or having the browser automatically transfer me to a special Thank You page that tells me more about how my submission will be processed. (Thank you for your order. We will e-mail you when the order is ready for shipment. . . .)

In most cases, creating and configuring a forwarding Thank You page is as easy as creating the Web page, adding a hidden field or two to the form, and inserting the URL of the forwarding page in a specific location inside the script that encrypts and processes the collected form data.

A good Thank You page will look structurally like the rest of the pages on the site, including navigation buttons and branding, and will contain text that acknowledges the visitor's submission. How that particular text will be worded is up to the site owner. The rest of the page can include other information that might be helpful to the visitor, such as shipping policy information for a retail purchase, store hours, sale information, additional products the consumer might be interested in purchasing, or other special news that the visitor might not otherwise be aware of.

Because every script or program is different, I can't instruct you on exactly how to configure your particular Thank You page, but I can tell you generally what to do and where to do it:

1. First off, you'll create the Thank You page based on another existing page on the site. Name it something like `thankyou.html` so it will be easy to remember.

2. When that's completed, you'll probably need to add a redirecting hidden form field at the top of the form, directly following the opening `<form>` tag.

   The particular script you're using might instruct you to add recipient and subject hidden fields to the form, too:

   ```
   <form action="cgi-bin/email.pl" method="post" name="MyForm" id="MyForm">
   <input type="hidden" name="redirect"
      value="http://www.example.com/thankyou.html">
   <input type="hidden" name="recipient" value="info@example.com">
   <input type="hidden" name="subject" value="Company Info Request">
   ```

3. Specify the SMTP server, domain name, recipient e-mail address, and forwarding URL inside the data processing script file.

   Good scripts will include comment tags that clearly indicate what needs to be changed in the script and exactly where to make those changes.

   The *SMTP server* is your domain or the domain of the host provider, such as `$smtp_server = "smtp.hostdomainname.com";`.

   The *recipient address* should be the address at the Web site that will receive notification of a form submission, such as `@recipient_addresses = ('info@mydomain.com');`.

   The *recipient domain name* is the address of the Web site that will be submitting the form data, such as `@recipient_domains = ('mydomain.com');`.

4. After you've customized the script file, upload the script to the domain host's cgi-bin folder (which the host provider should have already installed on the domain, inside which the form script should be placed), and upload the form and Thank You pages to the root level of the live server for testing.

   Remember, you can modify the form filename, SMTP server, and recipient e-mail address for testing purposes and then change that information to the correct names when the form is ready for publishing. For example, you could use your own e-mail address while configuring and testing the form and then change the e-mail address to the client's right before the site gets published.

Most host providers have some kind of uncomplicated form-processing software to handle simple form data transmission and encryption with a Perl or CGI script. Typically, the script comes preinstalled with the hosting plan, or the host provider can install it for the domain upon request. Two of the most popular scripts are the `formmail.pl` script created by Matt Wright at `www.scriptarchive.com/formmail.html` and the enhanced `formmail.pl` script by Brian Evans at `www.geocel.com/webMail`. To work properly, most scripts must be installed in the cgi-bin folder on the server hosting the site, and you must do a tiny bit of code customization so that the script will forward the visitor to a particular page (`thankyou.html`) in the browser, and securely transmit the collected data to a specified e-mail address.

Scripts like these are extremely straightforward to use if you're willing to put in a little time to read any accompanying README file that comes with them and do the testing necessary to ensure the form is processed as desired prior to publishing.

Building Web Forms

Forms use only a small handful of tags, yet because each is tag is fully customizable, you can create an infinite number of form layouts with them. The main tags and elements used to build forms are `<form>`, `<input>`, `<select>`, `<textarea>`, `<label>`, `<fieldset>`, and `<legend>`. With the addition of specific tag attributes, you can customize each of these tags to create all the different types of form fields, such as hidden fields, text fields, text areas, check boxes, radio buttons, lists, menus, and buttons.

Information Kiosk

The last three form elements, `<label>`, `<fieldset>`, and `<legend>`, along with access key (which assigns keyboard shortcuts to particular form fields) and tab index number (which advances a visitor through form fields using the tab key) attributes, are accessibility-enhancement tags that you can use in conjunction with other form tags to facilitate assistive devices like screen readers with accessing the information on the form:

```
<input type="checkbox" name="checkbox" value=
"checkbox" accesskey="c" tabindex="3" id="checkbox">

<label for="checkbox">Chocolate</label>

<fieldset><legend>legend</legend></fieldset>
```

Use `<label>` to help screen readers find control fields like radio buttons and check boxes, add `<fieldset>` to group sets of related controls, and add `<legend>` to include a caption with any `<fieldset>`.

Structurally, you can add the form fields to the form in any configuration you need, as long as the entire form is encased in `<form>` tags. The opening `<form>` tag is where you'll provide processing instructions and other information to the server.

Start a good new habit by beginning the creation of all new forms with the insertion of the `<form>` tag:

```
<form>
</form>
```

Between the `<form>` tags, you can add a table with any number of rows and columns to house the labels and form fields for the information being collected.

The following exercise walks you through the steps of creating a simple Web form with Dreamweaver that's configured to process collected data with a dummy Perl script installed on a mock server:

1. In Dreamweaver, choose File → New to open a new blank HTML document and save it with the filename `formdemo.html`.

To help keep track of the file, save the file into a new folder on your desktop called Forms. Then manage a site to that folder before proceeding to Step 2.

To create a managed site, select Site → New Site. When the Site Definition dialog box opens, click the Advanced tab. In the Local Info category, enter a name for the site in the Site Name field, and in the Local root folder field, browse to and select the Forms folder you just created on your desktop.

2. With your insertion point positioned at the top of the page, choose Insert → Form → Form to insert a set of `<form>` tags on the page.

In Design view, the `<form>` tags create a bounding area with a 1-pixel, dashed, red, rectangular border. The line is meant to help you visually demark the bounds of the form data within the Dreamweaver workspace and won't be visible in a browser window. If the line doesn't appear in Design view, you can enable it by choosing View → Visual Aids → Invisible Elements.

In Code view, the inserted code contains the `<form>` tags and several tag attributes, including the `id` and `name`, which should be identical and will be used to assign JavaScript and apply CSS styles to the form. The code also includes the `method`, which tells the server whether this form will collect or transmit data, and the `action`, which instructs the browser where to send the transmitted information.

```
<form id="form1" name="form1" method="post"
action=""></form>
```

By default, all newly inserted forms use the `post` method of data transmission, but you may change that to `default` or `get` if desired. For this exercise, leave the method set to `post`, but read the following descriptions of both methods so you'll know for future use what each one does:

- `get`: This method appends the URL of the form page with the value of the collected information when the data is sent. When the form is gathering simple data, this is usually okay, but this method has some drawbacks. The main drawback is that the `get` method makes the URL bookmarkable so that the page data is vulnerable to spybots and hackers. Also, the URL can contain only a maximum of 8,192 characters, which limits the length of form data you can process with this method.

- `post`: This method hides collected data during the HTTP request but doesn't encrypt it. Therefore, whenever possible, try to use a secure server connection (using SSL) when transmitting private information, or at the very least, use a script or program to encrypt the data from transmission to receipt.

- default: This setting relies on the browser's default settings to choose the transmission method. But because the default form data transmission method can differ from one browser to another, it's much better to choose either post or get instead.

3. Replace the default identical form name and id (form1) attributes with the unique form name and id of "inforequest".

```
<form id="inforequest" name="inforequest" method="post"
action=""></form>
```

Naming forms both identifies the particular form so that the script can be easily attached to it, and helps you more readily identify a form when a site includes more than one.

4. In the Action field on the Properties Inspector, type the filename and location (relative to the root level of the host server) of the script that will process the collected form data.

CGI and Perl scripts must be placed inside the host server's cgi-bin folder, so in the Action field, type a path to a script inside that folder, such as **cgi-bin/email.pl**. Your code should now look like this:

```
<form id="form1" name="form1" method="post"
action="cgi-bin/email.pl"></form>
```

If you'll be using another type of form processing (such as sending the collected data to an application on the same or on another server), check with your system administrator and/or host provider about how to properly configure the <form> tag's action attribute.

5. In Design view, place the insertion point between the opening and closing <form> tags, choose Insert → Form → Hidden Field to add a hidden field to the form, and on the Properties Inspector, change the Name from "hiddenField" to "subject" and the Value to "Company Info Request".

```
<input type="hidden" name="subject" value="Company Info
Request">
```

6. With the insertion point between the opening and closing <form> tags, select Insert → Table to insert a seven-row, two-column table with cellpadding=0, cellspacing=5, and border=0.

The table will provide the structure to organize the form fields and labels.

7. Along the left side of the table, enter the following text in each of the cells starting from the top: *Name, *Telephone, *Email, I am a, I am interested in (check all that apply), Join Mailing List, and *Required fields.

Labeling the form before inputting the fields will assist you in selecting the right form field for the data being requested.

Next you'll add individual form fields in the cells next to the labels along the right column of the table.

8. **Place your insertion point in the top-right table cell and choose Insert →**
Form → Text Field.

If Dreamweaver's Input Tag Accessibility Attributes dialog box appears, you may input a label, an access key, and a tab index number if desired.

9. **With the newly inserted text field selected, use the Properties Inspector to**
change the `name` attribute of the text field to `"Name"`.

When you modify the default text field name to anything else, Dreamweaver automatically inserts both the `name` and `id` attributes with the new name provided. Both fields are inserted so that CSS and JavaScript can be easily applied to the field. It also readily identifies the collected data.

10. **In the next two table cells down, insert two additional form text fields and**
use the Properties Inspector to name the new text fields after the label in
the table next to them.

Name the text field next to Telephone `"Telephone"` and the field next to Email `"Email"`.

To set the width of the form field, select the form field and add a number in pixels, such as 15, to the Char width field on the Properties Inspector. If desired, you may also enter a number in the Max Chars field on the Properties Inspector to set the maximum number of characters allowable for the specified form field.

11. **With your insertion point in the empty cell to the right of "I am a," choose**
Insert → Form → List/Menu.

An empty List/Menu field is inserted in this cell. This type of form field can appear either as a list or a menu. Leave it as a menu, and you'll enter a series of options, from which the visitor will select one.

12. **With the new List/Menu selected, click the List Values button on the**
Properties Inspector to open the List Values dialog box. Select a value and
click the plus (+) button to add each of the items and values to the menu, as
shown in Figure 16-2. Click OK when you're done.

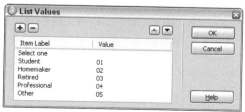

Figure 16-2: Use the List Values dialog box to quickly enter in the items that will appear in the List/Menu form field.

The first item in the list is instructional, "Select one," so you may enter a value of your choosing or leave the value blank (value=" "). The rest of the list items correspond to options the visitor can select.

Next you'll add check boxes to the form, which allow visitors to select as many options within a particular category as desired. To help keep the information neat and organized, you'll insert a nested table.

13. **With your insertion point in the cell to the right of the cell containing "I am interested in," insert a nested table with two rows and two columns and enter the following text labels in each cell of the nested table:** Web Design, Print Design, Illustration, **and** Other.

14. **Place your insertion point to the left of the label called Web Design and choose Insert → Form → Checkbox. After inserting the field, use the Properties Inspector to change the Checkbox name to "Interests" and the Checked value to "Web".**

```
<input type="checkbox" name="Interests" id="Interests"
value="Web">
```

Dreamweaver adds the id attribute to match the name attribute when you change the name.

15. **Repeat Step 14 to insert check boxes next to each of the remaining cells in the nested table. Change the Checkbox name to "Interests" for all of them, but set the Value to "Print", "Illustration"," and "Other", respectively.**

 Information Kiosk

By giving the check boxes the same name, the browser will understand that all the check boxes belong to the same group.

If you'd like visitors to be able to describe what other things they might be interested in, add a text field next to the word "Other" with the name attribute of "Interests".

16. **Place your insertion point in the cell to the right of "Join Mailing List" and choose Insert → Form → Radio Button. When the Input Tag Accessibility Attribute dialog box appears, enter Yes in the Label field, select the Wrap with Label Tag option as the Style, and set After Form Item as the Position. If desired, also enter an access key and tab index number. Click OK. Repeat the process to insert another radio button but enter No in the Label field.**

Your code should look like this:

```
<label>
<input name="radiobutton" type="radio" value=
"radiobutton">
Yes</label>

<label>
<input name="radiobutton" type="radio" value=
"radiobutton">
No</label>
```

You need both radio buttons to be in the same group so that a visitor can make only an either/or selection, and you can do this by using the `value` attribute.

17. Use the Properties Inspector to edit the `value` attribute in both radio buttons from `"radiobutton"` to `"mailinglist"`.

If desired, you may also set the Initial state of the Yes button to Checked. On form fields that have a default selection enabled, that selection will remain in effect unless the visitor notices and changes it.

18. In the last cell on the right of the table, insert a Submit button by choosing Insert → Form → Button.

Submit buttons are the default button type for forms. To change the label displaying on the button, you may modify the Value field from Submit to anything else, such as Send.

Step Into the Real World

Working with Hidden Fields *Hidden fields* are special form fields that allow you to store and send information on the form along with the information the visitor inputs and submits. Hidden fields are invisible in a browser and are often needed to assist scripts with processing the form data. The only down side to hidden fields is that anyone (including spambots) can view hidden fields by looking at the source HTML, so be careful about using hidden fields for private information like e-mail addresses and passwords. Here are some additional examples of how you can use hidden fields:

As a redirect to another page after form submission:

```
<input type="hidden" name="redirect" value="http://www.mysite.com/
  thankyou.html">
```

As an identifier of the e-mail address to receive notice of a form submission:

```
<input type="hidden" name="recipient" value="info@mysite.com">
```

As an e-mail subject line prescript for the recipient hidden form field:

```
<input type="hidden" name="subject" value="Company Info Request">
```

As a title for the collected data to be sent along with the data:

```
<input type="hidden" name="title" value="Website Info Request">
```

That's it! Your sample form is complete. Figure 16-3 shows the finished form in Dreamweaver's Design view. Save the file and preview it in a browser to see the full effect. When you're sure the form is laid out to your liking, you can style the form with CSS, add a validation script, test it, and publish it.

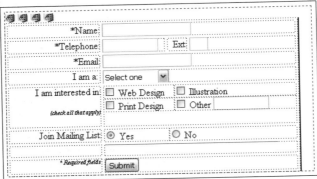

Figure 16-3: Dreamweaver's Design view shows roughly how the finished form will appear in a browser window, but to see the form in action, you must upload it to a server.

Transfer

The upcoming sections in this chapter explain validation and testing. Refer to Chapter 12 and Appendix A for a refresher on CSS.

Validating Forms

Validating a form means that special code or script, which verifies whether the visitor has correctly completed all required fields on the form before the data gets transmitted over the Web, has been added to an existing Web form. When a visitor submits incorrect or incomplete information in a form that contains a validation script, an error message appears either somewhere on the page or in a special pop-up message window above the open browser, identifying the problem or omission. This error message helps the visitor correct the form input and resubmit the form.

Validation on dynamic Web sites (sites that use programming to display content from a database) is typically done with a programming language such as ASP, JSP, PHP, or ColdFusion. For small, nondynamic sites, however, more often than not, validation is performed with JavaScript.

Dreamweaver users can automate the task of adding a JavaScript validation script to any form by using the special Validate Form behavior. You can customize this script to look at all the fields in a form and make sure the user filled in all the fields correctly. The validation script comprises a series of validation events that you can add to any or all of the fields on a Web form. This means you can choose whether the error message appears

- **As the visitor completes individual fields** (so they can correct mistakes as they go from field to field)
- **After the visitor clicks the Submit button** (so they can correct mistakes all at once)

The nice thing about both options is that the validation is done on the client-side, before the form is submitted to the server, to ensure that the server won't collect any data until the form passes validation.

Information Kiosk

You can hand-code validation scripts into any form, but that can be a lengthy process that requires some knowledge of JavaScript, especially if you intend to configure a validation rule for each field in the form. The easier and faster method of validation is the aforementioned Dreamweaver validation behavior, which doesn't presuppose any knowledge of JavaScript.

The following exercise describes how Dreamweaver users can add the Validate Form behavior to an existing form on a Web page. You may use the form you created in the preceding exercise, your own form (adapting it to the numbered instructions that follow), or a sample form page (available from this book's companion Web site or from `www.luckychair.com/1-line`).

1. Open the `formdemo.html` page (or your own form page) in the Dreamweaver workspace.

The form contains several fields, including a place for the visitor's name, phone, and e-mail address.

2. To validate individual form fields, select the first form that needs validation. Otherwise, to validate the entire form, select the opening `<form>` tag.

To select the `<form>` tag, you might need to manually select it in Code view.

3. Check to see whether the Behaviors panel is open. If not, choose Window → Behaviors to open the panel in the workspace.

4. Click the plus (+) button on the Behaviors panel and select the Validate Form option from the resulting pop-up menu.

The Validate Form option should be all the way at the bottom of the pop-up menu. Upon selecting it, a Validate Form dialog box like the one shown in Figure 16-4 will appear, listing all the named form fields in the form.

5. When validating a single form field:

Pick the field by its label, such as "Name", from the Named Fields list and configure the rest of the dialog box as desired, such as making the field required or specifying that only a numeric value may be entered in the field.

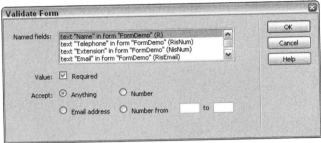

Figure 16-4: Specify which forms fields require validation with the handy Dreamweaver JavaScript Validate Form behavior.

When validating the entire form:

Specify the Value and Accept fields for each named field in the form.

The following is a description of the Validate Form dialog box elements:

- *Named Fields:* All the fields on the form will be listed here. Select each form by name and assign validation preferences using the rest of the dialog box options.

- *Value:* Check the Required box when the field selected in the Named Fields area must be completed by the visitor.

- *Accept Anything:* When this option is selected, the field in the Named Fields area will accept any type of input.

- *Accept Number:* With this option selected, the field in the Named Fields area will accept only a numeric value.

- *Accept Email Address:* Choose this option when you'd like the validation script to check for proper e-mail address syntax. It won't verify that the entered address is valid, only that it meets the *someone@somewhere. extension* format.

- *Accept Number from/to:* Select this option to allow visitors to input a range of numbers predetermined by you, such as between 0 and 5.

6. Click OK.

With both methods, Dreamweaver automatically adds the appropriate JavaScript validation code to the <head> of the page, along with additional script either inline with the form field or within the opening <form> tag at the top of the form.

The head script is the same for both methods:

```
<script type="text/JavaScript">
<!--
function MM_findObj(n, d) { //v4.01
  var p,i,x;  if(!d) d=document;
if((p=n.indexOf("?"))>0&&parent.frames.length) {
    d=parent.frames[n.substring(p+1)].document;
n=n.substring(0,p);}
  if(!(x=d[n])&&d.all) x=d.all[n]; for
(i=0;!x&&i<d.forms.length;i++) x=d.forms[i][n];
  for(i=0;!x&&d.layers&&i<d.layers.length;i++)
x=MM_findObj(n,d.layers[i].document);
  if(!x && d.getElementById) x=d.getElementById(n);
return x;
}

function MM_validateForm() { //v4.0
  var
i,p,q,nm,test,num,min,max,errors='',args=MM_validateFor
m.arguments;
  for (i=0; i<(args.length-2); i+=3) { test=args[i+2];
val=MM_findObj(args[i]);
    if (val) { nm=val.name; if ((val=val.value)!="") {
      if (test.indexOf('isEmail')!=-1) {
p=val.indexOf('@');
        if (p<1 || p==(val.length-1)) errors+='- '+nm+'
must contain an e-mail address.\n';
      } else if (test!='R') { num = parseFloat(val);
        if (isNaN(val)) errors+='- '+nm+' must contain
a number.\n';
        if (test.indexOf('inRange') != -1) {
p=test.indexOf(':');
          min=test.substring(8,p);
max=test.substring(p+1);
          if (num<min || max<num) errors+='- '+nm+'
must contain a number between '+min+' and '+max+'.\n';
    } } } else if (test.charAt(0) == 'R') errors += '-
'+nm+' is required.\n'; }
  } if (errors) alert('The following error(s)
occurred:\n'+errors);
  document.MM_returnValue = (errors == '');
}
//-->
</script>
```

When validating single fields, Dreamweaver uses the onblur or onchange
validation event inline with the code, so that visitors will see any error message
as they input data.

```
<input name="Name" type="text" id="Name" onblur=
"MM_validateForm('Name','','R');return document.
MM_returnValue">
```

By contrast, when validating the entire form, the `onsubmit` validation event handler will be used, and any error messages will appear to the visitor after he or she clicks the Submit button.

```
<form action="cgi-bin/email.pl" method="post" name=
"FormDemo" id="FormDemo" onsubmit="MM_validateForm
('Name','','R','Telephone','','RisNum','Extension','','
NisNum','Email','','RisEmail');return document.MM_
returnValue">
```

Testing Validated Forms

After configuring the form with the validation script, the next step is to test the form. The validation script in most cases shouldn't affect how the form gets processed, only how the fields are validated before being submitted to the server for actual processing. For best results, follow these steps:

1. Upload the form to a testing server.

The *testing server* can either be the server hosting the site or another server that mimics the hosting environment of the hosting server. I prefer to test directly on the hosting server to ensure the form will work without error when the site is published. The form page will need to be uploaded to the host server for testing, but unless someone knows the direct URL to that test page, no one should be able to access it during the testing.

 Information Kiosk

When testing, try to upload the file to the root level of the intended host or test server, especially when the encryption will be performed by a Perl or CGI script specified in a particular directory (`cgi-bin/filename`) on the host server; otherwise, the form might fail testing. Also, if the new form page will be replacing an existing file on the site with the same filename, change the filename on the test page until you're ready to publish it. For example, if the test page will be called `contact.html`, change the filename to `testcontact.html` until it's ready for publishing.

2. Input correct data in each field and click the Submit button to make sure the form can handle correct input.

Check to ensure that data is being sent to the proper recipient e-mail address (which can be yours, for testing purposes) or database at the Web site collecting the data. Also check to see that any return information to the visitor gets displayed or is e-mailed as specified within the script.

If you encounter any issues processing the collected data after uploading the form to a test server, the trouble will most likely be with the script or programming code being used to process the data. Reread any configuration files that came with the script and continue testing until you get the form to work. Otherwise, contact the host provider or system administrator in charge of the host site or test server for assistance. Often the reason the script isn't functioning properly is because you forgot to configure part of it or else some kind of software needs to be enabled on the host end. At worst, you might need to hire a programmer to assist you with processing the form data.

3. **Enter incorrect data at every step to ensure the form can handle mistakes. Test for every scenario you can think of and make any changes necessary before publishing the page.**

Check also to see that the validation script worked properly, and if not, make adjustments to that script in the Validation Form dialog box by double-clicking the yellow spoke icon for the Validate Form behavior in the Behaviors panel.

Watch Your Step

Whatever you do, do not publish a nonworking form. It's better to allow visitors to send a simple e-mail to a site than to display a broken form. Take the time to work out the kinks; then publish it.

access key: This tag attribute assigns a keyboard shortcut to any element on the page.

CGI: Common Gateway Interface. An interface that lets Web pages communicate securely with server-side Web applications for both data collection and data feedback.

cgi-bin folder: A folder at the root level of a host directory inside which scripts that process collected data must be placed.

check box: A Web form field presented in groups that enable visitors to select several options from a single category. For example, if the field is "I enjoy:" the options might be Hiking, Biking, Swimming, Pilates, Yoga, and Kickball.

form: A section of a Web page using special form tags that allow visitors to input and submit any data being requested by the site.

continued

 **continued**

forwarding: Automatically sending the visitor's browser to a different page (such as a Thank You page) upon submission of a form.

hidden field: A special form field that is hidden from view in a browser window and contains special information required for form processing.

Perl: Practical Extraction and Reporting Language. A programming language used for building CGI programs that perform server-side information processing such as encrypting data submitted to a server from a form. Perl scripts can also be configured to output data securely to another source such as an e-mail address or database.

radio button: An option on a Web form typically presented in pairs or in multiples that allows visitors to select only one of the options, such as Yes or No.

recipient address: The e-mail address specified in a hidden field to which the collected form data will be sent.

recipient domain name: The domain name of the host site. For example, if your site is called `www.mysite.com`, the recipient domain name would be `mysite.com`.

SMTP: Simple Mail Transfer Protocol. The protocol used on the Internet to send e-mail messages.

tab index number: An attribute of a form field or other HTML tag that, using a number between 0 and 32,767, sets the tab order of that tag relative to other form fields or objects on the page.

validation: A process to ensure that a page functions properly and conforms to a predetermined set of standards. With regard to forms, validation means ensuring a visitor properly inputs data prior to submission.

Last Stop

Practice Exam

1. True or False: Forms can be nested inside other forms to create unique form page layouts.

2. True or False: Validation scripts submit incomplete form information to the server, and the server returns the error message when the data is incorrect.

3. JavaScript validation code must be placed in the _____ of the code to work properly along with either a function in the opening _____ tag or _____ with the rest of the HTML.

4. Suppose you're going to create a form that will allow visitors to sign up for a monthly newsletter. Name three possible pieces of information that would be reasonable to request on the form.

_____

5. What is the best method for securing collected data on the Internet?

_____

6. What are the two different ways of validating a form?

_____

_____

7. How can visitors tell whether an SSL certificate is installed on a Web site?

_____

_____

8. How can a site inform a visitor that the submitted data has been transmitted successfully?

_____

_____

9. If you wanted visitors to select one answer from a list of several possible answers on a form, would it be better to use radio buttons or check boxes for each of the answer items? Why?

_____

_____

CHAPTER

17 Making the Site Interactive

STATIONS ALONG THE WAY

- Creating unusual rollover effects and building image maps
- Using JavaScript for interactive effects
- Opening a new browser window from any text or image link
- Inserting multimedia files such as Flash, QuickTime movies, sound, and other plug-ins
- Adding daily visitor magnets such as free games and daily tips

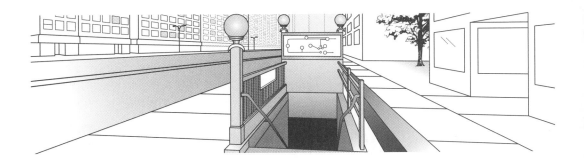

 # Enter the Station

Questions

1. What fun interactive things can you do to a Web page with JavaScript?

2. What is the difference between a rollover button and a rollover effect?

3. How do you transform a regular image into an image map with hotlinks?

4. How do you use JavaScript to launch a new browser window?

5. What's the trick to inserting media such as Flash movies into a Web page?

6. What are three different ways to get site visitors involved with the content on your pages?

Express Line

Site interactivity, as cool as it is, isn't absolutely necessary for every site. If you know your site will not be using any of the techniques described in this chapter's introduction, move to Chapter 18, where you'll find information on code cleanup, browser testing, and fixing common code problems.

The Internet becomes a more interesting and appealing place to explore when a user can interact with Web pages in some way. There are several ways to make sites interactive, from the very simple (such as rollover buttons) to the very complex (such as Flash components, QuickTime videos, and interactive games). You can whip up the simplest actions in JavaScript; for more complex interactivity, you'll have to obtain multimedia components or plug-ins, some of which are free, and properly insert them onto your page.

If you've already got the skills to create special multimedia files and write customized JavaScript, kudos to you! If you're just getting started, however, you'll need a good working knowledge of a few key areas that are beyond the scope of this book. Here are some places to get basics and pointers:

- **Building Flash components:** For a quick, practical introduction, check out *Flash 8 Accelerated: A Full-Color Guide,* by Youngjin.com (Wiley).

- **Creating video for the Web:** For a quick overview and how-to, try *50 Fast Digital Video Techniques,* by Bonnie Blake and Doug Sahlin (Wiley).

- **Creating MP3 sound files:** You can approach this topic from various angles, but if you're among the legion of aspiring podcasters, take a look at *Podcasting: Do-It-Yourself Guide,* by Todd Cochrane, an e-book from Wiley.

- **Creating JavaScripts:** *JavaScript in 10 Simple Steps or Less,* by Arman Danesh (Wiley) will get you off to a fast start.

To find those free multimedia files, you can do an online search for (you guessed it) *"free multimedia files"* — but as with anything that's free, it's always a good idea to read the fine print to ensure that you're not infringing on any copyrights by adding those files or their contents to your site. Better routes to getting multimedia files include learning how to build them yourself, hiring a third party to develop the needed components, or getting them from a reliable source. In that latter department, you're in luck: FlashKit.com and FlashFoundry.com (which requires a subscription costing anywhere from $9.95 to $99.95) are great resources for finding Flash movies, animations, sounds, and other Flash elements. That said, you must remember that whomever creates the multimedia files for you will be the rightful owner of those files unless or until those rights are expressly granted to you by contract, purchase, or licensing agreement. CorbisMotion.com offers beautiful, *rights-managed* (selectively licensed for a fee) QuickTime movie clips.

After you get hold of the multimedia files, all you need to know is how to insert them into your Web pages — and that's mostly a matter of getting the right tools. If you use a good HTML code editor such as Dreamweaver, you can insert multimedia files by selecting them via the Insert menu and configuring how they'll look in a browser. If you're working on JavaScript interactivity, Dreamweaver can help you insert several fairly common built-in scripts through the Behaviors panel. Beyond that, it will be up to you to install the scripts, customize them when necessary, and test them for accuracy before publishing.

This chapter introduces some ways of using JavaScript to make Web sites more interactive — such as creating multi-image rollover effects, building complex image maps, and opening new browser windows. You'll also see how easy it is to insert multimedia files on a page and add the free Google search bar to any site, which lets visitors search either just the site they're on or everywhere on the Web. Other interactive tutorials in this chapter include adding a daily tip and a free JavaScript Sudoku game to entice visitors to return to the site daily.

Exploring the World of JavaScript

JavaScript is one of the fastest and easiest scripting techniques, and it can turn static, ordinary Web pages into interactive, interesting — sometimes extraordinary — Web pages.

 Transfer

Realistically, however, about 10 percent of all Internet traffic comes from visitors who use assistive devices that can't understand JavaScript — and/or browsers with JavaScript disabled. Those visitors can't experience these neat effects or, as is sometimes the case, access the information that the JavaScript reveals. For those visitors, you should always try to provide alternate access to the same content; refer to Chapter 9 for tips on accessibility.

The most common uses for JavaScript scripts include making rollover buttons, opening new browser windows, turning status bars into message tickers, displaying the current date and time, creating simple interactive games, and turning static images into slide shows. Other scripts can be used to generate cookies and navigation bars, create special-effects images and sounds, add computer utilities and perform math functions, and even play interesting background and cursor DHTML animations.

Dreamweaver users have automatic access to about 22 of the more common JavaScript effects via the Behaviors panel; these include the Swap Image and Validate Form effects you've encountered in previous chapter exercises. In addition to these, scads of Web sites on the Internet offer free JavaScript — of which the top resources are listed in Table 17-1 — in exchange for leaving their contact information as comment tags (<!) inside the script when you use them. An example is this one from 24fun.com; it creates a snowlike animation effect on the background of the page:

```
<script>
// CREDITS:
// Snowmaker
// By Peter Gehrig
```

```
// Copyright (c) 2003 Peter Gehrig. All rights reserved.
// Permission given to use the script provided that this
notice remains as is.
// Additional scripts can be found at http://www.24fun.com
// info@24fun.com
// 11/27/2003
```

Information Kiosk

JavaScript, like many Internet technologies, can be used for good purposes as well as really annoying (unsolicited pop-up browser windows) and sometimes computer-damaging (installing ad-ware on a visitor's computer) purposes. The bad reasons prompted software developers to create pop-up blockers for your computer (which unfortunately can prevent your honest JavaScript windows from being displayed) and some people to disable JavaScript altogether in their browsers. To make sure you're getting your scripts from reputable sources and not from any sites with depraved hidden agendas, stick with the sites in Table 17-1.

Table 17-1   Free JavaScript Resources

JavaScript Resource	JavaScript Resource Web Address
24Fun	www.24fun.com
DynamicDrive	www.dynamicdrive.com
EarthWeb JavaScripts	http://webdeveloper.earthweb.com/webjs
Internet.com's JavaScript	www.javascript.com
IRT.org	www.irt.org/articles/script.htm
JavaScript Kit	www.javascriptkit.com/cutpastejava.shtml
JavaScript-FX	www.javascript-fx.com/index.php
JS Examples	www.js-examples.com/page/javascripts.html
The JavaScript Source	http://javascript.internet.com

Learning JavaScript is relatively easy when you understand its syntax and structure. You can find several online tutorials by searching for "JavaScript tutorial" in your favorite search engine, as well as working through the tutorials offered by the resources listed in Table 17-1.

To show you how easy it is to use JavaScript on your Web pages, the next part of this chapter will introduce you to creating multiple rollover effects, opening new browser windows, and setting up complex image maps.

Creating multiple rollover effects

When you learned about creating navigation systems in Chapter 13, you completed a short, six-step exercise on adding a simple rollover button to a page in Dreamweaver. That type of rollover took two same-size graphics in different link states (a normal state and a rollover state) and used JavaScript to swap the images in a browser window. When a visitor moves his or her cursor over the original graphic, the rollover state graphic appears in its place; when the visitor moves the cursor away, the original graphic returns to view. The rollover button is simple to implement — and it's an effective way to add a dynamic feel to a site.

But what if you want to make multiple parts of a Web page change in response to *one* visitor action — say, jazzing up a button graphic with a rollover effect while at the same time changing a color on the layout, displaying a small animation, and showing a special advertisement slogan? (That ought to get their attention.) Could you do it? How?

The answer is yes — and you do it with JavaScript. With a little bit more code than the simple rollover button — and a few more graphics for the new rollover states of all the graphics that will be swapped — you can get a single mouseover movement to control a slew of image changes! What's more, if any of those images are animated GIFs, the animation can be played for either or both the normal and rollover graphic states.

The next exercise will teach you how to create a multiple graphic rollover effect using Dreamweaver. You may use your own graphics for this demo or download the Chapter 17 sample files from this book's companion Web site or `www.luckychair.com/l-line`. (Non-Dreamweaver users can examine the JavaScript and HTML code in the completed sample file that comes with the sample file download.) Here's the Dreamweaver sequence:

1. **Download the `Multiroll demo` file from the *Web Design: The L-Line* Web site and save them into a folder on your desktop called Multiroll Demo.**

   The Multiroll Demo folder should contain the demo file, a completed demo file, and an images folder containing four graphics.

2. **Create a managed site in the new Multiroll Demo folder.**

   To create a managed site, choose Site ➔ New Site and click the Advanced tab of the Site Definition dialog box that appears. In the Local Info category, enter a name for the site (such as Multiroll Demo) in Site Name field, and in the Local Root Folder field, browse to and select the new Multiroll Demo folder. The name of the site is for your use only and won't appear anywhere on the published site; therefore, name the site after the client. The local root folder tells

Dreamweaver where to find the files for this site to perform special functions like sitewide modifications.

Managing a site allows you to leave (and return to) a project more easily, and it gives you access to Dreamweaver's advanced site-management capabilities. Failing to manage a site can cause broken links and inaccurate paths to graphics.

3. Open the `multirolldemo.html` file in the Dreamweaver workspace and select the graphic that says `"Services"`.

The file consists of a table with five graphics, each of which is sitting inside its own table cell. In the images folder there are additional graphics that will be used to create the multi-image rollover effect.

4. On the Dreamweaver Behaviors panel, click the Actions (+) button and choose Swap Image.

The Swap Image dialog box opens, listing (by `name` or `id` attribute) all images in the open file. Unfortunately, none of the images (except for one called `Services`) have been given identical `name` and `id` attributes, either by hand-coding or applying that attribute with the Properties Inspector. Without names to identify each image, it would be difficult to know which images are the right ones to call with the JavaScript to create your desired effect.

5. Click the Cancel button to close the Swap Image dialog box.

You have no use for that box just now. For this particular technique to work, you must name all images before applying any behaviors to them.

6. Select the top image that says `Nutmeg Group` and name the image `Nutmeg` in the text field at the top-left corner of the Properties Inspector, as shown in Figure 17-1.

Figure 17-1: Label all the images before applying JavaScript.

While you're at it, use the Properties Inspector to give the graphic some descriptive `alt` text, such as **Nutmeg Group**.

7. Select, name, and add `alt` text to each of the remaining graphics. Name the images About, Services, Contact, and Bottom, and add the `alt` text About Us, Services, Contact, and <empty> to each.

The <empty> alt text entry in Dreamweaver, as you might recall, inserts an empty `alt` attribute (`<alt=" ">`) to the image tag, making the image compliant with Accessibility.

8. In Design view, select the Services graphic, click the Actions (+) button on the Behaviors panel, and choose Swap Image.

The Swap Image dialog box opens. Now that you've named all the images, the dialog box neatly displays each of the images with the names you set with the Properties Inspector, as seen in Figure 17-2.

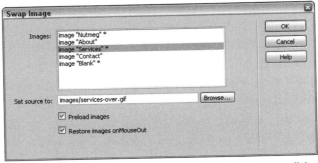

Figure 17-2: Labeled images are neatly listed in the Swap Image dialog box.

Now you can use this dialog box to set the rollover state for as many graphics as you like — all triggered by the visitor with a single mouseover event.

9. With the image `Services` selected in the Images area of the dialog box, click the Browse button next to the Set Source To field and choose the graphic called `services-over.gif` from the images folder.

An asterisk appears next to the word `Services` in the Images field in the dialog box indicating that the `Services-over` graphic will appear when a visitor moves the cursor over the normal Services graphic in a Web browser.

Watch Your Step

Leave the Preload Images and Restore Images onMouseOut options enabled, as both are necessary for Dreamweaver to add the correct JavaScript to the page.

10. Click OK, save the page, and preview the page in a browser window to test the rollover effect.

Moving your cursor over the Services graphic should now display the button's rollover state, showing the word `Services` with a white, rectangular border.

11. Go back into the open `multirolldemo.html` file in Dreamweaver and reselect the Services graphic. Then, back in the Behaviors panel, double-click the yellow gear icon next to the action called Swap Image.

This reopens the Swap Image dialog box for the Services swap image behavior. Now comes the fancy footwork!

12. **In the Images part of the open dialog box, select the image called Nutmeg and click the Browse button to set the source for that image's rollover state to `nutmeg-over.gif`. Next, select the Blank image and set its source for the rollover state to `blank-over.gif`. Click OK.**

The JavaScript that Dreamweaver has inserted into the code now has instructions to alter three different graphics when a visitor mouses over the single Services graphic.

Though the mouseover effect will work, clicking the Services graphic will not yet take a visitor to an adjoining Services page. To do that, you have to assign a hyperlink behavior to that graphic.

13. **To add a hyperlink, select the Services graphic in Design view, click the plus (+) button on the Behaviors panel, and select Go To URL.**

The Go To URL dialog box appears and displays two areas: an *Open In* box that lists Main window and a URL field. Because this page is not part of a larger frameset, only the Main window option is listed in the box. However, when the page is part of a frameset, the frame names would be listed here, from which the target destination within the frameset could be selected. Frames, if you'll recall from Chapter 9, is a technique that uses `<frameset>` and `<frame>` tags instead of `<body>` tags to make two or more pages display in a single browser window.

14. **In the URL field, type in or browse to select the destination page URL. For demonstration purposes, type** http://www.google.com **and click OK.**

When the URL is local (such as `services.html`), only the filename and extension are needed. However, when the file resides in a subfolder off the root level, type the path and filename (for example, **services/main.html**), and when the URL is external to the site, type the complete URL (for example, **http://www.mysamplesite.com/services.html**).

15. **Save the page, launch it in a browser, and move your cursor over the Services graphic.**

You should get these results:

- ◉ Upon mouseover, the Services, Nutmeg, and Blank graphics should all change — and you should see an animation within the Nutmeg graphic.

- ◉ Upon mouseoff, all the graphics return to their normal states.

- ◉ When you click the Services link, the page should transfer to Google.

If the page doesn't function as expected, you might have missed a step or accidentally typed the wrong character somewhere along the way. Go back into the code of your page to see whether you can identify and correct any errors; then test the page in the browser again. If you're still having trouble after that, take a look a the `multirolldemo_complete.html` file. Then to isolate the problem in your code, compare your page side by side with the code in the `multirolldemo_complete.html` file.

You can use this multiple-graphic rollover technique on any series of graphics within the same page — and really showcase your creativity while enhancing the visitor's experience on the site. Use this effect whenever you want to reveal several new graphics at once — for example, to display a descriptive sentence in a fancy font about what's at a particular link, to showcase special deals or events, or to spice up a presentation with an animated GIF.

Launching a new browser window

The world of Web design is divided into two camps on the issue of opening new browser windows. The upshot of their positions looks like this:

- Some believe you should launch a new browser window — displaying the linked URL or document — any time you provide a link that takes visitors away from the domain they're visiting. They also prefer to launch a new browser window any time a visitor opens a non-HTML document from a Web site.

- Other designers adamantly believe that any new browser windows that open without the express consent of the visitor are a nuisance — akin to the spamlike pop-up advertising windows that appear automatically when you visit certain Web sites (or even worse, the pop-up windows spawned by other pop-ups that plaster the screen, completely against the visitor's will, and sometimes can only be stopped by shutting down the computer).

To me, the solution that's the most respectful of visitors falls somewhere on the border between the two camps:

- Open new windows for links to external Web sites and links to non-HTML documents.

- Notify the visitors of what's going on (using an icon or screen tip of some kind, such as *View Close-up* or *Page opens in new window*).

- Never, ever, *ever* launch an advertising window.

Let me give you a few good examples of when you might need to open a new browser window:

- To display a close-up image or detailed views of a product

- To provide technical data or other information in a printable format

- To launch a PDF, PowerPoint, Word, or Excel document

- To display special notices, sale information, or shipping details

To open a link to a resource page on another Web site

To provide a special login area for registered visitors

Information Kiosk

You should realize that pop-up windows launched with JavaScript might be inaccessible to visitors who use screen readers and other assistive devices. As a workaround, you can include special `<noscript>` tags in the code that appear only to visitors who have disabled JavaScript — and provide a direct link to the pop-up page's content so those visitors can still experience that information. Other enhancements to accessibility include putting the notification of a new window opening in the `alt` text for linking images, adding the `title` attribute to text hyperlinks, and ensuring (as often as possible) that all pop-up windows' contents include a Close button or Close link to make closing the window as easy as possible for the visitor.

As you've already learned, opening a new browser window can be as simple as including the `target` attribute (`target="_blank"`) within a hyperlink. This method opens the target URL inside a new browser window with the same attributes and dimensions as the parent window that spawned it. In other words, if the parent window has no status bar and is 500 x 500 pixels, the child pop-up window will also be 500 x 500 pixels and contain no status bar.

To control the size, browser attributes, and screen position of pop-up browser windows, you must turn to the know-how of JavaScript. Here's a set of steps that creates a simple pop-up window with JavaScript; it also lets you set size, location, and browser attributes:

1. Open a new or existing HTML file in your favorite HTML code editor and convert any word, phrase, or image on the page into a null link.

For example, type the word **Google** and create a null link around it, using the number symbol (#) or the `javascript:void(0)` syntax, like this:

```
<a href="javascript:void(0)">Google</a>
```

2. In the head of the page, drop in the following script:

```
<script type="text/JavaScript">
<!--
function MM_openBrWindow(theURL,winName,features) {
//v2.0
  window.open(theURL,winName,features);
}
//-->
</script>
```

The script tells the browser how to handle the JavaScript request that you'll add to the hyperlink in the next step.

3. **Append the hyperlink with the following script, which tells the browser to open the link in a resizable pop-up window named MyWindow that is 300 x 300 pixels in size and includes a toolbar, location bar, status bar, menu bar, and scroll bars:**

```
<a href="javascript:void(0)" onClick="MM_openBrWindow
('http://www.google.com','MyWindow','toolbar=yes,
location=yes,status=yes,menubar=yes,scrollbars=yes,
resizable=yes,width=300,height=300')">Google</a>
```

Information Kiosk

Browser window attributes such as the toolbar and menu bar can be easily omitted from the pop-up window — simply don't include those attributes in the JavaScript. So, for instance, if you want to open a pop-up window in a precise size but without any browser attributes, the code would look like this:

```
<a href="javascript:void(0)"
onClick="MM_openBrWindow('http://www.google.com',
'MyWindow','width=300,height=300')">Google</a>
```

4. **Save the page and test it in a browser window.**

   Click the link to see how a new 300-x-300-pixel browser window pops open, displaying the Google Web page.

5. **To control where the pop-up window appears on the visitor's screen (relative to the top-left corner of the parent browser window), add the top and left attributes by hand to the JavaScript:**

```
<a href="javascript:void(0)" onClick="MM_openBrWindow
('http://www.google.com','MyWindow','width=300,height=
300,top=150,left=150')">Google</a>
```

Watch Your Step

Pay attention to the syntax used in the JavaScript here. There are no quotation marks around the top and left pixel attributes (as you'd normally use in HTML code), and the entire sizing area is enclosed between two apostrophes.

Dreamweaver users can simplify the process of adding pop-up windows to a page by using one of the built-in behavior scripts. Here's the complete procedure:

1. **Select a null link from an open page in the Dreamweaver workspace, click the plus (+) button on the Behaviors panel, and select Open Browser Window.**

   The Open Browser Window dialog box opens, as shown in Figure 17-3.

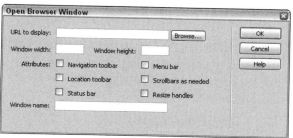

Figure 17-3: Set target destination and window attributes for pop-ups in Dreamweaver.

2. **Type in the filename and path of the destination link, input the pixel dimensions for the window's width and height, select any desired window attributes, and provide a unique name for the pop-up window.**

Select check only the window attributes you want. Attributes left deselected will be omitted from the new window automatically.

3. **Click OK.**

Dreamweaver automatically inserts the proper code on your page to make the pop-up window work. Look at the code and you will see JavaScript in the <head> area as well as inside the hyperlink tag in the body of the page:

```
<!DOCTYPE html PUBLIC "-//W3C//DTD XHTML 1.0
Transitional//EN"
"http://www.w3.org/TR/xhtml1/DTD/xhtml1-
transitional.dtd">
<html xmlns="http://www.w3.org/1999/xhtml">
<head>
<meta http-equiv="Content-Type" content="text/html;
charset=iso-8859-1" />
<title>L-Line: Web Design</title>
<script type="text/JavaScript">
<!--
function MM_openBrWindow(theURL,winName,features) {
//v2.0
  window.open(theURL,winName,features);
}
//-->
</script>
</head>

<body>
<p><a href="javascript:void(0)"
onclick="MM_openBrWindow('http://www.google.com','','')
">Google it!</a></p>
<p>  </p>
</body>
</html>
```

Information Kiosk

What Dreamweaver does not do, however, is provide for the option of controlling the pop-up window's position. That must be hand-coded after the JavaScript has been inserted. (See Step 5 earlier in this section to find out how to insert that code.)

Building complex image maps

Making any image into an image map is pretty straightforward: Add coordinates to the code that map out a shape somewhere on top of the image; then add a hyperlink to it to make it into a link. Hotspots can use the area-shape attributes of `"circle"` or `"rect"` (short for *rectangle*) or `"poly"` (short for *polygon*).

Transfer

Image maps were briefly explained in Chapter 11 in the section on creating hyperlinks.

Step into the Real World

Opening Pop-Ups When JavaScript is Disabled   Even though the scripts in this section are fairly benign examples of JavaScript usage, be very careful if you use JavaScript in combination with null links. When a visitor's browser has JavaScript disabled (and/or when visitors using special devices can't read JavaScript), a null link goes nowhere — and is likely to cause confusion and frustration.

To get around this issue, on JavaScript-independent devices, you can rewrite the JavaScript so the link to the pop-up content appears in the same browser window that contains the link. As with the other script, you can include or omit any browser attributes as desired — and specify the size and position of the pop-up. Here's what the code looks like:

```
<a href="http://www.google.com/" onclick="window.open
  ('http://www.google.com','MyWindow','resizable=yes,width=100,
  height=100,top=100,left=100');return false;">Google</a>
```

This script does not require any script in the <head> of the HTML code. Instead, it uses basic JavaScript instructions to open the specified page in a pop-up (`window.open`) for JavaScript-enabled browsers; even though the page is also specified in the HREF, the `return false;` statement tells the browser to ignore that specification. For devices with JavaScript turned off, the same script ignores the `onclick` statement and opens the file specified in the HREF — inside the same window.

This script was developed by Marja Ribbers at flev00w@re and is available as a free Dreamweaver Extension at `www.flevooware.nl/dreamweaver/extdetails.asp?extID=8`. The extension, however, uses slightly improved JavaScript syntax which includes script in both the head and body of the page.

Take, for example, the odd-shaped logo for Joe's Tiny Diner. If you wanted to create a hotspot on the rectangular graphic that matched exactly the logo's borders, you'd add the coordinates to a <map> tag to specify a hotspot shape relative to the top-left edge of the graphic, set a link for the hotspot, add target and alt attributes, and then link the image to the map with the map attribute that specifies the map's name, and *voilà*:

```
<img src="images/joestinydiner.gif" alt="Joe's Tiny Diner"
width="212" height="115" border="0" usemap="#MyMap">
<map name="MyMap"><area shape="poly" coords="5,2,104,31,206,
4,175,63,208,112,107,100,4,111,37,64" href="joestinydiner.
html" target="_self" alt="Joe's Tiny Diner"></map>
```

Here are instructions for adding a simple image map to a graphic with Dreamweaver:

1. **Open a new Web page and insert an image into it by using the Insert →
Image command.**

Use any image you like for this exercise, whether it be one of your own or one of the sample graphics you've downloaded for doing other exercises in this book.

2. **Select the image in Design view, and in the Map field at the far left side of the Properties Inspector, provide the image with a map name.**

This step is optional, but a good idea to do — especially if you're putting more than one image map on the same Web page. (Unspecified maps are automatically given default names such as Map1 and Map2.)

3. **Select one of the Hotspot tools in the Properties Inspector and create a hotspot shape on top of the image.**

Both the Oval and Rectangular Hotspot tools allow you to create shapes by clicking, dragging, and releasing the mouse. To use the Polygon Hotspot tool, click as many times as needed to draw the outline of the desired hotspot shape.

Hotspots, when drawn, appear in Dreamweaver's Design view as light blue, semitransparent cloaks on top of the graphic — with anchor point squares at each angle along the hotspot path.

4. **Select the Pointer Hotspot tool to select the hotspot you just created and use the Properties Inspector to add a link with target and alt attributes, as shown in Figure 17-4.**

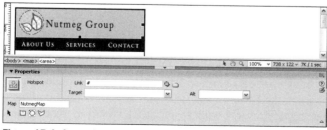

Figure 17-4: Create image maps with the hotspot tools in Dreamweaver's Properties Inspector.

5. **Deselect the image and hotspot by clicking outside the image, anywhere inside the page in Design view.**

If you want, you can continue making additional hotspots on the same image by repeating Steps 2–5. Otherwise save the file and launch the page in your favorite browser to make sure the hotspot works.

That's how you create a simple image map, but you can actually use this technique to create more complex linking systems, especially when combined with other JavaScript behaviors. For example, check out the instructor group photo on the home page of the Noble Desktop Web site at www.nobledesktop.com, also shown in Figure 17-5.

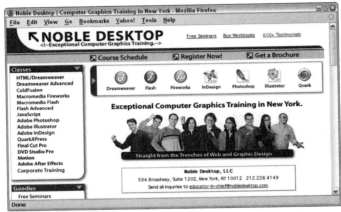

Figure 17-5: Use multiple image maps on the same graphic to link to separate pages.

Each instructor in this image has a unique hotspot that links to an individual instructor page. What's more, when you mouse over any instructor's picture, the animated black bar graphic below the instructors' pictures (Your Instructors . . . Straight from the Trenches of Web and Graphic Design) gets swapped with a black bar identifying the selected instructor by name.

To make multiple hotspots on the same image, follow the steps as outlined earlier in this section. Once that's set up, you can make any particular hotspot cause one or more images change on mouseover — just follow these steps:

1. **Select each of the images on the page, one at a time, and add a name to each graphic in the Name field at the top-left corner of the Properties Inspector.**

All the images on the page must have unique names to identify the graphics before you add the Swap Image behavior. If you're hand-coding, add identical name and id attributes to each image, such as <img src="images/cat.gif" name="cat" id="cat">.

2. Select the first hotspot on the graphic, click the Actions (+) button on the Behaviors panel, and choose Swap Image.

When the Swap Image dialog box appears, you should see each of the named graphics on the page.

3. In the Images area of the dialog box, choose the named graphic that you'd like to swap with another image. Then click the Browse button next to the Set Source To field and choose the desired rollover state graphic.

An asterisk appears next to the selected image in the Images field to identify that the image has a graphic assigned to its rollover state.

Leave the Preload Images and Restore Images onMouseOut options enabled; both are necessary for Dreamweaver to add the correct JavaScript to the page.

To make more than one graphic change with the same Swap Image behavior, set the source graphic for additional named images.

4. Click OK to close the dialog box.

Dreamweaver adds the appropriate JavaScript to the page to make the effect function in a browser.

5. Repeat Steps 2–4 for each hotspot on the image, then save and test the file in a browser.

Moving your cursor over the hotspot areas on the graphic should make the rollover state graphics appear.

Information Kiosk

To enhance appeal, use animated GIFs for any part of the image map configuration. To view examples of both simple and complex image maps, see the Image Map Demo at www.luckychair.com/1-line.

Adding Multimedia Files

Multimedia refers to any kind of file that can be viewed or listened to on the Internet — including videos, music, animations, and games. Unfortunately, because Internet browsers have been developed by different companies over time, not every browser or browser version is equipped to handle media files in quite the same way. For example, some browsers allow you to insert the media file in the code similar to that used for an image — others require that special plug-ins, applets, or ActiveX controls (specified in the code along with the media file) are also installed to play properly in the browser window. To make matters even more complicated, every media file has its own format, as indicated by its file extension — and not all formats are playable in all browsers. Some are even meant only for PCs and not for Mac computers!

The good news about media files, however, is that as Internet users have gotten more savvy, so have browser developers — and over the past few years, certain media formats have become more standard than others. Examples are MP3, WAV, and RAM for sound, and QuickTime, Shockwave, SWF, and MPEG for video. What's more, the newest versions of the most popular browsers (Internet Explorer, Firefox, and Safari) come equipped with the right stuff to play these popular media-file formats without requiring any additional downloads from third-party vendors (even when free, installing those can be a bit of a hassle).

The fastest and easiest way to insert multimedia files into a Web page is to use an HTML editor that automatically writes the appropriate code for each type of file. Dreamweaver, for example, makes it super-easy to add QuickTime movies, Flash animations, Flash buttons, Flash text, Flash paper, Flash video, Shockwave movies, Java Applets, ActiveX controls, and other plug-ins to your Web pages.

To add a multimedia file to your page in Dreamweaver, place a copy of the media file in the local root folder of the managed site you're working in, open the HTML file in the Dreamweaver workspace that you'd like to insert the media file into, and follow these steps:

1. **With your cursor at the spot on the page where you'd like to insert the media file, choose Insert from the main menu and choose the desired media type from the drop-down menu.**

   Alternatively, you can click the Media button on the Common tab of the Insert panel (shown in Figure 17-6) to access that same list with helpful icons next to each media type.

Figure 17-6: Drop multimedia files into any Web page with Dreamweaver's Insert Media command.

   After you choose the desired media type, Dreamweaver opens the Select File dialog box.

2. **Navigate to and select the media file you want to insert, and click OK.**

   Dreamweaver uses the filename and location of the selected file to ensure that the appropriate path to the file gets added to the inserted code. For example, when inserting a Flash SWF animation file, Dreamweaver adds code that enables the visitor to view the animation in most browsers; that code appears in **bold** in this listing:

```
<object classid="clsid:D27CDB6E-AE6D-11cf-96B8-
444553540000" codebase="http://download.macromedia.com/
pub/shockwave/cabs/flash/swflash.cab#version=7,0,19,0"
width="150" height="30">
  <param name="movie" value="button1.swf">
  <param name="quality" value="high">
  <embed src="button1.swf" quality="high" pluginspage=
"http://www.macromedia.com/go/getflashplayer"
type="application/x-shockwave-flash" width="150"
height="30"></embed>
</object>
```

For some media files, after you click OK, the Object Tag Accessibility Attributes dialog box might prompt you to type Accessibility attributes. Type any desired information and click OK to proceed.

3. **With the media file still selected in Design view, enter any desired additional parameters, attributes, and dimensions for the media file.**

On an inserted Flash animation media file, for instance, you can change the quality, scale, alignment, dimensions, V and H space, and background attributes.

Information Kiosk

To learn even more about adding media files to your Web pages, refer to *Dreamweaver 8 Bible*, by Joseph W. Lowery (Wiley) and check out the free online tutorial at www.w3schools.com/media/default.asp.

Increasing Visitor Interactivity

Fundamental to successful Web sites (and described in Chapter 1) is *stickiness* — the different ways Web sites can entice visitors to stay at a site for a long time and revisit the same site as often as possible. These techniques include (for example) using JavaScript to increase visitor interactivity; adding Flash movies and games; offering visitors polls and poll results; requesting feedback from visitors by using forms; adding a site blog; sending out a daily, weekly, or monthly newsletter with links back to the site; including free online tools for visitors to use (such as calculators and converters); publishing regular site-related articles and tips; offering free printable coupons for products and services; and hosting special contests and sweepstakes.

Step into the Real World

Searching Any Site with Google   What better way to make visitors feel in control over their experience on your Web site than allowing them to search for specific words and key phrases using a site search tool? Although some site search methods are admittedly costly and difficult to configure, the free Google search bar is free and requires only a simple cut and paste to install.

Google actually offers three types of free search bars, depending on your site's specific needs:

- **Google Free:** Google's original Free search bar allows visitors to search the Web from your site; it displays the Google logo, a search box for entering keywords and phrases, and a Google Search button.

- **Google Free SafeSearch:** This search bar prevents search results from returning pages with any sexually explicit or adult-themed content. Like the Google Free search bar, this one displays the Google logo, search box, and Google Search button — and also includes the label SafeSearch modestly displayed beneath the Google logo.

- **Google Free with Site Search:** This search bar has all the parts of the Google Free search bar and also includes a feature that allows visitors to search your content or the entire World Wide Web by choosing (respectively) the YOUR DOMAIN NAME or WWW option before clicking the Google Search button.

To install the Google Free search tool with Site Search, follow these steps:

1. **Type the following code at the spot on your page where you'd like the search bar, shown in this sidebar, to appear:**

```
<!-- SiteSearch Google -->
<FORM method=GET action="http://www.google.com/search">
<input type=hidden name=ie value=UTF-8>
<input type=hidden name=oe value=UTF-8>
<TABLE bgcolor="#ffffff"><tr><td>
<A HREF="http://www.google.com/">
<IMG SRC="http://www.google.com/logos/Logo_40wht.gif"
border="0" ALT="Google"></A>
</td>
<td>
<INPUT TYPE=text name=q size=31 maxlength=255 value="">
<INPUT type=submit name=btnG VALUE="Google Search">
<font size=-1>
<input type=hidden name=domains value="YOUR DOMAIN NAME"><br><input
type=radio name=sitesearch value=""> WWW <input type=radio name=
sitesearch value="YOUR DOMAIN NAME" checked> YOUR DOMAIN NAME <br>
</font>
</td></tr></TABLE>
</FORM>
<!-- SiteSearch Google -->
```

2. **Replace the words YOUR DOMAIN NAME in the code in all three spots with the full URL of your Web site's home page, such as** http://www.mydomain.com/.

To have the search feature appear on all the pages of your site, include this code on each page in the same location for consistency.

To get the code for this as well as the other three Google Free search bars, go to `www.google.com/searchcode.html`.

In addition to the three basic search bars, Google also offers two more specialized versions: the Customizable search (which lets you customize the colors of the background, text, and links) and the Site-Flavored search (which returns search results that are more geared to your specific visitors' interests). To learn more, visit these sites:

Customizable: `www.google.com/services/free.html`

Site-flavored: `www.google.com/services/siteflavored.html`

Though not every technique is suitable to every Web site, some function well on nearly any site. You can (for example) offer daily tips, wisdom, coupons, information about sale items or new items, or other desirable content, and post a free game of some kind that visitors can return to each day (or several times a day) to play or replay. Coming up are instructions for adding both types of traffic grabbers to your pages.

A daily tip

Giving visitors a reason to return to your site each day will increase the chance of them wanting to learn more, and perhaps purchase, your site's products or services. One of the quickest ways to get visitors to return is to post some kind of relevant information for them on your site every day. This could be in the form of a daily tip or suggestion, horoscope or fortune, poem, joke, famous quote, special image, coupon, or details about a new product. It honestly could be anything you like, as long as you customize the JavaScript to accurately display the desired information.

The JavaScript in the next exercise was originally developed by Mike W. at dvol.com and can be found in its entirety at The JavaScript Source (`http://javascript.internet.com`). The script contains two parts; one part must be placed in the `<head>` of the code; the other will go inline, between the `<body>` tags of the code, at the location on the page where the daily tip content should appear.

To add a daily tip to a page on your Web site, follow these steps:

1. Type the following script between the opening and closing `<head>` tags of your open HTML file:

```
<SCRIPT LANGUAGE="JavaScript">
<!-- Original:  Mike W. (mikew@dvol.com) -->
<!-- Web Site:  http://www.dvol.com/~users/mikew -->
<!-- This script and many more are available free online at -->
<!-- The JavaScript Source!! http://javascript.internet.com -->

<!-- Begin
var msg = new Array();
Stamp = new Date();
today = Stamp.getDate();
msg[1] = "Tip 1";
msg[2] = "Tip 2";
msg[3] = "Tip 3";
msg[4] = "Tip 4";
msg[5] = "Tip 5";
msg[6] = "Tip 6";
msg[7] = "Tip 7";
msg[8] = "Tip 8";
msg[9] = "Tip 9";
msg[10] = "Tip 10";
msg[11] = "Tip 11";
msg[12] = "Tip 12";
msg[13] = "Tip 13";
msg[14] = "Tip 14";
msg[15] = "Tip 15";
msg[16] = "Tip 16";
msg[17] = "Tip 17";
msg[18] = "Tip 18";
msg[19] = "Tip 19";
msg[20] = "Tip 20";
msg[21] = "Tip 21";
msg[22] = "Tip 22";
msg[23] = "Tip 23";
msg[24] = "Tip 24";
msg[25] = "Tip 25";
msg[26] = "Tip 26";
msg[27] = "Tip 27";
msg[28] = "Tip 28";
msg[29] = "Tip 29";
msg[30] = "Tip 30";
msg[31] = "Tip 31";

function writeTip() {
document.write(msg[today]);
```

```
}
// End -->
</script>
```

Watch Your Step

Please note that to use this script, you must include the four comment tags (`<!--`) at the beginning of the code, or else you'll be in breach of the copyright.

If you'd rather *not* retype all this code, you can copy and paste it from the free online version posted at

```
http://javascript.internet.com/text-effects/
daily-tip.html
```

2. **With your cursor at the location of the page where you'd like the daily tip to appear, type the following JavaScript into the code:**

```
Daily Tip:   <script>writeTip();</script>
```

This bit of code calls the JavaScript in the `<head>` of the page. If today is the eighth day of the month, for example, the daily tip named `msg[8]` appears on the page when viewed in a browser.

Watch Your Step

Dreamweaver users must take care to add this script in Code view and not in Design view.

3. **Back in the JavaScript in the `<head>` of the page, customize each of the tips between the opening and closing quotes.**

For example, change

```
msg[1] = "Tip 1";
```

to

```
msg[1] = "There is nothing wrong with America that
cannot be cured by what is right with America. &#8212;
Bill Clinton";
```

To display an image instead of or in conjunction with text in the tip, add the `<img>` tag between the quotation marks of the JavaScript tip area, and replace quotation marks for attributes inside the inserted image with apostrophes. The result looks like this:

```
msg[1] = "Text and a graphic <img src='images/
coupon1.gif'>";
```

Information Kiosk

This script can also be placed in an external JavaScript file. Like a Server-Side Include, this external file helps minimize code by centralizing the instruction for the JavaScript into one location that an unlimited number of HTML files can access and use via a link in the HTML code to the external file.

To convert this script into an external file, follow these steps:

1. **Cut the JavaScript code from the `<head>` of the page, paste it into a blank file, and save it with the extension `.js` at the root level of the Web site it will be used in.**

   To keep things easy to remember and in the spirit of semantic HTML, name the external file after the function in the script. In this case, you might name the external file `dailytip.js`.

2. **Within the new external JS file, delete the opening and closing `<script>` tags.**

   The comment tags should stay in, and will not affect the functionality of the script.

   Save and close the external JS file and go back to the HTML file.

3. **Add a link to the external JS file between the HTML file's opening and closing `<head>` tags, like this:**

   ```
   <head>
   <script language="JavaScript" type="text/javascript"
   src="dailytip.js"></script>
   <noscript>
   This page includes a daily tip using JavaScript.
   </noscript>
   </head>
   ```

   To make the script more accessible, the example includes a set of `<noscript>` tags with descriptive information about what the JavaScript does, and (when applicable) how visitors can access that information.

After you've updated all 31 tips in the JavaScript, you can virtually forget about it for about 27 days or so — until it's time to change all the tips again for the following month. Keeping your site fresh keeps your visitors interested.

Daily Sudoku

The latest craze in mind puzzles, hands down, has got to be Sudoku — so why not treat your site visitors to a free daily game? The friendly folks over at

SudokuHints.com are now offering free sticky content for those who are willing to add the code to their pages. When you use their code, puzzles appear on your page(s) wherever you have space for them — and when a visitor plays the game, a new browser window opens with special-hint tools to assist gamers with solving puzzles.

Puzzles can be included on any site in about six different formats, depending on your preferences and available page space. The game board can be presented inside a larger landscape rectangle, in a square, or in a vertical format — as well as in smaller, grid-only formats with columns that measure 120, 155, 227, and 272 pixels wide.

To insert the default Horizontal Format Sudoku game, shown in Figure 17-7, on your page, follow these steps:

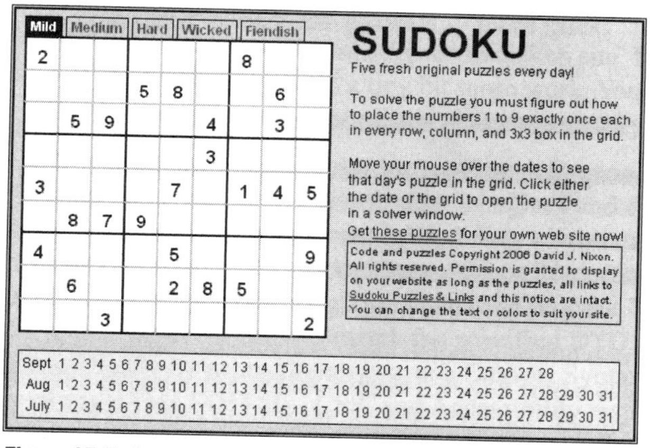

Figure 17-7: Keep visitors coming back often by adding a free Sudoku game to your site.

1. **Place your cursor in the code of your page, at the location where you'd like to insert the free Sudoku puzzle.**

2. **Then add the following code:**

```
<iframe name="sudokuhints1"
src="http://www.sudokuhints.com/free-sudoku.html"
width="587" height="423" frameborder="0"
marginwidth="0">
</iframe><br>Sudoku by <a
href="http://www.sudokuhints.com/">Sudokuhints.com</a>
```

The code uses the `<iframe>` tag to insert an inline frame on the page inside which the puzzle, pulled from the `sudokuhints.com` Web site, gets displayed.

If you'd like to display one of the other game formats (instead of the horizontal format), you must insert slightly different `iframe` code that uses a different HTML file on the SudokuHints.com site as a source — and specifies the size of the frame in pixels. This one (for example) specifies the mini 120-pixel format for the game board:

```
<iframe name="sudokuhints1"
src="http://www.sudokuhints.com/free-sudoku-mini1.html"
width="119" height="123" frameborder="0" marginwidth="0">
</iframe><br>Sudoku by
<a href="http://www.sudokuhints.com/">Sudokuhints.com</a>
```

The colors and fonts used in the free game can also be customized by downloading and hosting a few different files on your site. To download the pages to customize in a Zip file, go to www.sudokuhints.com/free-download.html and click the Zip file link.

advertisement window: Any of those pesky advertising pop-up browser windows that appear without the visitor's consent when visiting certain Web pages.

browser attributes: The normally visible parts of a browser window that can be hidden using JavaScript: toolbar, location bar, status bar, menu bar, scroll bars, and resize handles.

Flash: A vector-based animation program the creates small files with the .swf file extension. SWF files can contain motion, graphics, and sound — and can provide complex interactivity with a site visitor.

frames/framesets: Framesets allow the presentation of two or more pages inside a single browser window using special frame and frameset tags in place of the traditional body tags of a regular Web page.

hotspot: On an image map, an area defined by rectangular, circular, or polygonal coordinates. It activates an assigned hyperlink through the use of special HTML code that defines the area with numerical coordinates.

iframe: Working similarly to framesets, the <iframe> tag creates a window within a Web page, inside which a visitor can view another HTML file.

normal state: The default state of a rollover button or hyperlink, which appears when the page loads in a browser.

 **continued**

preload (preloading script): A type of JavaScript script that runs automatically when the page loads in a browser window and instructs the browser to preload files specified in the script (typically graphics for rollover buttons) into the visitor's browser cache so that those files are ready to use when the page is finished loading.

restore: In JavaScript, this term means "to return to the original state" when an event is triggered, as when a visitor moves the cursor off a rollover graphic button.

rollover state: The state of a rollover button or hyperlink when a visitor moves the cursor over the button or hyperlink.

search bar: A mini form containing a text field and Submit button that allows visitors to search the existing site or the entire World Wide Web. Results typically appear in the same browser window unless otherwise configured to appear elsewhere.

Last
Stop

Practice Exam

1. True or False: Everyone on the Web can experience JavaScript-enabled files.

2. Multimedia files use special file extensions such as `.wav` and `.ram`, and at times require _____ to play in a browser window.

3. Name five things that JavaScript can do on a Web page.

_____

_____

4. Why is it important to name images with the `name` and `id` attributes when you use JavaScript?

_____

_____

5. When might it be necessary to open a new browser window? Give two examples.

_____

_____

6. Name two ways to make content on a JavaScript-enabled pop-up window accessible to visitors using assistive devices.

_____

_____

7. How many hotspots can be created on a single graphic image?

_____

_____

8. Based on the information you learned in this chapter, list three possible ways you might increase visitor interactivity on your site.

_____

_____

9. Alter the following JavaScript so that the pop-up window appears at 250 pixels from the top and 300 pixels from the left of the parent window:

```
<a href="javascript:void(0)"
onClick="MM_openBrWindow('http://www.yahoo.com','MyWindow','width=300,
height=300')">Yahoo!</a>
```

Testing, Testing, Testing

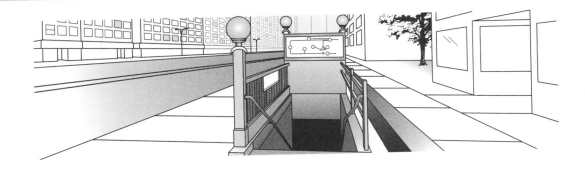

Enter the Station

Questions

1. What is the best way to clean up imperfect code?

2. Does it matter whether you test your pages on a Mac or PC?

3. What are the most common types of code errors, and how can you quickly repair them?

4. What kinds of tools can automate or partially automate site testing?

5. Are there any other platforms or devices you should test Web pages on?

6. Which different browsers and browser versions should you test pages on prior to publishing?

Express Line

Testing can take anywhere from a few hours to several days, depending on the number of issues identified that require fixing. Concurrent with that process, additional steps must be taken to ensure the site passes objective code validation tests and is compliant with the recommended W3C standards for Accessibility. Chapters 18 and 19 go hand in hand and should be read and addressed as a single unit. To learn more about code validation and compliance before doing the exercises in this chapter, move ahead to Chapter 19 and then return to Chapter 18 to begin performing all the testing methods suggested in both chapters.

You're almost to the Web design finish line, but you still have to do a few more things before your site gets published. The last thing you or your client would want is a Web page (or whole site) that doesn't quite work (or look) the way it should. Therefore, all the pages should go through a rigorous review to catch problems like spelling errors, code problems, broken links, and missing code attributes like `alt` text for images and `title` attributes for hyperlinks.

If you're using Dreamweaver to build your site, you're in luck because the program has some incredible tools to assist you with testing so that you can identify and fix any problems before visitors have a chance to see the site.

This chapter outlines how to use several of Dreamweaver's testing tools, including ones that clean up code, check spelling, find and replace text and source code throughout an entire site, use a special Paste command, clean up redundant and unnecessary code, apply uniform source formatting to pages, and fix some common coding problems such as identifying broken links and orphans using Dreamweaver's built-in validator.

Setting Up a Prelaunch Testing Method

Building Web pages is one of those activities that require you to remember a bunch of little details that all add up to a finished Web site. Besides designing the pages, optimizing all the graphics, building the pages, pasting in all the relevant content in every page, dropping in JavaScript and media files, and formatting everything with CSS, you have to remember to include Meta tags in the code, add customized titles to every page, give images alternate text, and add target attributes to links that should open in separate browser windows. The list could go on and on.

To help you remember all the things to do, try creating your own Web-testing check-list, like the starter list example shown here, and use it when reviewing every site you build prior to publishing:

Web Site Prelaunch Testing Checklist

1. Have you performed a spell and syntax check, included the correct DTD, applied source formatting, organized your CSS, and cleaned up any HTML and Word HTML coding errors?

2. Have you tested the pages in multiple browsers and browser versions on both the Mac and PC platforms and found solutions for any glaring errors?

3. Do all the pages on the site include Meta tags?

4. Does each page have a unique, descriptive title?

5. Do all the images include `alt` text or empty `alt` text attributes?

6. Do all the hyperlinks include `title` attributes?

7. Have you hand-checked all the internal and external hyperlinks for accuracy? Do they go where you want them to go? Did you find any broken links that need fixing?

8. When aligning tables, have you replaced `<table>` tag alignment attributes with surrounding `<div>` alignment tags?

9. Does the site have any unused files, images, or folders that can be safely moved to another location or deleted?

10. Are the site's forms and tables fully accessible and functional?

In the sections that follow, you learn about some of the best tools for completing all these tasks.

Information Kiosk

If you're looking for a fully comprehensive checklist that covers everything from code quality and accessibility to basic usability and site management, visit `www.maxdesign.com.au/presentation/checklist.htm`.

Cleaning Up Code

Some people might think that hand-coders must always make a practice of checking the hierarchical order, syntax, and spelling of their HTML code, but that designers using HTML editors need not worry about syntactical or other HTML errors. Not true. Even if you use the best program out there, your code will have errors because you're human and because the program was made by a human. No matter how carefully you build a site, the HTML in your pages might inadvertently become cluttered with redundant tags, unnecessary markup, and outright detrimental code that can negatively impact the presentation of your pages.

Many of the errors within the coding happen when you paste content from other sources like a Word or Excel file, from an online resource, or from another code editor or application. Other times, an error might just be an honest typo that wasn't caught or something that happened behind the scenes when moving elements around the page by clicking and dragging or cutting and pasting. One common code problem is empty hyperlinks, such as `<a href="http://www.google.com"></a>`, which some code editors occasionally leave in the code for no apparent reason when you move a link from one spot on the page to another. As is often the case, such extra code might not be noticeable during the building phase of your site, but it will often rear its head during the testing phase prior to publishing.

To minimize errors, perform code cleanup twice during the building phase:

1. Clean up any completed master pages or templates *before* the rest of the site is built.

2. Do another cleanup on all the pages of the site at the end of the building phase.

To do the cleanup, I highly recommend using an application like Dreamweaver, which offers several tools that can automate the process within any managed site. Besides Dreamweaver, quite a lot of online tools can check your pages for certain errors and help you identify those problems in the code. That, however, might be a lengthy process because you usually can input the URL of only one page at a time.

Dreamweaver's tools include a Find and Replace tool, a Spell Checker, a Word Clean Up command, a Code Clean Up command, a Source Formatting tool, and a Convert Syntax tool. I cover all these tools in this chapter, except for the Convert Syntax tool, which I cover in Chapter 19.

Finding and replacing global errors

One of my personal favorite features in Dreamweaver is the Find and Replace tool. With this single tool, you can search for and optionally replace any text, source code, or specific tag throughout an entire page, selected pages, a specified folder, or an entire managed site. Suppose, for example, you realize that the content provided by the client contains a certain word misspelled throughout the entire site. This tool can find that misspelling and fix it on all the site pages.

Watch Your Step

The only thing about this tool that might be a deterrent to some designers is that these operations can't be undone, which can be especially critical when modifying pages sitewide. Therefore, to ensure that you can revert innocent mistakes, make a backup copy of your entire managed site before using this tool. That way, in the event that something goes awry, you can always return to the state the site was in before you began making changes. After a few weeks, if you clearly won't be reverting back to that particular state of the site, you can safely delete the backup files.

To find a misspelled word and replace that text with the correct spelling throughout all the pages in a managed Dreamweaver site:

1. **With a document containing the spelling error open in the Dreamweaver workspace, select the misspelled word or phrase.**

   For example, the client might have misspelled the word *services* as *serbices* throughout all the pages on the site.

2. Choose Edit → Find and Replace.

This launches the Find and Replace dialog box shown in Figure 18-1. By selecting the misspelled word or phrase first, the dialog box opens with the selection automatically placed in the Find text box. If you forget to select the content before launching the dialog box, simply type the word, phrase, tag, or source code you want to find into the Find text box.

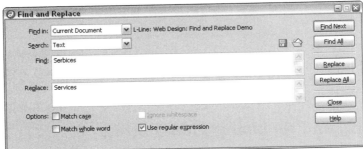

Figure 18-1: Use Dreamweaver's Find and Replace tool to fix coding errors in the content, specified tags, and source code.

3. From the Find In drop-down list, select the Entire Current Local Site option.

You may also choose just the selection, the currently open document, all open documents, a specific folder, or selected files from within the Files panel.

4. In the Replace text box, type the word or phrase with the correct spelling.

Here you enter the replacement contents, such as the properly spelled word *services*.

To help refine the search when you need to match specific spellings of a particular word, enable the Match Case and/or Match Whole Word option. The Use Regular Expression option is enabled by default in case you know how to write regular expressions (a method of using special characters as search patterns to speed up the find-and-replace search process) and want to use them.

5. Click the Replace button or the Replace All button.

To change a single instance, click Replace. To change all instances, click Replace All. To just find but not replace other instances of the selection being searched, you can click the Find Next and Find All buttons.

Watch Your Step

Similar to working with Word documents, try to always be wary of using the Replace All command in Dreamweaver when the word being replaced is contained inside of another word that you wouldn't want replaced. For instance, if I misspelled *rice* as *ice* and I used Replace All to replace *ice* with *rice*, all instances of *dice* would be changed to *drice*.

If there is any question about the replacement term you've used, consider selectively replacing each match of the search term, one at a time, by clicking the Replace and Find Next buttons. Or, to find all instances of the word in question in a single document, click the Find All button, which opens the Results panel listing each of the words that match your query. That can help you identify whether any strange matches were included with your replacement term. From there you can double-click each instance in the Results panel to have that particular word highlighted in the text on the page, where you can make the changes by hand.

After clicking the Replace All button, Dreamweaver displays an Alert box to remind you that the operation can't be undone. Use this as an opportunity to verify that you've accurately spelled the correction and selected the appropriate files in the Find In drop-down list.

6. **If you have any doubts about your selections, cancel out of this operation by clicking the No button. To proceed, click the Yes button on the Alert box.**

As the operation quietly runs in the background, the Results panel opens and displays all the filenames that are being modified, along with the line of matched text that contains the fix for each file.

7. **Close the Results panel and save the changes to any open files.**

Repeat Steps 1–7 to run another Find and Replace operation.

Changing words and phrases is only one example of how to use this powerful tool. You can also edit whole chunks of code, replace filenames throughout the site, and remove tags and other unwanted coding like comments.

Checking spelling

Despite best efforts, spelling errors happen. Sometimes, they take the form of regular typos and grammatical errors, like *htis* instead of *this* and *they're* instead of *their.* Sometimes, they're commonly misused words, such as *accept* and *except.* And sometimes, they're accurately spelled words that are contextually wrong, like typing *moon* when you meant *noon.*

A good way to check spelling is to do it yourself, or even better, have a group of people, possibly including the client, read the site content to look for spelling and grammatical mistakes prior to publishing.

To help speed up the human part of spell checking, however, take advantage of any automated spell checking commands that come as a standard feature of your HTML editor. Dreamweaver has a pretty decent spell checker that works very similarly to the one found in Microsoft Word.

Information Kiosk

If you'd rather not be responsible for the accuracy of the site's spelling — especially because clients often provide content that is rife with spelling errors! — you can include a stipulation in your design contract that states the client will be ultimately responsible for the accuracy and substance of the content. But even if you do so, consider running a spell check anyway to correct any obvious mistakes, such as *the* spelled as *teh.*

To run the spell check command in Dreamweaver, choose Text ➜ Check Spelling. The Check Spelling dialog box appears, as shown in Figure 18-2, and you may Ignore, Change, Ignore All, or Change All the instance of the word in question. If desired, you may also add any word to a personal dictionary within Dreamweaver so that the spell checker will bypass future instances of that word. After you select an option, Dreamweaver will move on to the next questionable word, and you can again select an option on how to treat the word. The process will continue until Dreamweaver can't find any more instances of problematic words, at which time the program will display a Spelling Check Completed alert window.

Figure 18-2: Dreamweaver's Check Spelling command is similar to the spell checker found in Word.

If you initiate the spell checker when text is selected or from any place other than the top of the file, Dreamweaver will also ask whether you want to continue checking the rest of the file or continue checking for potential spelling problems from the beginning of the document.

Watch Your Step

Currently, the Check Spelling command verifies text only in one file at a time, but hopefully the folks at Adobe can figure out how to make it possible to check all the pages on a site so you won't have to open and check each page manually. Until then, you'll need to open and check your pages individually.

Cleaning up unwanted formatting

The Clean Up Word HTML/XHMTL command in Dreamweaver is a must for any Web file that receives pasted content from Word and any other Microsoft documents, including Word HTML, PowerPoint, and Excel files. Because Microsoft files often embed extra markup to make the file retain its formatting, you need to use this tool to strip that out, ensuring that the Web site code — and only the Web site code — dictates the look of the site to the visitor's browser.

To access this feature in any open document in Dreamweaver, follow these steps:

1. **Choose Commands → Clean Up Word HTML.**

The Clean Up Word HTML dialog box will open, as shown in Figure 18-3.

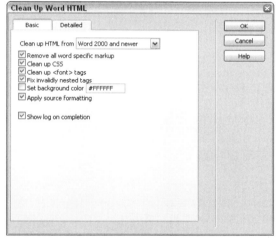

Figure 18-3: Use the Clean Up Word HTML command any time content is pasted into a Dreamweaver file from a copied Microsoft document.

2. **Modify the cleanup settings as desired on both the Basic and Detailed tabs of the dialog box.**

Most of the options in the Basic tab and all the options in the Detailed tab will be automatically enabled to provide the most robust form of cleanup. Ignore the Detailed tab and leave all the options enabled on the Basic tab for this exercise, with the exception of the Set Background Color option on the Basic tab, which should be deselected.

- **Remove All Word Specific Markup:** This option deletes any special markup that is required to format the page in Word and Word HTML files, but is unnecessary in a normal HTML file.

- **Clean Up CSS:** Enable this option to delete any Word-specific CSS markup.

- **Clean Up <font> Tags:** This setting deletes any instances of old `<font>` tags.

- **Fix Invalidly Nested Tags:** Word sometimes adds markup to a page outside normal heading and paragraph tags, which don't conform to valid tag nesting standards. This option will remove those tags.

- **Set Background Color:** If you're styling pages using CSS, be sure to deselect this option. Otherwise this function will add a background color attribute, using the color specified (`bgcolor="#ffffff"`), to the opening `<body>` tag in your code.

- **Apply Source Formatting:** Source formatting is determined by the options specified in Dreamweaver's `SourceFormat.txt` file as well as the Code Format settings in the Preferences panel.

- **Show Log on Completion:** Select this check box to see a summary of the cleanup results.

3. **Click OK.**

Upon completion of the cleanup process, Dreamweaver displays an alert box, like the one shown in Figure 18-4, with details about the cleanup.

Figure 18-4: Dreamweaver displays Clean Up Word HTML results in a handy alert box at the end of the cleanup process.

Information Kiosk

To avoid copying formatting embedded in Microsoft files in the first place, use Dreamweaver's Paste Special command when copying and pasting content into the Web site. After copying content from the source document, simply choose Edit → Paste Special in Dreamweaver and choose the option that pastes only the content and options that you want to include.

Cleaning up HTML/XHTML syntax

Another useful tool that should be applied to every page on a completed site prior to publishing is the Clean Up HTML/XHTML command, which looks for problematic code and automatically cleans up those errors. This is especially helpful when

Dreamweaver uses one markup language (XHTML) and you used another (HTML) but you'd ultimately like all the code to be consistent.

The Clean Up HTML/XHTML command takes its cue from the stated Document Type Definition (DTD) in the file and will convert any tags that are inconsistent to the proper format.

Use these steps to access this feature in any open document in Dreamweaver:

1. **Choose Commands → Clean Up HTML or Commands → Clean Up XHTML.**

   Dreamweaver automatically recognizes the DTD in the page code and displays the right Clean Up command in the Commands menu to match that DTD.

   The Clean Up HTML/XHTML dialog box will open.

2. **Modify the cleanup settings as desired.**

   A few of the options are automatically enabled, but you can disable them to suit particular cleanup needs. For instance, you can use the tool to clean up only empty <span> tags.

   If you'd like to see cleanup results, be sure to enable the Show Log on Completion option.

3. **Click OK.**

   When the Show Log on Completion option has been enabled, a small alert box appears listing a helpful Clean Up summary.

Applying consistent code formatting

Dreamweaver is such a highly customizable program that users can choose specific source formatting options for all newly created documents. Dreamweaver has several preference categories that you can customize, including code coloring, code format, code hints, and code rewriting. For example, by adjusting some of the settings in Dreamweaver's Code Format preferences, you can tell Dreamweaver to automatically create closing tags around selected content after typing </ at the end.

Knowing how Dreamweaver will format the code for new documents is great, but what can you do about code format conformity in already created files? Use the Apply Source Formatting option, of course. This command will apply the formatting options to the code of your page as specified in Dreamweaver's HTML format Preferences and in the application's SourceFormat.txt file (itself an editable document that helps Dreamweaver determine how to code new files), thereby over-writing any coding inconsistencies that might have come about since the file was originally created.

To apply source formatting to any open document in Dreamweaver:

1. Choose Commands → Apply Source Formatting.

Dreamweaver applies the settings in the Code Format preferences to the HTML, automatically updating any code that didn't match those preferences.

2. Choose File → Save to save the changes.

Continue working or close the document.

If desired, you can also apply the source formatting to a selection of contiguous code instead of an entire document.

Checking the Code for Common Problems

When you're done with the basic code cleanup, you can move on to your initial tests of how the code works. These tests help you check for things that need remembering but are easily forgotten and so must be done at the end of the site-building phase. At the top of the "Oops, I forgot to . . ." list are tasks like verifying that all the images on a site include `alt` text attributes and checking to see that links work properly.

Fortunately, testing for most of these to-do items can be automated when working in a managed site in Dreamweaver. Nonetheless, you simply must perform some tasks by hand. In those instances, using a conveyer belt/repetitive task methodology works best. For example:

- To check whether all the pages on a site include unique titles, open each page in the Dreamweaver workspace one at a time and verify the `title` attribute is complete. (You could also run a Dreamweaver report to check specifically for untitled documents, but the hand check is a more thorough method of verification because you might find typos that the report simply wouldn't identify.)

- To check for Meta tag information, either check the template file (which would automatically insert the same Meta information in all template-based files) or start the process by checking the home page file for Meta information. Add or edit the Meta content there, copy it to the computer's Clipboard, and then open each page, again one at a time, and paste the updated Meta information into the `<head>` area of each file's code. Save everything and close the files.

To use Dreamweaver's built-in testing tools and reports, you need to open Dreamweaver's Results panel by choosing Window → Results or pressing F7. The Results panel contains eight different tabs, which each provide access to different types of site information and testing tools. Four of them in particular are extremely useful for prelaunch testing: Validation, Target Browser Check, Link Checker, and Site Reports.

The tools all work in a similar way. Each can be

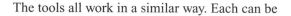 Activated by clicking the green Play button at the panel's top-left edge

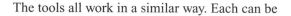 Set to perform the task on the currently open file, all open files, a specified folder, selected files in the Files panel, or on all the files in the currently managed local site

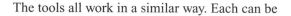 Customized to meet specific testing needs

After running any tool, the results are displayed in the results window, filename first, then by the line of code containing the issue in question, then by description and any other pertinent details. Each issue identified also displays with one of three icons next to each line, the Error, the Warning, and the Message, as shown in Figure 18-5. Errors should be addressed and corrected, Warnings need to be looked into but might not cause serious display problems, and Messages typically identify code issues that although incorrect might not affect how the page displays.

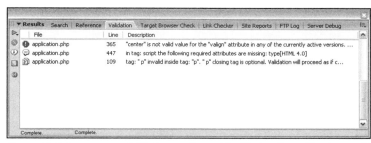

Figure 18-5: Dreamweaver Validation results are identified as Errors, Warnings, or Messages.

For each problem identified in the code, you can right-click (Windows) or Control+ click (Mac) to access a contextual menu from which you can select further options, such as requesting more information about a particular issue. Even better is that if you click any error in the Results panel, Dreamweaver takes you directly to the page containing the error and highlights the exact line(s) of code containing the error, making it a snap for you to correct.

Read on to learn more about the powerful Validator, Target Browser Check, Link Checker, and Site Reports features in Dreamweaver.

Validating the markup

You can set the Validator to check code accuracy in the currently open file, a series of selected files, or the specified managed site, and you can use this tool to validate a number of markup languages including HTML, XHTML, JSP, CFML, XML, and WML.

To run the Validator on a single open HTML file, follow these steps:

1. **From the Validation tab in the Results panel, click the green arrow button in the top-left corner and select Validate Current Document.**

To validate the whole site or selected files, choose the appropriate option from the pop-up menu.

Dreamweaver automatically runs the report and displays any results in the bottom part of the panel.

2. **To view or correct any of the errors, warnings, or messages listed in the results area, double-click the filename in question.**

Dreamweaver automatically opens the selected document and highlights the line(s) of code containing the error.

3. **Correct any errors in the HTML as needed and rerun the report.**

Occasionally, fixing one error can result in another, so it's always a good idea to rerun the report at least once.

When no problems are found in the code, Dreamweaver displays a message that states `No warnings or errors found [DTD]`.

Checking for browser support

The Target Browser Check looks at all the tags in your files and determines whether those tags and any attending attributes are compliant with the latest W3C recommendations (for example, the code doesn't contain any deprecated tags like `<center>` and `<b>`) and are supported in the most popular browsers. Though this test doesn't show you how any found errors will look in browsers that don't support a particular tag, the test results will list the browser type and version so that you can do your own testing to correct the error. For instance, you might get an error like the following one, which identifies the `tab-stops` property in the CSS that isn't supported by ten browser versions:

CSS property tab-stops is not supported [Firefox 1.0, Microsoft IE for Macintosh 5.2, Microsoft Internet Explorer 5.0, Microsoft Internet Explorer 5.5, Microsoft Internet Explorer 6.0, Netscape Navigator 6.0, Netscape Navigator 7.0, Netscape Navigator 8.0, Safari 1.0, Safari 2.0]

In the following steps, you'll run the target browser check on a single open HTML file:

1. **From the Target Browser Check tab in the Results panel, click the green arrow button in the top-left corner and select Check Target Browsers for Current Document from the drop-down menu.**

To check an entire site or selected files in the Files panel, choose one of the other options from the drop-down menu.

2. **Depending on the number of found issues, the report might take a few minutes to generate. Be patient.**

Like the other tabs on the Results panel, the results for this tool will display in a list at the bottom of the results panel with an Error, Warning, or Message icon next to each issue found.

3. **To correct any issues found, double-click the line in the Results panel containing the issue, and Dreamweaver automatically opens the page containing the error.**

The code in question will be highlighted and/or displayed with a red wavy underline to assist in making a correction or adjustment.

Placing your cursor on top of the red underline will reveal a tip window that identifies the error and lists the browsers that don't support it.

Keep in mind that this tool checks only for the validity of code within a subset of browsers and browser versions and doesn't verify the accuracy of the code or of any functionality of any JavaScript or other code used in the file(s).

Checking links

Use the Link Checker tab in the Results panel to check your pages for broken internal links (for example, you misspelled index.html as inddex.html), to see a list of all the page's external links, and to identify any *orphaned files* (unused or unlinked to files) that you can remove from the site to help save room on the server.

To run the Link Checker on a single open HTML file, follow these steps:

1. **From the Link Checker tab in the Results panel, click the green arrow button in the top-left corner and select Check Links in Current Document from the drop-down menu.**

To check links in an entire site or selected files in the Files panel, choose one of the other options from the drop-down menu.

2. **By default, broken links (if any exist) will be displayed in the bottom of the Results panel. To correct a link, click the URL under the Broken Links column and edit the text to correct the link.**

Corrected links automatically disappear from the listing.

If no broken links are identified, congratulations!

3. **Click the Broken Links drop-down menu at the top of the Link Checker area, below the tabs, and choose External Links.**

Any links going to pages outside the site to a different URL are listed here. Though you can't test these links from within Dreamweaver, the list can be a useful tool for identifying the links that need to be verified.

4. **Click the External Links drop-down menu at the top of the Link Checker area, below the tabs, and choose Orphaned Files.**

This report feature can only be used for an entire managed site, so when the Alert box appears, click the OK button.

5. **Click the green arrow button on the panel again, but this time choose Check Links for Entire Current Local Site from the drop-down menu. When the results appear, click the Broken Links drop-down menu and choose Orphaned Files.**

Any file, image, or other asset saved into the local managed site that isn't being referenced by another file (linked to) is displayed.

6. **If you know that file is unnecessary to the functionality of the site, either archive it in another location or delete it.**

7. **As a practice, rerun the report after making any changes to ensure that you've caught and corrected as many errors as possible.**

Generating site reports

Dreamweaver has a series of HTML Reports that can help you find common code problems that can affect page download time and create performance and display issues. Run the reports for every site to make sure you catch those little problems that might otherwise slip through the cracks.

The reports can identify the following elements:

- **Combinable nested font tags** such as `<font face="verdana, arial"> <font size="2">Hello</font></font>`, which could be rewritten as `<font face="verdana, arial" size="2">Hello</font>`

- **Accessibility** issues, which identify ways the code can be improved

- **Missing alt text** for any `<img>` tags

- **Redundant nested tags** that can be safely removed, like deleting the extra `<strong>` tags around the word *pumpkin* in the following sentence: `<strong> Halloween is a time for ghosts, <strong>pumpkins</strong > witches, and spooky creatures of the night</strong>`

- **Removable empty tags** that are totally unnecessary and can be deleted from the code, such as empty `<font>` or `<span>` tags

- **Untitled documents** and files with empty `<title>` tags

- **Workflow** for designers working within a group setting. These special reports help identify files that have been checked out by particular teammates, find files with associated Design Notes, and display files that have been recently modified

In the following steps, you run the HTML Site Reports on an entire managed site:

1. **From the Site Reports tab in the Results panel, click the green arrow button in the top-left corner.**

   In the Reports dialog box that appears, you can select which report options the results should display.

2. **Select each of the options under the HTML Reports area of the dialog box.**

   Leave all the Workflow reports options deselected.

3. **Click Run to run the report.**

   Results are listed in the bottom of the panel identified by filename, code line number, and a description of the found issue.

4. **Make corrections directly inside the Results panel or double-click an entry to directly edit the document in question.**

5. **When you're finished making corrections, rerun the report with the same settings to ensure all the errors have been addressed to your satisfaction.**

Testing Web Pages on Different Platforms and Browsers

Viewing pages in a browser is the best way to evaluate how the page will look to visitors, to determine whether there are any mistakes in the code, and to help pinpoint where in the code the problems are. Browser testing should be done throughout the master page and site-building process and again at the end of the project prior to publication. Presuming you've been previewing your pages in one or two browsers during the building phase of the site, at this stage the focus will be on how well the site displays in different browsers. When it comes to page testing, most Web novices test their pages only in Internet Explorer and Netscape on a PC, completely ignoring any other popular browsers and platforms. People with more schooling do a little better by testing on both Mac and PC platforms.

Transfer

To be as thorough as possible when testing Web pages on different platforms and browsers, upload your site to a test directory on the same server that will be hosting the site and test it from there. Chapter 20 includes instructions on creating a test directory and on uploading files by using File Transfer Protocol (FTP).

Although definitely commendable, that strategy doesn't cover all the bases, and unfortunately, it's difficult to do thorough testing without using third-party software (like the free tool at AnyBrowser.com or the fee-based tool at BrowserCam.com) or hiring an outside service.

In fact, according to the statisticians at W3Schools.com, as of September 2006, 88.5 percent of all Internet users use PCs running some version of Windows, 3.8 percent of all Internet traffic comes from Mac OS users, and another 3.5 percent comes directly from Linux OS users. The remaining percentage of Web users experience the Internet with alternative tools, such as hand-held devices, WebTV, and text-only assistive devices. This tells you that to be fully thorough in your testing, you must simulate how all visitors experience the site and correct any glaring mistakes prior to publishing.

Realistically, such a noble effort isn't an affordable solution for the average Web designer. As such, you should at minimum test on both Mac and PC in the most popular browsers and browser versions, namely

- **PC:** IE 5–7, Netscape 7 and 8, and Firefox 1.5
- **Mac:** Safari 1.0 and 2.0, Opera 8.5, and Firefox 1 and 1.5

The reason for testing so many browsers and browser versions on both Mac and PC is that one version of a browser can differ drastically from another depending on the platform. Case in point is the IE 5 browser. On a PC, IE 5 worked great, but on a Mac, it had tons of display issues. In fact, that version of IE for Mac was so problematic, it was nearly impossible to find a coding and CSS solution that worked in both that one and all other browsers. As a solution, this one browser version forced designers to include browser detection and CSS chooser scripts on their sites so that visitors running IE 5 on a Mac would see their pages as they intended them to look. The people at IE got a lot of flack for this, so much so that rather than try to solve the problems, the IE developers chose to abandon the Mac platform altogether. As a result, today most Mac users surf with Safari, Firefox, and/or Opera.

The bottom line when it comes to testing is to test on both Mac and PC platforms on as many browsers and browser versions as possible. For example, you might want to test a bunch of browsers on a PC first, and then test several on a Mac. For each page you review, ask yourself if it looks as you intended it to. If you need to resolve any display issues, go back into the code and make the appropriate changes:

- Review the home page.
- Review any pages that include HTML forms.
- Review any pages containing dynamic data.
- Review the rest of the pages on the site and check the functionality of any interactive elements using JavaScript or other scripts, programming languages, or applications such as rollover buttons, links, and multimedia files.

Another great testing tool is the Web Site Viewer at AnyBrowser.com, which can help you identify coding issues based on slightly modified HTML 3.2 coding specifications. Test all the pages on both Mac and PC platforms.

1. Go to `http://anybrowser.com/siteviewer.html` and type the URL of the page online that you would like to test.

The page must be already on a live server before it can be tested. Therefore, in the URL field you'd enter the full path to that page, such as `http://www.mysite.com/test/index.html`.

Transfer

Refer to Chapter 20 for instructions on setting up a test directory.

2. Click the View Page button.

The browser window will refresh and display the page you entered. If you see any display errors that simply can't be ignored, you'll need to go back into the code and make some changes.

3. Repeat Steps 1 and 2 for the rest of the pages on the site.

The site viewer tool also provides testing results based on different HTML Levels, such as HTML 4.0 Transitional and Strict syntax rules.

When you identify problems with how the pages appear, exactly how to correct those issues might be a matter of trial and error. In some instances, the problem will be easy to correct, as with a glaring coding mistake. However, in other instances, finding a way to make the page look right might involve several different solutions. Be patient and persistent, and remember that the more mistakes you make and correct, the better designer you'll be.

Information Kiosk

Another helpful tool for testing is the Lynx Viewer, the text-only browser simulator at Delorie.com, which was briefly mentioned in Chapter 10. The simulator identifies how visitors using text-only browsers will see your site, so that you can correct any issues that those visitors might experience. To use the free simulator, designers must register on the Delorie site (`www.delorie.com/web/lynxview.html`) and install a test file on the hosting server before the simulator will function. Delorie also offers a WebTV simulator (`www.delorie.com/web/wpbcv.html`) for visitors using legacy WebTV units or new WebTV users using the updated MSN TV boxes.

broken internal link: A hyperlink that doesn't work, either because the link contains a typo, incorrect path, or improper syntax, or the linked file is not on the server.

empty attribute: A tag attribute with no value between the quotes, as with `alt=""`.

empty tag: A tag pair that surrounds no content, such as `<a href="peanut.html"></a>`, or an opening tag that is missing its closing tag, such as `<p>Hello world`.

Firefox: A popular free PC, Mac, and Linux Web browser put out by the folks who developed Mozilla. Free downloads are available at `www.mozilla.com/en-US/firefox`.

Internet Explorer: Microsoft's free Web browser, now available only for the PC (`www.microsoft.com/windows/ie/default.mspx`). Mac versions were abandoned in 2005.

Link Checker tool: A tool in Dreamweaver's Results panel that tests and identifies broken internal links and lists external links on a page, specified folders, or an entire site.

Netscape: One of the first free Web browsers, originally developed for PC, Mac, and Linux OS, which is now only available for Win PC users at `http://browser.netscape.com/ns8/download/archive80x.jsp`.

Opera: A powerful free Web browser for Windows, Mac, Linux, FreeBSD, and Solaris operating systems at `www.opera.com/download/index.dml?custom=yes`.

orphan: In Web design terminology, any file, image, or other asset in a Web site that isn't linked to any other files in the site and may therefore (in most cases) be deleted or otherwise relocated to a backup location.

redundant tag: An instance where one tag pair is nested inside another set of the same tags and provides no functional use, as with the extra `<strong>` tags in the following example: `<strong>Explore the world of <strong>cheese.</strong></strong>`.

regular expression: A method for representing data with specific strings of alphanumeric and special characters used in text search patterns for finding and replacing data more rapidly than with other methods. Examples include using the ^ character to represent the start of an input string or $ to identify the end of a line of input.

Safari: Apple's OS X Web browser, which has become the preferred browser for most Mac users. Available from `www.apple.com/macosx/features/safari`.

 *continued*

Site Reports tool: One of several Dreamweaver tools that evaluate HTML code and report the results, which identify common coding errors like missing title tags, alternate text, and empty tags so that you can more readily fix them. Workflow reports can also be generated to assist designers working in groups.

source code: The code of an HTML document in Dreamweaver, as opposed to the Design view version of the content.

Target Browser Check tool: A Dreamweaver testing tool that evaluates HTML/XHTML code against W3C recommendations and identifies by browser name and version when particular browsers won't support certain tags.

Validation tool: Any tool that examines HTML/XHTML, CSS, JavaScript, and other code used on a Web page for proper usage and compliance against recommended W3C standards for accessibility and interoperability.

1 | Last Stop

Practice Exam

1. True or False: Most site testing can be performed in less than two hours. Explain your answer.

2. Dreamweaver's Link Checker tool will identify any broken _____ links and will list but not verify _____ links.

3. Name at least three common types of coding errors.

   _____

4. Provide an example of when it would be resourceful to use Dreamweaver's Find and Replace tool.

   _____
   _____

5. How do you access Dreamweaver's testing tools for Validation, Target Browser Check, Link Checker, and Site Reports?

   _____

6. What are the differences between the tasks performed by the Clean Up HTML/XHTML and the Clean Up Word HTML/XHTML commands?

   _____
   _____
   _____
   _____

7. Describe what you should do, at minimum, when testing how Web sites will appear to visitors?

_____

_____

_____

_____

8. Create your own Web Site Prelaunch Testing Checklist based on the one in this chapter and add at least three other items to the list.

_____

_____

_____

_____

9. How does the Target Browser Check tool differ from viewing pages in test browsers?

_____

_____

_____

_____

EXIT

Code Validation and Compliance

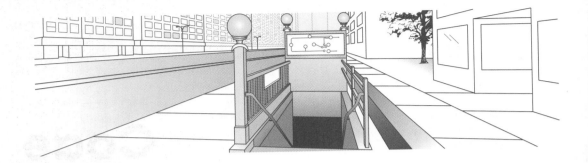

Enter the Station

Questions

1. How difficult is it to convert HTML to XHTML and vice versa?

2. What are online code validators and how do you use them?

3. When pages fail validation testing, what kinds of coding issues typically need to be addressed?

4. What does it mean when a page "fails acceptably"?

5. Where can you obtain proof of validation for sites that pass validation and compliance tests?

Express Line

If you're one of the lucky ones whose site passes validation testing quickly or if you've handed off the testing to a third party so you can keep moving ahead with your project, read on to Chapter 20, where you'll gain knowledge about transferring files with FTP and publishing your finished Web site to a remote hosting server.

Cleaning up code can be an arduous task! And believe it or not, even when you think you've found all the potential problems in your coding, you're likely to find new ones when you take the next step in the testing process — that is, putting your pages through the rigors of code validation and compliancy testing. In truth, performing the validation testing is relatively easy; it's fixing the problems found during the validation process that might take you some time, research, and more testing until you reach the ultimate goal of having all the pages on your site successfully pass validation.

So why undergo the rigors of validation? Well, making your pages pass validation offers a handful of important benefits:

- Validation makes the site more accessible to more visitors, which can translate into more visitors and potentially more sales.

- Pages download faster.

- Clean code improves search engine accessibility.

- You'll be able to maintain and update pages more quickly in the future.

When you validate code, do so methodically so you can keep track of your progress in case you need to break up testing over the course of several days. This chapter will walk you step by step through the validation process. You'll begin by converting all the syntax on every page to match the specified DTD in the code. You can do this automatically by using Dreamweaver's Convert Syntax command. After that, you'll perform HTML/XHTML, CSS, and Accessibility testing on every page. Then you'll fix any errors that need fixing and retest to ensure that you've either fixed everything or that problematic code fails acceptably. Then you're done. As a final step, if desired, you can display proof of validation on your site to show the world that you cared enough to spend the time doing the testing in the first place. It's the Web design world's way of giving you a merit badge for a job well done.

Keeping Syntax Consistent with the Convert Syntax Tool

When most designers select a DTD for their Web docs, they have all the intentions in the world of writing code that's compliant with that DTD's syntactical rules. Sometimes, however, with all the cutting and pasting and inserting and hand-coding, the syntax gets out of whack here and there, and when the time comes to test pages, you might find errors that cause the pages to display not exactly as you intended.

Watch Your Step

This is especially true when designers make the shift to using an XHTML DTD but are still in the habit of hand-coding tags in HTML syntax. One of the easiest mistakes to make in this regard is forgetting to add the extra space and backslash for certain tags in XHTML when their HTML counterparts don't require it, like forgetting to write `<br />` instead of `<br>` and `<hr />` instead of `<hr>`.

Once again, Dreamweaver users are in luck. Dreamweaver has a handy little tool called Convert Syntax that automatically converts all the code in a single document to conform with the syntactical rules of any selected DTD, such as changing all the HTML syntax into XHTML. The code on any page — regardless of the original DTD and syntax used to code the page — can be automatically adjusted to match the syntax for any of the following DTDs:

- HTML 4.01 Transitional
- HTML 4.01 Strict
- XHTML 1.0 Transitional
- XHTML 1.0 Strict
- XHTML 1.1
- XHTML Mobile 1.0
- XSLT 1.0

Listings 19-1 and 19-2 show an example of how the Convert Syntax tool converts a page using HTML into the proper syntax for the XHTML 1.0 DTD.

Listing 19-1 Before Syntax Conversion (HTML)

```
<!DOCTYPE HTML PUBLIC "-//W3C//DTD HTML 4.01
Transitional//EN" "http://www.w3.org/TR/html4/loose.dtd">
<html>
<head>
<meta http-equiv="Content-Type" content="text/html;
charset=iso-8859-1">
<title>Convert Syntax</title>
</head>
<body>
<p>This is a simple page using the <br>
HTML 4.01 Transitional DTD!</p>
<hr>
</body>
</html>
```

Listing 19-2 After Syntax Conversion (XHTML)

```
<!DOCTYPE html PUBLIC "-//W3C//DTD XHTML 1.0
Transitional//EN" "http://www.w3.org/TR/xhtml1/DTD/xhtml1-
transitional.dtd">
<html xmlns="http://www.w3.org/1999/xhtml">
<head>
<meta http-equiv="Content-Type" content="text/html;
charset=iso-8859-1" />
<title>Convert Syntax</title>
</head>
<body>
<p>This is a simple page using the <br />
 XHTML Transitional DTD!</p>
<hr />
</body>
</html>
```

To convert the syntax of any open document in Dreamweaver — which includes having Dreamweaver automatically insert the selected DTD when one isn't detected or overwrite any existing DTD — follow these simple steps:

1. **With a document open in the Dreamweaver workspace, choose File →**
   Convert and choose a DTD from the submenu, as shown in Figure 19-1.

   Upon releasing the mouse button, Dreamweaver changes the DTD in the open file to match the one you just selected and converts any tags in the code of the page to match that DTD's syntax rules.

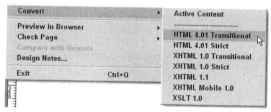

Figure 19-1: Select a DTD from the submenu.

2. **Save the file and repeat this process on any additional open files to ensure**
   that they use the same DTD and coding format.

   I'm sorry to say that, at this time, a sitewide conversion isn't possible in Dreamweaver. The conversion must be applied by hand to every document in a managed site.

You can apply this process to both normal documents and templates. When using templates, be sure to also apply the Convert Syntax command individually to all the template-based files on the site so that the content inside any editable regions of the template-based files will also be converted to match the selected DTD.

Validating CSS, HTML, and More with Online Tools

Hopefully you're working with Dreamweaver and have already used its Convert Syntax tool to locate and correct as many syntax errors as you can on all the pages of your site. If you're working in another program, check to see whether it has a similar feature. Otherwise, your options include reviewing the code on all your pages by hand, one at a time, or skipping this part of the process.

Information Kiosk

Dreamweaver has a set of built-in code validation tools to help designers improve their code prior to publishing. To access the tools, open the Results panel by choosing Window → Results. The panel, shown in Figure 19-2, is divided into several tabbed areas. You can find the code validation tools under the Validation, Target Browser, and Link Checker tabs. All the tools work similarly in that they allow designers to validate or check code in the currently open page, all open pages, all selected files in the Files panel, or an entire managed site. Although using these tools isn't mandatory, they can definitely help designers identify and fix problem code before using the online validation tools described in this section.

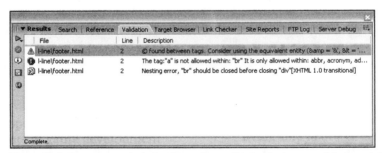

Figure 19-2: Dreamweaver includes three robust validation tools, accessible through the Results panel.

Your next step is to use the free online validation tools that the W3C and WDG provide. These tools conform to and validate against the W3C's latest recommended standards for CSS, HTML, XHTML, and 508 Accessibility. Table 19-1 lists the URLs for each of the recommended free online validation tools from the W3C, WDG, and others.

Table 19-1 Online HTML, XHTML, and Accessibility Validators

Validator Name	URL
W3C Markup Validator	`http://validator.w3.org`
W3C Link Checker	`http://validator.w3.org/checklink`
W3C CSS Validator	`http://jigsaw.w3.org/css-validator`
W3C Log Validator	`www.w3.org/QA/Tools/LogValidator`
Web Design Group (WDG) HTML Validator	`www.htmlhelp.com/tools/validator`
WDG CSS Checker	`www.htmlhelp.com/tools/csscheck`
WebAim WAVE 3.0 Accessibility Tool	`www.wave.webaim.org/index.jsp`
WatchFire WebXACT (formerly Bobby) Accessibility Tool	`http://webxact.watchfire.com`
HiSoftware Cynthia Says Accessibility Validator	`www.contentquality.com/Default.asp`
AnyBrowser Web Site Viewer for Browser Compatibility Verification	`www.anybrowser.com/siteviewer.html`
A listing of free HTML, CSS, and link validators	`www.thefreecountry.com/ webmaster/htmlvalidators.shtml`

You can typically test with these online validators in up to three different ways, depending on the location of the files being tested and the particular validator being used:

- **Validate by URL:** To test by URL, you must upload the page you're testing to a live, working server. However, because you want to test on a live server anyway before visitors can come look at the site, you could upload the files to a testing server or a hidden directory on the actual server that will be hosting the site, such as `http://www.mySite.com/test/`, and validate by URL from there.

- **Validate by upload:** This method allows you to browse for (on a local computer or at some remote destination), select, and upload a single HTML file for validation. For more advanced options using the W3C validator, go to `http://validator.w3.org/file-upload.html` (which might not work in Internet Explorer on PCs running Windows XP SP2).

- **Validate by direct input:** To test the code on a single Web page before it's uploaded to a live server, copy the entire document — from DTD to closing `</html>` tag — and paste it into the Direct Input or other appropriate testing text area on the online validation page.

Now, depending on the number of pages on the site, actually performing the validation on all the pages might take awhile because you can validate only a single page at a time. The exception to that rule is the WDG batch validation option at `www.htmlhelp.com/tools/validator/batch.html.en`, which allows you to input multiple pages by separating each URL with a new line in the input area.

To show you how easy it is to use any of the free online validators, follow these instructions to do validation testing with the W3C Markup validator:

1. **Open a browser window to `http://validator.w3.org`.**

   This is the W3C's main Markup Validation page.

2. **In the Validate by URL Address field, shown in Figure 19-3, type the complete path of the following test page:** http://www.luckychair.com/l-line/imagemap.html.

   This is the Image Map demo page that you referenced in Chapter 17.

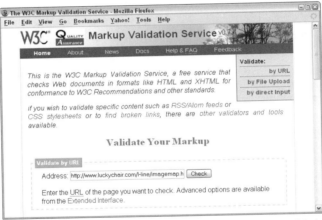

Figure 19-3: Type the URL to begin validating your code and then click the Check button.

3. **Click the Check button to validate the page.**

   The W3C server will process the validation and return results in the same browser window.

   The page should return a Failed Validation notice, along with details about three found errors on lines 56, 57, and 58 regarding the omission of `alt` text attributes on the image map's hotspot areas:

```
Error Line 56 column 149: required attribute "ALT" not
specified.
...,1)" onMouseOut="MM_swapImgRestore()">
```

4. In a new browser window, go to `www.luckychair.com/1-line/`
`imagemap.html` and save a copy of the **Image Map** demo Web page to
your local computer from the browser's File menu.

The save option in your browser is typically something like File → Save Page
As or File → Save Page.

You're now going to correct the errors and retest the page.

5. Open the downloaded `imagemap.html` page in your favorite HTML editor and add the `alt` attribute to each of the images as indicated in the W3C
failed validation results.

The validator identified three errors where the code is missing alternate text for
the image map shapes. Insert descriptive (or empty) `alt` text attributes to the
code as follows:

```
<area shape="circle" coords="66,51,39" alt="Love"
href="#" onmouseover="MM_swapImage('bottom','','images/
marigold_love.gif',1)"
onmouseout="MM_swapImgRestore()">
<area shape="circle" coords="112,125,38" alt="Honor"
href="#" onmouseover="MM_swapImage('bottom','','images/
marigold_honor.gif',1)"
onmouseout="MM_swapImgRestore()">
<area shape="circle" coords="157,51,38" alt="Service"
href="#" onmouseover="MM_swapImage('bottom','','images/
marigold_service.gif',1)"
onmouseout="MM_swapImgRestore()">
```

Information Kiosk

The W3C validator returns line numbers in the error descriptions.
To see which line numbers the validator is testing against in the
actual code, you'll need to resubmit the test page. At the top of the validation
failed page (the URL should be something like `http://validator.`
`w3.org/check?uri=http%3A%2F%2Fwww.luckychair.com%2F1-`
`line%2Fimagemap.html`), you should see an area labeled Validate With
Options. Inside this box, enable the Show Source option and click the
Revalidate button. When the results are returned, you will see a Source
Listing area below the results, containing the line numbers in the code.

6. Save your updated `imagemap.html` file and then select and copy all the
code on the page (from DTD to closing `<html>` tag), paste it into the
Validate by Direct Input field at `http://validator.w3.org`, and click
the **Check** button.

Pasting in the HTML code from a local copy of a file is sometimes faster than
the Validate by URL and Validate by File Upload methods.

7. When the results appear, you see a Passed Validation notice, like the one shown in Figure 19-4.

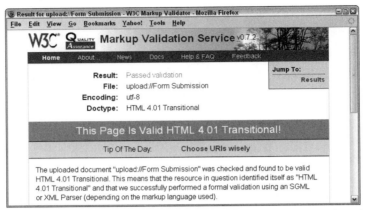

Figure 19-4: Successful HTML validation results will display a large notice decreeing the page uses valid HTML or XHTML.

The results also list the detected DTD in a message on the page using white text against a bright green background saying something like, `This Page Is Valid HTML 4.01 Transitional!`

Watch Your Step

Remember, unless you're doing batch processing to validate all the pages on a site with the WDG tool, you'll have to check and correct every page one at a time. What you might find is that the same few errors appear on all the pages, which can make identifying and correcting them go that much faster. Consider, too, in those cases, using an automated process like Dreamweaver's Find and Replace tool to find the problematic code and replace it with the corrected code in all the pages of a managed sited.

Information Kiosk

Using the CSE HTML Validator   Lastly, I want to mention another validation tool that claims to offer a more thorough type of validation than the free tools on the W3C site. The tool not only checks for interoperability like the W3C tools, but it also identifies illegal tag usage, potentially bad attribute values, and syntax and spelling errors. In point of fact, the tool is actually a software program called the CSE HTML Validator (www.htmlvalidator.com) that both edits HTML and validates code. Currently, it's available only to Windows users in both a free Lite version and a licensed Full version that ranges in price from $49 to $69 for standard usage and $69 to $129 for professional usage.

After playing around with the Lite version for a few hours, I found it to be a very robust HTML editor and validation tool. When it finds errors during validation, it displays the results in the code using red and yellow highlighting for easy identification, and because the program is also an editor, you can quickly make corrections directly to the HTML of the page you're testing. The program offers several levels of customization, and if you have the Pro version, you can even perform batch processing on an entire site's worth of pages and view the results in HTML format. The program has been highly rated by both PC World and ZDNet, among many other reputable software review sites, and seems like a good tool to use in place of or in addition to the W3C validators.

Fixing Noncompliant Code

For each coding issue identified by a validator, you need to determine what course of action to take. Although some culprits that will repeatedly crop up are easy to fix, like missing `alt` text and `<noscript>` tags, you're bound to find coding issues that stump you. For instance, if you get an error message about a particular tag not being supported in Safari 1.0 and IE 5 on a Mac, what do you do? Should you change the way the code is written so that the page works properly for all users, regardless of the browsing tool, or should you leave it as is and let visitors using those browser versions see the page in a slightly skewed way?

In the coming sections, you will find help with common code problems and learn how to retest your code after you've fixed it.

Fixing common coding mistakes

You can fix noncompliant code by hand or by using an HTML editor of your choice. While you're busy making all the corrections, remember that making your pages pass validation will make the site more accessible to more visitors, which can translate into more visitors overall and potentially more sales. Cleaner code also means faster page downloading times, improved search engine accessibility, and quicker page maintenance and updates in the future.

Ultimately, the best way to learn how to code better and make fewer mistakes before validation testing is to make mistakes and figure out how to correct them on your own. Nevertheless, Table 19-2 shows a list of the most common noncompliant code problems and suggestions on how to fix them, which should help you get started.

When you're completely finished identifying and adjusting all the noncompliant code identified by the validation tools, it's time to move on to the retesting and acceptable failure phase, discussed in the next section.

Table 19-2   Common Noncompliant Code Fixes

Problem	Solution
`alt` attribute missing from `<img>` tag	Add alternate text, as in `<img src="images/cookies.jpg" width="239" height="117" alt="Sue's Famous Salted Peanut Oatmeal Butterscotch Chocolate Chip Cookies">`
`<noscript>` tags missing from code when JavaScript is present	Add `<noscript>` tags below each instance of inline JavaScript and/or at the end of the content before the closing `<body>` tag. Between the tags, include content that describes the function of the JavaScript and, when appropriate, how visitors can access the information revealed by it, as shown here: `<script language="JavaScript" src="bookmark.js" type="text/javascript"></script><noscript>JavaScript is used on this page to provide a quick link that allows visitors with JavaScript enabled to automatically bookmark this page. Please use the Bookmark this Page menu option in your browser to bookmark this page.</noscript>`
Flashing or flickering element(s) detected, such as animated GIFs, Java applets, and other multimedia plug-ins	Adjust the speed of any animations to "avoid causing the screen to flicker with a frequency greater than 2 Hz and lower than 55 Hz." Anything beyond these two measures might cause seizures in visitors with photosensitive epilepsy. For further details, see `www.access-board.gov/sec508/guide/1194.22.htm#(j)`.
No DOCTYPE specified	Add a valid DOCTYPE above the opening `<head>` tag.
No HTTP charset parameter specified	This special `<meta>` tag specifies the character set used in the HTML code. Some HTML editors include it automatically when generating new blank Web pages. If validation finds that this tag is missing from your code, fortunately it's easy to insert. Add the default HTTP charset tag for HTML, `<meta http-equiv="Content-Type" content="text/html; charset=iso-8859-1">`, or visit `www.w3.org/International/O-charset.en.php` for further information.
No `<title>` tag specified	Add a unique title between `<title>` tags on each page.
No `<meta>` tags specified	Add Meta `Keywords` and Meta `Description` tags to the head of each page. These can be identical on every page on the site.

Problem	Solution
No `Robot` tags specified	Add the `Robots` Meta tag to instruct Web spiders and robots whether or not to index the page and follow any hyperlinks, such as `<meta name="Robots" content="All">`.
Deprecated `<font>` tags detected	Move all the presentation of the HTML (page, fonts, tables, links, and so on) to an external CSS file and remove all `<font>` tags and formatting attributes.
Deprecated table height attribute detected	Control cell heights, when necessary, with CSS styles.
Style attributes detected in the opening `<body>` tag	Move styles, like margin attributes and background page color, to an external CSS file.
`type` attribute not specified for JavaScript or CSS	Add the `type="text/css"` attribute for `<style>` tags and the `type="text/javascript"` attribute for `<script>` tags.
Entity name used instead of entity number	Change entity name to entity number, such as using `$#169;` instead of `&copy;` to create the copyright symbol ©.
No background color attribute was specified for a CSS style that specifies text color	Provide each style that contains a text color attribute with an attending background color attribute. The background color should match, or closely match, the background color upon which the text will display.

Retesting and failing acceptably

When testing your code, the ideal goal is to get a clean bill of health from the various HTML, CSS, and Accessibility validators for each page on your site. To achieve that, you might need to spend most of that time retesting the page after each adjustment to the code. Some issues, however, might just be unfixable, especially when you employ special HTML and CSS hacks to make the page look a particular way in most browsers.

When a coding error causes a page to look slightly askew in a browser but the page is still readable, it's known as *failing acceptably,* and when an error in the code makes the page look completely jumbled in a browser, the page has *failed.*

One good example of a page failing is a page that contains a form with text fields. On most browsers, form fields can be fixed in size when the `size` attribute is assigned to the fields, such as

```
<input name="Name" type="text" id="Name" size="45" />
```

But in the AnyBrowser.com compatibility viewer, those fields seem to expand nearly a full half size more in width, and in Web pages using a fixed width layout, that expansion can cause the main content area to shift, which in turn can give your page a very unprofessional look, as shown in Figure 19-5.

Alternatively, a page that fails acceptably can be one that doesn't display an object exactly as you intended, but the lack of styling doesn't alter the overall layout of the site. A good example of this would be when a deprecated attribute, like the table cell border attribute, isn't supported by all browsers.

Step into the Real World

Fixing Deprecated Tags with CSS   Even though the newest versions of HTML editors should write code that conforms to the latest standards proposed by the W3C, some online tutorials might still be teaching old methods that rely on deprecated tags to format the content in a particular way.

You learned in Chapter 12 that you should avoid using <font> tags and do all your site styling and positioning with CSS. Nonetheless, <font> tags aren't the only things that have been deprecated in HTML 4.01; plenty of other tags and tag attributes for formatting and layout have been thrown out too, like using the marginwidth and marginheight attributes in the <body> tag to remove margin space from the page, marking text with the old <b> and <i> tags for bold and italic text (you're supposed to use the new <strong> and <em> tags now), or adding the blink attribute to a CSS style, when that attribute is supported only by an old version of Netscape.

One of the most-used deprecated attributes that gets identified by HTML validation tools is the percentage-relative height attribute for tables and table cells. With height attributes set to percentages relative to the browser window (height="100%"), the vertical scale of a table or table cell becomes expandable in much the same way the horizontal scale of a table or table cell is automatically expandable when using percentages for relative widths (width="100%").

With this single attribute, designers used to be able to create pages with expanding content areas and a footer that always stayed at the bottom of the browser window. Now that it's deprecated — though it's true most browsers are backward compatible and will still usually display deprecated tags — it really shouldn't be used anymore, especially because once certain DOCTYPEs are defined in the page, most browsers stop supporting (ignore) the deprecated attributes. Today, to achieve the same expanding page effect in a standards-compliant way, designers must layout pages using a series of layers (<div> tags) in conjunction with advanced CSS techniques for precise styling and positioning.

As part of your validation and testing process, you must try to identify and correct any instances of deprecated tags. To help with this, Dreamweaver users can quickly identify deprecated tags and attributes in Code view by looking for any code that is underlined by a red wavy line, like the example shown in the following figure.

To see how deprecated tags work with and without a DTD, go to www.luckychair.com/l-line and open the two deprecated tags sample files under the section marked Chapter 19.

```
<BODY BGCOLOR="#CDD8D8" leftmargin="0" topmargin="0" marginwidth="0" marginheight="0">
<table height="100%" cellspacing=0 cellpadding=0 width=700 border=0 valign="top" align=
"center">
```

Figure 19-5: Some coding choices might look good in most browsers but fail in others, like this form page when tested with the AnyBrowser.com Web site viewer.

When you absolutely cannot or will not adjust a found error, it is up to you to determine whether you can live with the consequences of having a site that is either aesthetically inconsistent or not as accessible as it should be. Certainly if the page looks good in IE but looks bad in all the other browsers, your work isn't finished. Yet if the page looks good in IE, Safari, Opera, and Firefox but just won't seem to display correctly in Netscape, perhaps you can live with that audience (approximately 2 percent of all Internet users) not being able to see your page in its ideal way. The judgment call is yours. I wish you the best of luck!

Obtaining Proof of Validation

Congratulations to you if you passed most if not all the validation tests! Now that you're almost ready to publish your site, you can decide whether to add icons to the site as proof of validation.

For successful validations, most validation sites contain directions on how to add a validation icon to your page. For example, the W3C offers several free validation icons, like the ones shown in Figure 19-6, that you can proudly display on your site for HTML 4.01, XHTML 1.0, CSS, and WCAG 1.0 (Grades A, AA, and AAA) code compliance. WCAG is a set of recommended accessibility guidelines that can help designers make Web pages more accessible.

Figure 19-6: Use the honor system when displaying any of the free W3C validation icons.

Information Kiosk

The W3C states that validated pages are those that have stated DTDs against which validation using either an SGML or XML parser took place. Valid pages, thus, are considered *interoperable* and are granted permission to display the appropriate validation icon.

Watch Your Step

Be advised that claims of compliance and validity of your pages are not in any way verified or endorsed by the W3C and that you are entirely responsible for the proper usage of these validation icons.

Follow the steps shown here to place the HTML 4.01 validation icon on a sample Web page. After you learn how easy it is to insert, you can visit the validation logo information and usage page on the W3C Web site to get the code for the other icons: `www.w3.org/Consortium/Legal/logo-usage-20000308.html`.

1. Open a blank HTML file in your favorite HTML editor and add the following HTML code to the location on the page where you'd like the icon to appear:

```
<p>
 <a href="http://validator.w3.org/check?uri=referer">
 <img src="http://www.w3.org/Icons/valid-html401"
 alt="Valid HTML 4.01 Transitional" height="31"
 width="88"></a>
</p>
```

This code will display a Valid HTML 4.01 Transitional icon.

2. Save the file and launch it in a browser window.

The W3C HTML 4.01 Transitional validation image should appear on the page. As long as the entire paragraph of code remains intact, the logo can be placed anywhere inside a valid page. What you can't do is alter the look of the image or add any special formatting to it.

The code provided by the W3C contains a URL to the W3C for the source of the graphic. If you'd prefer to have the graphic display from your own site rather than having to access the W3C site to display, you may create a copy of the desired graphic in either GIF or PNG format, place it in the images folder of your own site, and change the source within the code to reflect the graphic's new location, like this code showing proof of valid CSS:

```
<p>
 <a href="http://jigsaw.w3.org/css-validator/">
  <img style="border:0;width:88px;height:31px"
  src="images/vcss" alt="Valid CSS!"></a>
</p>
```

compliance: Writing code that meets the recommended standards for HTML, XHTML, CSS, and Accessibility.

fail acceptably: When code doesn't meet the recommended compliancy standards yet still looks okay (or looks acceptable enough) when viewed in a browser.

interoperable: On the Internet, Web pages that conform to standards and can be accessed with a variety of devices such as Web browsers, search engine robots, text-to-speech applications, and other assistive devices.

syntax conversion: Modifying all the code syntax in a Web page to match the specified DTD.

validation: An evaluation process to test for conformance to a set of standards. In Web design, you can do validation on Web pages to test for HTML/XHTML, CSS, and Accessibility compliance to suggested recommended coding standards.

WCAG: Web Content Accessibility Guidelines. The recommended guidelines on how to make the content on Web pages more accessible to people with disabilities. Learn more about the WCAG at `www.w3.org/TR/WAI-WEBCONTENT`.

Last
Stop

Practice Exam

1. True or False: Using both HTML and XHTML code syntax in a single XHTML Web document has little to no effect on how the page displays in a browser.

2. What three things should you test for with online validation tools?

_____

3. Describe one common noncompliant code problem and the solution to it.

_____

_____

4. What kinds of proof can you use on your site to show visitors that the pages have passed interoperability validation?

_____

_____

5. When is it okay to use deprecated tags in your Web pages?

_____

_____

_____

_____

6. Test the Yahoo.com home page (`http://www.yahoo.com`) with the following validators. What are your findings?

W3C Markup Validator	`http://validator.w3.org`
W3C Link Checker	`http://validator.w3.org/checklink`
W3C CSS Validator	`http://jigsaw.w3.org/css-validator`
WDG HTML Validator	`www.htmlhelp.com/tools/validator`
WDG CSS Checker	`www.htmlhelp.com/tools/csscheck`

Taking the Site to the Web

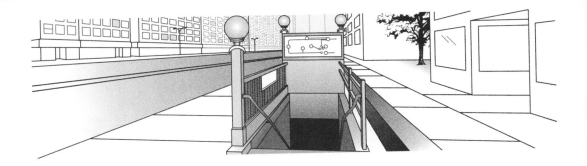

Enter the Station

Questions

1. What does FTP mean?
2. Which FTP programs are the best and least expensive to use?
3. What's the difference between an FTP program and an FTP host console?
4. How can you set up a secret directory on a host server for testing?
5. What does publishing a site entail?
6. How do you let the world know the site is online?

You've made it to the last chapter. Hopefully, this means you've planned, organized, designed, optimized, built, and tested an entire Web site and you're now ready, at last, to show it to the world. To get the site online, you'll need to transfer all the site files — all the HTML documents, images, CSS, external JavaScript files, SSIs, media files, and any other documents that you used to support the site — to the remote server hosting the site.

If you didn't select a domain name and secure hosting as instructed back in Chapter 5, now is the time to choose and register the domain and pay a host provider for a hosting plan. If you already acquired a hosting plan, go dig up the information the host provider sent to you that shows the plan's username and password and includes any special instructions about FTP (File Transfer Protocol) and transferring files to the host's remote server.

Information Kiosk

In addition to FTP, you can connect to a remote server using other methods, such as Local/Network, RDS (Rapid Development Services), WebDAV (Web-based Distributed Authoring and Versioning), and Microsoft Visual SourceSafe. However, the most common way is with FTP, so that's the one you learn about here.

In addition to learning about how to set up a remote connection to a host server with FTP, this chapter will demonstrate how to transfer files (both to and from the server), create a test directory on the server, upload your site to the test directory for a final round of testing, and lastly, upload the site to the root level of the remote server to officially publish the site on the Internet.

Uploading with File Transfer Protocol

File Transfer Protocol, or just FTP for short, refers to a standard TCP/IP Internet protocol that allows for the exchange of files between remote computers over the Internet. To initiate an FTP session, a client (you) must use special software or some kind of Internet interface to log in and gain access to the remote server. Logging in typically requires the input of a special username or ID and password that the host provider furnished when you purchased the hosting plan. For example, if your name is Phil Jenkins and your site is called PhilosophyIsCool.com, your host provider might generate a username/ID and password such as *pjenkphilo* and *th23ejo8*. Some hosts give you the opportunity to select your username/ID and password after logging in with the auto-generated username and password, so you can reset them to something you'd remember later.

After access to the remote server has been granted for the FTP session, you may begin *getting* (downloading) and *putting* (uploading) files between your local computer and the remote server. Remember, the remote server is the live host, which means that as soon as files hit the remote server, they're publicly accessible on the Internet! When finished transferring, you'll simply log out or otherwise disconnect from the remote server and go about your other business.

Choosing an FTP application

FTP applications come in a few different flavors. Although all FTP applications essentially allow you to do the same things with files — such as view files by name, date, and size, and copy, rename, and delete files and directories on the server — the interface might be slightly different from one application to the next:

- **Software programs:** Standalone software, such as WS-FTP or Fetch, must be installed on the client computer and launched like any other software program each time the client needs access to the remote server. Server profiles can often be saved within the program for as many remote sites as desired. Saved profiles will remember the URL, username, and password information to make logging in each time run quicker. Though some FTP programs have a drag and drop interface, most consist of a single window with two panes representing views of the local site files and the remote site files, as shown in Figure 20-1. Data may be transferred in either direction using common controls such as Get, Put, Change Directory, Make Directory, Rename, Delete, and Refresh.

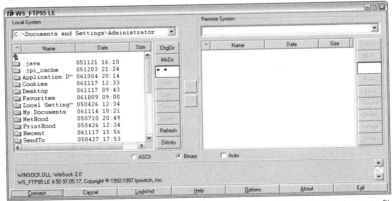

Figure 20-1: WS-FTP has a single window with two panes to display local and remote files.

- **Integrated:** Built-in FTP clients are components within other software programs, which allow you to transfer files to and from a specified remote server through a special FTP panel. Dreamweaver's expanded Files panel is a perfect example. The expanded Files panel provides views of both remote and local files and allows for transfers between the two in both directions.

Browser: These kinds of FTP clients use a browser interface (usually IE or Firefox) to access the remote server from the client's computer. You establish access by entering a special FTP address into the address bar, which prompts the client to enter in a username/ID and password. That information is passed to the remote server and authenticated when the login information is correct. That same browser window is then used to display files and directories on the remote server into which a client can drag and drop files into and out of from a local computer.

Transfer

In an exercise in Chapter 5, if you'll recall, you uploaded a place-holder page to the remote server using IE as an FTP browser client.

Internet control panel: Panels are customized Web interfaces developed by host providers that are composed of a variety of Web forms. These forms allow the host's customers (you or your client) to upload files to the remote server and occasionally also to select and download files from it. Most control panels restrict uploads to single files at a time, rather than enabling users to specify and upload several files or folders at once. Control panels also tend to rarely let clients have full control over the files on the remote server and restrict certain functions like renaming and deleting files.

Information Kiosk

Having used a standalone software program for FTP for several years now, that has become my personal preferred method for transferring files, even in light of the adept capabilities of Dreamweaver's expanded Files panel (itself a well-developed tool with an impressive site-synchronization option). Standalone FTP clients tend to provide the most control over the file transfer process, whereas browser-style FTP clients tend to transfer files too slowly and the various proprietary Internet control panels tend to be too restrictive. My recommendation, therefore, is that you do your file transfers through Dreamweaver or by using any of the myriad free or affordable standalone file transfer programs. Table 20-1 lists the names and URLs of some of the better FTP software programs for both Mac and Windows platforms. Visit each of the sites that interest you and download the software application that appeals to you the most.

Table 20-1   Standalone FTP Software Programs

Program	URL	Cost	OS
FileZilla	`http://filezilla.sourceforge.net`	Free	Win
FlashFXP	`www.inicom.net/pages/en.ffxp-home.php`	Free	Win
WS_FTP	`www.ipswitch.com/products/file-transfer.asp`	$89	Win
CuteFTP	`www.globalscape.com/products/ftp_clients.asp`	$39	Both
Cyberduck	`http://cyberduck.ch`	Free	Mac
Fetch	`www.fetchsoftworks.com/downloads.html`	$25	Mac
FTP Client	`www.ftpclient.com`	$35	Mac
Fugu SFTP	`http://rsug.itd.umich.edu/software/fugu`	Free	Mac
RBrowser	`www.rbrowser.com`	$35	Mac
Yummy FTP	`www.yummysoftware.com/?gclid=CJOY2puC5ocCFSRjWAodLilF_Q`	$25	Mac

Setting up a remote connection

Regardless of which application type you choose to use for the FTP process, to access the host server, you will need to set up a remote connection to it. This entails configuring the FTP client with a session profile for the connection. Profiles typically include

- The URL of the domain being accessed or a special FTP address provided by the host
- The registered username and password
- At times, additional information depending on the host server type

In WS_FTP, for example, each FTP session profile requires a name, host name/address, host type, user ID, and password before a connection to the remote server can be established. Figure 20-2 shows the dialog box for configuring a new profile in WS_FTP.

Dreamweaver users will have to take two extra steps when setting up a remote connection: managing the site and setting up the remote access information.

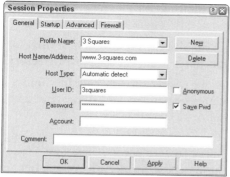

Figure 20-2: Most FTP applications request a host address, user ID, and password information to grant access to a remote server, like this session profile window in WS_FTP.

To set up a remote connection in Dreamweaver, follow these steps:

1. **From within Dreamweaver, choose Site → Manage Sites.**

The Manage Sites dialog box will open. If you have already managed a site for the files you intend to transfer, that site's name should appear in the dialog box. However, if you haven't managed a site for those files yet, you must manage a site before continuing.

To create a managed site, click the New button in the Manage Sites dialog box and choose Site from the drop-down menu. Then click the Advanced tab of the Site Definition dialog box that appears. In the Local Info category, enter a name for the site in the Site Name text box and the location of the site on your local computer in the Local Root Folder text box. The name of the site is for your use only and won't appear anywhere on the published site; therefore, name the site after the client. The local root folder tells Dreamweaver where to find the files for this site to perform special functions like sitewide modifications.

2. **Select the desired managed site from the listing of managed sites and click the Edit button.**

The Site Definition dialog box will appear for the selected managed site, open to the Advanced tab, Local Info category.

3. **Select Remote Info options under the Category area and choose FTP from the Access drop-down menu.**

The dialog box will refresh and display FTP configuration fields, as shown in Figure 20-3. The Access setting defines the protocol by which files will be transferred from your local computer to the remote server and vice versa.

4. **In the FTP Host text box, type the host name where the files will be uploaded to.**

This will be either the domain name preceded by www or ftp, such as www.*mydomain*.com or ftp.*mydomain*.com, or the domain's IP address.

When in doubt, refer to the information about FTP access furnished by the host provider or system administrator.

5. **(Optional) Some host providers require the input of a host directory. If this information was provided to you, enter it now in the Host Directory text box.**

A host directory is the location on the remote server where files for your domain will be housed. Typical host directories are often named www, `public_html`, or some specialized name such as `/c42/sitename`.

Your host provider should have furnished this information to you along with the user ID and password if it is required for FTP access. Therefore, if you don't have (or think your site doesn't have) a host directory, leave this field blank.

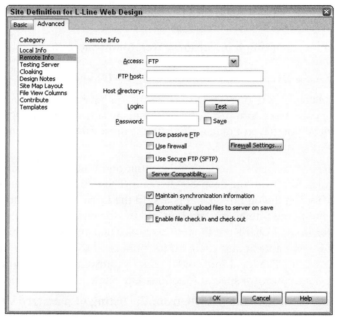

Figure 20-3: Set the remote access information in the Remote Info area of the Advanced tab in Dreamweaver's Site Definition dialog box.

6. **Enter the Login and Password information.**

Unless otherwise specified, the Login is often the same as the host-provided username or user ID.

7. **Click the Test button to verify the connection.**

When the Remote Information is accurate, Dreamweaver displays a Connection Established success message. Proceed to Step 8.

When the connection fails, an error message appears. Check the spelling of all the information in the dialog box to ensure the information is accurate. Typos and incorrect letter case can prevent the connection from being established. Test again until a connection is established.

If none of the preceding suggestions fix the problem, try using Passive FTP and/or some of the other options in the dialog box, such as Use Firewall and Use Secure FTP, and click the Test button after each configuration modification.

- *Passive FTP* tells the client to use the local computer rather than the remote server to establish a connection.

- *Firewall* settings allow you to custom configure the FTP connection, hosting preferences, and transfer options.

- *SFTP* (Secure FTP) uses encryption for a totally secure connection.

After a connection is established, Dreamweaver displays a Connection Established success message, and you can proceed to Step 8. If you can't establish a connection to the remote server despite your attempts, contact your host provider or system administrator for assistance.

8. To have Dreamweaver save this configuration, select the Save check box next to the Password text box.

9. The remote site configuration is complete, and you may click OK to close the Site Definition dialog box and click the Done button in the Manage Sites dialog box.

If you've decided to use a different FTP client than Dreamweaver, take a moment right now to configure the FTP client with the appropriate session profile details for your site. Most systems either allow you to test the connection or actually make a connection to verify the data you input is correct. If you need help, contact your host provider or system administrator.

With a successful remote connection, you're ready to learn how to transfer files between your local computer and the remote host. In the next section, you'll find instructions on setting up a test directory, transferring files, last-minute testing, and publishing your site.

Publishing a Site

By now, you must be very eager to publish your site online, and you're very close to doing it. There's just one more thing you might want to do beforehand. That is, set up a test directory where you can upload your site to the hosting server for one final round of quick testing. Many a broken link and spelling error have been found at this final testing stage, so I urge you to spend the few extra minutes, hours, or days, as the case may be, performing this most important second-to-last step before making your site live on the Internet. After testing, you can confidently publish the site and move on to your next Web project.

Setting up a test directory

A test directory can be a folder that sits at the root level of the remote server. By copying (or technically, uploading) all the site files into this folder, you can work with the files as though they are "live" for the final round of testing, but keep only the placeholder page (index.html) visible to actual visitors to the domain until you're ready to publish the site.

To create the test directory, follow these steps:

1. Launch your FTP client and establish a connection with the remote server.

2. Create a new folder with the name of your choice at the root level on the remote site. You should have an option somewhere in the interface to make a new directory (often called MkDir) or create a new folder (perhaps through a File → New Folder command).

That's it. You can name the folder anything you like. For instance, *test, temp, dev* (for development), *secret, lab, check, wip* (for work in progress), and *trial* are some temporary test directory names that many designers use for this type of testing. Alternatively, you could name the test directory after the abbreviation of the client's site, such as *MWD* for *Martin-West Design*.

 Information Kiosk

You might notice when you create the test directory that the server already contains some files and folders. Most host providers will have default home pages (index.html or index.htm) that are used as placeholders for your domain until you're ready to publish your site. And, if the host-provided placeholder pages use any graphics, you'll also see an images folder at the root level of the host server for your domain. Or, if you already designed and uploaded a customized placeholder page in Chapter 5, you can leave your index.html file and images folder in place at the root level until the fully tested site is ready for publishing.

 Watch Your Step

Other things you see at the server's root level are things like a cgi-bin folder which you can use to handle some form processing and other programming needs. Any additional files and folders you see there are usually required by the host provider for your site to be functional — leave them there and don't touch them unless you know what you're doing.

Now, with the test folder in place, you're ready to learn about the file transfer process so you can do a final round of testing. Then, when the testing is complete, you can transfer your site to the root level of the remote server.

Getting and putting files

File transfers are bi-directional, which means that you may both transmit to and receive files from the remote location. In Web-speak, another name for transmitting files to the remote server (putting) is uploading, and thus the other name for receiving files (getting) is downloading.

Occasionally, you might want to get a copy of some or all of the files from the remote server for your local computer to, say, restore a broken version of a file or to get a copy of the site onto a new computer. In most instances, however, you will simply put copies of your local files onto the remote server for testing and publishing purposes. Notice that I say put or get a *copy* of your files. Like a document through a fax machine, when transferring files via FTP, the originals stay in place and only copies are sent.

Putting files with an FTP client

To place your local site onto the remote server into your new testing folder, you will put your files there through the FTP client. Follow these steps to complete the task:

1. **Establish a connection with the remote server through your FTP client.**

You'll want to have access to both your local files and your remote files, so you'll need to configure the interface to display both locations. Or in the case of a drag-and-drop-type FTP client, have the remote folder accessible in one window on your computer and the folder with your local site open in another window on your computer.

2. **Open the test folder on the remote server by double-clicking the folder's icon.**

You want the folder to be open so that the files will be transferred into it, rather than into the root level of the remote server for your domain.

3. **Put an entire copy of the completed local site into the test folder on the remote server.**

Depending on your FTP client interface, this step will involve a drag and drop of the desired files or the selection of the desired files and the clicking of a Copy, Put, or Transfer button.

Information Kiosk

In some FTP clients, whenever HTML documents are transferred, the program might prompt you to also send *dependents*, a term that refers to any and all additional files associated with the HTML document(s) being transferred, such as images, media files, CSS, SSIs, external JavaScript files, and PDFs. When the transfer involves sending information for the very first time, sending dependents is a good idea. However, when sending updated files to the server during testing after the initial transfer, it might be faster to not send the dependents, unless they've been modified for testing, too.

Transferring files in Dreamweaver

You can transfer files in Dreamweaver in a few different ways through the Files panel. You can use the icons in the collapsed Files panel; the selections found in the Files panel's options menu; or a variety of methods including drag and drop, clicking icons, or using menu options in the expanded Files panel. The easiest method, which most closely mirrors the standalone FTP client way, is to transfer files through the expanded Files panel.

To use the expanded Files panel in Dreamweaver for FTP, follow these steps:

1. With Dreamweaver open to the managed site that you want to transfer, click the Expand/Collapse button on the Files panel, as shown in Figure 20-4.

Expand/Collapse

Figure 20-4: Expand the Files panel by clicking the Expand/Collapse button.

The expanded Files panel will be split into two panes. By default, the local files will display in the right pane and the remote files, after establishing a connection via FTP, will display on the left.

Information Kiosk

To flip the location of the local and remote files, collapse the Files panel by clicking the Expand/Collapse button and open Dreamweaver's Preferences by choosing Edit → Preferences (Windows) or File → Preferences (Mac). In the Site category, modify the *Always Show* and *On The* drop-down menus to suit your particular needs, such as Always Show Local Files On The Left. Click OK to close the dialog box and re-expand the Files panel before proceeding to Step 2.

2. Click the Connect (Connects to Remote Host) button on the expanded Files panel toolbar.

The button looks like a blue plug and socket. When clicked, the plug will connect with the socket and a green light will appear next to it indicating that the connection was a success. You will also suddenly see all the files on the remote server appear listed in the Remote pane of the Files panel, as shown in Figure 20-5.

3. In the local pane of the expanded Files panel, select the file(s) that you'd like to transfer and click the blue up arrow Put button on the panel's toolbar.

To select more than one file at a time, rather than holding down the Shift key as you normally would for multiple selections, click the Control button when selecting each additional file.

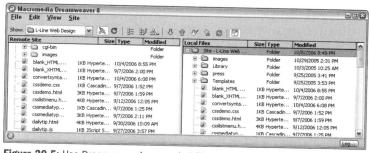

Figure 20-5: Use Dreamweaver's expanded Files panel as an FTP client.

Upon clicking the Put button, Dreamweaver displays a Dependent Files dialog box from which you may select whether or not to also upload dependent files.

4. Click the Yes button to upload dependent files or the No button to upload only the selected file(s).

Dreamweaver uploads the selected file(s). Depending on the size of the file(s) and your connection speed, the upload might take anywhere from one second to several minutes.

5. When you're finished transferring files, click the blue plug connection button again to disconnect from the remote host and collapse the Files panel by clicking the Expand/Collapse button once more.

The Dreamweaver workspace returns to normal with the panels lined up along the right of the screen and the document workspace on the left.

What's lovely about the expanded Files panel in Dreamweaver is the ability to sort and view both the local and remote files by size, type, and modification date. You can even set additional file attributes, including custom attributes, for this view in Dreamweaver's Site Definition dialog box by going to the Advanced tab and using the File View Columns category. Another useful feature is the Synchronize command, which evaluates both local and remote files and gets/puts files in both directions so that both locations contain the most recent version of each file in the managed local site.

Testing one last time

After you upload the site to the test directory on the remote site, you can view and test the site online. To access the files on the Internet, enter the domain and test directory into your browser's address bar. For example, if your domain name is joestinydiner.com and the test directory you created is called JTD, you'd enter **http://www.joestinydiner. com/JTD/** into your browser's address bar.

Step into the Real World

Custom 401 and 404 Error Pages   When a Web server receives a request from an Internet user that it doesn't know how to process, it typically returns one of several error messages to the visitor's browser window. Two of the most common errors are the 401 Unauthorized Access message, which gets displayed when people attempt to access Web pages that are password protected without permission, and the 404 File Not Found message, which appears when visitors click a broken hyperlink or type an incorrect Web address in the browser's address bar.

What a lot of people don't know is that these two message pages can be customized to match the design of the site they're served on, and with a little help from your host provider, can be installed and in service within 24 hours or less after transferring the site files to the remote server.

The 401 Unauthorized Access page typically contains the refresh `<mega>` tag, `<META HTTP-EQUIV="refresh" content="5;URL=http://www.YOURDOMAIN.com">`, and says something like,

```
You have attempted to access a page for which you are not
authorized. This page will automatically redirect to the [INSERT
DOMAIN NAME] Home Page in 10 seconds, or click the following link
to manually redirect this page to [INSERT DOMAIN NAME].
```

The 404 File Not Found message provides more room for customization but generally should read something like,

```
The page cannot be found:
The page you are looking for might have been removed, had its name
changed, or is temporarily unavailable.
Please try the following:
    * If you typed the page address in the Address bar, make
      sure that it is spelled correctly.
    * Open the www.DOMAINNAME.com home page, and then look for
      links to the information you want.
    * Click the Back button to try another link.
```

To customize your own 401 and 404 error pages, create two new Web pages based on existing pages on the completed site. That way, the new pages will use the same layout and graphics as the rest of the site. Edit the content areas for both pages by using the preceding examples and then customize the content to suit your site's particular needs. For example, rather than just displaying the URL of the home page on the 404 error page, why not also include links to all the pages on your site, similar to your site map page? The same technique would also work for the 404 error page. Or perhaps instead of or in addition to the site map links, you can offer a site search feature on the error pages. The content is entirely up to you, so be as creative and helpful as you can to the visitors (potential customers) that will be viewing these pages. Save these files with the filenames `error401.html` and `error404.html`.

Next you'll need to edit the existing `.htaccess` file on your server or create a new one. The `.htaccess` file needs to sit at the root level of your host directory to provide instructions to the server on how to serve up your new custom documents should either of these errors occur.

To see whether your server already has an `.htaccess` file, establish an FTP client session and take a look at the root level of your host server. If an `.htaccess` file already exists, download

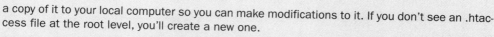

a copy of it to your local computer so you can make modifications to it. If you don't see an .htaccess file at the root level, you'll create a new one.

To create an `.htaccess` file, follow these steps:

1. **Open a text editor and type the following two lines of code:**

```
ErrorDocument 404 /error404.html
ErrorDocument 401 /error401.html
```

2. **Save the file as `htaccess.txt` into the root level of your local site.**

3. **Establish a connection between your host server and your FTP client and upload a copy of the file to the root level of your host server via FTP. While still connected change the name of the `htaccess.txt` file on the remote server to `.htaccess` by removing the `.txt` extension and placing a period before the filename.**

4. **Upload both your `error401.html` and `error404.html` files to the root level of your host server.**

The last step after creating your pages and uploading them to the root level of your remote server is contacting your host provider for further instruction on how to make these files replace the server's default error message pages. The host provider typically needs to configure some software on its end before the new pages will work. They might also request that you log into your site's control panel or site utility and make some adjustments to your site's configuration yourself.

To see examples of (and grab the source code for) both a 401 HTTP Protocol Unauthorized Access and a 404 HTTP Protocol File Not Found error, go to www.luckychair.com/1-line.

Watch Your Step

Pay attention to letter case of the address for the test directory because entering the correct letters and/or numbers in the wrong case can prevent you from accessing the files on some host servers. In other words, if the server only displays pages when the path uses the correct lettercase, you could access http://www.joestinydiner.com/JTD/ but not http://www.joestinydiner.com/jtd/.

No one else — including search engine spiders and robots — will know about the presence of these live, published files on this test directory unless you give them the specific Web address. Spiders and robots don't typically index sites unless you expressly request indexing or unless one or more of the pages is automatically indexed during a regularly scheduled crawl. For that reason, it is best to delete the test directory after publishing the site at the root level of the host server for your domain.

Share the URL to the test directory with your client if you like, to provide one final opportunity to review the site prior to publishing. I highly recommend doing so, even if it pushes back the publication date of the site by a few hours or days. Better to have more eyes previewing it for errors than to publish the site with even one minor typo or broken link.

During this final testing phase, you won't be looking so much for problems related to accessibility or validation (because you should be done with that by now, though of course if you find any issues like that you should certainly fix them), but rather for performance issues with links and forms and to catch any last-minute typos that might have been overlooked.

When you find an issue that needs correcting, modify the file locally first and then send the updated file to the test folder via FTP. Preview the updated page online again in the test directory to ensure that the error was corrected to your satisfaction or continue making adjustments and re-uploading the file until you get it to work right.

Unfortunately, there is one thing you can't test for within a test directory, and that's the functionality of any form-processing that uses scripts copied into the remote cgi-bin folder, such as a Contact page form with a forwarding Thank You page redirect. Those pages must be copied over and tested at the root level of the remote server. Even though these few files will be at the root level and are technically publicly accessible to anyone with an Internet connection, no one else will know about the presence of these files unless you give them the URL. In other words, you can safely test these files at the root level while testing the rest of the site in a test directory.

Information Kiosk

When providing the test directory URL to your client, have him review the entire site online and provide written approval of the site to you when he's satisfied with the work and agrees the project is completed. Getting a signed Project Completion form will officially mark the end of the Web project so you can submit any final invoices to the client for payment and confidently publish the site.

Finishing the site publication

To publish the site, establish an FTP client session and put a copy of the entire local site to the root level of the remote server, excluding any Template and Library folders that are necessary only for site management within Dreamweaver but including any additional folders with content to support the site, such as images, SSI, CSS, and JavaScript folders.

Immediately after publishing the site, access it online through the site's domain and test all the pages one more time. This time you'll be looking for missing images, broken links, and anything else that might suddenly jump out at you as not quite right. If you find any issues that need troubleshooting or fixing, fix them at once on your local version of the site and re-upload the corrected files to the remote server as quickly as possible.

When you're absolutely, positively sure the newly published site is 100 percent functional, delete the test directory from the server. Deleting files can be as simple as selecting the directory (folder) within the FTP client session window and clicking a Delete button. Likewise, some FTP clients require that you delete any contents in the folder before deleting the folder itself. Remember, the purpose of deleting the test directory is to prevent any visitors, human or program-based, from accessing and/or indexing those test pages. And, in the event that any of the test pages were indexed by search engines, when they're not found by the server, your new customized 404 File Not found error message page will display.

Contacting Search Engines

You've done it! You've published your first Web site. Now give yourself a big pat of the back and get ready to do a tiny bit more work. You should do a couple more things for the site to really make your design services stand out from the competition.

Back in Chapter 10, you learned some Search Engine Optimization techniques including how to submit a site to search engines and directories. Because some of the submissions are entirely free and only take a minute or two to complete, you can offer to do these things for your client as a value-added service. Refer back to the list of URLs for these services.

Most of the free submission tools request just the domain name to complete the submission process, but others require that you find a category to submit to that best matches the site's product or service offerings. Before submitting a URL to the Open Directory Project (`http://dmoz.org`), for instance, you must use their search feature to find the most appropriate category for your site, and from within that specific directory, submit the site.

To illustrate, suppose you've just created and published a site for a baker who's just finished her first cookbook on baking cakes and pies. What would be the best category to list this site in? One for baking or one that promotes the sales of the cookbook?

Go to `http://dmoz.org` and, in the search bar, enter the keywords **baking recipes**. What are some of the subcategories that appear? Are some more appropriate than others? Type another search with the keywords **cake cookbook**. Two suitable categories might be *Shopping: Home and Garden: Kitchen and Dining: Baking* and *Home: Cooking: Baking and Confections*. Because you may submit the site to only one category, get the client's take on what she thinks will best match her needs.

When you have the right category selected, click the Submit URL link at the top of the page and follow the online instructions for submitting the site.

What's Next?

Finishing up a project can sometimes be a little anticlimactic. You've put in so much work to create the thing, and now you must let it go and move on. Realistically, though, while you're working on all your new projects, the client will often come back to you to make minor (and major) adjustments to the site. Some clients will need regular weekly or monthly site maintenance, whereas others might only occasionally contact you for small edits like a change of address or modifying the copyright year in the footer.

The more responsive and friendly you are in making these changes, the more likely your clients will be to continue working with you and recommending your services to their friends, family, and colleagues. To help generate more business from your existing clients, consider sending out your own periodic e-mail newsletters or making personal phone calls once a month or so to check in and say hello. These little details really mean a lot in this fast-paced, impersonal, need-it-now society. If you really want to stand out, send your client a hand-written congratulations card with a note saying how much you enjoyed working with him or her and how pleased you are with the launch of the new site.

Another thing you should do after finishing each new project is add information about the project to your own Web site. Some designers simply put a small screenshot graphic of the completed site's home page with a link to it and the name of the client's site. Others create more in-depth case studies detailing the entire process from start to finish. (If you don't have your own Web site yet, you've just found your next project to work on.)

When word begins to spread about your services, hopefully you'll be able to spend less time and money on marketing your services. Until then, it's up to you to find new clients and build up your portfolio. The more projects you have under your belt, the more you can feel confident about your skills and possibly charge more for your services. Now go out and find some new clients and get to work on your next project!

.htaccess: A hypertext access file that provides directives to the server such as password protection and serving error pages.

401 error: An Unauthorized Access error message that appears in the browser when a visitor attempts to access a password protected area on the site without permission.

 **continued**

404 error: A File Not Found error message that appears in the browser when a visitor clicks a broken hyperlink or tries to access a page on the domain that either doesn't exist or has a misspelled filename.

client: A computer or other type of system that connects to a remote service on a different computer, as with an FTP connection whereby one computer connects to another for the purposes of transferring files.

dependent file: Any supporting file for another file, such as images, CSS, and JavaScript files for a Web page.

FTP: File Transfer Protocol. A method for establishing a connection and transferring files to and from a remote server.

getting: Downloading files from a remote server.

host server: A remotely accessible computer providing domain hosting for a published Web site.

putting: Uploading files to a remote server.

remote connection: The link established between two computers on a network or the Internet for the purposes of sending and receiving data.

test directory: A directory or folder established for the sole purpose of testing in a live environment prior to publishing.

Practice Exam

1. True or False: A directory on a server is different than a folder on a server.

2. Before files can be _____ to a _____ server, you must first set up a _____ connection.

3. What does FTP stand for and what does it allow you to do?

_____

4. Name the four types of FTP applications.

_____

5. What is the difference between *getting* and *putting*?

_____

_____

6. What information is typically requested to establish a server profile for an FTP session?

_____

_____

7. When using FTP to transfer files through Dreamweaver, what two steps must be done before a connection can be established?

_____

_____

8. When might you need to get a copy of a file from the remote host?

_____

_____

9. What is a dependent file?

_____

_____

10. If your domain name is JewelryByJess.com and your test directory is named jbj, what is the URL you'd need to enter in a browser's address bar to view the test site on your host server?

_____

_____

11. What kinds of files can't be accurately tested in a test directory?

_____

_____

12. Why is it a good idea to set up a test directory on the remote host before publishing a completed site?

_____

_____

_____

_____

13. Name two nice things you can do for your client after the site is published.

_____

_____

_____

_____

Index

C

calculator
  exercise, 26–28
  increasing traffic with a, 26–28
calculator.com, Web site, 26
capitalize attribute, A3
case, Type Property, A3
case attribute, A3
.cc Web Domain extension, typical usage, 107
cell alignment, tables and, 285–286
cellpadding attribute, 283–284
cellspacing attribute, 283–284
<center> tag, 294
cgi-bin folder
  defined, 423
  overview, 508
CGI (Common Gateway Interface), 97
Character
  defined, 73
  encoding Meta tags, 267
  formatting tags (HTML), 82
  palette, 157, 159
cheat, unethical practice, 240
check box, defined, 423
Check Spelling command, 464
Check Spelling dialog box, 464
choosing development tools and techniques,
    practice exam, 100–101
CHOW.com, Web site, 23–24
circle attribute, 440–442
class attribute, 290, 367–368
clause, Permissions and Releases regarding
    Copyrights and Trademarks, 66
Clean Up HTML/XHTML command, 467
Clean Up Word HTML dialog box, 465
Clean Up Word HTML/XHTML command,
    465–466
clear, Box Property, A8
click, drag, and type method, adding text to a
    document with the, 157
click and type method, adding text to a document
    with the, 157
ClickTracks.com, Web site, 38

client
  defined, 517
  questions used to discover needs of, 57–60
  side defined, 233
CliffsNotes, Web site, 21–22
clip, Positioning Property, A12
ClipArt.com, Web site, 65
CMS (Content Management System)
  cost of using a, 18
  defined, 29
CMYK (cyan-magenta-yellow-black)
  color mode, 181
  colors, 90
.cn Web Domain extension, typical usage, 107
code
  adding a <noscript> tag to, 254
  cleaning up, 460–468
  editors overview, 80
  example Meta tag, 68
  hacks defined, 233, 379
  Movies and plug-ins, 272
  semantics layer, 215
  structure layer, 215
  testing, 468–469
  testing for compliance, 222
  validating the markup, 469–470
  writing to add images, 277–278
code cleanup
  applying consistent code formatting, 467–468
  checking spelling, 463–464
  cleaning up HTML/XHTML syntax, 466–467
  cleaning up unwanted formatting, 465–466
  finding and replacing global errors, 461–463
  overview, 460–461
code testing
  generating HTML Reports, 472–473
  Link Checker tab, 471–472
  Target browser Check, 470–471
code validation and compliance, practice exam, 498
ColdFusion Markup Language pages, file
    extension for, 85
color
  adding to a mockup, 157
  Background Property, A4
  Border Property, A9
  Type Property, A3

D

E

registering a domain and getting a hosting plan, 125–126
taking the Site to the Web, 518–519
testing Web pages on different platforms and browsers, 478–479
using an HTML site map, 258–259
Web site planning, 31–32
working with Web standards (HTML/XHTML/CSS/508), 235–236
Preferences dialog box, 231
preload (preloading script), defined, 338, 356, 453
press releases page, questions, 59
primary color, defined, 146
print
  layout issues, 136
  media type defined, 311
print graphics
  quality of, 184
  Web Graphic versus, 180
printing process, getting a true black in the, 181
Privacy Policy, Web site component, 12
Privacy Policy Agreement, Web site for a, 12
PrivacyAffiliates.com, Web site, 12
processing, form data, 409–412
Product/Service Information, Web site component, 14–15
products page, questions, 58
programmer
  necessity of hiring a, 96–97
  steps for hiring a, 97–98
Progressive, JPG optimization, 197
projection media type, defined, 311
proposal, submitting a, 35
protocol, Web address component, 106
publishing, a site, 507–515
pulling together the content, practice exam, 75–76
purpose statements
  developing, 4–6
  examples of, 5
putting, defined, 517

Q

Quality, JPG optimization, 196–197
Quark 7, using for Web layouts, 87
QuarkXPress
  using for Web layouts, 87
  Web Graphics software program, 179

questions
  to determine a Web site's benefits, 8
  to determine a Web site's purpose, 4
  to determine whether to include a blog on a Web site, 23–24
  to determine whether a Web site needs a database, 18–19
  sample client, 57–60
  used to define the ideal site visitor, 43–45
  used to discover client needs, 57–60
  used to finalize a mockup, 166
  used when reviewing competitors' sites, 41–42

R

radio button, defined, 424
raster
  defined, 98, 173
  graphics application, 86
  program, 86, 179–180
raster images, vector images versus, 156
RBrowser, Standalone FTP Software Program, 504
Real World example
  401 and 404 error pages, 512–513
  adding special comments to CSS files, 354
  alternate text for images, 275
  copyright, 66
  creating a favicon, 248–249
  fixing deprecated tags with CSS, 494
  formatting HTML e-mails, 224–225
  forwarding visitors to a Thank You page, 410–411
  getting written client approval, 168
  hidden fields, 417
  making a new mockup, 162–163
  media types, 312
  multilanguage site, 50
  navigation systems, 142–143
  netiquette, 21
  opening pop-ups when JavaScript is disabled, 440
  protecting e-mail addresses, 119–120
  searching any site with Google, 446–447
  templates, 393
  using descendant selectors, 371
  Web site benefits, 7
  wireframes, 62, 63

recipient address, defined, 424
recipient domain name, defined, 424
`rect` attribute, 440–442
Rectangular Hotspot tool, using the, 291, 441
Rectangular Marquee tool, 91
redundant tag, defined, 476
refresh, Meta tags, 267
Register.com, domain name hosting services, 111
registering a domain and getting a hosting plan, exercise, 125–126
regular expression, defined, 476
`rel` attribute, 310
remote
  server defined, 52
  site search tool defined, 17
remote connection
  defined, 517
  setting up a, 504–507
  setting up in Dreamweaver, 505–507
repeat, Background Property, A4–A5
`repeat` attribute, A4
`repeat-x` attribute, A4
`repeat-y` attribute, A4
repeating regions, overview, 387
Replace All command, disadvantage of the, 462–463
resampling, defined, 86
research by proxy, defined, 43
resolution
  defined, 37, 174, 183
  Web Graphics, 183–185
  Web/Print Graphic comparison, 180
  Web site, 184
restore, defined, 453
Restrictive (Web), Color Reduction Algorithm, 195
retesting, noncompliant code, 493–495
Revised, Meta tags, 267–268
RGB (Red-Green-Blue)
  color mode, 181
  colors, 89
rights managed, defined, 74
robots
  defined, 241, 257
  Meta tags, 267
rollover
  button, 333, 338–344, 340–343, 343–344
  creating in Dreamweaver, 343–344

effects, 432–436
graphics, 169–172
outputting in ImageReady, 340–343
showing the, 166–167
state defined, 166, 174, 453
root level, defined, 52, 310
`rowspan`, attribute, 282–283, 364
royalty-free, defined, 74
royalty-free images CD, purchasing a, 65
RoyaltyFreeArt.com, Web site, 65
`run-in` attribute, A7

S

`<s>` tag, 294
Safari, defined, 476
samizdata.net, Web site, 29
satisfaction, of a mockup, 152
Save As dialog box, 117–118
Save As Template dialog box, 389
Save For Web - Powered By ImageReady dialog box, 194, 204
Save Optimized As dialog box, 203, 204–205, 342
saving, images, 189–190
`<script>` tags, 338–339, 450
screen media type, defined, 311
ScribeGroup.com, copywriting service, 64
script, converting into an external file, 450
scripting, hosting plan feature, 114
`scroll` attribute, A6
search bar, defined, 453
search engine
  contacting a, 515
  defined, 257
search index, defined, 257
search listing, defined, 257
searching, a site with Google, 446–447
secondary color, defined, 146
Section 508, Web site, 214
Section 508 amendment, HTML usage, 229–231
Section 508 Standards, Web site for the, 231
Secure Sockets Layer (SSL), defined, 95
secure transactions, planning for, 95–96
`<select>` tag, 412–417
selective, Color Reduction Algorithm, 194

tag. *See also specific tag*
  defaults, 316–317
  padding, 240
  redefine, 316
  redefine selector defined, 326
tags, basic HTML, 82
taking the Site to the Web, practice exam, 518–519
target audience
  data overview, 129–131
  defined, 52
Target Browser Check tool
  defined, 477
  running the, 470–471
`target` attribute, 288
.tc Web Domain extension, typical usage, 107
`</td>` tag, 280
`<td>` tag, 280, 285, 286, 336–337, 364, 368
technical, hosting plan feature, 114
Technorati.com, Web site, 25
template-based files, creating/editing, 392–393
template-based page
  creating, 392
  defined, 402
template-based Web design, advantage of having a, 387
templates
  Dreamweaver, 386–393
  Real World example, 393
  SSIs versus, 401
Terms of Service, Web site component, 15
Terms of Use Agreement, Web site for a, 15
test directory
  creating a, 508
  defined, 517
testing
  validated forms, 422–423
  Web sites for publishing, 511–514
testing server, defined, 422
testing Web pages on different platforms and browsers, practice exam, 478–479
`<textarea>` tag, 412–417
text. *See also* fonts
  adding to a Photoshop document, 157
  adding to a Web page, 272–274
  adding to Web page content, 272–274

alignment, 274
  using alternate for images, 275
text align, Block Property, A6
text editor, creating a page in a, 83–84
text indent, Block Property, A7
text layer, adding to a mockup, 159
text navigation menu
  creating a, 335–337
  ways to present a, 335
Text only, navigation systems, 333
text wrapping, adding attributes to graphics, 277
`<th>` tag, 286, 364
Thawte, SSL provider, 410
The Big Box of Art, 65
The Disability Rights Commission, Web site, 214
The JavaScript Source, JavaScript resource, 431
The Nature Conservancy, website, 7
The Web Standards Group, Web site, 214
The World Wide Web Consortium, Web site, 30
thecounter.com, Web site, 37
TheHostingChart.com, hosting review site, 115
thenoodleincident.com, Web site, 379
Third-Party Newsletter Services, contact information, 20
Third-party shopping cart, adding a, 94
tiered navigation menu, defined, 356
tiered text-based JavaScript navigation menu, creating a, 345–349
Tips and articles, increasing traffic with, 21–22
`<title>` tag, 265, 296
`title` attribute, 243, 257, 297, 351
tool
  Color Picker, 182
  Horizontal Text, 170
  Horizontal Type, 157, 158
  PDF file conversion, 73
  Rectangular Marquee, 91
  Slice, 198–199, 201–202, 204
  WDG, 490
Tool palette, 91
TopTenReviews.com, Web site, 16
Total Site Replication, content organization method, 46, 49, 50
`</tr>` tag, 280
`<tr>` tag, 280, 364

Wireframing V1.0.0 Dreamweaver Extension, downloading, 63
word spacing, Block Property, A6
WordPad, as a code editor, 80
working with Web standards (HTML/XHTML/CSS/508), practice exam, 235–236
World Wide Web Consortium (W3C), founding of the, 212
WriterFind.com, copywriting service, 64
writing, HTML and XHTML code, 220–222
.ws Web Domain extension, typical usage, 107
WS_FTP, Standalone FTP Software Program, 504
www, Web address component, 106
WYSIWYG (What You See Is What You Get)
   defined, 99
   editing, 80–81

Xara's Webstyle software, image-editing program, 87
XHTML
   capital letters and, 271
   code versus HTML code, 221–222
   code writing, 220–222
   defined, 99, 212
   DOCTYPEs, 218
   file conversion into a Dreamweaver Template, 388–392
   syntax clean up, 466–467
XHTML, HTML, CSS, and 508 compliance information, Web site component, 17
XML, defined, 234
XSL, defined, 234

Yahoo!, Search Directory, 241
Yahoo! Search Marketing, Search Directory, 241, 242
Yahoo! Shops, using to process payments, 16
Yummy FTP, Standalone FTP Software Program, 504

z–index
   defined, 380
   Positioning Property, A12
zdnet.com, image editing software, 87

Elevate your education.

The L Line puts learning on the express line. Each book gives you a crash course in the skills you need to master concepts and technologies that will advance your career or enhance your options. Discover how quickly you can reach your destination on The Express Line to Learning.

What you'll find on *The L Line*

- Pre-reading questions to help you identify your level of knowledge
- Real-world case studies and applications
- Complete tutorial coverage with plenty of illustrations and examples
- Easy-to-follow directions
- Practice exams that let you evaluate your progress
- Terminology overviews to clarify technical jargon
- Additional online resources

Put your career on rails.

Get where you want to go with The Express Line to Learning.

Game developers are in demand!
Learn concepts of game development and object-oriented programming for game design.

ISBN-10: 0-470-06822-1
ISBN-13: 978-0-470-06822-9

Being able to design and maintain effective Web sites boosts your marketability. You'll learn to create well-designed Web pages using Dreamweaver and manage live, working sites.

ISBN-10: 0-470-09628-4
ISBN-13: 978-0-470-09628-4

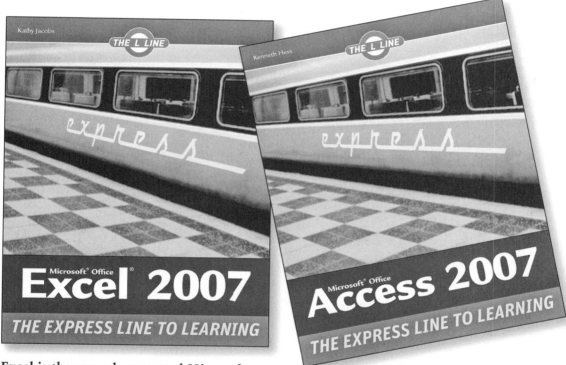

The more you know, the farther you'll go.

Jump aboard *The L Line*, the direct route to sharper skills and better opportunities.

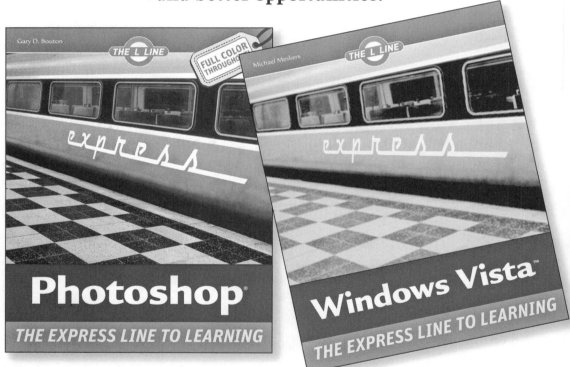

Whether photography is your business or your passion, Photoshop expertise is essential. Master the number one image-editing software, including painting and drawing, using layers, retouching, correcting color, creating Web graphics, and more.

ISBN-10: 0-470-09746-9
ISBN-13: 978-0-470-09746-5

Become an expert with Windows Vista, the first major Windows upgrade since XP. Here's what you need to become proficient with Vista's new features, including everything from the task-based interface to the Sidebar feature and the enhanced file system.

ISBN-10: 0-470-04693-7
ISBN-13: 978-0-470-04693-7

WILEY
Now you know.